PRAISE FOR *RIM TO*

"Tom Zoellner paints an evocative portrait of the Arizona Trail as it wends from the Grand Canyon across the Mogollon Rim. Read it and taste the magic of the high country."
— *Phoenix* magazine

"It's a book that blends Arizona legend and lore, like the Mogollon Monster, with a sobering dose of reality."
— Hank Stephenson, *Arizona Agenda*

"Zoellner marries the personal, the political and the geographic."
— Bill Goodykoontz, *Arizona Republic*

"He fulfills his promise and takes us right to the heart of Arizona. I'd never, ever been there before."
— Jana Bommersbach, *True West* magazine

"Powerful, moving, clear and accessible prose. . . . You won't be disappointed."
— Jon Talton, *Rogue Columnist*

"Social history, personal stories, greedy developers, political maneuvering, environmental disasters, retirees, Native Americans, lonely teenagers, all clicked together seamlessly 'in a complex pattern' as Zoellner takes us with him down this trail."
— Jo Dean and Marion Vendituoli, *Patagonia Regional Times*

PRAISE FOR TOM ZOELLNER

"Zoellner is a beautiful writer, a superb reporter and a deep thinker."

—New York Times

"Spirited and bighearted."

—San Francisco Chronicle

"[A] dazzling display of intrepid reporting."

—Entertainment Weekly

"The author is expert with vivid prose."

—Publishers Weekly

"Zoellner is both a first-rate reporter with years of newspaper and magazine work behind him and a skilled stylist who makes you want to come back for more."

—Kirkus Reviews

"Tom Zoellner is one of my go-to authors. He has a clear eye, a deep soul, and a very sharp pen."

—Luis Alberto Urrea, author of The House of Broken Angels and The Devil's Highway

"Tom Zoellner writes like a dream and thinks like the best kind of realist—the kind whose truth-telling is infused with fundamental compassion, implicit empathy, and genuine curiosity."

—Meghan Daum, author of The Problem with Everything: My Journey Through the New Culture Wars

"To get where we're going, we need to know where we've gone, and Tom Zoellner is the best guide for our times that I know of."

—Ben Fountain, author of Billy Lynn's Long Halftime Walk

RIM TO RIVER

RIM TO RIVER

Looking into the Heart of Arizona

—

TOM ZOELLNER

THE UNIVERSITY OF
ARIZONA PRESS
TUCSON

The University of Arizona Press
www.uapress.arizona.edu

We respectfully acknowledge the University of Arizona is on the land and territories of Indigenous peoples. Today, Arizona is home to twenty-two federally recognized tribes, with Tucson being home to the O'odham and the Yaqui. Committed to diversity and inclusion, the University strives to build sustainable relationships with sovereign Native Nations and Indigenous communities through education offerings, partnerships, and community service.

© 2023 by Tom Zoellner
All rights reserved. Published 2023
Paperback edition published 2024

ISBN-13: 978-0-8165-5328-0 (paperback)
ISBN-13: 978-0-8165-4002-0 (hardcover)
ISBN-13: 978-0-8165-4856-9 (ebook)

Cover and interior design by Leigh McDonald
Cover photo by Daniel J. Carhuff
Interior illustrations by Porter McDonald
Typeset by Sara Thaxton in 11/15 Garamond Premiere Pro with Payson WF and Brother 1816

Library of Congress Cataloging-in-Publication Data
Names: Zoellner, Tom, author.
Title: Rim to river : looking into the heart of Arizona / Tom Zoellner.
Description: Tucson : The University of Arizona Press, 2023. | Includes bibliographical references and index.
Identifiers: LCCN 2022016010 (print) | LCCN 2022016011 (ebook) | ISBN 9780816540020 (paperback) | ISBN 9780816548569 (ebook)
Subjects: LCSH: Zoellner, Tom—Travel—Arizona—Arizona Trail. | Hiking—Arizona—Arizona Trail. | Arizona—Description and travel. | LCGFT: Essays.
Classification: LCC F815 .Z64 2023 (print) | LCC F815 (ebook) | DDC 917.9104—dc23/eng/20220525
LC record available at https://lccn.loc.gov/2022016010
LC ebook record available at https://lccn.loc.gov/2022016011

Printed in the United States of America
♾ This paper meets the requirements of ANSI/NISO Z39.48-1992 (Permanence of Paper).

CONTENTS

RIM TO RIVER

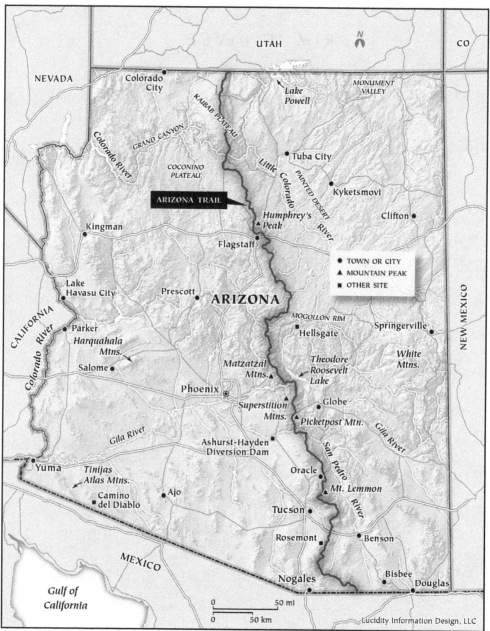

NEVADA

UTAH

CO

Colorado
City

Lake
Powell

MONUMENT
VALLEY

KAIBAB PLATEAU

GRAND CANYON

Colorado River

COCONINO
PLATEAU

Little Colorado River

Tuba City

PAINTED DESERT

Kyketsmovi

ARIZONA TRAIL

Humphrey's
Peak

Clifton

Kingman

Flagstaff

TOWN OR CITY
MOUNTAIN PEAK
OTHER SITE

Lake
Havasu City

Prescott

ARIZONA

NEW MEXICO

CALIFORNIA

Colorado River

Parker

Harquahala
Mtns.

MOGOLLON RIM

Hellsgate

Springerville

Theodore
Roosevelt
Lake

White
Mtns.

Salome

Matzatzal
Mtns.

Phoenix

Superstition
Mtns.

Globe

Picketpost Mtn.

Gila River

Gila River

Ashurst-Hayden
Diversion Dam

San Pedro River

Yuma

Tinijas
Atlas Mtns.

Ajo

Oracle

Camino
del Diablo

Mt. Lemmon

Tucson

MEXICO

Rosemont

Benson

Gulf of
California

Nogales

Bisbee

Douglas

0   50 mi

0   50 km

Lucidity Information Design, LLC

SOURCE: U.S. Geological Survey

ARIZONA BEGAN WITH A WINK of metal in a sun-splashed valley.

On November 20, 1736, a Spanish captain named Juan Bautista de Anza rode his horse to a ranch in a remote valley of the Sonoran Desert to investigate the origins of a silver rush. A Yaqui Indian, it was said, had dug up several big nuggets and hundreds of people had clustered in the valley to find their own fortunes. One had even uncovered a gigantic slab of silver—a *planchon*—that seemed like a freak of nature.

Anza interviewed a wealthy rancher named Bernardo de Urrea, a man of Basque ancestry who owned some land nearby and had pocketed some of the silver himself. He showed Anza the remnants of the big slab, which had been hacked into pieces for easier carrying.

Did a thief take the silver from the royal treasuries and hide it in the valley to "find" it later? That would be a serious crime. Anza took depositions in the name of the King of Spain from everyone who had gone into the valley. He named the site for his own patron saint, Anthony of Padua, but nobody paid attention. The wildcat miners were already using a more worldly name borrowed from Urrea's nearby ranch, which he called Arizona.

The four-syllable name, strangely beautiful, was becoming synonymous throughout Mexico with all things rich and extravagant, a version of what "Klondike" or "Comstock" would mean to later generations of mineral seekers.

A twinkle of wealth and then some hype. This was how Arizona was born.

The shallow dugout mines quickly exhausted themselves. People who had walked away from plows to chase the Arizona silver grumbled the property had been "salted," or deliberately seeded with nuggets from elsewhere to create a frenzy that benefited only local shopkeepers. Anza never concluded whether the silver had been pilfered from the treasuries, and the valley went quiet again, leaving only its name as a wistful marker of lost riches.

I wanted to see this valley that gave my state its name. But this would not be easy. For one thing, it was not even within the United States. Urrea's old ranch lay about fifteen miles south of the Mexican border. An irony: Arizona wasn't even in Arizona.

For another thing, it was difficult to reach. There weren't roads that went there anymore—not even Jeep trails. Finally, it was on private land behind a series of locked gates. Outsiders couldn't just walk in.

Before trying to go down to Arizona's nominal birthplace, though, I wondered if it wouldn't be better to see the real subject itself a little closer.

———

I had grown up in Phoenix and then Tucson, but I never felt my surroundings were "real." The desert seemed hostile and blasted, the neighborhoods too synthetic, the sunlight all wrong, the entire package a funhouse mirror of an ideal that lay somewhere else, maybe in the greener country of the East that I'd seen in photos and on television.

The dry surfaces of Arizona had made a similar impression on some of the first Anglos chasing the silver lying underneath the jagged rocks. The Irish writer J. Ross Browne traveled overland from the Colorado River to the former Spanish garrison town of Tucson in 1863 and professed to be appalled at the "scraggy thickets of mesquit, bunches of sage and grease-wood, beds of sand and thorny cactus," along with the threat of Apache raiders and the persistent heat. The new American territory, recently acquired from Mexico, received a tenth of the annual rainfall of New England.

Here was a land older than the Bible, wrathful as the Transjordan, but also a new slice of promise for those who could endure its aridity, lonesome spaces, and rawboned character. Riding alongside Browne was Charles Debrille Poston, a fanciful storyteller from Kentucky who had been appointed the first superintendent of Indian Affairs for the territory. When he was in Washington, he had told Abraham Lincoln the entire blank spot on the map should be named for the flash-in-the-pan silver rush in the valley called Arizona, a name he found in a secondhand book.

If I was going to go to that valley, it seemed a destination that should be earned. So on September 16, 2019, I drove north from Tucson with my parents to the border with Utah in preparation to walk all the way down to Mexico—across the entirety of Arizona, top to bottom. I wouldn't be blazing any original paths. In fact, I'd be mostly following the route of the Arizona Trail, a continuous 790-mile patchwork of state, federal, and private land that attracts many more casual tours on day hikes than people determinedly walking all the way through.

This book is an account of my pilgrimage toward the source of Arizona, which doubles as an attempt to understand the state better—to come to terms with it, perhaps even to make my peace with it. I have extremely complicated feelings for this place where I grew up, was educated, spent part of a career, fell in love with its people and places, and had my heart broken by some of its failures. I have despaired over elements of Arizona, even as I have taken inspirations in its dazzling vistas, the intriguing people who call it home, and the enduring spirit of fresh beginnings that for decades has made it one of the fastest-growing states in the nation as the newcomers put backbreaking pressure on its capability to support them.

This journey toward the source is interspersed with essays I've written in my lifelong effort to peer into the heart of this often-baffling geography of Arizona. Each corner of the state bears its own surprises. Every time I think I've seen or learned as much as I can about Arizona, I find new questions and revelations: mountains behind mountains.

To their credit, my parents didn't think I was completely crazy. They weren't outdoorsy types, but they had gotten used to some of my more improbable ideas. And together they represented rather well, in their own ways, the Anglo side of the state.

My mom was born into a family that farmed cotton in the Salt River Valley before Arizona was a state, and she grew up poor in a hand-built adobe house down a dirt lane. Her cowboy-obsessed stepfather made her answer the phone with the greeting "Hello, this is the Lazy B Ranch"—a name, as it happened, also taken by a cattle outfit near the town of Duncan, where future Supreme Court justice Sandra Day O'Connor grew up. My grandmother commuted in a dented Studebaker to the state capitol for a series of secretarial jobs, where she knew (and mildly distrusted) O'Connor, then a charismatic Republican state senator. The civil service wages were modest in those days, but my grandmother scraped together enough to send my mom to Arizona State University, where she got set up on a blind date with my father in 1961.

He was from another vital category of Arizona resident—a migrant from the Midwest. He had fled here from a small town in Kansas for a change of scenery and ended up working for one of the state's old-line institutions, Valley National Bank, which had been a prime mover in the mortgage business that flung stucco homes to the horizons and powered the real estate monster.

We crossed the Utah border right after the Glen Canyon Dam with about four hours of daylight left and then took U.S. 89 to a turnoff for House Rock Road, a rutty path that parallels the spectacular Vermilion Cliffs. Eight miles down this road lay a small campground at the Arizona line.

In the bed of the truck was a backpack containing maps, a water purifier, a notebook, pens, a pocketknife, first aid, sunscreen, a tent, sleeping bag, a stove, and a few other items that added up to twenty-six pounds of base weight, a lot more than I wanted. Add four liters of water and five days of food and it was a real load of bricks. But that was as light as I could reasonably make the pack.

I felt a jolt of anxiety as we drew close. Had I packed correctly? Would I be able to take the heat and cold? Would I run out of water? I busied myself with the pack while my parents read the words on a stone obelisk marking the northern terminus of the Arizona Trail.

Here it was at last. I would be hiking across the Kaibab Plateau, down and out of the Grand Canyon, past the cinder cone of Humphreys Peak, across Anderson Mesa, down the Mogollon Rim, through the Mazatzals and the Superstitions, across the Black Hills of Pinal County, and then up and over four major ranges in succession: the Catalinas, the Rincons, the Santa Ritas, and the Huachucas to the Mexican border and then—hopefully—the spot in the valley that poured forth silver for about a week and from which the state had taken it beguiling name.

It was fitting that my parents were with me at the start of this trek, as they were there at the start of my life. The image of a man walking away from his mother and father is one of the oldest metaphors for the trip into the world we all must take, or are forced to take. I was reluctant to leave them and wanted to find an excuse to delay. But the sun was fast retreating behind the ridge to the west, making the juniper shadows long, and I knew I should get at least five miles down the trail before I camped.

I hugged them goodbye, several times, took one last photo of them, and started walking across a sage plain to the base of a large rise without looking back. And by the time I had ascended halfway and looked across the House Rock Valley, their white pickup truck was already gone.

I got to the top of the ridge and saw classic Colorado Plateau country: chocolate- and pink-colored sandstone, junipers, sagebrush, rabbitbrush, small stands of pinons, through which the sun cast long shadows before disappearing. On a narrow part of the trail leading into a canyon bottom, I broke a hiking pole—the trip's first equipment casualty, though not its last—and struggled three miles further before making a first night's camp in the half-moonlight around 11 p.m. As it turned out, that hour was the latest I would be staying awake for most of that autumn.

The next morning, up at dawn, I slapped some duct tape on the snapped pole. The trail flattened out into Summit Valley, where Mormon renegade John D. Lee ran his cattle while he was operating Lees Ferry a few dozen miles away, in a mazelike valley of cliffs with "an agreeably confused appearance," in the judgment of the explorer Silvestre Vélez de Escalante in 1776. The sky seemed gigantic.

As I walked, the ground began to blacken underfoot and take on the character of crushed pumice. I passed through a burned-out area south of the small settlement of Jacob Lake, where a forest fire had come through two years ago. Some aspen trees that had survived were turning lemon-lime in the first crisp of autumn.

Through a break in the ridgeline to the east, I could look out onto a wide expanse of red rock country below the plateau and all the way to the stone barricade called Echo Cliffs over on the Navajo reservation.

THE GLITTERING WORLD

I'm not going to stop learning. I'm not going to stop moving forward.

Regina Parrish says this out loud while on a morning run out amidst the towers of Monument Valley. She's training for a marathon, and she gets to be out here in the sunshine with her friend Michelle Dawn Smith. They were teammates on a high school cross-country team from the Navajo Nation that bagged three state titles. Both quit running for more than two decades, and even lost touch with each other. But individual traumas led them back into friendship—and an old pastime.

"You sort things out," says Regina. "You can see things better. If you're in your house, you're thinking and crying. But when you're out there you have the air and the atmosphere and you're free. You're finding direction. You feel the high."

The two friends usually run from the town of Kayenta up the powerline trail to the jagged volcanic plug El Capitan. But today they're doing a six-mile circumnavigation of a burgundy-colored hulk called Gray Whiskers Butte, just a few hundred yards south of the Utah line. I'm tagging along with them today. Out of charity, they're going at about half their usual pace and letting me listen in on their conversation.

Regina is telling Michelle about the funeral for her grandmother, who died the previous month at the age of one hundred near the settlement of Inscription Rock. Fog and rain had moved in as Regina was giving the eulogy. The hard spring shower had the effect, she believes, of cleansing her grandmother's footprints from the ground, merging them into the earth. There was divinity in all of that.

Michelle said she agreed. The earth heals itself, just as people can heal themselves. She's in the midst of this herself, in fact.

Breathe, she often tells herself on these runs. *Breathe steady. Don't force it.*

Michelle lost custody of her two daughters several years ago. They remain estranged. She prays for her daughters on these runs. Sometimes she prays *to* them. She had a bad stretch involving an addiction to crystal meth, and a few situations where she and her boyfriend easily could have been shot by people coming to buy drugs. At one point, her weight was down to 109 pounds. But she's cleaned herself up and now manages a Chevron station.

Her employees love her. Michelle is the kind of manager who won't tell anyone to unclog a toilet; she'll do it herself. She sees some of her younger employees making the same mistakes she did when she was younger, and she tries to offer thoughts without seeming to lecture.

As part of her fight to keep sober, she joined a nonprofit group called Navajo YES and went on their charity runs. At an event to raise money for diabetes treatment in the town of Dennehotso, she had an unexpected encounter with Regina, a friend she hadn't seen for decades. And now, at a mutual forty-eight years old, they run again together, just as they had when they were girls, sharing in-jokes and teasing. When one goes too far, the other will tell her *ya dah ley*, stop that.

Michelle tells Regina about taking her grandchildren up to Black Mesa to help relatives moving sheep to another pasture. Three had gotten separated from the herd. The children had climbed a slope and found a ewe covered in blood. She had apparently died in the act of giving birth. But the grandchildren weren't bothered by the gory sight. They kept climbing until they located the other two.

Raising sheep is a signature of a traditional lifestyle of the Navajo, also known as Diné, "The People." Michelle wishes she had paid more attention to that side of her family when she was growing up. Her father had been white, a coach at Monument Valley High School, and her childhood had been one of relative isolation and bullying. Others jeered her as "half-breed," and she lived in the 1950s Beaver Cleaver–style housing complex reserved for teachers set behind the school. When she was sent out to her family's winter sheep camp, she didn't pay attention to the intricacies, though she has powerful memories of sitting on the back of an Appaloosa and watching her grandmother waving her skirt like a flag to move the sheep from one place to another.

Regina had a closer relationship with her grandmother, who lived in a mud and wood hogan, herded sheep, suffered the humiliation of government boarding schools where she was slapped for speaking her native tongue, and had grown up among people who had been on the Long Walk of 1864, when the U.S. Cavalry had moved them away from their spectacular home in northeastern Arizona to a dreary river flat in New Mexico. After much suffering and near-starvation, they were permitted repatriation, with bitter memories.

Regina thinks about her grandmother often, sometimes in relation to the suffering that carried forward to her. She gave up a scholarship to Prescott College to marry a high school boyfriend when she was eighteen. He was a certified welder and made good money at power plants. They had six children, and they moved to North Carolina and Illinois, among other places. But he was an alcoholic who got violent when he drank, and it took years for Regina to escape his grasp. For a while after her divorce, she found work as a caretaker for a man who had gotten sick with cancer from his work as a uranium miner in the 1970s. But then he died and the payments stopped.

Regina made a New Year's resolution three years ago to recommit to running, both as a spiritual practice and a way to keep sadness away. "You keep everything equal," she says. "You're equal to the landscape, you're in balance. You're not above it. You're not angry at anything. Everything has a purpose."

One of the great untranslatable words of Diné is *ho'zho*, which sums up both a cosmology and a personal philosophy. It means living in harmony with the natural world and recreating the same moderation and tranquility of the earth in one's own mind. Getting one's insides in tune with the outside. Running is a method of accessing *ho'zho*, finding balance in the wild places and healing what hurts.

We've now gone about three miles, steadily advancing south down a twist of two-track paths that wind around Gray Whiskers Butte, a boxy formation that took its name from an elderly doctor who used to live out here. You can see it through a doorway in the opening scene of *The Searchers*, the classic 1956 Western starring John Wayne.

Of the two friends, Regina is the one with a closer connection to traditional ways and a better command of the Navajo tongue. She is also more prone to observe the practice of rising before dawn and running toward the east to greet the rising sun—a constituent part of Kinaalda, the girls' puberty ceremony. After a girl gets her first menses, she becomes a kind of celebrity for four days, going for progressively longer runs toward the sun, with neighboring children trailing behind her like sports fans.

Just as the Christian ritual of the Stations of the Cross imitates the steps of Jesus, Kinaalda mimics the creative act of the deity Changing Woman, who made herself strong and healthy through four days of running when the universe was still forming. Endurance is the point because life is hard. "So you go into your womanhood and you begin to prepare for all the things like bearing children, you have to be strong," a Diné elder told an anthropologist in 1992.

Whenever footraces are held on the Navajo Nation, outsiders are surprised at the number of family members who show up to watch. Regina has memories of being rustled out of bed at 4:30 a.m., her parents urging her to go running in the dark: first toward the east, then in the three other cardinal directions. Neither she nor Michelle does this orthodox practice anymore; their view is more unstructured, a street spirituality made up of practical outcomes. It's a common outlook on the Navajo Nation.

Regina tells Michelle about an event from two weeks ago for which she has no explanation. She had been running at night through Kayenta, the crossroads town where they both grew up, the streetlights shining on her instead of the moon, when she felt a force blowing through her like a wind, coming from a distant place. Her body was only a conduit for this energy.

She was still pondering what it meant, especially in light of the race she was supposed to run in three days—a qualifier for the Boston Marathon, in which she aimed to finish in less than four hours. The night wind, she felt, was the Holy People signaling approval, in addition to the fabled "runner's high" of endocannibinoids released under stress that create a burst of euphoria.

This is part of the reason why Regina never runs with earbuds. Recorded music would separate her from what the world offers—the crickets, the birds, and the crunch of gravel under her sneakers.

The Diné share a collective fondness for running with almost all of the twenty Native tribes of Arizona that have reservations, more than any other state. Centuries before the first wagons and rifles arrived from the East, Native people were sprinting all over the region that would become Arizona: to deliver messages, hunt game, scout enemies, compete with their friends, and pray.

The Apache economy, with its reliance on raiding and rustling, put a premium on running as a military skill—both in stealth and as intimidation. The Tohono O'odham earned the respect of their neighbors for their ability to sprint over sand and rocks without shoes. When some of the Hopi villages conspired to revolt against the Spanish in 1690, they developed an espionage system based on messages sprinted from one mesa over to another.

The Hopis didn't just like to run; they had an imperative to run. Their society depended on it. Young men were expected to venture forth from the villages on a long-range hunt for juniper and pinon wood that kept the kiva fires burning; they bore the fuel with backpack-like contraptions of beams and blankets. Walking was not sufficient. Soon the practice became a religious ceremony, and a contest.

Competitive races in Hopi villages typically began when the sun first peeked over the top of a distant mesa; they became niche tourist events for Anglos willing to make the bumpy trek from the Santa Fe Railroad station in Winslow. The newspapers heaped coverage on Hopi runner Louis Tewanima's races at the 1908 London Olympic Games. But the superstar factor has never really been a part of reservation running culture. The collective outcome of the group is far more important than individual prizes. You don't run for yourself; you run for others.

Running was a way to bring the rain clouds for the whole community, an act often combined with singing. A U.S. anthropologist once asked a Hopi elder why so many traditional songs were about rain, with rich images of thunderclouds, rushing rivulets, and rain-slickened corn leaves. "Because water is so scarce," answered the elder. "Is that why so many of your songs are about love?"

The act of moving one's body around in harmony with nature is at the heart of the Diné's Blessingway ceremony, which contains the famous lines:

Beauty before us.
Beauty behind us.
Beauty around us.

In beauty we walk.
It is finished in beauty.

There are many here who read that sacred walk as a kind of marathon. High school basketball teams from Anglo parts of northern Arizona have learned to fear and respect the breakneck pace of the game typically played at Tuba City and Window Rock—a style known as "rezball" in which every play is a fast break, the ball moves up and down the court in seconds, and no guard pauses in contemplative dribbling while a pick gets set up. The Chinle women's cross-country team is legendary for its accomplishments. When Vincent Lee came in to coach the football team in the mixed Hopi-Diné town of Tuba City in 2018, he tried to teach a strong ground game—a smashmouth "five yards and a cloud of dust" strategy he'd learned from his years in Phoenix. His players rebelled, not wanting to do bench presses and weight training for hours and disliking the intense physicality of the line of scrimmage. They wanted to emphasize pass plays. They wanted to run.

We pause—at my request—to walk for a bit. We're now completely behind the monolith of Gray Whiskers and have gotten off the two-track road. A lone frame house is about a half mile away across the sands, and a few dogs frisk and nip in the yard. The two friends wanted to know if I had a leg cramp, and I said I was just winded.

"No problem," Regina told me. "I'm glad it's not a cramp. I had to push through one of those in a half-marathon last year at Shiprock. Painful. Then it just went away. You can't let that stop you. You just have to go from point A to point B."

She wasn't just talking about physical endurance. Running across the landscape, for traditional Diné, is also a way of making and following maps. A customary way to travel from point to point was to follow the path of a story told by an elder or a trusted relative. A journey from a grandparent's house at the base of a mesa across a plain and through a narrow canyon toward the gas station, for example, might be the physical manifestation of the story of how Owl once led White Shell Woman along the ray of a moonbeam, through the clouds and into a spider web, with the forms apparent in the physical world as it unfolded before the runner's eyes: a cairn of rocks, a sandy hill, the face of a cliff.

This intoxicating combination of mythos and geography meant that a Diné runner was putting their own sneaker treads into the footsteps of the Holy People. As one elder said to his nephew, Diné scholar Harris Francis:

> When a boy came of age, he was taken along and taught the location of those landmarks and that songs that told of them. He has to know of these things because one day he might have to come this way again. Even in travel one had to be in harmony with everything.

Michelle told us about a blood disease she contracted a few years ago that the doctors at Indian Health Service couldn't figure out. A relative took her to a medicine man in Many Farms who asked her to chant words in the Diné language along with him so he could make a diagnosis. She couldn't understand most of them and was skeptical—and even more so when he told her the sickness was caused by ants who were angry about the way she'd tortured them when she was a girl. Had she burned some with a magnifying glass? Michelle told him she had no memories of this.

The healer said she could atone for whatever she had done by tossing pebbles out to the ground and apologizing to living ants. She rolled her eyes but complied. That same day, her feelings of lethargy disappeared.

"There's no telling what happened," said Regina.

"I know there's something out there," said Michelle. "A higher being. I don't study the Bible or anything. I believe in science, in evolution. But prayers get answered. The older people have been telling us our whole lives that we need to get back to the old ways, we prayed for that. Maybe the COVID pandemic was our answer. The earth needs to be healed. People started gardens. They grew food for themselves again."

The street spirituality practiced by Regina and Michelle is a form of *ho'zho*, the balance woven into the fiber of the universe. There's a strong give-and-take element to it, almost like Newtonian physics. Actions get results.

Regina talks a lot about the concept of "protection"—a feeling of being watched over whenever she goes on runs, a security of not being hurt. At the same time, she is also watching over the earth and caring for her body. The good energy is flowing both ways.

Flexibility is a characteristic woven directly into the Diné tribal personality. Anthropologists believe they migrated to their current home from present-day Alaska and British Columbia in repeating waves during the thirteenth century. They picked up the tricks of dryland farming from the Hopi, who were here first, but placed a higher premium on sheep rustled and purchased from Spanish colonists—the tough-hooved *churro* who clattered easily up the steep inclines of the Four Corners region and made a feast of the desert scrub. Their wool was equally durable, lending itself to the art of weaving.

The Diné excelled at creating rugs and blankets in symmetrical patterns that drew together and drew apart, designs suggestive of their own sociology. More than sixty clan groups were spread out on a rugged plateau bigger than Connecticut and bounded by four sacred peaks on the cardinal points of the compass, each with a sanctified color: white, turquoise, yellow, and black.

Just as they appropriated Iberian sheep culture from the soldiers of Don Juan de Oñate, the Diné may also have borrowed elements from the Hopi religion in the origin story about themselves—the Emergence.

The world had been small and dark, but First Man and Woman led an exodus through successive planes of existence until their descendants, the Diné, moved into a present-day world of northeastern Arizona and parts of Utah and New Mexico, a place known as the "glittering world" that Changing Woman had created for them. She wove the edible and medicinal plants of the region into life from techniques she learned from a benevolent animal called Spider Woman, who lived among the sandstone pillars in the Y-shaped basin of Canyon de Chelly.

Anthropologists from outside the reservation have understood the Emergence as an allegory for the Diné move from polar shores and a mark of their supreme adaptability. They hate giving up. The "moving forward" that Regina Parrish told me about as we chuffed around the butte is entirely consistent with this sense of *becoming* that permeates the cosmology. She likes to use the phrase *danohsinigii, t'aa*—it's what you want to do. Set a goal and stick with it.

Though Regina's philosophy sounds a lot like the success ethic of the American corporate world, it has nothing to do with a profit motive. In fact, the Diné have had a tangled relationship with business culture, especially when it comes to natural resource extraction.

Uranium mining on the reservation during the Cold War sickened thousands of Diné, such as Regina's friend. And both women had relatives who worked at the strip mines on Black Mesa, in which a Missouri company pumped groundwater from the aquifer—an immensely precious resource—to use as slurry for transporting coal down a pipeline all the way to a generating station in Laughlin, Nevada. You might compare it to using cognac to wash the dishes. This was the only such water-wasting slurry line in the country, in a place that could least afford to have its water turned into dark gunk and piped away.

The last coal mine closed in 2019. Bad feelings linger. On the side of an abandoned gas station along State Route 264, the highway that connects the Hopi mesa villages, somebody scrawled graffiti that plays off lines from the Blessingway ceremony: *Don't just walk in beauty. Protect it!*

We had walked a bit off the trail and came to a maze of dry rivulets coming off the western slopes of Gray Whiskers, the ghosts of long-ago rain showers, half full of siltstone and manganese debris that had tumbled off the formation at some point in its 320-million-year history. The cliffs and spires here have always reminded me of cities from a different world, and in fact, the region of Monument Valley used to be underwater; it emerged into this world though wind, water, erosion, and the retreat of a shallow sea. "When you look over it," wrote N. Scott Momaday, "it does not occur to that there is an end to it. You see the monuments that stand away in space and you imagine that you have come upon eternity."

Michelle told us that one of the first adult runs she tried was up Navajo Mountain, a dome of igneous rock that functions as the symbolic northern border of the glittering world. The effort made her sore for days. Shortly after that punishing experience, she put a tattoo of a runner on her right calf, bouncing along an electrocardiogram line. And she was given a T-shirt of synthetic fiber from Navajo YES bearing the slogan *Resilience. The Navajo Way since the Time of Hoskinini.* This invoked the legendary warrior who dodged the U.S. Cavalry and refused to go on the 1864 Long Walk. He led a band of followers to the base of the mountain, where they survived on seeds and the occasional rabbit until their people were repatriated five years later.

In the same spirit, Michelle didn't quit. She learned—or relearned—not to run with her arms folded across her chest but to keep them lightly dangling at her sides to improve the flow of oxygen. She treated her leg cramps with pickle juice and kept running until the side stiches went away. Soon she became a regular sight on the streets of Kayenta. Even some of her old friends from the drunken days, the *glonnies*, gave her a shout of approval when they spotted her trotting through Kayenta.

Getting lost in Monument Valley is almost impossible because the vistas are so wide. We could see Michelle's car parked on the side of the road two miles away but had to scramble down the slopes of a dry creek to cut back to the two-track path. I slipped on siltstone talus and sharp rocks gashed my hand open.

"You okay?" asked Michelle.

"Nothing hurt but my pride." A slight elision of the truth, as I discreetly wiped blood from my palm onto my shorts. But I had already been humbled enough that day.

When we got back onto the Jeep road, with just about a mile to the end, I asked Regina to cease her kindnesses to a laggard and run at her customary marathon pace. She smiled at me. And then kicked away down the path with the grace of a gazelle, at roughly triple the tempo of my labored jog.

"You can do this," she told me at the car as I came panting up ten minutes later. "You can get there."

Michelle nodded her assent. Their own emergence wouldn't stop; they would keep running, even as they aged into elders, pushing their way through pain and the wounds of the past.

The Diné refusal to quit, or to call a matter finished, is reflected in a curious feature of almost all their artwork. Weavers typically include a small broken line in blankets or rugs, poking at an odd angle like a tiny stovepipe or snorkeling tube. No geometric pattern is left completely closed. The Diné do not like to be hemmed in; they always leave themselves room to maneuver, new ways of becoming. The deliberate flaw in the design is called "the spirit-way-out." They loathe the thought of anything being final.

One huge mistake that other Arizonans make when they pass through the Navajo Nation—almost always on their way somewhere else, typically to play on the azure waters of Lake Powell—is to get caught up in the surfaces.

They see the drab institutional housing, the broken cars in the yards, the stray dogs wandering around, the plastic sheeting over the windows, and they feel a kind of pity, perhaps mingled with historical guilt, fueled by a thousand newspaper stories about the poverty endemic to American Indian reservations. The conventional view fails to show what lies underneath. The first residents of Arizona are much stronger, tougher, more humorous, and more adaptive than a first look could ever reveal.

Michelle and Regina drive me back to the parking lot of Monument Valley High School. They hug each other as Regina says goodbye. She'll likely go for another run today in preparation for the Boston qualifier.

"Love you," says Michelle. "Love you," says Regina. They will run again soon.

I notice another of Michelle's tattoos, this one on her left bicep, and ask her about it. "That's of a Navajo wedding basket," she said. She got it years ago when she got married. The blue lines have crept together on her skin a bit in the intervening years, and the spirit-way-out has closed in.

The design on her other arm tells a different story. An eagle feather gives way to a riotous flock of birds wheeling skyward.

THE PORTION OF THE ARIZONA TRAIL that arrows toward the Grand Canyon runs parallel to a state highway that covers up a path used by some of the big game hunters, including Teddy Roosevelt, who used the area for their safaris in the first decade of the twentieth century. They'd likely wince at the condition of the forest: badly torn up by fire, a ravaged landscape of sticks and new underbrush. I paused by the hollowed-out stalk of what used to be an aspen and listened as the wind made a whine through the wood like a church organ.

My right side was stinging as though it had been cut by a surgeon's knife, and this seemed like a good place to drop pack and chug some water out of one of the four plastic bottles stuffed into the sleeves of my blue backpack. It lay sideways on the ground in front of me as I leaned over it, breathing deliberately, trying to make the pain go away. I had tried to get the weight down to a minimal burden, which now seemed like an anvil.

As down-to-the-bones as this burden seemed back at my parents' house in Tucson, all the gear was weighing me down, and I resolved to dump the Swiss Army knife and the gas burner into the mail once I hit Flagstaff. Same for the solar panel because it wasn't working at all, even strapped to the top of my pack and pointed upward for the whole day. That would shed about five pounds.

By this point on the hike, I'd learned to look for flat patches of ground about as big as a coffin. How much land does a man need? wondered Tolstoy. For the night, not much. The view doesn't matter because there's nothing to see after dark. So there no sense being perfectionist. Some nights the only flat spot available was *on* the trail itself, and I pitched the tent directly on top, lying lengthwise on the route.

But that night, there was a tidy little clearing at the base of some ponderosa pines. I had already eaten so the ritual was simple. Pack down, tent out, poles grommeted, hooks clipped, pad unfolded, bag unrolled, climb in, light off, settle down. I was ten miles from help. Small animals rustled gently in the unseen brush as I slipped into dreams.

When I made it to the northern boundary of Grand Canyon National Park, I had been walking for four days and had spoken to not a single other human being. Off a spur was a spindly fire tower once manned by seasonal ranger Edward Abbey, who wrote blistering essays about man's encroachment on the environment when he should have been looking for wildfires on the horizon. The trail cut out of the woods down a slope and went past the booth at the highway, where a ranger in a green uniform taking fees through car windows seemed confused by a man on foot. I had an annual pass. She reluctantly let me in.

A five-mile slog down old wagon roads took me to the edge of North Rim Village, a pleasant collection of dark stone lodge buildings run by a hospitality company called Forever Resorts. I made camp not far from the edge, in a permitted spot, and then headed over to the hotel in search of a tourist chuckwagon supper. On the deck, a mélange of visitors from Europe and Asia watched as the sun set over the immensity below.

"It's surreal," murmured a retired navy officer from Georgia. "Why even bother photographing it?" wondered another visitor out loud. "It will never show what it's really like." They were only echoing a certain hopelessness that comes over the viewer upon gazing at the chasm, which overwhelms the optic nerve with texture and depth.

The longer I stood here among my fellow travelers, the more that misanthropy began to blossom inside me, and I began to question how starved I am for conversation after all. A middle-aged woman from Colorado waved me over and asked if I might not photograph her with her outdoor youth group, of whom she was apparently the leader, and I obligingly took a few snaps with the iPhone she handed me. Perhaps it was a measure of my unwashed clothes, week-old beard, and generally unsavory appearance that she said to me: "Thanks for not taking my phone." It was enough to make me wish, for a moment, that there weren't a bitumen road to this transcendent place—that it should be reserved only for those truly determined to see it.

That cranky goat Ed Abbey sure thought so. He professed to hate the spaghetti twist of roads through the parks, even though the stream of tourists gave him a job and a purpose in his early career. "You can't see anything from a car," he complained at one point, "You've got to get out of the goddamn contraption and walk, better yet crawl, on hands and knees, over the sandstone and through the thornbrush and cactus. When traces of blood begin to mark your trail, you'll see something, maybe." I slept that night on the edge of the rim, overlooking an assembly of spires in the moonlight: Deva Temple, Brahma Temple, and Zoroaster Temple.

The best Grand Canyon mornings start in the dark. But I slept in and missed the sunrise and set off down through the sandstone layers and into the dazzling gash in the earth at about 10 a.m. The trail itself was coated with a powder of atomized dung, decades' worth of it. The mules step in the waste of their forefathers. The foul dust lasts all the way to Supai Tunnel, a narrow, dark passage blasted out of the wall in the 1920s, and it's not far from here to the hydrological cannon of Roaring Springs, in which the waters that soon form the bulk of Bright Angel Creek come pouring out of the canyon wall via multiple little waterfalls at a rate of four hundred gallons a minute.

Flakes of red sandstone protruded from the banks of the path, along with chunky aggregate that looked like a Pleistocene version of rocky road ice cream. The transition to desert flora—prickly pear cacti, yucca, and agave—happened with shocking speed. The creek to the right was choked with tamarisk, an invasive species with deep roots and a freakish talent for absorbing water too saline for any other plant. Ranchers call them salt cedars. I had to hike along for several hundred yards before I could spot a keyhole to the stream.

Maroon walls towered upward. I was close now to a vertical mile from the rim—a mountain inverted—and it seemed beyond ability for the mind to process how the ancestor of this little stream could have pounded this magnificent channel into existence. I lowered my face to Bright Angel Creek, took in long draughts, and let the chilly water run down my face.

On the way back out, I picked up a bulbous fruit from a prickly pear, plucked the thorns away, and devoured the ruby treasure in two bites.

HEIDEGGER AT THE GRAND CANYON

Has anybody truly seen the Grand Canyon? The first view into the gorge assaults the eye with detail and color, overwhelming the mind's capacity to focus on any one point in the mess of ruined sheet cake: a geological supernova quilled with soaring pillars, rounded temples, fallen battlements, gigantic toadstools, and high walls lacquered in colors of apricot, lava, bisque, mulberry, and umber. The canvas is so orchestral the viewer almost expects to hear urgent cymbals, bellowing woodwinds, and shouting arias from a Wagnerian end of the world. But the canyon keeps a terrible silence.

And there goes yet another attempt to translate the inexpressible sight of the Grand Canyon into the sanity of language. These descriptions are always hopeless. The ambition to match this landscape with a squirting of ink symbols is like trying to throw a paper airplane into the sun. But the struggles keep coming every day via articles, instant messages, letters, and emails, trying to render in words what amazing horror lies out there in the gash. "When a writer has tackled everything in the line of fancy descriptive writing, he crowns his life work with a pen picture of the Grand Canyon," observed John McCutcheon in *Appleton's Magazine* in 1909, just as the first railroad access brought in a flood of visitors and would-be poets.

No photo or painting has captured it, either, though there have been billions. None ever could. The canyon will always withhold the largest parts of itself, concealing its many worlds behind stone curtains no matter where the viewer stands. The knowledge makes any view of the canyon all the more graphic, almost profane, certainly alienating, the apotheosis of what John Keats said about "negative capability"—the power of totally ungraspable beauty. Comparing it to any other fissure is like what is said about the difference between seeing a partial and a total solar eclipse. One is like a kiss; the other is like lovemaking.

But this is just the visual problem. Now combine it with the intellectual blast of understanding of how this graveyard terrain formed when the Colorado River responded to the gravitational pull of the sea by shredding new channels through a plateau of loess and hardened lava, opening the Deep Time sandwich of fifteen geologic eras layered on one another and, beneath that, some of the oldest stone on the planet. The Vishnu Basement Rocks are 1.7 billion years old, making the Colorado River an interloping youngster.

And you there standing on the edge? *Pfft!* A blip. The sigh of a dying mouse. A sprinkle of dust.

Visitors who write of their first look often describe a profound sensual shock. Some are prone to enthuse over the handiwork of the creator, but some, especially pastors, come away almost trembling, their faith in a benevolent God shaken after gazing on the hellish wreckage of his sweet creation, discrediting the Genesis theory of a six-thousand-year-old earth and upending theology. Could humanity be the only consciousness in the universe?

Many take a stab at description before retreating to the sensible position of total futility.

A sampling:

"A combination of regions infernal and celestial. I am not going to try to describe it, for before its superhuman majesty, its splendor, its loveliness, words become as sounding brass and as a tinkling cymbal."—Edith Sessions Tupper, *Wilkes-Barre Record*, August 16, 1895

"It is understood that in a time long before this one there was a time of *koyaanisqatsi*, or life out of balance, a time of corruption, turmoil and chaos. Because of this, we fled to find a new beginning. After much seeking, we emerged into our current world, the Fourth World, at *sipaapuni* in the Grand Canyon."—Susan Sekaquaptewa, Hopi tribal member, 2018

"Man is a living lie—a bitter jest upon himself—a conscious grain of sand lost in a desert of unconsciousness, thirsting for God and mocked by his own thirst."—Henry Van Dyke, *The Grand Canyon—Daybreak*, 1914

"It seemed to me as if it were the burying ground of the universe. It is the delirium of nature. It seems both alive and dead. The mind at first stands aghast. There is a sense of terror that cannot be put into words. There is the silence of eternity."—Rev. C. B. Spencer, *Rocky Mountain Advocate*, 1905

"It flashes instant communication of all that architecture and painting and music for a thousand years have gropingly striven to express."—Charles Higgins, 1892

"You can feel the energy coming off it, you can feel it's alive."—Sarana Riggs, Diné tribal member, 2019

"One's powers of articulation are paralyzed. The artist stands aghast as he gazes on and pinnacles, with a wealth of coloring the secret of whose blending is known only in the infinite."—J. C. Martin, *Prescott Journal Miner*, 1894

"Men of rigid exterior and neglectful religious habits have been known to bend in reverence before this sublime mystery."—Frank Caughey, *Detroit Free Press*, 1902

"Mountain upside down"—Paiute name for the Grand Canyon

"Full of sunken mountains, gorges, terraces, domes, obelisks, precipices, cataracts and cliffs of every hue and color of the rainbow, carved in granite, quartz, sandstone, limestone, iron, marble, gypsum, alabaster, chert, agate and cornelian."—Emily Brown Helminger, *Houston Daily Chronicle*, 1927

"There is a sadness in the canyon, as in all great things of nature, that remove it from human experience."—C. M. Skinner, *Brooklyn Eagle*, March 24, 1901

The Grand Canyon is only an extension of one of the oldest ontological questions, which most people confront at some point. How can we understand anything at all? A view of the canyon puts that matter directly in front of the visitor like a sledgehammer to the face.

Against our will, the canyon exposes the rift between the world as it is, in all its terrible majesty, and the tiny world we experience in our heads, cloistered in our insect perceptions and equipped with feeble eyes that can barely see ten miles to the horizon, let alone give us a glimpse of the true existence we choicelessly inhabit. A canyon, indeed.

Can we touch or even approach that larger reality that the German philosopher Martin Heidegger called Being? In one of his more lucid passages, the famously difficult thinker wrote of walking up to a "well-shaped apple tree" growing by itself in a field. "This face-to-face meeting is not, then, one of these 'ideas' buzzing about in our heads," he wrote.

The tree, of course, has an independent existence. But we can never touch it—not really. Our neurology only wraps the latex glove of the five senses around the tree. We can look at it until our eyes burn, sniff its trunk, put its leaves in our mouth, run our palms over the bark until they bleed, and all of those experiences are *still* filtered through sense perceptions and not truly direct. The core always dances outside our grasp. We do not know Being, only the signposts that point toward it over the horizon. The tree—and the Grand Canyon—might as well be a hologram.

The same is true for the written word. You could build your house next to that apple tree, orient the study window toward it, open the blinds, contemplate it for hours each day, and write five million words dedicated to the tree. None of your encyclopedia would ever come close to the heart of that tree. Language can whiz around pure Being like a swarm of electrons, but it can never pierce the nucleus. And so strange that the language used to describe hard truth often reaches for geologic terms to describe the end of frivolous speculation and the beginning of the unchangeable. *Bedrock principles. Cornerstone. Foundational. Stone-cold truth. Ironclad. Rock solid.* The crumbled necropolis of the Grand Canyon puts the lie to that idea.

In a related thought, no less startling, the British physicist Roger Penrose has pointed out that three basic realities exist simultaneously: strict Euclidian mathematics, the physical world of objects, and the realm of consciousness. These three hard realms inform each other but do not touch. The geometric ratios of the apple tree are not the same as the wood of the apple tree, which are also not your own thoughts about the tree.

Immanuel Kant made a similar observation in *Critique of Pure Reason*. Standing between you and Ultimate Reality is a two-pound mass of wet processing equipment called the brain. We can watch the show from a distant edge. But we will never get close, never truly touch.

This is why all those failed literary attempts to describe the Grand Canyon bring us close to the mystery of existence.

—

We lack a precise linguistic record of what the first human residents of the canyon thought of their surroundings, though the rock art of the western Archaic culture of four thousand years ago offers some clues.

A panel of ocher marks on the sandstone—some of the oldest writing in civilization—shows elongated human figures against a backdrop of zig-zagging lines that may represent mountains, and beaded circles that may represent caves, or motherhood, or the canyon itself. The birth imagery, suggestive of a larger emergence, indicates these pioneer citizens may have seen the canyon as a source of their being.

The first Europeans who happened on it lacked any coherent grammar to describe what they'd seen. García López de Cárdenas y Figueroa sent some men down the canyon in 1540 to see about a Colorado River crossing, but it took them three days to make it even a third of the way down. They gave up, cursing their Hopi guides, who were almost certainly trying to mislead them. When they returned to camp, they told stories of boulders "taller than the great tower of Seville." Cárdenas himself viewed the magnificent split in the earth as nothing more than a tactical obstacle between him and rumored cities of gold.

Americans who arrived later also could not seem to process it in aesthetic terms, as if it were painted in a color not visible to the human eye. Lieutenant Joseph Christmas Ives explored the canyon 317 years after Cárdenas and found it curious, but not worthy of sustained attention. "The region is, of course, altogether valueless. It can be approached only from the south and after entering there is nothing to do but leave," he wrote in his withering *Report on the Colorado River of the West* in 1864.

Ives's bleak assessment came in for radical revision by John Wesley Powell, a Civil War veteran who had lost his right arm at the Battle of Shiloh. In 1869 he marshaled up supplies and took the railroad out to Green River, Wyoming, where he and ten companions set out to float down the Colorado River and report their findings. This epic journey, and another in the winter two years later, resulted in a celebrated report on what had previous been a *flumen incognita*.

What many forget about Powell's *The Exploration of the Colorado River and Its Canyons* was how light it was on geography and how lavish it was in descriptive prose that tried—as many would after him—to sum up the impossible. Powell made a ritual confession of literary inadequacy before launching into intricate sentences like this:

> When thinking of these rocks one must not conceive of piles of boulders or heaps of fragments, but of a whole land of naked rock, with giant forms carved on it: cathedral-shaped buttes, towering hundreds or thousands of feet, cliffs that cannot be scaled, and canyon walls that shrink the river into insignificance, with vast, hollow domes and tall pinnacles and shafts set on the verge overhead; and all highly colored—buff, gray, red, brown, and chocolate—never lichened, never moss-covered, but bare, and often polished.

His friend Clarence Dutton upped the literary ante even higher in 1882 with a tour de force entitled *The Tertiary History of the Grand Canyon District*, written for the U.S. Geological Survey after he spent months camped on the South Rim and studying the glorious disaster beneath him.

Though cheerfully agnostic, Dutton was a student of world religions and had an awareness that such an apparition should reach for otherworldly labeling. He bestowed exotic names on the metropolis of buttes and mesas: Vishnu's Throne, Zoroaster Temple, Rama Shrine. Other figures from world religions receive their due: Solomon, Apollo, Venus, Thor, Horus, Buddha, Krishna, Confucius. This seeming horror of the cosmos in Arizona was, in fact, "the most sublime and awe-inspiring spectacle in the world," disclosed late in history to the Western mind. And to glimpse it was to surrender to profound confusion.

"The lover of nature, whose perceptions have been trained in the Alps, in Italy, in Germany, or New England, in the Appalachians or Cordilleras, in Scotland or Colorado," Dutton cautioned, "would enter this strange region with a shock, and dwell there for a time with a sense of oppression, and perhaps with horror."

The Grand Canyon was no terrestrial atrocity, Dutton said, but instead a jewel of creation that deserved a radical new method of appreciation. The history of Western art would have turned out different if the canyon had been plopped on the plains of central Europe, he said, just as the imposing cone of Mount Fuji had influenced Japanese painting. The ugly gash of the canyon must be studied with patience, he argued, before the "the forms which seemed grotesque" can be revealed in dignity and grace. No fast views would ever suffice.

The Tertiary History was a masterpiece of geological specificity contained within richly descriptive prose, one of the finest government documents ever written. The public loved the report; it became a huge hit and opened the canyon for the type of mass appreciation Dutton suggested. A platoon of entrepreneurs then did their best to shrink the Grand Canyon down to human scale, to package and present it to visitors. In short, to sell it. This new frame of reality would put a cash register in the foreground of Vishnu's splendors.

One of the great capitalist rogues of Arizona, Ralph Cameron, tried to claim the entire canyon as his personal property. He came out from Maine in 1883, took an interest in the canyon, and dug a copper mine near Grand-view Point that turned him and his brother, in the eyes of a friend, into "ragged assed millionaires." But he realized more profit could be wrung from the tourists drifting to the area in stagecoaches. "I have always said that I would make more money out of the Grand Canyon than any other man," he remarked.

This took a little construction work. Havasupai sheepherders on the river had found a sloping fissure on the South Rim to drive their flocks up to summer pasture. Using frivolous mining claims to secure the old corkscrewing route, Cameron hired a crew to shovel and blast a wider lane and named it the Bright Angel Trail, charging visitors a dollar to descend. On a watered glade near the halfway point, he erected a few primitive shacks and called them the Indian Gardens Hotel. Mule train guides hit their passengers with a surprise here: it would cost them another dollar to be taken back. And an additional charge to use the outhouse.

A threat to Cameron's monopoly arrived in 1901 when the tracks of a spur line of the Atchison, Topeka and Santa Fe Railroad arrived at the South Rim, along with a vision of a luxury vacation haven for aesthetes and outdoorsmen. The railroad had seen pikers like Cameron before, but he promoted himself to the public as the little guy battling the *real* monopoly. "He could charm a bird out of a tree," observed a federal official. And he used more bogus mining claims to pin down strategic points in the canyon where he was betting a hydroelectric dam might one day be erected.

To the deep-pocketed Santa Fe and its allies in Washington, Cameron was a parasitical huckster trying to turn the canyon into a third-rate tourist trap, the "Niagara Falls of Arizona." They sought to drive him out by erecting a resort of limestone and pine logs—a blown-up version of a hunting cabin—called El Tovar, for one of the lieutenants on the 1540 Spanish expedition. Federal judges kept ruling against Cameron, but he refused to leave.

The railroad gave up and bought his dumpy hotel for a sum they refused to disclose but was almost certainly exorbitant. And then President Woodrow Wilson, not ordinarily a friend of conservationists, was persuaded to sign a bill creating Grand Canyon National Park in 1919. Administrators then ordered Cameron to cart all the "filth and refuse" out of Indian Gardens, replacing the typhoid-ridden accommodations with a set of stone bungalows called Phantom Ranch down at the river.

Cameron got revenge, of a sort, by getting himself elected as a U.S. senator from Arizona on a populist platform in 1921 and trying to withdraw appropriations for the park. But even as he maneuvered, the park was already being transformed by the vision of a onetime reporter for the *New York Sun* who, like Cameron, had a flair for promotion. Stephen T. Mather had made his fortune from helping advertise the 20 Mule Team brand of borax detergent. But he struggled with depression. Only walks in the woods, it seemed, cheered his spirit.

Mather accepted an offer to become the first director of the National Park Service in 1917 and set about democratizing the face of America's prettiest places, wanting everyone to "see" what he saw, selling the view like soap. Paved roads were the key to mass enjoyment, Mather believed, and he replaced old wagon paths with asphalt, centering them around visitor's centers, scenic drives, and concession stands. The customer base shifted from artists and hunters toward families in their cars and campers—the basic shape of the park as it is today. When you take a map at the entry booth of any national park, you're looking at Mather's vision.

"Leave it as it is," Theodore Roosevelt had said at the Grand Canyon on May 6, 1903. "The ages have been at work on it and you can only mar it." Conservators of the park have stayed mainly true to that idea. Mather's roads have a limited footprint on the North and South Rims. Harebrained schemes, such as the 2017 proposal to build an aerial tramway to the bottom, have been stopped in their tracks. Bids to extend uranium mining near the canyon have been rebuffed by Washington authorities in the name of protecting the watershed from radioactive debris.

One of the monuments on the South Rim is a National Park Service installation called the Trail of Time, which details the geologic formation of the canyon in a series of interpretive markers, starting two billion years ago and ending at the present. Each meter walked stands for a million years: as good as a futile representation as any piece of flowery writing.

My friend Laura Trujillo had the agonizing experience of visiting the spot close by where her mother leaped off the edge. Laura writes:

> I got lost in the geology for a moment, standing in a place that held rocks 2 billion years old, and my brain placed the two and six—no, nine—zeros to the right. That is not forever but an amount of time I could not understand. I focused on the facts. The trees and rocks, how the Colorado river snaked below almost exactly 1 mile down into the earth, the sound of a raven and the light rain that was slowly growing heavier and turning to snow. My mom fell 5 million years.

Perhaps the uncomfortable questions that hover over the abyss are what inspire so many people to rebel against the physical reality of the canyon—to attempt to defeat it with their own strength.

The "rim to river to rim" journey is a brass ring among ultramarathoners—a forty-two-mile ordeal that takes about eight hours for an Olympic-level athlete to complete. Others punish themselves in the tradition of Harvey Butchart, a math professor from Northern Arizona University who scaled the cliffs here in 164 known spots. But even the most intense physicality brings the visitor no closer to the heart of the matter. All the views are valid and none of them are complete.

The Grand Canyon is at the edge of perception where certainties drop out of sight, territory where even the strictest atheists must confess some simulacrum of religion, if only that of simple wonderment—the only place to retreat after all language collapses and all the achievements of science still leave us with a void of meaning. We'll never really *get it*.

Perhaps this is why a retreat into the El Tovar hotel to sit by the fireplace in the dark-logged room is such a relief. These are human dimensions we can understand. We can think about dinner, or how to load the car the next morning, or what's brewing back at the office. The drama of two billion years lies sprawled naked out there, but we must make peace somehow with the single day that we are allotted. Easier not to think of it much.

Perhaps it is merciful that we cannot really see the Grand Canyon. It is Arizona's most famous signpost into the unspeakable, the death of rationality, which is really just an unwelcome challenge to our tiny human view: the drunkenness of ordinary life jolted for a brief moment into awestruck sobriety.

A view of the Grand Canyon goes in more than out.

THE GRAND CANYON GETS QUIET in the early afternoon as the temperature peaks; there is no birdsong; and Bright Angel Creek narrows into a channel through obsidian cliffs as it gets closer to the Colorado. From the rim, the tops of these walls are but one wave in the stony sea of color and depth.

I ate dehydrated food at a campsite in the heart of the canyon in the company of a family from small-town Ohio, a retired lawyer and his wife plus their son and daughter-in-law, as the stone around us grew dark and we listened to the trickle of the creek. "You can't perceive this when you're in it," said the wife, gesturing all around.

The next morning, I knelt at a certain spot on the south bank of the Inner Gorge for the first time in sixteen years. I had been here on what was supposed to have been my wedding day. That engagement had fallen apart a few months before the intended date, and she had declined to move with me to Arizona. I didn't want to spend the day of ghost matrimony sitting in my apartment in Phoenix feeling sorry for myself. So I came here to the cleft of some of the oldest stone on the planet and marched five miles down to the river on a broiling hot day, wondering what would become of me.

Inner Gorge: was there ever a more evocative phrase? Our personal histories invariably merge with the land; we put our tiny marks on the rocks and they wash away in the next rain.

"The living of life, any life, involves great and private pain, much of which we share with no one," Barry Lopez wrote in an essay about this part of the river. "In such places as the Inner Gorge, the pain trails away from us. It is not so quiet or so removed that you can hear yourself think, that you would even wish to; that comes later. You can hear your heart beat. That comes first."

I like to think of this spot near Bright Angel Creek in the depths of Arizona as "mine" because of that private pain, though of course it is not. Innumerable caravans have passed here, both on foot and on water. In a few dozen or hundred years, this beach of rock and sand likely won't even be here, erased by the relentless river.

On August 17, 1869, John Wesley Powell and his corps camped near here. The crew had lost a crate a food in the rapids and had searched for wood to make replacement oars. They got lucky, chancing on a pine log that had floated down the river from the plateau. "On the way, it must have passed over many cataracts and falls," wrote Powell, "for it bears scars in evidence of the rough usage which it has received."

The Bright Angel Trail goes upward, past the site of Ralph Cameron's onetime "hotel" called Indian Gardens, and then starts a more relentless ascent through a fault-line crack. The crowds of tourists grew thicker as I got closer to the top, and my large backpack became more conspicuous. I staggered through switchbacks, and by 1 p.m. I gained the South Rim and announced my arrival to nobody in particular by thunking my one good trekking stick down on the sidewalk on the spot where Cameron's tollbooth used to stand.

After sundown, a brief eruption of luxury: a laundromat, some microwaved pizza, and eight hours' sleep in a park service campground. The sun rose too soon, and I moved onward through ponderosa pines on the blissfully flat Coconino Plateau toward the edge of the park and the burst of municipal acne called Tusayan, a smaller example of the kind of terrible Arizona city-building that flourished in the 1980s alongside highways in strings of linear commerce like Prescott Valley and Bullhead City. The steak was dry at an unfortunate cowboy restaurant called Yippie-Yi-Yay; the atrium of the Grand Canyon Inn smelled of Jacuzzi and bore an upholstered patina of 1980s Navajo kitsch. Like other Arizona profit zones, it clung to the edge of grandeur. Ralph Cameron's ghost haunted this place.

Fire roads took me the next morning through valleys of granite and past the fire tower at a place called Grandview, built in 1936.

From the top of it, I could see the red smudge of western Navajoland once again, a maze of red walls and canyons. And then the trail picked up the path of an 1890s stagecoach line for a two-day march across undulating ranchlands toward the lumpy triangle of Humphreys Peak: an unmissable Mount Doom, the tallest mountain in Arizona, and the remnant of a volcano that last erupted 2.8 million years ago. I stopped to smoke a cigar near the stony remains of the stage station at Moqui Springs to stare at the faraway pyramid.

Surveyors had named this remarkable mountain for the Civil War general Andrew Atkinson Humphreys, denying it the traditional Diné name of Dook'o'oslid, or Shining on Top. The snow-capped pinnacle is the home of Abalone Shell Woman, the lunar deity, who went there after First Man and Woman affixed the highest elevations with a sunbeam and made it shine with yellow twilight. Though I'd been walking toward the peak all day, it seemed to retreat before me. "The strong white shell is standing out," goes a traditional Diné chant about the mountain. "A living mountain is standing out."

I camped near the base of a cinder cone named Missouri Bill Hill and climbed to the top for a view the next morning. Dook'o'oslid had crept closer; the white shell of snow on its crest looked cool and inviting. Another day of walking took me up a broad slope into alpine forests dotted with aspen and green moss growing on the rocks. Not far away was the Snowbowl Ski Resort, where much of the snow in an era of climate change has been made with treated sewage water, inspiring years of federal litigation from the Hopi Tribe, who did not want melting piss on one of their holy sites.

The only people I'd seen for days were elk hunters bouncing down dirt roads in pickup trucks. Now came a young woman jogging past me engaged in a cell phone conversation about a sales quota, a sign of approach to the city of Flagstaff, even still inside the kingdom of pines spilling down from the tops of Dook'o'oslid. Before long I was walking past the climate-controlled storage units of the Museum of Northern Arizona on U.S. 180. Inside the crescent-shaped building, in the vague shape of a pueblo house, were tens of thousands of rugs, pots, bracelets, beads, and Kachina dolls, a dazzling horde of antiquities, all collected here since 1928, when the museum was founded by a zoology professor and his artist wife, both from Philadelphia.

Rather than walk along the noisy highway, I found a paved trail alongside the Rio de Flag that took me through a neighborhood of slant-roofed vaguely ski lodge–style houses that looked like they could have been situated in Aspen, and into the northern edges of town. There I bought a cup of coffee at a converted gas station called Late for the Train that I used to frequent when I lived not far from here, on Piute Street, a decade ago. I relished my cup.

At the next table, an energy consultant half-shouted into his cell phone. "I hate going to Scottsdale!" he told whoever was on the other line. "Just hate it. It's all self-dealing there. They all want you to promise points on the deal for nothing, just making an introduction to someone else. And they never write anything down. No ethics!" Northern Arizona always did view itself as a purer kind of place than anywhere else in the state. "Don't Phoenix my Flag," says a local bumper sticker, in protest of the creeping subdivisions and the nightmarish traffic on the retail drag of Milton Road.

The town had gotten more expensive and crowded since I lived here last, but it has an unpretentiousness that will never go away: the feel of a working-class lumber-and-rail town that happens to be blessed with close access to two major Native reservations, plus the Grand Canyon. The handsome and compact downtown is stuffed with brewpubs frequented by students and river-runners. The gabled old train station is a predawn stop for Amtrak's Southwest Chief; the motels near the crescent of track through town advertise "No Train Noise" on their marquees. On warm nights the scent of pinesap hangs over Northern Arizona University and its heart of gothic sandstone halls, a spillage of modernist dorms, and a giant timber-domed football stadium looking like a woman's ample breast crossed with a flying saucer.

Up on a nearby ridge is the observatory founded by Percival Lowell, the gifted scion of a wealthy Boston family who excelled in mathematics, wrote books about the Far East, and became obsessed with the idea that canals could be sighted on Mars. He was wrong about that, but it was in his Lowell Observatory in the high country air that Pluto was first identified as part of the solar system in 1930. The first two letters of its name, PL, are the initials of the patron who brought the furthest planet in the darkness into human consciousness.

A scouting party for some of Lowell's fellow Bostonians had passed by here fifty-five years earlier to raise an American flag spangled with thirty-seven stars up on a ponderosa. Then they departed in a search for better pastures, leaving only a pragmatic name for the future post office. Catholic families like the Riordans got here before the Atlantic & Pacific Railroad was able to erect its bridge over Canyon Diablo to the east, and got an early advantage in what became one of the rougher towns on the line. The *Arizona Champion* newspaper complained of "frequent forays of drunken cowhands, who love nothing better than to ride full tilt down Railroad Avenue, whooping and firing their six shooters into the air as the terrified populace scurries for cover."

Many of the country hooligans worked for the Babbitts of Cincinnati, four brothers who pieced together various parcels into a mammoth spread they called the CO Bar Ranch—Arizona's largest. The descendants still own a good portion of it. With the landed wealth came power. One of the grandsons, Bruce, was the governor when I was growing up in the 1980s.

I needed calories and found my way to a greasy spoon just south of the tracks named Mike and Ronda's The Place, where I've been a periodic customer since the afternoon I was introduced to it in 2001 by the *Republic*'s northern Arizona bureau chief on the day we both climbed Humphreys Peak. It's tough to get a table here because of its well-deserved popularity, and I sat at the bar next to an old Spanish-speaking cowboy in a leather vest who told me he spent most of his career working out at the Babbitt ranch. He was having biscuits and gravy; I had an omelet with hash browns. It was a perfect breakfast.

In a growth-obsessed state like Arizona, where erasure of history can seem like an organizing principle, such mainstays like The Place are a comfort. They reassure us that our constructed environment has at least some purpose and continuity. Communal places like restaurants and bars also help us understand a little bit more about who we are and where we came from. The food and drink of Arizona is edible culture.

ENCHILADAS AND WHISKEY

Is there such a thing as a distinctive Arizona cuisine? We have our taco stands that grill carne asada late into the night; family-owned diners open at sunrise with eggs and toast; the stinky old dives with graffiti on the walls; fresh seafood trucked up from Puerto Penasco; the fine dining with heirloom vegetables; the cowboy steaks; the norteño cuisine of northern Mexico, with its rock salt, tortillas, cumin, and chilis.

Arizona also has thirst written into its design: not just the arid country that cries for rain or the heritage of hard-drinking mining camps but the persistent yearning for a stiff drink when the sun goes down. Our drinking is often done in darkness—not merely in the gloom of night, but in the neon dusk of one of the 1,270 licensed establishments dedicated to the ancient habit of tippling.

Perhaps Arizona's restaurants and bars are darker, almost cave-like, because of the pitilessness of the sun. This is only appropriate because the heart of Arizona eating and drinking goes to the sun-drenched land itself. The original diet here grew from trees, fell from cacti, and sprouted underground.

The scientist farmers of the Hopi grew corn in shades of red, black, yellow, lavender, and white, along with beans equally as flamboyant, on plantations spread on the desert floor below the four ship-like ridges where they made their apartment dwellings. The corn was female, mother, *sonowi*—an object of religious communion, dispensing both life and tenderness. Hopi chefs patted the grain meal into cakes as thin as crepes and cooked them on stones greased with squash seeds to make a delicious bread called piki.

Further south, the Tohono O'odham perfected the *ak-chin* method of planting corn kernels and tepary beans into streambeds to catch brief summer floods. They enlivened their diet with blossoms from saguaro and prickly pear cacti, which delighted a Swiss Catholic missionary sent to work among them in 1732. "For me these fruits take the place of cherries, plums, sour cherries, and many pears," reported Father Philipp Segesser. "God sends and provides in every place that which refreshes man."

Father Segesser watched the Tohono O'Odham pound the seed pods of the mesquite trees that grew everywhere in southern Arizona to make a sweet-tasting flour, packed with protein and amino acids, sometimes mixed with water for an electrolyte drink during long desert crossings. The acorns of scrub oak had a similar staple function for the Apache further to the northeast: both bread-meal and energy paste. When bow-and-arrow technology surpassed that of spears and darts around 1,600 years ago, the Apache menu grew to include more generous helpings of deer, gopher, rabbits, and javelina.

And then came the chili: a relative newcomer, yet one of the signature Arizona tastes. The word comes from the Nahuatl people of central Mexico, and so does the combustible fruit brought to Arizona by Spanish settlers in the sixteenth century. The chemical irritant capsaicin burns the tongue and mucus membranes, triggering a pain-pleasure release of endorphins. Red and green flavorings created by the terroir of alkaloids in the local soils made legends of household chefs and created tests of sweaty fortitude at the supper table.

Laguna Pueblo writer Leslie Marmon Silko has defined *culture* as "an entire worldview complete with proven strategies for survival," which is certainly true of the intimate entanglement of territory and dinner among Arizona's first residents. They were literally "eating the landscape," in the words of Enrique Salmon, turning the beauty of the earth and its plants into sustenance, grinding out bread meal from the flower buds of cholla cacti.

Nightly feasts came with a feeling—all too fleeting—of oneness with the very flesh of creation, as well as a knowledge of terrible fragility: a religion in itself. The lifeway and the landway and the foodway became all as one. "Lost travelers and lost pinon-nut gatherers have been saved by sighting a rock formation they recognize only because they once heard a hunting story," wrote Silko.

The fusion of this landscape-based food culture with the Iberian tastes of the European newcomers provided the kettle for an entirely new way of eating that came into flower in the eighteenth century—the norteño style of Mexico, which incorporates pinto beans, cornmeal, chili, onions, cumin, and tomatoes into a heavier base of beef, cheeses, sour cream, and sausages.

Many Anglo visitors turned up their noses or felt their tongues burning off. And Mexican elites to the south disdained norteño cooking, considering it hillbilly slop not fit to serve to dogs. But it proved both durable and malleable: hardy ranching fare for a tough country that nevertheless contained a thousand varieties of flavors, heat, and piquancy within its basic forms.

Norteño made a twist on flat Hopi piki bread. The Southwest rancheros of the seventeenth century grew more wheat than corn, so the finely ground white flour became the staple of the flatbreads that settlers called tortillas. Leavened with oil and mineral lime, shaped on a stone, and cooked on a metal griddle, it served a function like a hand utensil to pick up bits of meat—a Mesoamerican style of table manners that can be traced to 500 BCE. In the cattle empire of the northern parts of New Spain, tortillas with the diameter of dinner plates could be folded once over strips of grilled beef to make a taco or rolled around beef and beans to make a burro.

The Spanish-speaking cowboys laid strips of cow flesh out under the desert sun, in cages to keep the flies away, to make a jerky called *carne seca* (dried meat) that could be reheated in the field camp. Chunks of pork or goat fared better after they marinated in the vinegar-chili concoction called *adobo.* The signature blast of taste most associated with norteño cuisine lent itself to the most versatile entrée in the repertoire: a tortilla rolled around fish, beef, chicken, greens or any number of fillings, baked, and slathered with sauce made from green or red chili—the verb *enchilar* means "to add chili," hence, the enchilada.

For those raised on norteño, the ancestor of Mexican food served up in today's Arizona, nothing would ever compare again, and they would speak about it in exultant terms usually reserved for the deepest affections of family and home. "Homemade white cheese sizzling in a pan, melting inside a folded tortilla," wrote Gloria Anzaldúa. "My sister Hilda's hot, spicy menudo, *chile colorado* making it deep red, pieces of panza and hominy floating on top."

Different ingredients arrived with the Anglo prospectors and livestock growers—many of them from Kentucky and West Virginia—who sought riches for themselves in Charles D. Poston's land of Arizona after the end of the Mexican-American War in 1848.

The former Spanish garrison of Tucson became a pro-Confederate stronghold, as older men from slave states courted Mexican teenage brides and ingratiated themselves into prominent mestizo families. They grudgingly accepted hot norteño suppers even as they asked for the cornbread, poultry gravy, and peach cobbler of their youth. The larders of the hell-on-wheels camps like Tombstone, Bisbee, Wickenburg, and Oatman were likewise heavy on the starch and the proteins of Civil War rations: lots of bacon, lots of biscuits, lots of grease and fat. African American cooks in the cowboy wagons brought a distinctively Deep South taste to the ranch chow served in the open air, with pork-flavored stews and sorghum for sweetening. Arizona cuisine might therefore be described as a happy collision of two cooking traditions regarded by their nation's elites as not worthy of their attention. This is where Southern farm food meets Norteño.

The first Arizona restaurants founded in the nineteenth century were little more than crude mess halls where people wiped their hands on their clothes. "The lack of formality that has long characterized its table manners is of pioneer stock, induced by hard living," noted the author of a 1930s Federal Writers Project guidebook. Many of the first Anglo residents—including the Kentuckian Poston and my great-great-grandfather Evan Wilson from the coalfields of West Virginia—hailed from Appalachia and brought a fried chicken sensibility with them to their new mountain-miner's landscape. Perhaps that's why European-style fine dining was not established here until the postwar suburban boom. Not until 1973, in fact, did an Arizona restaurant win four stars from the Mobil Travel Guide: the Tack Room, which served haute cuisine with rhinestone cowboy flair.

America's oldest surviving Mexican restaurant is Tucson's El Charro, named for a particular type of spangled horseman. Monica Flin was the daughter of an immigrant stonemason from France who helped build Saint Augustine Cathedral. She married into a Mexican family, learned Spanish, picked up norteño techniques, divorced, and then opened a restaurant in 1922 that relied on a bit of leveraged creativity to help it squeak by. During lean times, Flin would sometimes take an order, run over to a grocery to get ingredients on credit, rush back and cook the meal, then quietly pay off the grocer with the customer's money.

El Charro also claims to be the birthplace of the chimichanga, that deep-fried burrito whose origins remain disputed. Flin's relatives always claimed that it got its name from a Spanish corruption of the word "thingamajig," which came out of Flin's mouth after she dropped a tortilla full of beef into hot oil, and then started to say a Spanish verb beginning with *ch-* that implies fornication. Other signature dishes include the *caldo de queso* and the *carne seca*, spiced beef dried in a special cage on the roof, and the *capirotada*, a Lenten dessert of bread pudding with cheese and cilantro.

Another story has the cheese crisp—that signature Arizona appetizer made of a tortilla, butter, and shredded cheddar—coming out of El Charro. But its origin was almost certainly from a private household in Tucson, a city whose history is suffused with norteño home cooking and household agriculture. "Anything you stuck in the ground would grow, the soil was so rich," recalled Gilbert Molina, whose family had come north from Sonora in 1910 to grow chilis. "We never had to add manure or fertilizer."

Another old Mexican standby can be found in Scottsdale, whose civic history can be conveniently divided into three parts. The founding era began in 1888 when U.S. Army chaplain Winfield Scott purchased some land next to the new Arizona Canal to grow citrus trees, and a little market village sprung up around him. The second era exploded after World War II when the first mayor, Malcolm White, hyped a mythical cowboy past with the slogan "The West's Most Western Town," encouraging a discretionary economy founded on snowbird golf resorts and cowboy gewgaw emporiums. The third era, beginning in the mid-1980s and continuing to today, featured the ridiculous hurl of luxury homes, stucco strip malls, and golf courses far to the north of the 101 Loop, and the carnivalization of its sedate downtown into a nightclub cavalcade of wasted frat bros and money-obsessed strivers.

Los Olivos Mexican Patio is a holdout from the first period, founded next to a metal shop and named for Scott's olive trees by the Corral family, who came up from Sonora in 1919 to get away from the Mexican Revolution and farm cotton in peace. The classic elements of Yaqui Mexican are here in generous quantities: chips and salsa, rocks-and-salt margaritas with triple sec, albondigas soup, combo platters with rice and beans.

Once considered a poor man's food, then an exotic treat, Mexican dishes became fully absorbed into the middlebrow Arizona mainstream in the mid-twentieth century thanks to welcoming establishments like Los Olivos. Tamale carts had been common sights in working-class barrios, but they migrated into the air-conditioned indoors. "Combo plate" family startups, like the inimitable Garcia's of Sunnyslope, began popping up on corners and in strip malls in urban Arizona during the midcentury craze for Tex-Mex, a blander version of norteño.

Not everyone loved it. The British author of *The Guide to Mexican Cooking*, Diane Kennedy, deplored these dishes as "an overly large platter of mixed messes, smothered with a shrill tomato sauce, sour cream, and grated yellow cheese preceded by a dish of mouth-searing sauce and greasy fried chips." Phoenix historian Jon Talton looked back with mingled fondness and queasiness at the "Sonoran goop" served up at chain restaurants like Macayo's.

Yet they thrived and multiplied. And those with liquor licenses served up margaritas on the rocks with salt, the preferred Arizona way to down the fermented heart of the agave plant called the maguey. The margarita, a citrus syrup product of 1930s border vice culture in Baja California, helped popularize tequila and make it, in the words of journalist and author Gustavo Arellano "alluring and fun, dangerous yet irresistible." The concoction of tequila and crème de cassis called Tequila Sunrise was invented at the Arizona Biltmore to satisfy a poolside day-drinker.

Fermented delights were enjoyed in Arizona, of course, long before statehood. The Tohono O'odham made wine from saguaro fruit. Roman Catholic missionaries brought in vineyard grapes under the watch of the Spanish crown, and American miners and cowpunchers packed in distilling equipment for rotgut whiskey. Tucson had a German brewery as early as 1864. But frontier beer was nasty and far less common than whiskey because a corn homebrew called tiswin—with a recipe borrowed from Apache ceremonies—could be boiled and re-boiled at home in metal milk can.

Only Arizonans of a distinguished age can now recall the old A-1 brand of beer, brewed on Madison Street in Phoenix and advertised with art featuring cowboys and cactus decorating Arizona's dim-lit taverns, or places like the classic Drift Inn in Globe, whose opening at 6 a.m. was timed for shift change at the copper mines. The indefatigable play-by-play man for the Phoenix Suns, Al McCoy, was encouraged to shout "Good! Like A-1 beer!" upon a player's successful basket. Our local beer joined another beverage brand launched after Prohibition—the non-alcoholic Citrus Club soft drink brewed up by Glendale grapefruit orchard manager Ed Mehren in 1936. He intended it as a fruity mixer for gin and whiskey, but it stood fine on its own and was soon called Squirt.

Squirt got sold off to a Michigan company just as the venerable A-1 went into decline in the 1970s. The final wrecking crew was led by Cindy Mc-Cain's father, Jim Hensley, a salesman who won the license to distribute Anheuser-Busch's beer on the condition of exclusivity. By the time future senator John McCain came on in 1981 as vice president of public relations, A-1 had all but evaporated. Local craft pilsners and ales from breweries like Four Peaks, Barrio, and Grand Canyon have replaced it on the supermarket shelves and in the Arizona taverns that come and go like monsoons.

The Native American tradition that gave Arizona such a harvest of delicious food is exceedingly difficult to find today outside of private homes. You can get a decent mutton stew at the Junction Restaurant in Chinle, and the food trucks that show up outside Sunday mass at San Xavier del Bac mission south of Tucson sometimes serve up Tohono O'odham tortillas called *ceme't* with red chili.

A more dependable Indigenous taste can be found at the unpretentious Fry Bread House on Seventh Avenue in Phoenix, where Native owners serve up the namesake puffy disks filled with chorizo or greens. A blend of flour, sugar, and lard, fry bread is a recent introduction to the Indigenous diet, an improvised use of staples handed out by U.S. government agents on nineteenth-century reservations. Some consider fry bread equal to prison food. Others see it as a testament to Native creativity and resilience in the face of adversity.

A word should also be said about Arizona road food: inexpensive and unpretentious, but a distinguished type of cuisine unto itself, served up with grease and care at venerable holes-in-the-wall like Tag's in Coolidge, the Ajo Café and Bobos in Tucson, Brownie's in Yuma, Rock Springs Café in Black Canyon City, and in several places just off the old Route 66. Juan Delgadillo built his Snow Cap drive-in in the town of Seligman from lumber salvaged from the nearby Santa Fe railroad yard. A fitting symbol indeed.

The highway and all its colorful roadside barnacles followed the train route that created northern Arizona's vine of jerkwater towns.

Delgadillo lavished his considerable sense of humor on the premises—a neon sign proclaimed "sorry, we're open," the menu featured "cheeseburger with cheese," and a phone booth outside housed a toilet. Delgadillo messed with his customers in other ways, by squirting "mustard" at them, which was actually yellow string from a bottle, or by serving an absurdly miniature portion of an order. The comedy went on all day long, and although the puns and insults were too much for some grumps, families tended to remember the Snow Cap, a preservation of a specific culture of Arizona eating: the majestic era of the roadside ice cream cone and grilled delectables wrapped in white paper.

Another living time capsule sits on the opposite end of Route 66 with its beginnings in an era of awful food: the time when western train passengers were given flyspecked slop and told to like it. Englishman Fred Harvey changed all that. He persuaded the Santa Fe Railroad to let him operate a string of eateries along the tracks that treated traveling guests like royalty, with haute cuisine to back it up: filet mignon, oysters, exceptional wine, and gourmet coffee, all of it brought in via the Santa Fe's refrigerator cars.

La Posada—"the resting place"—in Winslow was the last of the big Harvey Houses, designed by southwestern architect Mary Colter and built in 1930. Restoration artist Allen Affeldt saved it from oblivion at the turn of the century and reopened the Turquoise Room restaurant, which routinely wins accolades from the international foodie press. The attached hotel retains Colter's quirky touches like stained-glass windows, arched entryways, wrought iron bars, and ashtrays shaped like jackrabbits.

When the westbound Southwest Chief passes by with the rumble of a forgotten monarch, it reminds the entire room of the raison d'être for the churro lamb, saguaro cactus syrup, and seared elk medallions on the plates.

Raise a margarita here to Fred Harvey, America's original chain restaurateur, who was responsible for the popularization of norteño cuisine in middle America, serving up then-exotic tacos and enchiladas to fascinated eastern travelers. Harvey went light on the chili to avoid offending delicate palates yet did more to normalize the Mexican cowpoke tradition of food in the United States than any one Anglo person until hot dog cart entrepreneur Glen Bell. Bell's 1962 appropriation of pre-fried shells in his new Taco Bell restaurants planted a battalion of Mission-style cinderblock boxes across the West. Arizona has 171 of them.

For those looking for more distinctive norteño on the cheap, late night taco joints like Nico's, Losbeto's, Alberto's, and Filberto's—all descendant from the vision of an immigrant from San Luis Potosi named Roberto Robledo—cater to graveyard shift workers and woozy bar crawlers craving the protein in a tortilla pioneered by Mesoamericans of twenty-five centuries ago.

To truly appreciate Arizona, one must eat of its hard-won gifts, draw in the heat and flavor from the soil. Longtime food writer for the *Tucson Citizen* Alva Torres shared a family recipe for tortillas that was the essence of simplicity: flour, water, salt, and lard mixed, kneaded, and rolled into little balls, then flattened and cooked on the griddle for just a few seconds. Torres exulted in the fragrance, calling it one of the best on earth.

"There are some things that cannot be described accurately," she said. "They must be experienced."

T HE ARIZONA TRAIL CROSSES UNDER Interstate 40 in a concrete drainage tunnel that echoes with the rattle of traffic, and I emerged from the southern end facing a rise that soon plunges into the U-shaped basin of Walnut Creek, lined with dark boulders on both sides. The Sinagua people lived in pit houses here in the seventh century, within shouting distance of what would become the route of the first railroad through Arizona, and eventually, a continental highway identified by a number. Whatever name the Sinaguas may have given to their canyon home has been lost forever.

The urge to pin names to pieces of land—to give them significance—is a widespread urge among global societies, and a mark of pathos. We try to sink our nails into the ground for a bit of immortality, a sense of continuance.

Though I couldn't see it from the trail, there's a mound of Kaibab limestone seven miles to the southwest, a product of mountain building of 290 million years ago, and the subject of a memorable but eerie little book called *Biography of a Small Mountain* by a teacher named Donna Ashworth, who quit the classroom to watch for fires from the lookout tower on top.

Woody Mountain took its name from John Woody, who came out from Oregon in the spring of 1883 to raise cows at its base. "After a million wordless years, Woody Mountain gained a human name," Ashworth wrote. "If it hadn't been for that, he'd have disappeared into the past like smoke from his own campfire. A lot of men did."

Contemplating the mountain and its name drove Ashworth to melancholy thoughts of geology and mortality. "Solid, but not permanent," she wrote of the mountain. "Nothing is ever permanent."

In these lava-tossed regions of Arizona, with all its frozen magma humps, perhaps it is easier than other places to understand that the land is indeed moving imperceptibly, like colors on the spectrum of light that cannot be perceived by the human optical nerve, and that our brief lives unfold in the still-frame of a lengthy geological movie whose plot we don't get to enjoy. "What disorients most of us without formal geologic training is grappling with time," wrote naturalist David Yetman. "The vastness of the past is upsetting and incomprehensible on the face of it."

The trail atop this still-creeping soil leads on to Anderson Mesa, a bleak stretch of pines named for one of Woody's livestock-driving contemporaries—a settler named James Anderson partnered up with the father of one of the state's first U.S. senators, Henry Fountain Ashurst, raised here in a dirty sheepherder's cabin, cut off from the comforts of the world and dreaming of faraway cities and beautiful words.

Despite his scaly-handed background—or perhaps in revenge of it—he earned a reputation as a parvenu with a fancy for high-winged collars and rhetoric. He laced his congressional speeches with Latin and Greek and whatever else sounded pleasing to him. "I love auriferous words, and nothing delights me more than to pluck gems from the dictionary that otherwise might never see the light of day," he said.

Ashurst's love of political belles lettres concealed his true identity as an ethical shapeshifter. "There has never been superadded to these vices of mine the withering, embalming vice of consistency," he said. Except for one cherished principle: "When I have to choose between voting for the people or the special interests, I always stick with the special interests. They remember. The people forget." He lost a reelection bid in 1940, having failed to return from Washington to campaign. Like the Sinagua people, he bloomed like a wildflower and passed on to whatever is next beyond the earth.

An icy wind blew across the plain where Ashurst first opened a book, and I had to lean into the gust to make headway. The late-afternoon clouds tumbled and raced overhead, seemingly just a hundred feet off the ground. My side began to hurt. An hour after sundown, I gave up and threw down the tent on a rocky patch of ground with absolutely nothing to distinguish it from the rest of the dusky plain. Setting up the tent, bending the poles, and setting them into the grommets turned into a formidable chore as my hands shook.

I crawled into a cold bag and pulled the flap over my face. Sleep was elusive; my teeth wouldn't stop chattering. How many others had spent desolate nights out here? My sympathies mounted for the child Henry Fountain Ashurst, and all the other sheepherders of this plateau—Anglo, Mexican, and Native—whose names I'll never know.

My spirit didn't improve much the next morning when I climbed down off the mesa and into the wooded valley near the bottom end of Lower Lake Mary. I heard semiautomatic gunfire coming from an indistinct direction. It's not an uncommon sound in the Arizona wilderness, particularly in deer season, but the woods are flat, my clothes were in dull colors, and I began to wonder if an errant round was going to tag me like a wasp. I was forced to trust a person I can't see to be responsible.

These periodic gunshots became the percussive soundtrack for my walk down the ruined tracks of the Mineral Belt Railroad, a scheme from the 1880s to connect Flagstaff with the copper lodes surrounding Globe. But it petered out near here for lack of funds. The railbed is a berm of maroon earth topped with rotting square ties. I felt a bit better once I could get behind it as a dirt shield from whoever was shooting their semi-automatic rifle out there. Every now and then, the vanished track intersects a dead stream revealing stone bridgework. What hands built them? Immigrant laborers, most likely, whose anonymous contributions gave the state its abutments and paid for its growth with their sweat.

In time, the trail crests a ridge and comes down to a scene resembling the Florida Everglades or a tidewater marsh. This is Mormon Lake, not really a lake but a damp plain of clay and grass that fills up only in the wettest seasons. You can't really take a boat on it, but it's still surrounded with vacation cabins belonging mainly to Phoenicians.

That night, I sat at the bar at the Mormon Lake Saloon and talked with a retired detective from the Maricopa County Sheriff's Office. He had a cabin nearby and came up here to fish. Cops tend to have easy second lives, thanks to generous pensions.

He had served during the same period when I was working as a reporter for the *Arizona Republic* and we knew some of the same people in law enforcement. Then we got talking about some infamous valley cases.

"Hey," I said, after a while. "Do you remember when that house in Scottsdale exploded?"

HELLSGATE

I walked out of my rented house in Scottsdale on the morning of April 10, 2001, and squinted at a giant plume of smoke on the horizon. It was about two miles away and colored black, meaning that whatever was burning over there was still on fire.

Public safety was not my beat at the *Arizona Republic*, but I figured I'd drive by the fire on my way to work and pick up a few quotes for whoever would be doing the story. Assuming we'd even cover the blaze if it resulted in no big damages or injury.

I followed the pillar of smoke to a cul-de-sac called Seventy-Fourth Place just in time to see the roof of a house crash down in a confetti of flames and sparks. The Scottsdale Fire Department was spraying geysers of water onto the mess, and several police officers were busy stringing yellow tape around the scene. A couple of kids stood straddling bicycles nearby, arms across handlebars, looking stunned. The house had exploded about twenty minutes ago, they told me. Their friend, ten-year-old Bobby Fisher, lived there.

Houses catch fire all the time. But they don't just blow up. This would be more than a blotter item. I called the newsroom and told them I'd be staying awhile as a news helicopter clattered overhead, getting video. More police cars arrived.

I knocked on doors around the cul-de-sac and learned the obliterated home was the property of a couple named Robert and Mary Fisher. He worked as a heart catheter technician at the Mayo Clinic; she was a homemaker. They had two kids. One woman next door said she occasionally heard screaming fights, but it never got frightening enough that she called police. As I thanked her for talking to me, I could see a few technicians from

Southwest Gas rooting through the still-smoking rubble, lifting up objects. At their side were two besuited detectives from Scottsdale P.D.

Within the hour, a police spokesman came out to tell the growing scrum of reporters three corpses had been found inside the ruin. Robert Fisher, forty, was nowhere to be seen. Apparently he had left on a camping trip. By sunset, the police had identified his wife and two kids as the victims. But they insisted Robert was not a suspect, that they only wanted to talk with him.

None of us believed this. I went back to the newsroom, made some calls, and chanced upon a knowledgeable leaker. He told me the gas line had been deliberately cut and an ignition source had been left burning in the house as a crude kind of fuse. We put that into the first front-page story. Then came another piece of information we were not supposed to have: the cause of death.

My colleague Judd Slivka and I ripped out another A1 lede:

Mary Fisher was shot in the back of the head and her children's throats were slashed in the hours before their Scottsdale home exploded Thursday, law enforcement sources said Friday.

The city editor, Kristin Gilger, winced as these words pecked into being on the green monitor screen in front of us. She normally did not look over the shoulders of her reporters, but this was a hot one: a "good murder," in the parlance of newsrooms, a sordid impulse festering within a tract house and bursting into ugly flower. Monsters dwelt in the suburbs. All the TV stations were leading with it; we had better details.

"Do we have to say it like that?" she said. "So bluntly?"

"But that's what happened," I replied. "We can't be in the business of covering it up." The right-to-know argument: a favorite of every reporter. Gilger relented.

A group of four reporters congregated that evening in the ninth-floor conference room as the sun made triangular shadows on the Hyatt Regency and the Chase Bank tower outside the windows. We speculated on where Robert Fisher might be, proposed unusual angles we might pursue, spat laughing contempt for the Scottsdale police who had been outraged at the leaks we had secured. Dennis Wagner drew abstract shapes on his legal pad that looked like peacock feathers.

Left unspoken among us was what journalists do not like to discuss: that writing about matters of somebody else's life and death can feel like living inside a novel. The details can be tremendous fun to a close-in observer with no real stake in the matter other than the pure *interestingness* of it all.

Judd covered the funeral for Mary and her two children in the same Scottsdale church the family had attended. The pews had been salted with plainclothes cops in case Robert decided to show his face. After talking with many of his friends, we started to assemble a profile of the suspected killer: he was a controlling husband with a liking for massage parlors and a mania for guns. He fancied himself an outdoorsman and liked to brag about how he could "live off the land" for months. He favored Copenhagen chewing tobacco and harsh discipline for his kids. Mary dreaded having sex with him and had threatened to leave him. Robert apparently could not bear the thought; his own childhood had been scarred by his parents' divorce.

One night, I drove home from work with the creepy realization that Robert Fisher—wherever he may have been hiding—was almost certainly reading the stories I was writing, either in hard copies of the *Republic* surreptitiously obtained or perhaps online, trying to learn what the police had found out.

After I parked my Jeep in the carport of my rented brick house on Hopi Way, I went to the side door and found it unlocked.

An improbable thought stood up urgently in my consciousness. What if he had been displeased by my coverage, found out where I lived, and was lying in wait inside? Calling the police seemed unwise: my local agency was Scottsdale P.D., the same agency we were feuding with, and my skittishness would have been a source of bemusement. So feeling like a gigantic chump, I crept to the hall closet where I kept a pistol, clicked off the safety, and went methodically from room to room, leading with the muzzle, and ascertained that Robert Fisher was not hiding in my house. I had apparently left the door unlocked that morning while leaving for work.

The case fell off the front page. We learned that Fisher had been photographed at an ATM on Thomas Road at approximately 10:40 p.m., about an hour after the surmised time of the triple-murders, and had withdrawn the limit of $280. The state Department of Public Safety at last named him a suspect in the murders, putting out an alert that suggested he was heavily armed. Then the information pipeline went silent for more than a week. Scottsdale police weren't telling us anything, of course. The leakers had no further tidbits.

Ten days after the explosion, I was at my desk working on something else when an alert came over the police scanner from the Arizona Highway Patrol. Fisher's sport-utility vehicle had been found off Forest Road 41 in the woods of the Tonto National Forest some thirty miles from Payson. State police had surrounded a limestone cave where they thought they had him cornered; Scottsdale P.D.—the agency of record—was rushing to the scene.

I begged Gilger to let me go, and within ten minutes, I was tearing northeast. By the time I made it to the discovery scene near the Mogollon Rim, way off any paved roads, four police agencies had put up a bivouacked command post under a bank of generator-powered lights. About half the valley's press corps also showed up, and we spent most of that night in an improvised corral of TV vans and print reporters' cars, shivering and laughing together at a campfire ignited with highway flares. We made fun of the cameraman from Channel 15, who had gotten his remote broadcast van stuck in the mud. We laughed at the polished correspondent from Channel 5, Christian Kafton, who was so particular about his pants that he didn't want to sit on a log. "Hey Mr. Beautiful," yelled Dave Cruz, the *Republic*'s photographer. "Say hello to Mother Earth!"

We laughed, above all, that we were safe around a fire while the killer was cornered and doomed. We knew him not. His fate was not our fate. No civilians were around for us to pester for interviews; the cops were tense and not talking to anyone. This was only a deathwatch. I filed my story back to Phoenix over the phone and relished the thought of how a woman I had been seeing would read my dramatic words on A1 when she awoke. After 2 a.m., I crawled to my Jeep and dozed in the driver's seat, awakening at one point in a half-dream as I pictured the face of a grinning Robert Fisher filling the window, a hunting knife held at the side of his ear like an *American Gothic* pitchfork.

The next morning, the Scottsdale police confessed a mistake through clenched teeth. Their technicians had dropped flash-bang grenades into the darkness and searched the cave with a remote camera and found nothing but cobwebs. Fisher had probably abandoned his wife's SUV and left the scene—maybe by hiking out through Canyon Creek, possibly by hitching a ride. No footprints, no body, no trace. And that was the beginning of the end of the search. Gila County sheriff's deputies would be taking over, but they didn't show much inclination to go trudging through the woods looking for Fisher.

I left the media encampment on foot and found a side track stemming off Forest Road 512. With nothing better to do, I walked down the washboarded dirt for a mile, rounded a bend in the pines, and came upon a tow truck with Mary Fisher's SUV perched on the back halfway wrapped in green tarp. Scottsdale's two lead detectives—T. J. Jiran and Joe LeDuc—stood by it, looking exhausted.

"Hey!" I said brightly. "Did you find anything in that vehicle?"

Jiran fixed me with a death stare. He was a Brooklyn native, a "cop's cop," as he had been described to me, a street tough who took no shit from anyone and was an expert in breaking down suspects during interrogation.

"I'm not answering your questions," he said.

"But you've clearly searched this vehicle?"

"You have fucked up this case," he told me.

"Way too much information has been put out there," added LeDuc. "Totally compromised this investigation."

"You want to have this debate, I'll have this debate," I answered.

"Get the fuck out of here!" screamed Jiran, and I shrugged and retreated down the road.

"Jerkoff!" he yelled at my back.

Gila County enlisted the aid of some amateur spelunkers who knew the cave system in the Tonto National Forest. But they called off a second search after the county attorney warned them of liability problems if a barricaded Fisher happened to be lurking and shot at one of the volunteers.

I wrote several stories for the *Republic* exploring the possibility that Fisher had simply walked a good distance away from his vehicle to kill himself. But no corpse materialized to prove the theory. The FBI put him on their Ten Most Wanted list with the assumption he had slipped across state lines, possibly to a tropical location to work at a menial job under a pseudonym.

The television show *America's Most Wanted* did a segment on Fisher. One week later, somebody with a menacing baritone called the show's 1-800 tip line from a payphone outside a pizza joint in Chester, Virginia, and said: "This is Robert Fisher. I'm glad I killed the bitch and you will never find me." Local police staked out the phone for the next seven days, but nobody resembling Fisher came back.

More time passed. I left the *Republic*. Calls continued to trickle in to the FBI from tipsters who thought they saw someone who resembled his wanted poster. Police in Vancouver, Canada, nabbed a forty-two-year-old suspect who seemed a dead ringer for Fisher and had a missing bicuspid in the same spot where Fisher had a false gold tooth, but the fingerprints were no match. Somebody bought the empty lot at 2232 Seventy-Fourth Place and put a new house on it. Scottsdale's detective supervisor on the case, John Kirkham, died of a massive stroke. Jiran and LeDuc found a massive blown-up photograph of Robert Fisher tacked to the inside of his closet door.

As the five-year anniversary of the explosion drew near, something motivated me to reach out to Jiran, the detective who had cursed at me in the woods. He responded to an email with more friendliness than I had expected. And a month later, to my huge surprise, I found myself smoking in a leather easy chair with him in a members-only Scottsdale cigar club inside a nondescript industrial park. He'd retired from Scottsdale P.D. and was now working as an airport courier, so he was free to speak with ease about past events.

We laughed a bit about the yelling incident, and he told me he'd worried I'd file a complaint against him with Internal Affairs. I told him his frustration was justified.

"But you know why we were so pissed off at you?" he asked.

"Why?"

"We were pretty sure he blew up the house thinking it would destroy the evidence that he'd killed them. People try to burn corpses all the time, but they never succeed. They don't know how much water is in a human body. Crematoriums require temperatures of about 1,500 degrees. No house fire gets that hot for sustained periods. All it does is make the body a little crispier. So our whole intent was to put out the message that we didn't think he was a suspect and we thought it was an accident. We'd hoped that he'd read the papers and think that he fooled us. That he could come back pretending not to know what happened."

I tried not to let any expression show on my face, but I felt like covering it with my hands. My career as a reporter had always been suffused with certain principles. Readers deserve to know. Government agencies need to be accountable. Print the truth as you know it. These ideas weren't wrong. But here was a case where they had collided with a more compelling interest.

My reporting might have let Fisher get away. Our collective pleasure in this crime—the instant press mythology around Robert Fisher—had likely been complicit in the mishandling of justice. The indescribable pain behind the killings took a backseat to the excitement of the manhunt. I felt sick.

More time passed. Tips stopped coming in to the FBI. I found myself thinking about the case more often than I liked. The *who-ness* of the crime was a slam-dunk, the *how-ness* had been well-established, and the *why-ness* wasn't hard to surmise: a bad marriage, a violent personality, a fatal snap one night.

But the *where-ness*—that was the trouble. Fisher's fate might never be learned.

The "escape" theory still seemed ludicrous to me. Fisher's butchering and burning of his family had all the marks of an impulsive act. He hadn't planned it; he hadn't packed; he'd withdrawn a small amount of money on the fly. How could anyone—sane or insane—go on living with the image of slaughtering his own children burned into his memories?

He had clearly shambled off into the Tonto National Forest and put his treasured .357 into his mouth. Rough justice served. If this were true, my reporting hadn't made a bit of difference in the end.

But where was the evidence?

That was why, more than eight years after the explosion, I stood at the edge of Canyon Creek not far from where Mary Fisher's SUV had been discovered.

The entrance to the cave was beyond a stone cairn. Fixed inside the crevasse was a surprise: an old wooden door, looking like a relic stolen from a prairie farmhouse. Beyond that, the unmistakable ebony hole of a volcanic cave with a slight breeze pouring out, as if aspirated from inside, signifying a corresponding opening that may be miles away.

Some of the late nineteenth-century settlers in Pleasant Valley used to come up here on horseback and play in the cave during picnics. Its name was the 41 Club cave, though it was marked on the topo map with only a Y symbol. This was where the police had been convinced Robert Fisher was hiding, and where they dropped flash-bang grenades in the darkness, hoping to flush him out.

I had a flashlight with two D batteries. The light seemed pitifully weak. I crawled through the mud-smeared opening until the blackness was complete.

What would it have been like to be stoppered up in here like a cork with the sound of police and dogs outside? Clearly he didn't die in this spot—this wasn't the place. But what of the deeper caverns that are up to a hundred feet below the surface?

Not a hundred feet inside and already I could feel the beginnings of severe claustrophobia, an insistence that I didn't belong here. What if the entrance should somehow collapse, pinning me inside? I crawled out, defeated, and when I returned to the truck, a smell hit me as I opened the door. A bag of peaches that I'd bought at a Payson supermarket had rotted, filling the cab with their odor.

Three weeks later, I came back. This time I brought a two-day food supply and hiked into the gully of Canyon Creek, picking my way carefully down a small drainage sinew lined with boulders. If I could find anything that hinted at a death scene for Fisher, it would mean my words in the *Republic* had not let him get away with a triple murder.

Among the burned pine trees, there were some that had been felled by chainsaws. One tree off to the side, still standing, appeared to have been decapitated. A giant blob of amber-colored sap mushroomed out of its top, like a frozen gush of blood. If Fisher had fled into this canyon to take his life, would his corpse have burned? This seems possible. Temperatures of forest fires have been known to reach eight hundred to a thousand degrees. Not hot enough to consume a fresh body, as T. J. Jiran could testify, but enough to obliterate everything but bones. I kept my eyes open.

At a spot about five hundred feet down from the western lip of the canyon, a small promontory afforded a view of the slope below. From here I saw the twinkle of the water in the creek. And a strange metallic sound split the air: an elk, making a piercing bleat that zoologists and hunters call a bugle. Males over four years old sound it as a mating call for unattached cows, who tend to choose those who can screech the loudest. It sounded like a giant sheet of tin being dragged against concrete.

There had to have been a hundred promontories like this in the Canyon Creek drainage, a hundred more over in Cherry Creek, thousands in the Hellsgate Wilderness seven miles behind me. A million places to stretch out under the stars and the sky and think about eternity. Think about dying and going to join it in its boundless whirl. Robert Fisher might have been here, propped up against this ponderosa, trickling blood from his knee, dun-colored cargo pants torn, a wound from a fall down a staircase of boulders. His back stinging from the hike, an old firefighting injury come back to torture him. The trees shafting over him like a chamber of judges.

I could walk with head cast down in a precise zigzag pattern over all this country every day for a year and still not cover 5 percent of this forest. And even so, there is no guarantee that I wouldn't have walked directly over the spot of transmutation for Robert Fisher. The blue-steel remains of his pistol may have still been visible, or partially covered by forest duff. But that, too, could be easily stepped over. His bones would have been long scattered by animals.

In Flagstaff I once talked to a Zuni elder who told me about the secret names of the rivers and outcroppings on the reservation and how knowing them was a mark of trust and power, an election to a high fraternity. The elders shared these secret names with only a select group of the younger, their favorites, and it was not uncommon that some of the most important names pass into oblivion with the death of the last elders who refused or forgot to share them. They are never written down because that would be a profanation.

I asked him if this was considered a kind of tragedy, and he said, no, not at all. If the names are forgotten and go to the grave with the elders, it is only a sign that the earth has shifted and the name deserves to be consigned to nothingness—the spot on the map of oral tradition gone to white, so to speak. Withered leaves must be cleared for new ones. This is the relentless way of the world. Even names are like flesh.

The shadows were falling longer on the granite cliffsides and the elk had gone silent. I descended another thousand feet to the side of Cherry Creek and picked a flat spot in some grass. The meadow was plush and almost like a carpet. The insects left me alone.

Before going to sleep I took a short walk to the creek. The moon was full and fat and cast reflected ivory light down everywhere, making the valley a camera obscura of shadows, and it occurred to me again how radically a landscape is altered when light is drained from it. What had appeared open is closed. The woods were a fabric of dark gray where insects ticked. I lay there in the grass looking upward.

———

This country has known violence before. A few miles down the road from where Fisher had parked the 4Runner is a place called Pleasant Valley, the epicenter for a series of murders between two rival families in the 1880s.

The Grahams and the Tewksburys started picking each other off in a series of ambushes after a rich cattleman named James Stinson accused men from both families of stealing his horses, then paid off the Grahams to testify against their former friends in a Prescott courtroom. Gunplay escalated when the Tewksburys imported herds of sheep, notorious for chewing grass down to the roots, creating a dead zone that would take years to replenish. The Grahams drew in the arrogant cowboys from the Aztec Land and Cattle Company, known as the Hashknife Outfit, the monopolistic Standard Oil of the rangelands with a blood vendetta against sheep. Killing and lynching mounted up—at least eighteen separate incidents—in this southwestern version of the Hatfield-McCoy conflict, until only Tom Graham and Ed Tewksbury were left alive. And then the latter shot the former in the back in Tempe in 1892, an event fictionalized in the Zane Grey novel *To the Last Man*.

No physical monuments have been erected from this time. The site of the Tewksbury family cabin lies in the woods, known only to a few locals.

Here the wife of John Tewksbury was said to have walked out in the midst of a siege, in the sights of the Grahams' rifles, to bury her husband and a friend so that hogs would not eat them. "Strangers who went into the valley, adventurers lured by the tales of the fighting, disappeared and their fate was never known," wrote Earle R. Forrest in his 1936 history of the feud entitled *Arizona's Dark and Bloody Ground*, "but one thing is certain, they found the trouble they were looking for—some in unknown and forgotten graves in a lonely wilderness."

The feud was only an extension of other violence in Arizona: the long Apache Wars, in which forces led by a series of U.S. Army generals pushed the various bands of Athabaskan-speaking peoples toward miserable reservations where government agents sought to wipe out their former lifeways and self-sufficiency. In mining towns like Tombstone and Wickenburg, sordid little conflicts over sex and money turned into southern-style duels of honor. The nineteenth-century newspapers delighted in exaggerating these stories and turning them into morality plays with recognizable heroes and villains. But there wasn't much honorable here. Profits rather than principles were at stake. Arizona was a fine atmosphere for sociopaths. "Innocent and unoffending men were shot down or bowie-knived merely for the pleasure of watching their death agonies," wrote a disgusted newspaperman, John Cremony. "Men walked the streets with double-barreled shotguns and hunted each other as sportsmen hunt for game."

All of these historical influences—the Indian removals, the range wars, the street gunfire, the incessant publicity, people rolling into town and rolling out—created a mystique of violence in Arizona that has never fully disappeared, even after the heyday of the dime novels and television shows that enshrined the idea of western bloodshed as purifying, even noble. You can pay six dollars to gain admission to the site of the O.K. Corral gunfight in Tombstone. "Walk where they fell!" leers an advertisement.

Arizona is still among the bloodier states in the country, thanks to a transient population and a high rate of gun ownership. Statistically it ranks as the ninth most dangerous state in the United States (Louisiana is number one), with 508 violent crimes committed for every 100,000 people in 2020. Rates spike in the summers. In a sociological study subtitled "A Field Study of the Heat/Aggression Relationship," researchers idled a car at a Phoenix stoplight and timed the inevitable honks, which they found grew louder and angrier depending on the temperature. The "interpersonal hostility" index rose in accordance with the heat of the day. Valley police reporters consequently have a lot of material.

The summer sun that washes the mountains bone white, the social isolation, the drowning open spaces, the heritage of bloodshed, the strangers next door—under the wrong circumstances, this Arizona pressure cooker can create an aura of nihilism, the conditions that lead to "regeneration through violence," in the words of Richard Slotkin. This is more than just random bloodshed. This is systemic.

Five months after the Fisher murders, in the shellshocked days after the September 11 terror attacks, my colleague Dennis Wagner and I were sent to Tucson to track down the addresses of a few of the hijackers and their associates who had lived there. It was a grim tour of sunbaked apartment cubes, cheap one-bedroom digs that could be had for four hundred dollars a month, where turnover was fast, and where nobody, of course, had any memories of Hani Hanjour or Wadih el-Hage. What I remember most from those days was the look of latent violence in those bright and shabby places.

Here is another story, this one from my childhood nightmares. Dad loaded the family into our van-conversion camper for the annual road trip from Phoenix to Kansas to see Grandmother in the summer of 1978. Newspapers had become a grade-school fascination for me. The *Republic* blared headlines that weekend about a gang that had broken out of the penitentiary in Florence on July 30. They were on a murder spree: a Charles Starkweather blood-odyssey in the desert.

Gary Tison, three of his sons and a portly accomplice named Randy Greenawalt had already killed a family outside Yuma, including a two-year-old boy hiding between his mother's legs as bullets poured in the backseat of the car. Nobody knew the location of the killers, only that they were almost certainly prowling the roads. I could see a little anxiety on my parents' faces as we set out, and perhaps some relief we would be leaving Arizona for a while.

We camped on the side of a road near Durango, Colorado, and the next morning, at breakfast in a diner, my mother brought a copy of the *Denver Post* to the table and said simply: "He's here."

An Associated Press wire story in the paper carried speculation that Tison and his henchman were in southwestern Colorado, perhaps on their way to link up with Tison's brother, who had promised to help them escape to Mexico. We pressed on to Kansas and later learned that, sure enough, the gang had murdered a married couple who had also been camping on the side of the road near the town of Pagosa Springs.

I will never know how close we came to being the van they picked.

By the time we returned, the Tison rampage had ended. The gang tried to run a DPS roadblock south of Casa Grande near the settlement of Chuichu on August 11. Two of the boys were killed in a hail of police gunfire that sent their stolen van careening off the road. Gary Tison—the mesmerizing sociopath—yelled "every man for himself!" and ran off wounded into the desert as his only surviving son and Greenawalt gave themselves up.

Tison had sworn he would never go back to prison, and he didn't. Dehydration took him. They found his corpse under an ironwood bush eleven days later.

The garish bloodshed had freaked me out. But it wasn't until years later—after I went to work for the same Arizona newspaper that had fascinated me—when I learned the Tison episode went deeper and reached higher than had been reported at the time. It was as tangled as the Pleasant Valley War, and even more insidious.

Phoenix in the 1970s—so bright and polished to me at the time—concealed a stratum of corruption under its prosperity. Selling worthless land to suckers was the big game, and nobody was better at it than a lanky charmer named Ned Warren, who lived in a rambling estate on the side of Camelback Mountain and drove a Rolls-Royce. He ran multiple scams: selling the same vacant lot to multiple customers, creating fake neighborhoods up in Prescott Valley without water or electricity, handing out mortgages to drunks for the sake of building a stack of instant debt that could be sold to unwitting investors.

Despite the sleaze, Warren traveled in elite circles, drinking with politicians at Durant's, the Central Avenue power-lunch spot. He hired washed-up actor Cesar Romero, who had played the Joker on the *Batman* TV series, to make celebrity appearances at his land sale events.

Murders trailed Warren like bad cologne. His accountant Ed Lazar was shot to death in a stairwell of a parking garage at 3003 North Central Avenue. One of his managers, Tony Serra, got beaten to death in the license-plate factory in the penitentiary at Florence. A short time later, Gary Tison told one of his sons that he'd been paid fifty thousand dollars to "take care" of Serra, who had been found with a drill hole punched into his forehead. The blood money had been placed in a safe deposit box in a Scottsdale bank.

Amazingly, Tison—who had made a successful breakout from the Pinal County Jail in 1972—was then transferred to the minimum-security unit. This allowed him to have occasional lunchtime visits with his sons. On July 30, one of them smuggled in a pair of shotguns tucked into an ice chest and freed him.

Had Tison been allowed to escape? Had his transfer out of maximum security been an institutional reward for killing Tony Serra and keeping him from telling what he knew about Ned Warren, whose fraud schemes had hazy connections to U.S. Representative Sam Steiger and to the brother of Senator Barry Goldwater?

The byzantine story—which really required thumbtacks, a corkboard, and several lengths of yarn to keep straight—got even weirder.

Investigative reporter Don Bolles of the *Republic* had written several blockbuster stories about Ned Warren's fake neighborhoods in Prescott Valley and his empire of shell companies, one of which—the Great Southwest Land and Cattle Company—had been managed by Tony Serra. The county attorney later admitted to a Phoenix police detective he'd held off prosecuting Warren because top Republicans had pressured him to go easy. "A sorry goddamned mess, this town," the detective mourned later.

On June 2, 1976, Bolles went to the Hotel Clarendon off Central Avenue to meet a source named John Harvey Adamson who promised information on top-level corruption. When he didn't show up for the appointment, Bolles went back out to the parking lot to his Datsun. It exploded when he turned the key. He died eleven days later.

Adamson had been a drinking crony of Ned Warren and had helped carry out the hit on Lazar. He and two other lowlife functionaries went to prison for rigging up the bomb in Bolles's car, supposedly because a liquor distributor named Kemper Marley had complained about stories in the *Republic* concerning the Arizona Racing Commission. The murder of the reporter, testified a corrupt attorney named Neal Roberts, was an example of "old-style Western justice." He evidently liked the phrase and repeated a version of it in his deposition: "it was just a kind of rangelands justice."

The scuzziest elements of Arizona and the cream of its society were here united in a Mobius strip. The dining room at Phoenix Country Club had links to a highway killing rampage that ended at a desert roadblock.

When I went to work for the *Republic* two decades later, a framed photo of Bolles hung from a pillar fifteen yards from my desk. Which is where I was sitting when the news about Robert Fisher came crackling over the police scanner.

—

A Gila County sheriff's deputy told me his theory that Fisher hadn't really headed east to hide in the Fort Apache Reservation. He might have gone west to the more formidable backcountry of the Hellsgate Wilderness Area, a confusing tangle of canyons where few backpackers ever traveled.

If ever there was a place where a man could hide himself, it would be Hellsgate, which took its name from a strange geologic feature—a set of cliffs in a cataract that tower over a series of pools.

Unlike the flatlands of the Gila River into which it drains, very few artifacts from thirteenth-century Indian cultures have been found here. Even they considered it too difficult a place to live. In 1984 it was classified a federal wilderness. Only eight cattlemen can graze their cows on the edges. No logging, mining, or motorized vehicles are permitted. No sheep in there, either: the legacy of the Grahams and the Tewksburys lives on.

Other than those scant facts, Hellsgate is a blank page—at least in human terms. "We know very little about it," Michael Smith, an archaeologist with the U.S. Forest Service, told me flatly. "None of it has been documented. I have flown over it and there's some pretty stuff in there, but we have nothing on it."

I drove my pickup inside a barbed wire gate near a place called Little Green Valley, shouldered my pack, and started walking down a trail that looked like it had been torn up by the tracks of all-terrain vehicles. Then I came to a wooden sign that read "Hellsgate Wilderness" in front of a vast cordillera, scrim after scrim of metamorphosed granite.

To the approximate southeast was Leo the Lion Canyon, a dry tributary that took its name from one of the only incidents out here ever to make a newspaper headline. In the autumn of 1927, Metro-Goldwyn-Mayer hired a stunt pilot named Martin Jensen to fly a promotional tour to movie theaters with the studio's trademark, an African lion named Leo, caged in the back.

Leo's original name wasn't Leo. The studio had purchased a lion named Slats from the Dublin Zoo in Ireland and filmed him blinking lazily with a regal bearing; the shot appeared in all MGM films with the lion framed in an elaborate setting of gold. Jensen set off from Los Angeles in a B-1 but flew too low over Hellsgate on the night of September 16 and couldn't summon the altitude to climb a ridge. He made a calculated crash on top of a tree and struggled out of the wreckage unhurt. The lion seemed okay, too.

Jensen fed Leo a few sandwiches and tried to hike out of the confusing wilderness. The studio grew concerned and then frantic before Jensen knocked on the door of the H-Bar ranch on the evening of September 19, begging for food and a telephone. The studio publicity head bellowed through the receiver: "Jensen, if you've hurt that lion, I'll personally break your damned neck!" A team of cowboys rode out and found the lion hungry and irritated. They fed him a butchered calf and dragged him out in the cage with a team of mules. Slats went on to live nine more years. Somebody from the Forest Service with a sense of humor changed the name of Flat Wash Gulch to Leo the Lion Canyon.

It was not inconceivable that Fisher could have died in that canyon, just as he might have taken his life not very far from his parking spot off the forest road. The 2001 police search had been so haphazard, and even diligent cops can miss evidence of a corpse in the wild. Hadn't the body of Gary Tison, avatar of my childhood dread, lain for eleven days just a half mile from where the highway patrolmen had shot out his tires? There were those who claimed the cops had deliberately not combed the desert for Tison as a sign of their contempt, knowing he would die of dehydration out there rather than turn himself in. Was that also the reason why this forest was never canvassed?

The path to Hellsgate is a dry lifeline to anyone who comes out here. Wander too far away and you're cut off. I wonder if Fisher tried to survive here as a fugitive. Could he have lived in a wickiup just a mile off the trail? The emerald pools at the base of Hellsgate are said to be rich with trout.

Sitting there under the agave and looking into the eroded sink of Hellsgate, as the heat poured down and unseen insects buzzed, I thought of that exercise that I used to play in childhood—to repeat an ordinary word over and over again—*sink, sink, sink*—until the moment when the word slipped from its signified and became a meaningless pronouncement. I could see the trail winding on down toward the cathedral spires of Hellsgate, though the river was tucked far away. The gorge looked like teeth.

An abundance of place-names bearing the mark of hell bespeckle the maps of America. According to the U.S. Geological Survey, the nation has a total 987 place-names that hearken to the devil's lair, including, most prominently, the town of Hell, Michigan, and New York City's relatively placid river crossing of Hell Gate. Of all those names, 571 are located in the West, where the arid geology more resembles the caverns and fires of pre-Renaissance imagination.

There was nobody around to speak to, nobody around to hear. I gathered up a little pile of deadfall in the colorless gloom after sunset and built a fire. Pockets of moisture within the wood sizzled with reproach. This was a vanity fire. I wasn't cooking anything. I just wanted something to do and not be lonely. Words of Heraclitus: "The universe, which is the same for all, has not been made by any god or man, but it has always been, is, and always will be an ever-living fire, kindling itself by regular measures and going out by regular measures." I wondered what the fire looks like from the air above, a sparkle in a plain of darkness.

Later in the tent, I clutched the sleeping bag around me and lay still in the waterproof skin that separated me from the stars, a nymph in a lake nursing a flame, breathing carefully in and out.

—

As the rocks get looser closer to Hellsgate, a sound comes: the cretinous drone of cicadas. Yet they are also a sign of some kind of water, and past the bend stands a line of cottonwood trees, a splash of lemon-lime in the maroon cataract. The river must be very close.

A scramble over huge river boulders and I am at last at Tonto Creek, which is flowing lazily winding between the rocks. I splash water on my face, under my arms. Up the creek, there are high cliffs and a narrow slot too tight to walk through: the Hellsgate.

Before I came here, the only printed description I could find of it was in a self-published book called *Pleasant Valley* by a cowboy named Frank V. Gillette. "No one had ever thrown a line into these big blue holes and the fish were gullible and unafraid of the sight of a man on the bank," he wrote. Properly prepared, Robert Fisher might have found this an easy spot to hide for a time.

The cliffs are lovely and strange, colored ocher with dark streaks that might be malachite. It takes fifteen minutes to struggle up the side of one of them before I reach a drop-off to the river that is perhaps one hundred feet high. Sunscreen drips into my eyes and I stumble a bit.

This can't go on much longer. I find a small bush that casts a little shadow and sit beneath it, determined to blink and cry the bitterness out of my eyes. A wave of dizziness comes and makes me feel like vomiting.

I have taken such a foolish chance on this trip. We try to create meaning in the face of uncertainty. This is the reporter's imperative. But I know now I will never have any answers to what happened to Robert Fisher, just as the true story about Don Bolles and Ned Warren will likely remain concealed from history, just as many of the victims of the Pleasant Valley feud and the Apache Wars will never bear names above their unseen graves.

I can see at least three natural punchbowls below me, a chain of them, each occupying its own slot. I creep down to the edge and step into the first pool. The sunlight is savage on the water. Jumping into unknown water always comes with a stab of fear. Will it be cold? Will it hurt? What really lies down there?

But I make myself do it from weak legs, and then I am immersed, covered in the water, feeling the shock on skin like the last tearing of essence, cliffs hanging in watch, the zigzagging slabs bearing down onto this improbable pit, and I lie floating there in the fissure, in liquid that seemingly has no bottom. This is the place.

WHEN I WAS A BOY in summer camp in the White Mountains near the border of New Mexico, the counselors liked to tell us ghost stories. One of them involved a creature called the Mogollon Monster, which sounded to my cynical ears like something they were making up on the spot. Turns out, they weren't.

A body of folklore about a shambling humanoid in the woods of north central Arizona has been circulating for more than a century. He lives, supposedly, amid the dense forests of the Mogollon (pronounced *Muggy-yon*) Rim, the dramatic escarpment that separates the northern third of the state from the basin and range country to the south.

In 1903 the *Arizona Republican* ran a story about the harrowing experience of one I. W. Stevens, who reported seeing a bigfoot-like man with "long white hair and matted beard that reached to his knees. It wore no clothing, and upon his talon-like fingers were claws at least two inches long." Other encounters described a stinking beast about eight feet tall, sometimes wielding a club. How many of the reports were hoaxes or cases of excitedly misidentified elk or bear is impossible to tell.

Trudging through these lonely ponderosa forests near the rim, though, it was easy to see how those stories grew up around here. Not even the Native people treated it as much more than a byway to pass through: it was an old trading link between the Hopis and the Yavapais down in the Verde Valley. Though the forest has been logged out and regrown multiple times, it seems haunted with the apparitions of previous travelers.

This region is called Happy Jack, after a vanished lumberman's camp, and the road is hard going, strewn with ankle-twisting lava rocks and rutted by last season's rains. The only landmarks are the cattle tanks, the silted-up ponds behind earth dams piled up long ago by Mormon ranchers with rented bulldozers. Land here was a commodity, not a romance. I began to develop a lack of feeling in my soles, a condition that would only get worse the further south I traveled.

But the bedrock changed, almost infinitesimally, from lava loam to a pinkish kind of granite and I could also see ferns growing in the forest duff. I was getting closer to the edge of that two-hundred-mile escarpment named for an eighteenth-century Spanish governor of New Mexico, Jose Ignacio Flores Mogollon, who stayed barely three years before he was removed in minor scandal. His flatterers left his name on a massive geologic wedge at least three hundred million years old. How fast the frost melts off the rocks.

The next afternoon, I stood at the base of a stone monument with this legend in raised letters on a metal plaque:

Seven miles north of this point a band of Apache Indians were defeated by United States troops on July 17, 1882. A group of tribesmen from the San Carlos Apache reservation had attacked some ranches in the vicinity, killing several settlers. Cavalry and Indian scouts were immediately sent into the field in search of the hostiles. Five troops of cavalry and one troop of Indian scouts converged on the Apaches, surrounding them at the Big Dry Wash. The resistance of the Indians was broken after four hours of stubborn fighting. The casualties numbered two soldiers and more than twenty Apaches.

Across the plaque, somebody has stenciled a simple counternarrative in white paint: "Settlers had it coming."

This marker sits on the wagon road that made the massacre possible: a military thoroughfare built by soldiers of General George Crook during the war to chase the Apaches onto reservations and open the territory for white settlement. Arizona was then less a U.S. territory than a vague grouping of buckets: a provisional government operating in a log house, some clusters of miners in the gold pockets, a few hopeful farmers, a vibrant mestizo trading center in Tucson, and a chain of U.S. Army forts in a restive majority-Indigenous land.

Crook had been put in charge of pacifying what Washington called the Department of Arizona, a place-name that had only recently been decided upon. Its roots, of course, were in the Arizona ranch that I'm walking toward, the place where the slabs of silver had been found in 1736. That old Basque name meaning "good oak trees" would go through a misspelling and a rethinking that ripped it far out of context and almost completely erased its original intent.

The modern appropriation of the name "Arizona" was a feat of linguistic alchemy by one of the great hucksters of the nineteenth century, a talented self-promoter and propagandist who came to be called the "Father of Arizona," a man who could tell stories that would make the creators of the Mogollon Monster look like bush-leaguers.

Charles Debrille Poston was a Kentuckian with a fecund imagination who joined the tide of young men his age who went out to California in the first wave of gold exploration. But he spent more time telling funny stories to his friends in a San Francisco boardinghouse than he did looking for minerals. That was the same time in 1853 that the U.S. government was negotiating with Mexico the purchase of the southern third of what would become the state of Arizona, not for any virtues of its own right but as a warm and relatively flat place to extend an all-weather railroad from the slave states to the Pacific Ocean. The Pierce administration sent James Gadsden, a South Carolina railroad executive, to negotiate a $10 million deal with the weakened government in Mexico City.

When the news arrived in San Francisco, it set off immediate speculative thoughts among Poston's friends, all of whom were looking to get rich quick. But what was this place like? Did it have any gold or silver? Nobody seemed to know—trading caravans hadn't been allowed past Santa Fe—and barely anything had been written about it in English. The boardinghouse gang grabbed any book they could find and enlisted some Spanish speakers to translate what they couldn't understand. Poston recalled:

> Old Spanish history was ransacked for information, from the voyages of Cortez in the Gulf of California to the latest dates. That the country north of Sonora, called in the Spanish history "Arizunea" (rocky country) was full of minerals with fertile valleys washed by numerous rivers and covered by forests primeval.

This is incorrect, on multiple fronts, and Poston's salesmanship is on display. What seems to have really happened is somebody at the boardinghouse found a copy of a popular book by Jose Francisco Velasco published just three years prior, a romanticized account of the country titled *Sonora*. Though written in Spanish and distributed in Mexico, it evinced the same tendencies toward exaggeration as Yankee rhetoric of its time.

In his chapter on minerals of the region, Velasco excavated the old story of the fabulous silver discovery on the Arizona ranch that had quickly petered out. But he added a twist: there was a second expedition there in 1817, led by a man named Don Dionisio Robles, who was determined to dig for the vein of silver that had eluded the previous generation of shallow diggers. The Robles group found only a small amount of silver before being intimidated out of the valley by lurking Apache Indians. And then Velasco added a tantalizing paragraph that must have leaped off the page to Poston when he read it in a San Francisco parlor:

> From these reports, it is evident that there can be no doubt that these enormous masses of silver did exist in the Arisona and, if the expedition to which I refer did not find them, it does not prove to the contrary, if one considers that they were in the Arisona only a week since they observed parties of Apache in the vicinity who

were about to attack them and for this reason were forced to abandon the country.

Velasco had misspelled the ranch name, and Poston made it worse with his reference to "Arizuena." And he also failed to appreciate that the legendary valley with its promised deep vein of silver wasn't even included in the Gadsden Purchase. But what did that matter? Facts were hard to come by, especially about a faraway territory with the hint of a lost Spanish treasure. When it came to seeking investors, the story was always king.

Poston and his friend Herman Ehrenberg got an exploratory party together and purchased bunks on the ship *Zoraida* sailing down the Pacific coast to Guaymas, Sonora, where they would go inland to find their El Dorado in this unknown desert they were still calling Arizunea, eighteenth-century Mexican slang for a place of great wealth. All it would take to succeed was displacing the Apaches, a project that would find its culmination three decades later in the campaign led by Crook and the vigilante actions commemorated right off the wagon road he ordered built on top of the rim. That ugly-beautiful name took on a new aura after the war. "For years the very word 'Arizona' has had a gruesome sound to the Easterner," wrote state official John A. Black in 1890. "At the mention of the name of this Territory visions of bloodthirsty Indians, white desperados, barren mountains, and alkalai deserts would spring up before one's eyes."

Stories that begin with romantic mythologies and end in violence—these, too, are monuments to "Arizona" and what it meant to so many people in its past. No coincidence that one of the most extravagant vistas in this natural art gallery of the state, the Mogollon Rim looking south, should be the locus of shameful acts that went down in history's first draft as heroism and adventure.

Also perhaps no coincidence that this corner of Arizona was the favorite writing retreat of one of its primary bards: the dentist-turned-cowboy novelist Zane Grey, who had come here chasing stories with the zeal of Charles Poston going after lost Spanish silver.

Grey wrote incessantly of the healing spiritual powers of the land and the grit of plain-talking settlers in an era when asphalt roads were paved over the trails and the forces of modernity were scrubbing away the greed and the bloodstains of the era of Poston and Crook. But no novel he wrote ever really got to the bottom of it all: the beauty and the hypocrisy and the terror.

Has any novel about Arizona ever done that?

THE CANON

Arizona yearns for a good novel like the soil wants water; poetic expression flourishes best in uncertain times. But no summary work exists, no *one book* that captures the state.

A review of Arizona's longform fiction since the mid-nineteenth century shows it to be much like the place itself: assembled in pieces over the years; full of slapdash constructions and half-starts; occasionally spectacular; concerned with the extremes of nature; pockmarked with stereotypes and burdened with contradictions regarding race and class; perforated with moments of real grandeur. But there is no Great Arizona Novel. Only a handful of major novels have ever been set here, despite an abundance of subject material.

"Arizona's hallmark is individualism," says Alberto Álvaro Ríos, the state's first poet laureate. "And what marks our literature is that it has no overlying set of individualists. We have this insinuation here that history is all behind us. And so we echo that idea: that there isn't anything left to say on a grand scale."

There have been a few attempts. One commonly cited aspirant is *Blood Meridian* by Cormac McCarthy, even though less than seventy-one pages are set in Arizona. McCarthy fictionalizes the story of the Glanton gang, a real-life band of marauders paid to scalp Apaches who start inflicting their deep haircuts on Mexicans and then anyone else unfortunate enough to cross them. After wandering through Sonora, they pass up through the Santa Cruz Valley and over to Yuma. McCarthy clobbers the reader with his tortured and bloody syntax. "The man in the floor was dying and he was dressed altogether in homemade clothes of sheephide even to boots and a strange cap," goes one typical line.

Another contender for the Great Arizona Novel also concerns itself with Indigenous people, except in a much gentler way. *Laughing Boy* by Oliver La Farge won the 1930 Pulitzer Prize in fiction and tells the story of a young Diné athlete who falls in love with a boarding school student named Slim Girl, who is in an unhappy prostitution arrangement with a white man. La Farge's nature writing was first-rate, and his examination of the inner lives of Native people was a corrective to the dime Western novels that had their heyday between 1910 and 1940, as the last remnants of the frontier were dissolving into a fever dream of railroads, dams, copper mines, and telephone wires.

Americans seemed to recognize they had slain a wilderness that could never return, and pulp writers responded with cheaply printed "blood and thunder" biographies that celebrated the deeds—often exaggerated—of adventurists like Kit Carson, Billy the Kid, and Buffalo Bill. The king of the Arizona mythologizers was the amateur baseball player and serial womanizer from Ohio, Zane Grey, who studied Owen Wister's 1902 Wyoming gunfighter saga *The Virginian* for pointers. He bought a cabin outside Payson and churned out romantic novels and stories at a febrile rate. The question that opens Grey's archetypical 1921 novel *The Call of the Canyon* could stand as a summary of his considerable life's output: "What strange subtle message had come to her out of the West? Carley Burch laid the letter in her lap and gazed dreamily out the window."

No gunfire is exchanged in *Call of the Canyon*, only smoldering glances and misunderstandings as Burch takes the train out to Oak Creek Canyon to pursue the love of Glenn Kilbourne, a war veteran who finds the high desert a tonic for his broken body and spirit. After a few catty misunderstandings with a voluptuous ranch girl, Burch wins her man.

Gray expended his most lavish writing not on human relationships but on the landscape. In a moment of romantic despair, Burch goes out on horseback and climbs "a stupendous upheaval of earth-crust, grown over at the base by leagues and leagues of pine forest, belted at the middle by vast zigzagging slopes of aspen, rent and riven at the heights to canyon and gorge, bared above to cliffs and corners of craggy rock, whitened at the sky-piercing peaks by snow."

Not every midwestern migrant to Arizona did it so well. Harold Bell Wright was a Missouri pastor who became a celebrity novelist, moved to

Tucson in 1914, and turned out a hokey story of a trove of riches in the Santa Catalina Mountains called *The Mine with the Iron Door*, complete with a noble savage named Natchee who dispenses sorrowful ancient wisdom and wears a costume that sounds like it was purchased at a truck stop. It was a best-selling contributor to defective Arizona myth-making.

A more realistic treatment of frontier life was Marguarite Noble's *Filaree*, which begins with a pregnant and resentful wife named Melissa riding in her husband's wagon toward the Roosevelt Dam and feeling as "bloated as a dead cow." Melissa goes on to fall in love with a ranch hand—only occasionally a good idea in books like these—before her boozehound husband abandons her. Melissa finds work running a boardinghouse in downtown Phoenix (as my own great-great-grandmother had done in the 1920s) and epitomizing the tough desert grass of the book's title. *Filaree* echoes a slew of nonfiction memoirs from southwestern pioneer women like *No Life for a Lady* and *Woman in Levi's* that constitute an important genre in Arizona literature.

All of them are better known than *Dark Madonna* by Richard Summers, published in the grim Depression year of 1937. It tells the story of Lupe Salcido, the pudgy daughter of a Tucson speakeasy owner. She yearns for a real boyfriend but encounters only abuse and neglect before a final scene with notes of Steinbeck. While *Dark Madonna* suffers from stereotypes and overwrought dialogue, it nonetheless explored territory on the margins that almost every other author of the time was afraid to travel.

Later years demonstrated more sophisticated portraits of Arizona's tripartite collision of Anglo, Latino, and Native cultures. Among the best of them was a 1993 novel by Alfredo Véa Jr. called *La Maravilla*, which takes place in the nether reaches of the Phoenix metropolitan spillage, among the shanties and poverty of the "unofficial trash heap" of Buckeye Road, where few nonlocals venture unless they have good reason.

There's not much of a plot to *La Maravilla*, as the soul of it is the narrator's experiencing the "sumptuous ample embrace" of food and love from his grandparents and witnessing a series of disturbing incidents, but it deserves a place alongside Arizona's other great work of revolutionary post-Vietnam fiction. Edward Abbey's *The Monkey Wrench Gang* is a rollicking adventure novel about a band of four friends who aim to halt the electrification of the

Colorado Plateau by vandalizing construction equipment and plotting the destruction of the Glen Canyon Dam near the town of Page (which Abbey memorably calls "the asshole capital of the universe"). Besides featuring one of the greatest finishing chase sequences of any Western novel, which is no small feat, the novel introduced "monkey wrenching" to the language as a term of extralegal technique.

Much has been written about Abbey's life as an activist and a rough camper—among American authors, he may be second only to Ernest Hemingway in the importance of his personal story to his work—but his biography fades to insignificance in the philosophical depth of the story and the giddy propulsive force of what amounts to an ensemble crime thriller in Arizona's northern backyard. Luis Urrea called it "an insanely violent and hilarious novel. It still feels subversive."

Only half the novel takes place in this state, but the details are finely observed, from the stern notice on the door of a Kayenta Holiday Inn to the pine-crisp air of the Grand Canyon's North Rim to the ugly alabaster slab of the Glen Canyon Dam, the novel's true villain, which goes unpunished.

—

Modern Arizona fiction is concerned not just with landscape but loneliness. The novelist Mark Jude Poirier grew up in Tucson and has set some of his most important fiction in Arizona's second city, most vividly in *Modern Ranch Living*, a 2004 ensemble novel about a gated community called Rancho Sin Vacas, or "ranch without cows," where bored teenagers struggle to connect with each other.

"What's always fascinated me about Arizona—and it's something that I play with in my own fiction—is this idea that Tucson is a really ugly city," Poirier has said. "There's no good zoning, strip malls everywhere, nothing prohibiting giant inflatable gorillas in front of used car lots. They don't give a shit what the cities look like. There's the imposing Catalina Mountains. But in front of them is a Whataburger."

The ugly-beautiful dynamic of Arizona looms large in another notable twenty-first-century novel—the phantasmagoric *Drowning Tucson* by Aaron Mark Morales, in which interlocking stories show the disintegration of the Nuñez family. The book ends in a Joycean pages-long sentence; a sex worker named Rainbow clutches a statue of Pancho Villa mounted on a downtown median and wishes for the apocalypse of this "damned city." Another cynical view can be found in *Spent Saints*, a collection of short stories from Brian Jabas Smith, who writes glittering and unforgettable nonfiction portraits of the down-and-out in *Tucson Weekly*. In this collection, he draws on his own history as a drug-addicted musician living in a Phoenix slum.

Terry McMillan's highly successful *Waiting to Exhale* is one of the very few novels that deal with the lives of African Americans in Phoenix. Four women seek husbands in *Jane Eyre*–esque narrative amid Circle Ks, real estate offices, and red tile roofs. "Why would anyone in their right mind want to live in Arizona?" a sister asks the main character. That question is posed in Barbara Kingsolver's *The Bean Trees*, the story of a refugee from a grim coal town in Kentucky who picks up an orphan girl along the way and names her Turtle. Their car breaks down in Tucson near Jesus Is Lord Used Tires, which might be a front for Central American immigrants seeking sanctuary, a signature progressive cause of the 1980s.

There are points where Kingsolver appears out of control of her story, not knowing where to turn, but near the end, she pulls off a wonderful narrative coup de grace that puts all the wandering events into sudden order. Taylor adopts Turtle through some extralegal sleight-of-hand. They go to a library to kill time between appointments and look up a horticultural definition of the wisteria that Turtle calls "bean trees" and that thrives because of the microscopic bugs in the soil that give it nitrogen.

"'There's a whole invisible system for helping out the plant that you'd never guess was there,'" Taylor says to Turtle. "'It's just the same with people. The way Edna has Virgie and Virgie has Edna and Sandi has Kid Central Station and everyone has Mattie. And on and on.' The wisteria vines on their own would just barely get by, is how I explained it to Turtle, but put them together with rhizobia and they make miracles.'"

What Kingsolver is writing about, of course, are the interlocking bonds of friendship and mutual support that make life bearable. A place like Arizona, where neighborhoods can be sterile, transient, and impenetrable, needs this reminder more than just about any place in the nation.

There is so much left to say, and many readers will find fault with this roundup for sins of omission.

What about the rising tension of small-town desire in Judy Troy's superb *Quiet Streets of Winslow*? Or the specimen of 1944 fancifulness called *Crazy Weather* by Charles McNichols, in which a child named South Boy takes a Huck Finn–like trip down the Colorado River on a journey of "glory hunting" in which he becomes a man? Or the stark 1983 debut from part-time valley resident Denis Johnson, *Angels*, in which two losers meet on a Greyhound bus bound for Phoenix and get tied up in a bank robbery?

Peculiar tales of the past and future have also taken root here, but without capturing the complicated heart of Arizona. An editor at the *Star*, Charles G. Finney, wrote a hallucinatory tale called *The Circus of Dr. Lao* about a traveling show of exotic animals that comes to the made-up town of Abalone, Arizona. It won a National Book Award in 1935. The distinguished writing professor Oakley Hall was a Pulitzer Prize finalist in 1958 for *Warlock*, a gunfighter morality tale set in a mining town similar to Tombstone but with a subversive plot that makes conventional American notions of justice a bad joke.

Or what of the cactus noir tradition? The David Mapstone novels of Jon Talton plumb the grotesqueries hiding in plain sight in the land of Phoenix boosterism. Or the police procedural corpus of J. A. Jance, whose red-rock version of Cochise County looks only intermittently like the real thing, but never mind. Former *Republic* copyeditor Bryn Chancellor wrote the haunting novel *Sycamore*, which hinges on the discovery of old bones in a northern Arizona cliffside. And Ryan Harty's short story collection with the unforgettable title *Bring Me Your Saddest Arizona* contains a tale, "Crossroads," in which a character on a quest to find a missing brother experiences what almost every Arizonan has felt: "Ahead was the glow of Phoenix. It changed as I approached, growing wider and higher until finally, and without even noticing, I became a part of it."

Belgian novelist Georges Simenon, eager to get away from questions about his Nazi friendships in the 1940s, took a long vacation to the Santa Cruz River Valley, where he wrote the booze-soaked novel *Bottom of the Bottle*, and in Tucson, staying in a rented house at 325 West Franklin, where he banged out one of the novels he was known to write in ten days—*Maigret at the Coroner*, in which his signature detective visits the Old Pueblo and becomes intrigued with a dismal local homicide: five air force servicemen stomp a woman to death next to the railroad tracks alongside the Nogales Highway.

The uninteresting court case plays out against a backdrop of earnest American faces, red electric coolers of Coca-Cola, and bouts of heavy drinking relieved by morning doses of Alka-Seltzer. Between laments of ennui, Maigret observes:

> Aside from the center of town, where the few buildings of over 20 floors were profiled against the sky like great towers, the rest of Tucson was like a development, or rather like a series of developments juxtaposed to each other. Some were richer, some poorer, but all were made up of equally new, tidy-looking ranch-style houses.

These Arizona novels occupy the fulcrum between cities and mountains, between thrown-up civilization and cold natural brutality. Arizona's literary tradition is not so much impoverished as it is disunified: still on the lookout for a clear expression of an organizing principle.

There is no widely circulated magazine of ideas, no strong newspaper book review, no literary "establishment" to imitate or rail against, no identified group seeking to create superior regional fiction, and just a handful of well-stocked independent bookstores. Soul-searching analysis has never been one of Arizona's strengths.

Gregory McNamee, former editor-in-chief at the University of Arizona Press, has thought about an architectural theory for such a book and has laid out four principles. First, it should deal in an honest way with the Native Americans who came here first. Second, the land should become an unmistakable presence. Third, it should revise and subvert the traditional idea of the lone hero taming the West. And fourth, it should have layers of depth and meaning that academics can love while retaining a straightforward prose style that the general reading public can admire.

Urrea wonders if such a task is even possible. "Maybe it's too hard to capture the Arizona landscape without fitting it into easy clichés," he says. "A number of people here came because of the images—and those aren't always accurate. But we remain caught in those images."

The job of a novel is to demystify reality. Now into its second century as an American state, Arizona needs this novel as much as it needs freeways and swimming pools and school referendums and health spas and air-conditioned groceries and dazzling magazine advertisements. After all that has been achieved, we need to know who we really are.

'M RELUCTANT TO LEAVE THIS vista atop the Mogollon Rim, but the sun is lowering and I've got to find some level ground down below before dark, so I start making my way down a rough ramp through the Paleozoic sandstone, an artifact carved by the construction crews working on James Eddy's bold attempt to create the Mineral Belt Railroad from Globe to Flagstaff in the 1880s.

When the Southwest's most famous incline proved too steep for locomotives, Eddy tried to blast a tunnel through the walls. It went in only seventy feet before he blew through his savings. Another Arizona bust; another monument to a lost future.

The ramp eases down to a truly lovely spot, East Verde Spring, a clear pool with a lacing of watercress, surrounded by a small pine forest. I drink deeply without filtering. And outside the pine grove, I see the landscape now looks more like Sedona or southern Utah than the Black Forest of Germany. There's sandstone, manzanitas, alligator junipers, yucca plants, strange rock formations, a few wild blackberry bushes in the creeks, some invasive fountain grass that recently migrated up the Verde River system from seeds blown off the front yards of faraway Phoenix.

The cattleman's path toward the old Mormon settlement of Pine is called the Highline. And it's hard going. By midafternoon, my water is running low again and the sun is cascading down on the exposed trail, and it takes several hours to round the final bend of the flattop rim and see the veiny streets of Pine. The LDS ward chapel is now a museum where the names of the four founding families of this valley settlement—Hunt, Allen, Fuller, and Randall—show up multiple times. Retirement cabins for the middle class loom in the thinned woods on either side of Highway 260.

I stay that night with a friend's brother, a retired cop, in the nearby settlement of Strawberry and load up on calories at a diner called Early Bird. At the table next to mine, a group of Pimas from the Ak-Chin reservation inquire about my backpack leaned up against a chair, and I tell them I'm walking to Mexico. The youngest of them, a man named Avery, tells me they just came from the shores of the Sea of Cortez, where they had been collecting salt for ceremonial purposes. He wants to give me a chunk as a good token and I follow him out to the truck for it, gratefully accepting. It's also good sprinkled on food, he says.

In front of me is Hardscrabble Mesa to the west and the beginnings of the Mazatzal Mountains—the hardest stretch of the trip. They are barely one hundred miles from metropolitan Phoenix and yet one of the least known and visited ranges in the state. The name is from the Nahuatl indigenous language of Mexico and means "place of the deer," and the local pronunciation is *Mad-as-Hell*.

Historian Thomas Sheridan wrote this passage about these mountains that has always haunted me: "If you hike into the Mazatzals, you pass jagged outcrops of rocks that are two billion years old. These rocks were Arizona before Arizona had a name and they will be Arizona long after the name has disappeared. All of us—Paleolithic mammoth hunters, Hohokam famers, Mexican ranchers, Anglo American dam builders, and city dwellers—are light dust on those rocks. The land should make us humble but it rarely does."

The trail winds through meadows, over a ridge, down the service road for a humming power line, then up and over a vicious malpaís littered with sharp volcanic rocks. I fill up bottles at Whiterock Spring, go past the LF Ranch with its bunkhouse, and then up and over the northern edge through the steep drainage of Bullfrog Canyon, littered with yellow wildflowers. Sweat tumbles out from me relentlessly and helplessly, and I stop to chug down an entire liter of water.

This walk has forever changed my relationship with water; I now understand it as a substance like gasoline or motor oil, and I am acutely conscious of how close I am to death should I ever run out. The locations of active springs are loaded on a crowdsourced phone app made by a Flagstaff company called Guthook, which has saved me time after time. Because not every spring listed on the paper maps still flows. In fact, many have long dried up.

Why does this happen? What governs the underground motions of water as it flows through the veins of the ground beneath us? Springs emerge when subterranean water gets pushed up via a crack in the caprock, sometimes at the pace of a slow seep and other times with the force of a stream. This can take centuries to achieve. They can dry up in times of drought or when nearby users lower the groundwater through overpumping, even though the ventricles remain. *The Lord giveth, the Lord taketh away.*

As the shadows descend and the burning sky begins to cool, the limestone cairns on the faint trail begin to look like scattered bones, and I spot a hole that looks like a lunar crater. Up on a ridge, I can perceive the lemony glow of metropolitan Phoenix to the southwest. Perhaps it was the exertion of the day, or perhaps it is feeling reasonably secure with water for the first time in a while, but I experience a moment of peace, almost to the point of intoxication, that I hadn't felt in some time.

All of what surrounded me—the stars, the moon, the weeds, the bugs, the mountains, the shine of the unseen city—felt connected in a giant design whose scaffolding lay all around but could not be physically perceived. The separation of all the world's parts, what the classic Chinese text *Tao Te Ching* calls "the ten thousand things," can seem like the greatest of delusions in certain moments of ecstasy. And then just as quickly, you are out of it. The feeling of unification does not last.

I reluctantly leave this ridge, whose name I do not know, to look for a campsite in the lower valley, my flashlight prodding the dark. The morning takes me up near the crest of the Mazatzals, a series of stone heads that looks like a line of Cenozoic spark plugs. The trail is littered with broken chips of slate, and bees buzz in the yuccas with dismayed stems, like they are surrendering themselves to the heat. There is nothing to be seen of humanity's mark except the trail itself, which winds in unpredictable directions. I lose sense of compass points. And at length I come to another ridgetop and it all clicks back into place.

I can now see the faraway blue coxcomb of the San Francisco Peaks north of Flagstaff that I thought I left behind more than a week ago. To the west is the Bloody Basin. And to the south are the slabs of the Superstition Mountains. Here is a gigantic chunk of Arizona all on one screen: like looking at how the state's massive jigsaw geology fits together from the vantage point of a space satellite.

The spell ends too soon, once again. I descend though oak forests down to distinctive Upper Sonoran landscape and by 2 p.m., I'm at the side of Highway 87—what old-time Arizonans call the Beeline—trying to hitch a ride into the vacation town of Payson, once famous for its bootlegging scene during Prohibition. I'm drained from the four-day march and craving a bowl of chili. Maybe a beer afterward. Eventually an orthopedic surgeon vacationing from Alaska picks me up and drives me the twenty miles into town. And I find my way to the Pinon Café, a roadside diner that's been here for ages.

Dining with a newspaper is one of life's signature pleasures, and I read in the *Payson Roundup* about the district's congressman—a dentist who formed ties with white nationalists and helped encourage the attack on the U.S. Capitol on January 6, 2021. Such a person could never have been elected in a different era in Arizona, when the Republican Party stood for rethinking decrepit institutions and casting a hopeful light on the future.

I might have been tempted to have been a Republican during the first term of U.S. Senator Barry Goldwater, who took office in 1954 and, by the end of his career, lamented the strident turn his party had taken. Arizona's reputation for crazy politics has only accelerated since then, and the state was even a harbinger of what later happened to the whole country.

How populist blight crept into the once-great Arizona Republican Party is an instructive story.

THE FOUNTAIN

The city of Fountain Hills took its name from a gimmick: a jet-powered geyser in the middle of a lake of reclaimed sewage.

The heir to a chainsaw fortune, Robert McCulloch, had it installed in 1970 as an attention-grabber for his new housing development on the east side of the McDowell Mountains. "It's not enough just to sell land," he explained. "You must get people to move into the community. It's a chicken and egg situation."

McCulloch had a reputation as a showman. He had already made a deal with British officials to purchase London Bridge and was having it shipped, brick by brick, to Lake Havasu City. His water toy at Fountain Hills was a cheaper stunt, but it was still impressive to watch a column of water get blasted six hundred feet high, multiple times a day, in the spirit of Old Faithful. There was a touch of defiance in this display of conspicuous hydrology, an element of *Yeah? Watch this!*—a king flaunting riches to the poor, an upraised middle finger to the desert.

On March 19, 2016, presidential candidate Donald Trump held a rally in the park next to the fountain. The city had matured into a middle-class showcase of golf and afternoon cocktails, the good life in the desert, but it was also a place where ethnic minorities said they felt watched and uncomfortable, unless they were clearly part of a landscaping crew. The population was 95 percent white; the audience was of the same cast.

Cable networks carried Trump's anti-immigrant speech live that day but did not cover a protest several miles away, where dozens of Latino activists had chained themselves to their cars to create a blockade. *Dump Trump*, they chanted. *Get this clown out of our town!* Maricopa County Sheriff Joe Arpaio—who happened to live in Fountain Hills—had been riding with the future president to the rally, and he ordered his deputies to cut the chains and make arrests.

"Wow, what a crowd this is," exclaimed the future president. "What a great honor. Sheriff Joe, I want to thank you. You have some sheriff, there's no games with your sheriff, that's for sure."

Then he laid into the "total disaster" of the national budget. "It funds Obamacare, it funds Syrians coming into the United States—we have no idea who they are—it funds illegal immigrants coming in through your border, right through Phoenix and right through, right through, it comes right through Arizona."

This horsepowered incantation rose in energy, creating a kind of tribal sway in the crowd out by the fountain: a group ecstasy that transported the listener from the boring world of restrictions and laws into a realm of apocalyptic threats and cinematic triumph. It seemed at Fountain Hills that the Republican Party was truly entering what one conservative observer called its "hippie phase"—a quasi-religion of romantic individualism, with contempt for American institutions and experts, tinged with a whiff of violence.

Trump had launched his campaign with the famous ride down the golden escalator and the branding of Mexican immigrants as "rapists," but he was then still regarded as a stunt and temporary amusement. It was only three weeks later at his packed anti-immigration rally at the Phoenix Convention Center, July 11, 2015, when the D.C. ring of donors, consultants, and journalists witnessed the energy for the first time and realized, *my God, there's a market for this stuff out there.*

"This has become a movement," Trump said from the podium. A seventy-five-year-old woman in the audience named Mary Przbylo told a reporter: "He says everything that's in our hearts. No baloney. He's got to keep it up. Keep it going." After the Phoenix event, cable networks began to carry his events live. And he seemed to recognize a second political home. "I am so glad to be back in Arizona," he said two months before his election. "Now you know this is where it all began for me."

The Arizona Republican Party embraced Trump for many reasons. He was a familiar archetype here: the outsider businessman from the East who rides in with a pile of money to fix things. He licensed hotels adorned with tacky gold plating and smoked glass, a well-known architectural vocabulary here. He lied—gleefully and blatantly—in the spirit of the nineteenth-century mineral huckster Charles Poston, "The Father of Arizona." And he appealed to an irrationality and demagoguery that had been long percolating underneath a respectable surface of country club lunches, crew cuts, and real estate boosterism.

How did the Arizona brand of conservatism get to this cultish place?

It took seventy years.

—

Arizona had been a U.S. state less than four decades when it was hit by a burst of government spending during World War II on a level not seen since General Crook was on the trail of Geronimo.

The old governing regime of cattle ranchers, cotton growers, and out-of-state copper interests gave way in the 1940s to a motivated group of younger professionals, many of them veterans who had been stationed at one of the many new airstrips built by the Pentagon: Luke Air Force Base, Williams Air Force Base, Davis-Monthan Air Force Base, Thunderbird Field, Yuma Proving Ground. The clear and arid weather had made for a splendid flying environment. "Planes could be flown and tested every day of the year," enthused Goodyear Tire executive Paul Litchfield to the War Department.

Arizona's capital city already had a streak of booster aggression written into its character. Much of the previous hype had been founded on the everlasting promise of cheap land, hydrology, and the weather. Midwestern farmers had been lured out to grow citrus and cotton with the promise of "dirt that yields all year round." The chamber of commerce promised "a modern town of forty thousand people, and the best kind of people, too. A very small percentage of Mexicans, negroes or foreigners."

Golf resorts and high-rise hotels sprouted up for winter vacationers. Chewing gum kingpin William Wrigley built a lavish mansion next to the Biltmore resort, attracting other monuments of wealth to the slopes of Camelback Mountain, which had once been a part of the Salt River Indian Reservation until real estate speculators decided they liked the way it looked and convinced the federal government to take it away from the Natives. A local ad agency came up with the branding term "Valley of the Sun" in 1935 to dispel old images of the Apache Wars and sleazy mineral promoters in favor of the new Hollywood-style resorts like Westward Ho, Jokake Inn, and the San Marcos Hotel. "Let's do away with the desert," enthused a local committee, encouraging its members to plant roses and oleanders to make the town look like Pasadena.

One wealthy snowbird of the 1940s, Eugene Pulliam, made a permanent home in Arizona and tried to shape it in a distinctly midwestern conservative image. He purchased the *Arizona Republic*, held court at the Phoenix Country Club, and put the voltage into what had been a sluggish Republican Party, finding an ally in one of his newspaper's primary advertisers: Barry Goldwater, the handsome forty-year-old heir to a family department store fortune. Pulliam instructed his editors to run flattering coverage of Goldwater—"he has a vote-getting personality," enthused one dispatch—and get him elected to the Phoenix City Council with a mandate to keep taxes low, rebuild the corrupt police department, and install a nonpartisan city manager.

Goldwater's own family had gotten rich off the government. His grandfather Michel "Big Mike" Goldwater had fled Poland in 1835 to avoid conscription into the army of the Russian czar, apprenticed as a tailor in London, then set off for the California gold fields to supply the miners with food and clothing. When that enterprise failed, he turned to Arizona, hauling goods on U.S. Army contracts to the military-and-mining settlement of Prescott. He founded a dry goods store that evolved into Arizona's signature department store with a mezzanine level, the latest women's fashions, and a touch of big-city flair—a Saks for the middle class.

Big Mike Goldwater's grandson Barry grew up pampered in Phoenix's verdant North Central neighborhood: gregarious, a bad student, half Jewish but raised Episcopalian, a tinkerer with radios, a practical joker, a lover of tequila and Old Crow bourbon, the maker of many friends, teller of dirty jokes, and never needing to carry cash because he could sign his father's famous name to any credit slip. He said later that he'd grown up in a log cabin—if the cabin featured a swimming pool and a billiard room. "I was one of the lucky few who was born with a silver spoon in my mouth," he acknowledged, "and I am doing my best to keep it there."

Goldwater preferred one-line witticisms to lengthy policy discussion. When council speeches grew longwinded, he set a windup set of chattering teeth on the desk to signal his irritation. He was, in the judgment of Mayor Nicholas Udall, "a young merchant prince who liked to get his picture taken and fly airplanes." But he was able to set forth a vision of a union-free Arizona that didn't want help from the federal government—except for military spending and the river-damming projects that made growth possible.

The Goldwater-Pulliam alliance had an inside fixer: attorney Frank Snell, the cofounder of the white-shoe firm Snell and Wilmer, who exhorted Goldwater and his fellow reformers to "stand up and be counted if we are to continue to be the masters of our fate rather than servants of an all-powerful government." Helping spread cash around the state was Walter Bimson, the president of Valley National Bank, who viewed homeownership with a religiosity like that of George Bailey in *It's a Wonderful Life*. "Make loans!" he commanded his lending officers, who offered walk-through home inspections to point out where swamp coolers could be installed, roofs resurfaced, or a dishwasher added. "The biggest service we can perform today is to put money in people's hands," Bimson liked to say.

Prosperity minted new Republican stars. Attorney Sandra Day O'Connor soon became the first woman majority leader of a state legislature. My grandmother's high school classmate, radio host Jack Williams, won the governor's office and refused federal redevelopment money for a downtown ravaged by suburban flight, increasingly defined by seedy bars and vacant offices. "The city can regenerate itself as the phoenix bird regenerated itself from the ashes," Williams said breezily, a fine talk-radio sentiment.

The postwar conservatives could afford this kind of insouciance; they had caught a tailwind of Sunbelt growth that showed no signs of ceasing. Demography tipped away from farmers and miners toward newcomers from Chicago and Los Angeles, to the dismay of leathery old Democrats. A local joke made the rounds: "With refrigeration came Republicans." Goldwater liked to take distinguished visitors up in his Piper Cub and show them the lights of metropolitan Phoenix reaching to the horizons. "If you'd dropped a five-dollar bill down there before the war," he told them, "it would be worth a couple hundred now." All those twinkling lights represented a state unclenching itself from the grip of copper and cows, moving into lifestyle-based wealth.

Land sales boomed. Homebuilders like John F. Long and Del Webb tore down orange groves and replaced them with closed-loop subdivisions featuring curvy streets, exotic names, cinderblock exterior walls, fenced-in backyards, kidney-shaped pools, minimal tree foliage, well-watered rectangles of lawn, and big garages fronting the street for a "go away" feel.

Defense contractors located new plants near the military airfields—Sperry, AiResearch, Honeywell, Motorola, Reynolds Metal, Hughes Aircraft, IBM. Computer-literate migrants of the new Arizona frontier told their relatives they wanted to escape smokestack towns like Detroit and Pittsburgh, with their corrupt mayors, wallet-busting taxes, union overlords, aging rowhouses, and dreary skies. Arizona offered a bright alternative. Even the sulfurous social critic Ed Abbey found something to admire when he went out to Fountain Hills in 1976 and talked to housewives, out watering their flowers, who saw their new home as "a step upward toward the fulfillment of the American Dream."

That the state was flat-out beautiful did not hurt, nor did a nostalgia for the Old West. *Arizona Highways* magazine spread color photos of movie-like vistas around the world, and a reporter from *Business Week* likened the state's corporate gunslingers to Wyatt Earp. One of Barry Goldwater's personal contributions to his department store was a line of skirts decorated with cattle-branding irons, and he loved to show off his collection of the sacred Hopi figurines called Kachinas in a spaceship-like house in Paradise Valley that he named Be-Nun-I-Kin, Navajo for "house on a hill." Out front was a flagpole equipped with a gadget that sensed the first rays of the rising sun and automatically raised Old Glory in response, echoing the tech-enabled pillar of water that would soon rise in Fountain Hills. He had himself photographed wearing a cowboy hat and brandishing a rifle while standing near a swimming pool for a publicity shot in 1963. A more perfect Arizona image could not have been snapped. Old and New West had become fused.

Goldwater had edged out Eugene McFarland for the U.S. Senate in 1952 and then captured the GOP nomination for president twelve years later on a platform of strident anticommunism, opposition to federal enforcement of civil rights, and nuclear aggression—"lob one in the men's room of the Kremlin," was one of his pet expressions. When asked what he'd do about insurgents carrying weapons down the Ho Chi Minh Trail in Vietnam, he suggested low-yield nuclear blasts could defoliate the trees and make the

Viet Cong easier to pick off. The extremist statements were just an extension of the snappy retorts he'd perfected on the Phoenix City Council, but they terrified voters and he lost to Lyndon Johnson in a drubbing.

The Arizona brand of conservatism had moved away from business-friendly optimism into suspicion of any government initiative, no matter how inoffensive. Andrew Kopkin visited in 1965 and concluded the older generation of conservatives like Goldwater had created a "Frankenstein's monster which no longer does their bidding" because the imaginary figures of socialistic terror they kept talking about "have so long been accepted as real that any step forward is suspect." When the city of Phoenix modernized its home inspection unit, some residents treated it as an outrage on the level of Yalta. The Arizona legislature had once been greased by compromise and had done a decent job at funding the universities, highways, parks, and schools. Now it began to admit more populist mountebanks.

In 1986 a car dealer from Glendale named Evan Mecham pulled off a surprise victory in the Republican primary for governor over Burton Barr, a winsome state senator known as Mr. Magic for his facility at getting things done. Almost half the voters hadn't even been living in the state for longer than six years—such was the thermonuclear power of the real estate growth machine. They didn't know of Mecham's history as an extremist crank who wanted to sell off public lands, pull the United States out of the United Nations, and eliminate almost all government programs except the post office and military. The voters had taken Goldwater's antigovernment rhetoric all too seriously.

Mecham's Pontiac dealership made its name with an ingenious radio slogan: "If you can't deal with Mecham, you just can't deal," implying that any problem was the fault of the buyer. Arizona government went into circus mode as Mecham governed like Trump, using his office as a bludgeon to strike at his perceived enemies.

He said, among other things, that the attorney general was using a laser beam to listen to his conversations, that Martin Luther King Jr. didn't deserve a holiday, that it was fine to call Black children "pickaninnies," that Japanese businessmen's "eyes got round" when they got a load of Arizona's golf courses, that the opposition was made up of "homosexuals and dissident Democrats." Before he could be recalled from office, he was indicted by a grand jury for taking an unreported loan of $350,000 from a municipal bond salesman he had met for only ten minutes. Impeachment soon followed.

The comic-strip reign of Mecham lasted little more than a year, but it revealed some important dynamics of Arizona politics that presaged the embrace of Trump. Voters here have typically given deference to loud talkers in command of a payroll. Walter Bimson of Valley Bank had lionized the mythic entrepreneur who "constructed new plants, re-equipped his factories with new machines, built millions of new homes, poured out an endless stream of cars, radios, refrigerators." But government is not a business. The governorship of wealthy real estate developer J. Fife Symington also ended with scandal, indictment, and removal.

The sleaze in the governor's office highlighted a semi-criminal pattern lurking under the surface. Barry Goldwater had been friends with the Mafia accountant Gus Greenbaum and served as an honorary pallbearer at his funeral after he was slain by hitmen from Detroit at his house at 1115 West Monte Vista Drive in revenge for skimming from Las Vegas casinos. Arizona political culture became so known for its moral flexibility that the FBI found little trouble in catching seven state lawmakers taking bribes in a 1990s operation called AzScam. "There isn't an issue in the world I give a shit about—I do deals," said Representative Bobby Raymond on a hidden camera. He spoke for many. One-tenth of the legislature had to resign.

One of Mecham's key insights was his vilification of a shadowy group of rainmakers he called "The Phoenix 40," generally understood to mean the Goldwater cronies and the aerospace poohbahs. He called them "powerful secret enemies" and provided a foretaste of the permanent schism in the Arizona GOP between the establishment base that held the money and the populist voices wielding the power of anger.

Goldwater did not create or embody this rage within Arizona, but he helped stoke the irrational suspicion of government interference that laid down a pathway for demagogues like Mecham and then Trump after him. The state's astonishing population growth without the structures of common association had created what former governor Terry Goddard called "a community of strangers" willing to turn over the steering wheel to those with raucous manners and easy solutions.

They had come to Arizona wanting to be left alone, after all, an attitude that tracked with a Don't Tread on Me mentality. "Within such a population there is no civic stability or sense of place," observed local government consultant Neal Pearce about Arizona in 1992. "It's an adolescent place, and like all adolescents [it's] awkward, thrashing about, searching for an identity. And often, it's the wrong identity."

Alexis de Tocqueville had thought the inherent genius of the United States lay in the willingness of its citizens to take charge of their own affairs through local boards, committees, and informal society. But the quest for individual freedom embodied by the New Old West in Arizona tended to shun the modalities of care for those down the street. The politics of independence had become the politics of loneliness: liberty without responsibility.

"Perhaps it is the splendid isolation of being alone in the air which fascinates me," said Goldwater, explaining the allure of flying over the lights of Phoenix.

—

In the same era when Robert McCulloch was decorating empty lots with eye-catching features like fountains and nineteenth-century bridges, other promoters were trying to sell their own hardscrabble desert as the next Beverly Hills. One of the most questionable schemes played out in a dehydrated valley northwest of the Route 66 town of Kingman.

A California real estate agent named Chrystal Collins bought some high desert rangeland from a retired cowboy, rebranded it Paradise Acres Estates, and sold it off to buyers through the mail for $795 per lot. Brochures enthused about utilities and mountain springs in the new city she called Golden Valley. "A land rich in value today, even richer in its potential as America surges westward," one boasted.

In reality, Golden Valley looked like the drained shell of the Dead Sea: a classic high desert basin with a water table a thousand feet below the surface. Those who had bought sight-unseen were in for a shock. There were no lights at night because there was no electricity in the moonscape. There were no homes, only trailers that a few hardy souls had dragged in. Bankers in Kingman laughed at those who asked for a mortgage to build a real home. One newcomer bumping through the desert got his car bogged down in sand and suffered a heart attack.

Chrystal Collins scored a major publicity win after *Look* magazine ran photographs of her in multiple poses—vamping by a swimming pool at a motel in Kingman, running her hands through desert soil as though it were coins, at the wheel of her luxury car with a rack of clothes fixed in the back so she could change outfits several times a day. "I say it's not so much what the land costs," she said. "It's what the blue sky overhead is worth. It gives me a great feeling to go up there and see happy people in their little trailers."

The hype attracted the attention of Lucille Ball's production company, and a screenwriter drafted a treatment for a television show called *Lady Land Developer*—a comedy that would follow the adventures of "a modern day pioneer woman" who had nothing motivating her but "a sincere conviction that everyone should be offered the opportunity to own a small piece of Arizona." The series was never produced. And as it happened, Collins had not developed much of anything except mortgages and deeds. Water and sewer hookups, she explained, would have made the land too expensive to sell to buyers of modest means. This was a classic scam of the sort that had been playing out in Florida swampland, only with a cowboy twist.

Officials at Mohave County, hoping for eventual property taxes, were complicit. They commissioned Bill Stockbridge to hundreds of miles of dirt roads with a bulldozer—a maze of empty "streets" in which they planted a few aboveground telephone boxes here and there that could not work because they had no electricity. They shrugged when aggrieved buyers complained about being hoodwinked. Robert Caro of *Newsday* painted a withering picture of Golden Valley. "There is nothing on the vast site but a huge sign advertising the rancheros and a few sticks representing street signs," he wrote. "The desert stretches away endlessly. Standing there, broiling in the hot sun, you feel like an ant on a huge tan rug."

Embarrassed lawmakers in Phoenix began to talk about tougher regulations on mail-order land sales. Collins formed a lobbying group called the League of Arizona Land Developers to stop it. The *Republic* ran a story about it on the same page as an item about a beef-and-beans dinner speech at the state fair by a U.S. Senate candidate named Evan Mecham. "Co-existence is a lot of baloney," said the car dealer, railing against the Soviet threat. "The world can't exist half-slave and half-free."

Chrystal Collins made $2.5 million before departing, leaving Golden Valley to find its own way. Some disappointed buyers sold off their bare lots at a loss, but others chose to hang on and build in the yucca-specked gravel. Real houses began to sprout up here and there on the dusty checkerboard, though plans for a community center kept falling through for lack of willingness to spend public money.

Today's Golden Valley has a distinct Alaska-like feel to it: a ramble of incongruous homes on wide lots, with lots of chain-link fences and an abundance of older men who moved here to be left alone—lots of desert rats and misanthropes. Wildcat RV parks sit amid yucca and creosote, giving off an aura that uninvited visitors should not come knocking. A flag high on a pole outside one house reads: *Fuck Biden. And fuck you for voting for him.* Aerial photos show a massive grid of "streets" bladed into the desert in the 1960s and almost never used: a cartographic monument to wild dreams and corruption.

Though few outsiders may be tempted to stop here, Golden Valley is a consequential place, representative of a pillar of Arizona's political culture. This is where you can find the exemplar of the rural consensus formed by hardcore conservative notions of liberty that dominates the legislature and holds philosophical sway over at least three congressional seats. The state's politics cannot be truly understood without understanding the view from Golden Valley.

There are no sidewalks or parks here. There is no discernible center. The strip of Highway 68 that functions as a main drag hosts an eczema of retail businesses spaced as far apart as the residential lots that stretch far away beyond them: Bucky's Swap Meet, Dollar General, Earl's Hot Rod Shop, Kokopelli Storage, a saloon called Jus' One More.

One of these establishments, All-American Pizza, is festooned with red, white, and blue paraphernalia and played host to a campaign event called Trumpstock in the days leading up to the 2020 election. It became a flashpoint of controversy during the COVID pandemic when the owner, Robert Hall, refused to abide by a county mask ordinance and was briefly shut down as a result. When I showed up to talk to him, I found a lengthy message taped to the door. It began:

> Dear Official: I am aware that you are only here to "do your job" but I am WARNING you not to proceed any further. You are attempting to deprive me of my rights under the color of law and are also committing an act of domestic terrorism by attempting to "intimidate or coerce" me.

The notice went on to cite several irrelevant laws, including the antiterrorism Patriot Act of 2001, insinuated the death penalty might apply, and ended with a threat to sue health department officials. "You are subject to lose EVERYTHING in your private capacity, including: houses, cars, all of the money in your bank accounts, and anything else you own."

I kept my mask on my face and talked to Hall, an intense man in his midfifties who wore a sidearm in a holster and a temper that seemed barely in check. "This is the real Arizona out here," he told me. "You want to do your government bullshit, do it somewhere else, we'll be fine out here."

Mohave County is already the reddest county in the state, and no precinct in it voted more heavily for Trump in 2020 than Golden Valley, except for the one on the Utah border encompassing the theocratic settlement of Colorado City, home of a cult of fundamentalist Mormons who vote as a unified bloc. Both locations are fiercely antigovernment, despite high rates of personal dependence on government benefits.

"Now this is the conundrum," acknowledged Laurence Schiff, a genial baldheaded psychiatrist who used to chair the local GOP. "Why do they vote Republican out there when 75 percent of them are on Medicaid or Medicare?"

I had first met Schiff at the 2016 Republican convention in Cleveland, where he had been on the armed security detail for Sheriff Joe Arpaio. When I went to see him at his office in Kingman, he offered me a detailed theory on Golden Valley from behind his expansive wooden desk.

"There are different types of Republicans, those who vote for economic reasons and those for cultural reasons," he said. "I believe in small government and low taxes, for example. But most of the people in GV are not paying taxes. They are not concerned with how the stock market is performing.

They're voting Republican on the cultural issues. Guns, first of all. I have four of them sitting here within reach, by the way. I could get to them in megaseconds. Half the women in Walmart are carrying guns in their purses. Then there's abortion. And there's 'Americanism.' They don't just stand for the flag. They *kneel* for it. People could get shot over that issue here."

He is Jewish by heritage with a Brooklyn accent, and though he is not observantly religious, he keeps a portrait of the rabbi Maimonides in his office. I asked him if any of the anti-Semitic beliefs at the fringes of the conservative movement gave him any concern, or if any of his Mohave County political acquaintances had ever said anything disparaging to him.

He paused.

"There can be an undercurrent," he allowed. "But they recognize me as a conservative. I'm like them. They say to themselves, 'but he's carrying a .45. How bad could he be?'"

Internal Republican dissension takes other forms, said Schiff, mainly the "constant recall elections, arguments, fights," that ensure that its commissioner district is one of the most contentious and least organized in the county. Golden Valley may vote en bloc in presidential elections, but finding agreement on anything else is an epic struggle, given the lack of community fiber. Perhaps this may be attributed to its origins as a land swindle: a legacy of fraud begets even more suspicion.

I spoke with the head of the Northern Arizona Militia, Rick Armstrong, the son of a casino security chief. "A lot of us believe that even requiring a permit for anything is like taking your rights away from you and then selling them back," he told me. His militia requires its members to attend regular training sessions, keep at least six months of food in storage at their homes, and bear arms in preparation for a possible invasion of Golden Valley by those who would seek to steal their supplies in case of a global crisis.

The once-toxic word *militia* has lost some of its electricity in Mohave County in the quarter century after the FBI swarmed in looking for ultraconservative associates of Timothy McVeigh, who had lived in Golden Valley in the months prior to the 1994 truck bombing of the federal building in Oklahoma City. He worked as a five-dollar-per-hour employee at the True Value hardware store on Stockton Hill Road and smoked marijuana with his army buddy Michael Fortier and Fortier's wife, Lori, in their trailer at 3035

East McVicar Avenue, which had a Don't Tread on Me coiled rattlesnake flag flying out front. It was in that trailer where McVeigh stacked up some soup cans on the floor to show Fortier the blast-and-collapse pattern he intended to create.

Right-wing militias are no longer a stigma in Kingman, with the Oklahoma bombing long in the past, and Armstrong made a credible run for county commission in 2016. But he failed to get enough votes to ride the Trump coattails. His irrigated yard has a row of fruit trees, a source of food in case of social apocalypse, but I met with him outside a drive-through Mexican restaurant that sits less than a half mile from where Timothy McVeigh used to live.

Politics in Golden Valley can get vicious, Armstrong said, especially around matters where a "liberty" question may be perceived. This is why the highway lacked a median for so long: too many people vocally worried that such an improvement would herald a socialist takeover. The one thing Golden Valley can be counted on to deliver with one voice, however, is the election of far-right Republicans at every level. "The Democrats are irrelevant here," said Trump's local campaign chairman, Steve Robinson, a bit wistfully, with a fighter's affection for a vanquished rival.

Candidates who want to win Mohave County must out-crazy one another in the Republican primaries. My friend Anne Marie Ward, who grew up in Prescott Valley, decided to make a run for Congress against the incumbent Paul Gosar, who had embarrassed some in the district with his embrace of conspiracy theories and alliance with quasi-criminal groups like the Oath Keepers. Ward crisscrossed northwest Arizona, holding listening sessions in public parks, taking about rural health care, and trying to get traction, but she got blown out of the water by twenty-five points. The experience gave her a deeper insight into the psychology of what its residents insist is "the real Arizona."

"They've lived busy lives elsewhere and now they want to live a quiet life," she told me after the election was all over. "They're not terribly social. They understand that life is hard and tough."

—

The most conspicuous statue outside Arizona's capitol is that of Frank Luke Jr., bronzed in a leather jacket and flying cap, a World War I ace who came second only to Eddie Rickenbacker in the number of confirmed kills by an American pilot and had a nearby U.S. Air Force base named for him. But the most revered fighter pilot here is John McCain, who held one of Arizona's U.S. Senate seats for six terms. Governors Mecham and Symington had both flown planes in the military. A Luke Air Force Base general elected to the legislature liked to wear his dress blues on the floor.

McCain sometimes got lost on the way to his own campaign events when he ran for Congress after only two years of living in Phoenix, but he shut down doubts about carpetbagging by saying the longest time he had lived anywhere was in a Vietnamese prison after his A-4 Skyhawk was shot down over Hanoi in 1967.

The style associated with fighter pilots has a special appeal to Arizona voters, especially military retirees who know the centrality of defense spending to the state's hypersonic growth. The technological triumph over nature has an element of Fountain Hills defiance about it—a lofting over the gravitational restrictions that would otherwise keep a person on the ground.

A retired military pilot loyal to a Republican president would have been a dream candidate in the Arizona of Barry Goldwater, himself a veteran of the Air Transport Command who loved to take his Piper Cub to speaking engagements. So thus it came as a shock when retired lieutenant colonel Martha McSally—the first American woman to fly a combat mission—lost back-to-back races for the U.S. Senate.

McSally's 2020 defeat in a race for Goldwater's old seat provided a vivid display of how the Arizona Republican Party was hitting a wall, and how the state's brand of conservatism had become a parody of itself.

McSally is a native of Rhode Island who retired in Tucson, the site of her last military posting. She won election to the U.S. House four years later, yet another demonstration that one doesn't need to be in Arizona very long to assume high office. The sole highlight of her tenure was her effort to save the local fleet of A-10 Warthogs—which she once called "a badass airplane with a big gun on it"—from being scrapped.

She ran for Senate in 2018 to replace Senator Jeff Flake, who had committed the unpardonable sin of suggesting the Republican Party brand should not be built on racism and extremist rhetoric. He said so in a book titled *Conscience of a Conservative*, an explicit paean to a 1960 book ghostwritten for Barry Goldwater. Trump took it as a personal insult and called Flake "toxic" and "weak." That was enough to sink Flake's reelection bid before it began. McSally absorbed the lesson and turned the dial to Full Trump in her campaign against conservative Democrat Kyrsten Sinema, even accusing her of "treason" in their sole televised debate. She lost by two points but went to the Senate anyway as an appointee to McCain's seat after he died of brain cancer.

The can-do Warthog pilot seemed wary of a fight, avoiding town halls and kicking small-town reporters out of booster lunches. "She is uniquely scared of her own shadow for someone in politics," one conservative talk-show host told me. When beloved former University of Arizona basketball coach Lute Olson went into hospice care on August 25, two days before his death, McSally misspelled his name in a consolatory tweet: "My prayers are with Luke Olson and his family tonight." Either this longtime resident of Tucson didn't know the name of one of its most famous citizens, or she had assigned the tweeting (maybe even the praying) to a hapless staffer.

The demographic wind had shifted. New residents fleeing housing costs and traffic in Los Angeles, Chicago, and Seattle were streaming into the once-dependable GOP suburban heartlands of Ahwatukee, Paradise Valley, and Chandler. Here was an echo of the migratory patterns that had swept Goldwater into office in the 1940s and put the GOP into a long-lasting majority. But now these newcomers were voting Democratic.

The antigovernment paranoia of Golden Valley seemed to be the tail wagging the old dog of what had been Barry Goldwater's Arizona Republican Party, which after 2019 was chaired by an osteopath named Kelli Ward who earned the nickname Chemtrail Kelli after she convened a meeting to hear out Golden Valley residents worried the government was spraying bio-engineered weapons on them through the contrails of high-flying aircraft.

The corporate Phoenix money that propelled Goldwater and his descendants took a pass on McSally. She had to plead with supporters to "fast a meal" so they could give her money. *Arizona Daily Star* cartoonist and former admirer David Fitzsimmons told her: "You flew your Warthog to the dark side." Most humiliatingly of all, Trump showed her no respect in exchange for the kowtowing. He rushed her to the stage at a rally in Goodyear, as if embarrassed. "Martha, just come up fast," he said. "Fast. Fast. Come on. Quick. You got one minute! One minute, Martha! They don't want to hear this, Martha. Come on. Let's go. Quick, quick, quick. Come on. Let's go."

On Election Day, she took a beating from Mark Kelly, a retired astronaut who—*quelle* Arizona—had been a fighter pilot in the first Gulf War. For the remaining GOP pragmatists, blame for the lost dogfight fell on the Trumpians. "Nobody wants to invest in the Arizona Kelli Ward represents," GOP lobbyist Kevin DeMenna told me.

The contempt was mutual. Under Kelli Ward's direction, the party voted to censure Jeff Flake, Governor Doug Ducey, and John McCain's widow, Cindy, in a trifecta of symbolic purging. Then Ward's staff put out bizarre tweets. One admonished voters they should be prepared to die for the sake of proving Trump's false claims that he won the election. "As the sun sets on 2020," said another, "remember that we're never going back to the party of Romney, Flake, and McCain. The Republican Party is now, and forever will be, one for the working man and woman!"

They might as well have included Barry Goldwater in their list of excommunications. He eventually split with the far-right elements of his party, coming out in favor of abortion rights and gay people serving in the military and denouncing the leader of the Moral Majority, Reverend Jerry Falwell. "I think every good Christian ought to kick Falwell's ass," he said. Goldwater also urged the right-wing populist Evan Mecham to resign before he could embarrass the state any further.

For all the energy he brought to the Arizona conservative movement, Goldwater never achieved much in the way of governing. His colleagues in the Senate considered him charming but disorganized, far more adept at telling stories over an afternoon glass of Old Crow bourbon than assembling floor votes. Goldwater didn't disagree; he had a self-deprecating streak along with a salty tongue, calling the Defense Department Reorganization Act of 1986 "the only goddamn thing I've done in the Senate that's worth a damn." If he is known for anything outside Arizona, it would be for his 1964 run for president that electrified hardcore conservatives, as well as a misfired riff on Cicero made at the party convention: "Extremism in the defense of liberty is no vice."

Goldwater's shadow still lies across today's Arizona GOP: the snappy one-liners, the demagogic style, the allergy to taxes and unions, the paranoid crusades against "socialism." But his party today lacks his innate optimism, passionate love of the landscape, and willingness to—however gingerly—confront the uglier quarters of the conservative movement that favor quasi-autocracy. On August 7, 1974, he was one of three Republican members of Congress tasked with going to the White House to tell Richard Nixon he didn't have the ability to survive an impeachment vote. Goldwater insisted he didn't tell Nixon he should quit.

"I don't think it would be proper for me to say what I think," he told the *Tucson Citizen*. "And, anyway, I'm not sure the president would pay much attention." Still, he confessed to being "very, very disappointed and upset" with Nixon, who resigned two days later. Goldwater was hailed then for his patriotism and pragmatism.

What is less remembered today was that he had sponsored a campaign-style rally in Phoenix for the floundering Nixon just three months earlier, on May 3, 1974, heaping praise on the president and telling reporters the American people didn't care about the disturbing revelations about Watergate. He was lying through his teeth.

That now-forgotten rally for a doomed president was held at the Arizona Veterans Memorial Coliseum, a distinctive saddle-shaped arena built for the Phoenix Suns basketball team and known to sports journalists as "The Madhouse on McDowell" for its location at the state fairgrounds on McDowell Road. The Suns left for a downtown indoor stadium in 1993, and the coliseum—once the height of futurism—grew dowdier as the years went on, hosting the occasional concert or pro wrestling match. It was impressed back into political service in 2021 when the state senate paid $150,000 to sponsor an "audit" of the presidential votes cast in Maricopa County that showed a clear defeat for Donald Trump.

On the same floor where a secretly doubtful Goldwater had introduced Nixon to a cheering crowd, citizen volunteers conducted a remarkably incompetent hand recount of 2.1 million ballots managed by a conspiracy theorist named Doug Logan and funded by $5.7 million in donations through various right-wing groups.

One official said the auditors were looking for paper ballots with bamboo fibers to prove their Chinese origin. Others spoke ominously of secret watermarks and deleted databases. The county's elections chief called the allegations "insane lies" and "unhinged," even as partisans wearing T-shirts reading "God, Guns and Trump" demonstrated outside the coliseum with a banner that read "Board of Supervisors is the enemy of the nation." In the end, only 184 ballots were found to be potentially defective. The expensive cuckoo show only confirmed Biden's victory by a wider margin.

The entire exercise had been an attempt to soothe Trump's fragile ego while casting broad suspicion of democracy and creating a roadmap for other states for how Democratic victories might be nullified. Senate President Karen Fann, who had authorized the farce under pressure from Trump, declined to run for reelection. The ethnonationalist fringe elements of conservatism that Goldwater had tapped into and then rejected had taken total control of the Arizona Republican Party.

Their strategy for hanging on to power used to be a reliable influx of new voters from elsewhere who shared their philosophies, or who could be persuaded. But now that Arizona's growth depended on more liberal-minded Anglos, along with ever-increasing numbers of Latinos, the tactics had turned to Jim Crow–style vote suppression.

A state representative from Fountain Hills—the venue for Trump's 2016 groupie fest—summed up the prevailing attitude of the Arizona Republican Party toward the will of the people. "Not everybody wants to vote, and if somebody is uninterested in voting, that probably means that they're totally uninformed on the issues," said John Kavanaugh. "Quantity is important, but we have to look at the quality of votes, as well."

Driving that weird racial euphemism about "quality" was a basic fact about Arizona that has always terrified the Republican Party. And that's an important story for a bit further down the road.

BACK ON THE TRAIL AFTER my break in Payson, I trudged up a dry channel cut by Boulder Creek and past a wildcat junkyard with the remnants of some 1930s automobiles dumped here for mysterious reasons. And then up a path of red quartzite, through watercuts in the stone, and at last to a summit where the blue amoeba of Roosevelt Lake can be first glimpsed.

Here was the most consequential body of water in Arizona, even more than the Colorado River, because it gave the state a modern boomtown character.

Farmers in the Salt River Valley lobbied heavily for this big-government project, which put up a masonry wall in this narrow gorge and filled up what was then the biggest artificial lake in the world. Theodore Roosevelt came out for the dedication in 1911 and pushed a button to send the first ceremonial waters over the spillway in a "mighty roar." He wore a black hat and tall riding boots for the occasion, and said he hoped tens of thousands of visitors would come by to see it "just as they go to Yosemite, to the Grand Canyon and Yellowstone Park."

As if following orders, my own great-great-grandfather, a physician turned cotton farmer, made the bumpy drive up from his farm near Papago Buttes to gaze on the 280-foot pharaonic slab, and he must have marveled at the federal gift that was going to make his farm even more productive. Within a year, the dam became the dominant image on the official state seal, under the Latin motto *Ditat Deus* ("God will provide").

Water infrastructure had already been provided for the alfalfa-and-cotton town of Phoenix some fifty-six miles down the gorge. The townsite had been plopped on a crisscrossing of silted-up canals first dug by the Hohokam people of the fourteenth century who had vanished after the soil became too encrusted with salts to coax any more corn, squash, or melons out of the exhausted earth.

An ex-Confederate morphine addict named Jack Swilling saw the potential for re-excavating the abandoned canal network and sluicing in water from the Salt River for the first time in half a millennium. This was a time of florid public rhetoric, and the image of a repurposed city from antiquity proved an irresistible bit of poetry. An erudite local drunk named Darrell Duppa proposed naming the settlement after the mythical Greek phoenix bird rising from the ashes, a more glamorous name than its first one: Pumpkinville.

The water impounded at Roosevelt Dam flowed down an ordered channel of five lesser reservoirs and then into an expanded version of Swilling's municipal honeycomb, trickling into main canals with names like Grand, Crosscut, Highline, and Western and into smaller ditches called laterals parallel to city streets. The canals became a center for public life: children swam in them, rope swings hung over them from Fremont cottonwood trees, families picnicked next to them, women did laundry in them, and a coupe speeding along the banks could tow a water-skier.

My great-great-grandmother dipped bedsheets in the Grand Canal and hung them over the windows in the family boarding-house on summer nights for a swamp cooler effect. Citrus orchards replaced alfalfa. And the lasting purpose of the Salt River Project, as the dam and canal company came to be known, soon emerged: the valley would be advertised "as a place for home building," in the 1907 words of the *Arizona Republican*, even though it lay far from any transcontinental railroad. The hulk of the Superstitions and the Mazatzals had cut off Phoenix in that way, but the automobile would soon correct for the capricious verdict of topography. Homes grew over cotton fields and orange orchards as the city crept outward like wine spilled on a tablecloth.

A favorite Arizona conversation involves comparing the relative merits of its two major cities, Tucson and Phoenix. Though both are saturated with production home subdivisions and inhumanly wide streets, they are indeed distinct places.

If you want to understand the soul of a city, look to the economic reasons for its founding. Tucson was a multicultural clump of different people—Tohono O'odham, Spanish, Apaches, and eventually Anglos—huddled in the eighteenth century around a frontier military garrison, Catholic mission, and supply post. Phoenix, by contrast, was a convenient flat place where bulk water could be disaggregated and spread around, a mammoth depot of hydrology: the most enviable combination of arable land, plentiful ditch water, and frost-free climate between the Louisiana rice fields and California's Central Valley. Its roots are burrowed deep in canal-watered soil. Whatever "Old World charm" resides in Tucson versus the glitzy boomtown nature of Phoenix can be directly attributable to this difference in their foundational characters.

I filled my water bottles from a weed-choked sinkhole at a spot called Little Pine Flat and had a quiet supper of cold ramen noodles soaked in a plastic jar. A little more elevation and by sundown I achieved a plateau of tall ponderosas throwing spikes up into the moonlight. The Edwards and Crabtree families had ranched up here in the nineteenth century, leaving their names on a creek and an isolated valley, and the bone dust of their lost cattle long mingled with the common earth.

Ten miles from any human and inside dark woods, but a few weeks of crossing Arizona had dispensed with any doubt or hesitation. If I lost my way, so be it. I could sleep on a flat spot and find the right way when the sun comes up. The spine of the ridge is easy enough to follow, and it eventually leaves the forest for a dirt road that affords a spectacular view of the eastern suburbs of Phoenix glittering to the horizon.

Here is the nation's fifth-largest metropolis in the unlikeliest spot of any big city, made possible through the hydrological rigging of a valley where every human is responsible for the consumption of 175 gallons each day via drinking water, cooking, dishwashing, lawn maintenance, golf courses, construction, and sewerage.

I paused to drop my pack and summon scattered visions of the city: my childhood in a dimly lit modernist home; Mexican restaurants and freeways; the solar assault of summer afternoons; golf courses smelling of reclaimed water; creosote bushes and mourning doves; mountains littered with pumice; and wealthy migrants coming in from Elsewhere, USA, who coveted low taxes and dry winter air.

MONOTONY RULES

The house on West West Wind Drive was built in the R-1 model configuration, like most of the others on its block, and it faces a patch of grassy space called an "amenity area" with a plastic jungle gym. A few paloverde trees have been planted nearby in concrete tube sections.

The four-bedroom house with a tile roof is near the back of the Rancho Mercado subdivision at the northwest edge of Surprise, once a jerkwater stop on the road to Las Vegas and now the fifth-fastest-growing incorporated city in the United States, with a super-bloom of houses spreading into rangeland so dry that even cattlemen used to shun it. Signs in Rancho Mercado point the way to a "community exit" so newcomers don't get lost in the maze of lookalike streets.

The snout-houses on West West Wind Drive were built all at the same time in 218 days, an example of the precision-oriented production home business. Almost no other enterprise has put such a distinctive stamp on the face of Arizona, filling out once-empty patches of malpaís with polygon colonies of stucco boxes colored in different shades of toothpaste.

Critics look at these oceans of clay-shell roofs and lament the relentless monotony of Arizona's residential empire, which feels stuck in the 1980s, in both mentality and aesthetics. Others see a welcome mat for families of modest incomes who would otherwise be stuck renting and fuel for the humming economy that keeps the state on the front lines of Sunbelt prosperity.

Rancho Mercado means "market ranch," but the nearest grocery store is fifteen minutes away. Nobody doubts one is coming, likely an Albertson's or a Safeway. A space has already been selected for it on Happy Valley Drive, and the customer base is already here. Retail follows roofs, as the old saying goes.

This home on West West Wind, about twenty-five miles from downtown Phoenix, has a "great room," a rear-facing kitchen, a suite of three bedrooms off to the side, a garage facing the street, and a front door set down a passage that feels like a brief tunnel. The exterior is in one of three styles available for the "Prairie" R-1 model with its vague Frank Lloyd Wright touches.

Some of the neighbors who bought their houses before the first board was nailed chose the "Santa Barbara" or "Cottage" designs, but they all have the same floorplan. The appearance of diversity is in accord with the home-builder's *Monotony Rules* tacked up in the show model. They specify no more than three homes with the same exterior appearance can be in a row together—a guideline reminiscent of backgammon.

A young couple from Minnesota on the verge of starting a family purchased the house on West West Wind Drive in August of 2020 for $339,990. The husband works as a technician for a logistics company that moves goods around the nation; the wife as a nurse in a behavioral health clinic. They've had hardly any contact with their neighbors.

Folks don't seem terribly outgoing in Rancho Mercado, the husband told me, a different atmosphere than what he grew up with in his midwestern hometown. Privacy and social distance appear to be the governing principles here. None of the R-1 models, nor any other house in Rancho Mercado, comes equipped with a front porch. The primary countenance facing outward is the garage door, which few here keep open for fear of thievery. Patios are in the back, protected by cinderblock walls.

"People aren't peering over your backyard wall to talk to you," he said from his darkened entry door. "It's not a warm or friendly place."

One of the only neighbors with whom he has a nodding relationship is an elderly woman next door who bought the "Tuscan" model house when her husband died. She lives on a retirement pension from a thirty-seven-year career with the phone company that used to be called US West. She also knows almost nobody in Rancho Mercado.

"It's the society we live in," she said. "Stranger danger and all of that. People prefer to be inside with their Xboxes and their phones."

While she stood in her driveway on a Thursday morning, holding a broom to sweep away mesquite pods, a woman pushing a stroller passed by on the sidewalk on her way to the "amenity area." The new mother gave a brief wave.

"See, that almost never happens here," observed the retired phone company employee. She held out hope that Christmas, then four months away, might bring a similar gesture of outgoingness, a chance for a conversation. "Maybe somebody will bake a few things and bring them over," she said.

The sun rose higher, the temperature crept toward one hundred, and the few pedestrians out for morning walks disappeared.

—

When Arizona homebuilders acquire land for a new master-planned community, they frequently put up a landmark near the entrance called an "image element," like a waterfall or a European-looking bridge to provide some texture to the new labyrinth of pastel dwellings.

In the case of Rancho Mercado, the homebuilder Taylor Morrison erected an arch made of flagstones about twelve feet tall in an empty lot that fronts Happy Valley Road. Nobody can explain its meaning. The arch is a portal to nowhere.

Developers had first scented the opportunity out here in 1985, back when Maricopa County voters approved a sales tax increase that funded—among other goodies—a limited-access freeway known as the Sun Valley Parkway in lonesome territory far to the northwest of Phoenix, out in the useless caliche by Lake Pleasant. As any fool knows, new freeways can make such nonplaces suddenly valuable, especially if it's close to one of the exits. And just as the old Hollywood joke says that a movie producer is anyone who can put a quarter in a pay phone to bring a team together, an "Arizona land developer" is anyone who can convince bankers, attorneys, and zoning officials to buy into a vision of eventual profit.

A pharmaceutical salesman named Bill Bliss got three of his friends together to buy a 1,600-acre parcel out by the route of the future parkway. It had just been sold off at an auction by the State Land Department, the custodian of nine million acres of rural territory seized from Native American tribal groups in the late nineteenth century.

Bliss was a happy-go-lucky bachelor with an endless stock of anecdotes about growing up in Chicago and a self-deprecating streak to his humor. "Ignorance is bliss," he liked to say. The land out by the proposed freeway had some surface problems: it was crisscrossed by arroyos, which meant whoever built on it would have to do extra flood protection. They called it Fox Trails for lack of a better name. Then the Arizona Department of Transportation shelved plans for the Sun Valley Parkway at the same time as a real estate depression in 1989. Bliss and his friends cut their losses and sold out for $16 million to a trust called Sunbelt under the management of Andy Kunasek, a future county commissioner. He had juice and could get things done.

Kunasek also had interests in subdivisions named Rancho Cabrillo in Peoria, Rancho Gabriela in Surprise, and, as he put it, "Rancho this-and-that."

The land near the Bliss parcel soon became Rancho Mercado. Nobody remembers exactly who named it that, or why. "It was just a name people liked," Kunasek said. The property sat remote and undeveloped during the recovery of the late 1990s, even as the nearby town of Surprise was hitting a thermonuclear period of growth, flinging new master-planned communities north and west like a radioactive atom throwing off subatomic particles.

Surprise itself was once a particle, a shabby dot on the highway to Las Vegas that came into legal existence in 1938 when Flora Mae Statler filed a plat for a triangle of land and told people she'd be "surprised it would ever amount to much." But there was agricultural opportunity there: sluice gates could be cut into the newly dug Beardsley Canal and cotton and oranges could be grown in mass quantities on the dusty flats. Statler and her husband sold three-hundred-dollar lots to those who wanted to build frame houses within earshot of the rattling Santa Fe freight trains. The city hall was a renovated root beer stand. Mexican families were politely but firmly steered to neighboring El Mirage.

The era of production homes arrived in 1986 when developers like Bliss found it a cheap place to buy up massive parcels of state trust land too remote to grow cotton. "Stop paying rent!" said one ad for Happy Trails Resort. "Own your home and lot at a country club resort for only $39,800!" New master-planned communities brought in rubber-lined fake lakes that created a Florida maritime feeling. Their names promised safe exoticism: Sun Village, Corte Bella, Mountain Vista Ranch, Arizona Traditions, Coyote Lakes. Palm trees, oleanders, bluegrass lawns, and bougainvillea flourished— none of it native to the Upper Sonoran Desert, and all of it thirsty.

Behind the cold language of planning and paving lies the home—the physical expression of family, a shield and comfort for the most basic unit of society. A private fortress of board game nights, blue corn enchiladas in the oven, safe marital erotics, school lunches packed in the mornings, a gas grill on the patio out back. Homebuilders operated like any other corporation, but they were striking at a chord close to the heart.

A previous generation of Arizona builders had grasped the enormous profitability of cookie-cutter building techniques on former cropland. In 1953 John F. Long bought up some cabbage farms west of Phoenix, named the plot Maryvale for his wife, and left blank spaces on his map where the government could fill in schools and parks and where chain stores could locate. By the time he was through, Long and his associates had built thirty thousand houses, mainly generic California-style ranchers with open-air carports, "all-electric kitchens," and porches facing the backyard. Rumors of shoddy construction did nothing to staunch the sales.

Even as Maryvale grew shabbier and aged poorly, its swimming pools gone to green algae, the methods of its creation were held up as a gold standard for Arizona production home maestros. The *Arizona Republic* ran a series of reports named for the average rate of land then being gobbled up and transformed: "An Acre per Hour." Sleepy towns like Peoria, Glendale, Buckeye, and Surprise mounted signs at their borders directing visitors not to city hall or parks but to the corporate master-planned communities: Fulton Homes, CantaMia, Taylor Morrison, Terrata Homes, Estrella by Newland.

"If you make the wrong turn, you'll get lost because all the houses look the same," said Ramiah Israel, an engineer, who lived in an Avondale subdivision for two years before moving to downtown Phoenix. The only neighbors he ever talked to there were the kids next door who occasionally kicked a soccer ball into his backyard by accident.

By the turn of the century, ADOT had rebooted plans for a freeway called the Loop 303, and Kunasek's partnership laid out specifications for Rancho Mercado. One of the consultants told me it was an "entitlement exercise built on small lot sizes" and that not much thought had been put into it. Rancho Mercado was the ham-on-rye of neighborhoods: a faithful replication of what had worked in hundreds of other places throughout Arizona. "This client had no interest in the history of the land," the consultant told me.

The Surprise City Council approved the plans on October 11, 2007, just three months after a fund full of subprime mortgages failed at the investment bank Bear Stearns. The timing couldn't have been worse. Arizona got hit especially hard in the ensuing meltdown; two-thirds of its mortgaged homes went underwater, as compared to the national rate of 21 percent. The average home in Surprise lost half its value. Weeds sprouted in untended yards, graffiti blossomed where it had never been seen before, and cities struggled to clean up the mess. Some frustrated homeowners punched out wallboard and flushed M-80 firecrackers down their toilets before handing in the keys to the lenders. Banks merged and folded into each other until there were only nine left in the Phoenix metropolitan area. All the willpower and financing behind Rancho Mercado evaporated.

"This is the nature of speculative real estate," said Kunasek. "You might see land worth $3,000 go to $30,000 and then back to $3,000."

The completion of the Loop 303 in 2017 defibrillated Rancho Mercado back to life, as did an announcement that the Taiwanese Semiconductor Manufacturing Company would be building a factory nearby—exactly the type of "clean" electronics that Phoenix economic boosters had always coveted. Now there was a reasonable guarantee of property value and a market for the type of younger homebuyer "entering the family formation stage of life," as the consultants say, who would be looking for a starter home.

Tens of millions of dollars of hard capital would have to be laid in the ground before a single mortgage closed at Rancho Mercado. But the forecasts looked good; all lights were green. Earthmovers arrived in 2018 to level the soil and dig the retention basins. A team of subcontractors built the meaningless arch in one day. Then came the homes.

Prokofiev ballets and Roman military campaigns have been staged with less precise choreography than the construction of a street-full of generic homes in a typical Arizona suburb. Taylor Morrison's predecessor signed extension agreements with the "wet utilities" (water and sewer) and "dry utilities" (electric power, Internet, telephone); arranged for the city to drill a new water well to the depth of 1,280 feet; and paid for the extension of Happy Valley Road into what had been *vacuum domicilium*.

Streets were laid out and given their Western names; the acreage got chopped into quarter-acre lots marked with wood stakes and pink plastic tape; ten slab-on-grade foundations went down on an average day. Then came a revolving cast of "trades"—the independent subcontractors who put up the wooden frames, laid the plumbing, hooked up the electricity, installed the wallboard and windows, affixed red tile to the roofs with adhesive, plugged in the HVAC, and put down the carpeting and laminate. As one team finished, the other moved in the same day.

The R-1 house on West West Wind was ready for occupation within seven months. The frame was stucco slathered over pine: a "stick house" or "balloon frame," in the lingo of the homebuilding trade. Pre-cut boards are easy lattices for stringing wires and inserting plumbing. They can be refitted on the spot by unskilled workers, and they're also nearly 40 percent cheaper than masonry.

In Rancho Mercado, the only remaining signs of a desert environment are the crushed granite in the front yards and the top of a nearby volcanic mound called Bunker Peak. The neighborhood could have been airlifted straight from Charlotte or Denver. "Nobody has figured out an appropriate southwestern desert aesthetic home," said Mark Stapp of Arizona State University. Even the colors fail to distinguish the neighborhoods. The spectrum of paint colors, according to historian Grady Gammage, radiates the sun in dull hues with manufacturer's names like Almond Mocha, Baja Breeze, Hazy Sunset, and Aged Tequila.

All the permitting paperwork for the house on West West Wind had to pass through the first floor of Surprise City Hall in the Development Services Center—a bay with ten windows and a false fountain in the middle. The pandemic transferred even more of its workflow online, so builders don't even have to show up in person to pull their permits. According to one of them, municipal functions at Surprise used to have a Podunk reputation—"kind of like dealing with Apache Junction," a specific term of insult among valley contractors. Those days are no more.

Surprise's economic development director, Mike Hoover, said the city's role is primarily that of a gatekeeper for more Rancho Mercados, annexing new lands to the north and west in response to developer demand. "This is a long-term play," he said. "Our primary responsibility is to get investment for the community."

The city, he acknowledged, is at the mercy of corporate homebuilders like Fulton, Pulte, KB Home, and Landsea. These out-of-state companies determine the direction of its growth and pay cash up front for most streets, sewers, water, power, and flood control. Municipal officials are there mainly to say yes or no to their decisions—mostly yes.

"When we bring in visitors, they're always telling us how clean, safe, and new we are," said Hoover. "Clean-Safe-New. It's a thing. We hear it all the time."

—

One Phoenix legend has it that home prices were always cheaper west of downtown because people would drive east toward downtown in the mornings and back west in the afternoon, with the sun piercing into their eyes both ways. John F. Long's Maryvale also set a tone of modesty for the giant slice of hardpan that promoters called the West Valley.

There's a world of Arizona property worship that deals in four-acre estates on the slopes of Camelback Mountain or the louche palaces of North Scottsdale: $10 million–plus price tags, garages with glass walls to display antique sports cars, actors whose names appear in the Page Six column of the *New York Post* discreetly snooping out a southwestern winter retreat.

The West Valley is not that environment. The dominant rock figurations are rhyolite mountains glowering in the distance rather than picturesque granite boulders scattered in intriguing patterns. Even though it sits a half-hour drive from the Camelback Esplanade, the topography seems more characteristic of the harsh basin and range of the Mohave Desert rather than the softer lines of the Upper Sonoran.

The West Valley functions as the San Fernando Valley of Arizona—irrigated farmland turned into a middle-class quilt of housing labyrinths, strip-mall supermarkets, sports bars smelling of fried wings, dust spores kicked up by the retreating cotton fields—a flat conurbation without vertical relief except for the Estrella Mountains to the west and the rounded hatbox of the arena in Glendale where the Arizona Coyotes play ice hockey. Major boulevards like Thunderbird, Bell, and Deer Valley are walled canyons of consumer monoculture: Home Depot to Bed Bath & Beyond to Taco Bell to Panera to Red Lobster.

Laced through as it is with blocs of lookalike houses, Surprise can recall Jane Jacobs's observation about the lack of casual walking in such environments that creates serendipity and friendships. "Almost nobody travels willingly from sameness to sameness and repetition to repetition, even if the physical effort required is trivial." There are few surprises in Surprise.

Those who feel a connection to Surprise talk about coming "over the river" from neighboring Peoria or Glendale, meaning the Agua Fria River, a bed of sand where steady water has not flowed since 1927, when the Carl Pleasant Dam was built upstream. And while urban theorists may complain about the dreary public spaces—the rare person on foot in the West Valley is generally seen as homeless or a security threat—there remains a logic and even a democracy to what happened here. In Surprise a person with a high school education and a working-class job has a reasonable enough opportunity to buy a house if they can scrape together three thousand dollars down and a monthly payment not too far off from an apartment rental.

Such freeholds are a major driver of Arizona population growth. They feed the economic furnace that alternately roars and sputters. The housing industrial complex provides more than a tenth of the jobs in this state: the people who put up the drywall, dig the pools, sell the properties, move the mortgages, zone the land, glue the tiles. But they all serve the animal spirits of the housing market, at the mercy of trends.

"Real estate is the most regulated business in the country," said Mark Stapp. "You have to work in narrow framework, but you can still make money, even within that tight envelope. One of the consequences of that is an abundance of sameness. There are ways to create quaintness. But you can't do that and make it affordable. Builders are struggling to build for those who make median income. There's no way to do that except to build on the fringes."

Surprise is now on a trajectory to grow bigger than Salt Lake City, Utah, within a few years. An entire way of relating to the airspace of society is being replicated each day, pushed further outward into desert land once considered worthless. Developers call it "The Phoenix Formula," a growth model built on the four pegs of air conditioning, shopping centers, cheap gasoline, and affordable ranch homes. This lifestyle factory in the desert that stamped out places like Rancho Mercado had created a new kind of American civilization.

In confessional moments, some developers repeat the fear they're building "tomorrow's slums today." Maryvale gets cited as a cautionary tale. Even in the *clean-safe-new* territory, there are signs of wear. Surprise's first strip mall, the red-tiled Crossroads Towne Center, opened amid hoopla in 1989 but has gone into decline. Everyone knows another mortgage meltdown could cut through the place like a neutron bomb.

Beyond the economic instability, do places like Rancho Mercado create a healthy sociological climate?

A striking number of Arizonans—more than half in some surveys—report feeling lonely on a regular basis, disconnected from others, and as though their neighbors don't care about them. The U.S. Census reports Arizona comes in last in the country when it comes to spending time with neighbors. The affordable detached ranch home contained a subtle but crucial design feature: the garage would be situated not to the side, but prominently out front for easy automobile access. An average street looks like a line of bent-over derrieres.

The porches common to the designs of the Midwest and South played an important social function in the neighborhood, the architectural equivalent of a welcoming smile. They are almost unknown in Arizona production home country. No more would drinking iced tea outside carry the risk of an awkward conversation with a windbag neighbor. But no more would there be any serendipity or impromptu friendships. All was made predictable and safe.

This is Capitalism 101. If any valley city tried to mandate costly improvements to encourage Danish Modern living amid the greasewood, the homebuilder would simply find another piece of vacant land in Queen Creek or Gilbert or whichever other competing city would be happy to welcome another Rancho Whatever to the tax base.

"Homebuilders keep doing the same thing that works," consultant Michelle Mace told me. "We've formulated and repeated. The speed at which homes need to be put out leaves no time for structures that are creative and disruptive. But when people don't know each other, there's a lack of safety.

Phoenix can be extremely disconnected as it is. You only go to your front door for Amazon or Doordash."

Teenagers often describe soul-crushing boredom within these tessellated colonies. For Sean Avery Medlin, a Black bisexual kid in Avondale's beige and ocher Rancho Santa Fe subdivision, the only relief from loneliness and monotony came through playing video games, listening to music, or taking his bicycle out to patches of the fast-disappearing desert.

"These houses were easy to make, quick to put up, they had garages in the same places, windows in the same places," said Medlin, the son of an officer at nearby Luke Air Force Base. "It's not a place that encouraged creativity. It kills the spirit."

But homebuilders aren't nannies or cruise directors. They may play a huge role in social engineering, but that role is forced and accidental. Their primary job is to put heads in beds, make it affordable, and keep shareholder value rising. It is possible to look out at the red tile oceans and see what Walt Whitman called "democratic vistas."

The Rancho Fill-in-the-Blanks tend to be more racially diverse than more settled neighborhoods; they are especially popular with educated immigrants from the Global South. A bounty of State Trust land and the efficiency of production homebuilding lets Arizona salvage an old American dream: here it is possible to work for hourly wages in service or manufacturing and still be able to afford a home of one's own, garden on one's own soil, steer one's own ship. That's the sweet spot in the market. Everything else is gravy.

"The issue comes back to affordability," said Greg Vogel, the founder of Land Advisors brokerage. "These places will have little to no social infrastructure. Three-quarters of it is going to be uniformly disgusting. But that's most of suburbia. You find your sociability in schools, churches, the fitness center. Up in Surprise, you see a lot of RV garages where guys store their toys and have their man caves, their boats they take up to Lake Pleasant. The answer lies outside the common subdivision. These people aren't in prison. They have options."

In Rancho Mercado, practically the only time residents can be spotted in public is when they come and go from work. In the evenings, the garage opens to admit them and then lowers like the hatch of a space pod.

On a recent Sunday morning, I sat on a decorative rock in the empty "amenity area" hoping to chat to someone about how they liked the neighborhood. A middle-aged woman walking her dog approached, and I stood up to greet her. She gave me a baleful look, held up a hand in a clear *don't approach* sign, and walked ten paces away dialing her phone. I sat back down on the rock, and heard her mutter, presumably to 911, *there's a guy here in the park . . .*

I took it as a cue to leave before Surprise P.D. arrived to investigate the case of a random guy sitting on a rock who tried to talk to someone on a Sunday morning. The encounter left me feeling gross, unsafe myself, fearful of being accused of something. Had I owned a home in Rancho Mercado, it likely would have been the last time I attempted a friendly conversation with a stranger.

"People are out here in Surprise for a reason," a man had told me the previous evening, as he paused between sprinting exercises on the street outside his RM-1 home on Faye Way. "They want to do their own thing. They keep to themselves, just enjoying what they have inside the house."

Another new homeowner down the street, fetching kitty litter from his garage, told me he liked Rancho Mercado, calling it "a working-class neighborhood," with no small amount of pride. He works as a correctional officer at a nearby prison and carries a commanding but gregarious presence, speaking in the inflections of his native Chicago.

His neighbor to the north also had a first career as a firefighter, a point of bonding, but they've only talked incidentally a few times. They have never been inside each other's houses.

"Back where I came from, you'd always come home after work and see people without a job, hanging out on their porches like they had nothing do to," he told me. "I hated seeing that. And that doesn't happen around here."

A FLAT SPOT OFF THE FIRE ROAD in the Superstitions seemed as good a place as any to flop for the night, though the partition in the rocks that let me glimpse Phoenix was also a natural conduit for wind blowing in, and the tent fluttered all night long. The smoldering electricity of the megacity made patterns on the vinyl. I lay awake, blinking, as the tent's envelope dances above me, making an occasional violent lurch. Were I not lying in it as an anchor, it would have blown down the ridge like a tumbleweed.

When I crawled out after sunrise, exhausted, the city lights had all disappeared, but a carpet of yellow wildflowers, *Pectis papposa*, among the foxtail barely stretched down a hill to the east. This variety of aster can be found all over the Southwest, its seeds carried in seasonal wind currents, and it was no surprise that it should be lighting up this breezy keyhole in the mountains. When combined with poppies and Indian paintbrush, the effect of wildflowers can be dazzling: a spray of rainbow gentleness. Passing near here with General Crook in the 1880s, cavalry captain John Gregory Bourke noted "a carpet of colors which would rival the best examples of the looms of Turkey or Persia."

The dirt Jeep trail underfoot was splotched with motor fuel and lubricant stains, but a thinner trail soon wound off into the Four Peaks Wilderness, named for the row of rhyolite and shale knobs that serves as a distant backdrop for the eastern suburbs and also appeared in 1996 as the purplish logo on the first state license plates to bear a graphic element under the letters and numbers. A typical Arizona scrum of manzanita, desert mahogany, and sumac lines the path that leads past the northernmost and highest summit, Brown's

Peak at 7,657 feet. I had tried and failed to climb it eighteen years ago in a high wind and had to stagger back down with blood on my face.

No time that day for a repeat engagement; the route hugging the southern slopes became monotonous, bulging with the peaks and then retreating into high canyon folds, and the oaks turned dark and indistinct. Off to the east under the Sierra Ancha mountains was the Tonto Basin, a broad bowl that Captain Bourke had described as "a weird scene of grandeur and rugged beauty" and "one of the roughest spots on the globe."

I wolfed a dinner of pepperoni and tortillas with my aching legs dangling over a precipice that seems to plunge five hundred feet in the lunar obscurity, then came to a valley an hour later that made my heart rise with happiness: a scattering of saguaro cacti pinned to the incline that leads down to the broad bowl of the Tonto Basin. They were the first saguaros I saw on the trail, which meant I was at the edge of the Sonoran Desert.

These ribbed green poles with arms held upward in hallelujah poses can rarely grow north of the thirty-third parallel, though they're astonishingly hardy once they find the right soil, sucking up the brief bursts of water from monsoons with root systems that go only six inches deep but can spread out thirty feet or more in all directions. When fully mature, they can weigh up to five tons and can live well past a century; it wouldn't be out of character for this stand to have sprouted before Arizona became a U.S. territory. Though I was exhausted, I exulted in seeing them under the bright bulb of the moon.

It was an easy walk to the Roosevelt Marina for coffee and eggs the next morning, on asphalt again crossing the bridge on the highway just a few hundred yards from the same masonry dam that my great-great-grandfather came up the dirt Apache Trail highway to see in 1911, almost certainly with wonder at what the future would bring. His farm was now underneath a Phoenix tract home neighborhood named Orangedale Estates, planted there more than a half century ago.

The Arizona leisure spirit was also on display at the marina, where dozens of long-hulled pleasure boats were tied to the wharves, and where potbellied men and women in T-shirts drank bloody marys and tallboy beers at the bar behind smoked glass windows with a panoramic view of the lake that made Phoenix.

A pregnant waitress brought me a drink and talked with me for a while. She was from Show Low and knew she couldn't count on the father, an auto mechanic who broke up with her when she got the positive test. Her friends and her family would be there for her, she said, but the future was frightening. I said encouraging things, knowing the answers were hidden and knowing the chances of my ever seeing her again were low, but wanting all good and redemptive things to rain on her when her baby arrived and they started out together. So many lives unfolding, all around us, disclosing themselves like winter stars.

I found a spot where a water tank used to stand on a hill above a trailer park. It was also uphill from the Roosevelt Cemetery, where up to seventy-five people who died of accidents or diseases during the construction of the dam were laid. Their remains had to be moved to this spot after the rising waters made the old cemetery obsolete.

A three-day haul through the Superstitions awaited, and I regarded it with dread. A fire had come through the previous year and made a charred wasteland out of large sections of it, and as I followed the dry drainage up Cottonwood Creek, I saw that the damage was even worse than I had feared. Debris loosened by the fire had cascaded down the wash during heavy rains and choked the passageway with branches and stumps. I had to take off my pack at least a half-dozen times and heave it over one obstacle or another, and crash my way through tangles that left bloody streaks on my arms. At points, I wished for a machete.

After a few miserable miles, the creekbed yielded to a disturbing landscape of baked yellow in all directions: charred stumps of sycamore and manzanita amid withered prickly pear. The fire had lasted more most of the previous June and had been of human origin, though its exact cause remains unknown.

FLASHPOINT

On June 4, 2021, a group of F-16 fighter jets took off from the Arizona Air National Guard strip near the Tucson International Airport. They headed up to the Pinal Mountains, a favorite spot for dogfighting exercises.

With its many canyon folds and fangtooth ridges, the region a few dozen miles to the east of metro Phoenix looks like Afghanistan, and the training sortie from the 162nd Wing was working on defensive maneuvers to avoid enemy air-to-air attack. Part of their protocol involves release of a type of flare to confuse a heat-seeking missile.

This charge is known as an M206—it consists of a square pipe eight inches long packed with a mixture of magnesium, Teflon, and Viton designed to burn in midair at a temperature of two thousand degrees Fahrenheit for about seven seconds, long enough to provide an incandescent mirage to draw enemy fire.

An unknown number of these flares were sent corkscrewing over Telegraph Canyon five miles south of the town of Superior, as the fighter jets darted around the white clouds of smoke, whirling and pitchbacking above a ceiling of eleven thousand feet, meaning the magnesium flares would drift at least twenty-five seconds through the air and burn out completely before they hit the uninhabited desert below. The detachment completed their mission around noon and then streaked back to Tucson.

At 1:32 p.m., the supervisor of the Superior Public Works Department, Anthony Huerta, had finished the lunch his wife cooked him at their home near the town cemetery and walked outside to his truck. He noticed a huge cloud of white smoke rising up in the hills to the south. *Oh boy*, he thought. *That's going to be a hot one.*

Huerta got in his truck and went out to U.S. 60 for a better look, then dialed the fire department. The dispatcher passed on the alert to the administrative office of the Tonto National Forest.

The summer of 2021 was already shaping up bad in Arizona. Fire managers were predicting big burns in what was the driest recorded season since 1895. Dead pine needles broke with the slightest touch—an indication of vanished moisture. Sun hammered down without relief; the heat alone had already killed at least thirteen people in mobile homes. A mining employee digging a trench with a backhoe near the copper town of Bagdad accidentally kicked up sparks and started a fire that wiped out a dozen houses.

Two major national forests, including the Tonto, were closed to all visitors, out of fear that some idiot camper would flick a cigarette. Arizona was parched to the point where even sparks flying from a blown tire into the ditch weeds could trigger a catastrophe. "Vegetation is stricken across the state; there isn't one area that isn't impacted by the drought," said Tiffany Davila of the state Department of Forestry. "It's pretty much kindling at this point."

This was a good description of fuel conditions in Telegraph Canyon, a little-visited place named for the route of the first telegraph wires to be strung up from Florence in 1902. The smoke Huerta had seen was coming from deep inside it, where the scrub oak and manzanita were vaporizing fast. Within twenty minutes of his call, the fire had blown up to more than a thousand acres.

Protocol dictates the fire be named immediately, typically for the first prominent landmark near the point of ignition. This one received the modern but antique name Telegraph Fire. Deputy ranger Adam Bromley put in the order for a Type 3 Incident Management Team of firefighters to contain what they could. Then he went up for a look in a Forest Service helicopter.

As he and the pilot chattered closer to Telegraph Canyon, the heat and the brightness intensified until, nearly underneath him, a carpet of flame writhed and danced like a living entity, surging eastward in heavy wind. The smoke filtered the sunlight in strange patterns, obscuring the view, but Bromley got a good enough look into the abyss to understand what was going to happen.

"It was charging through everything," he said. "It looked like it was burning rocks." Directly ahead of it lay the asphalt stripe of Highway 177 and the small ranching settlement of El Capitan, pop. 37. Plus lots more dry fuel.

Bromley got on the phone with chief ranger Tom Torres and gave him the news. "This is going to be a big one. And we've got a problem."

The two of them talked every twenty minutes or so, monitoring the weather, which promised forty-mile-per-hour winds the next day. But they still waited to see if the fire justified calling the Southwest Coordination Center in Albuquerque to "place an order," that is, make a request for hundreds of elite wildland firefighters, called Type 1 Hotshot teams, to form an army to attack the Telegraph Fire. An instant city would be created, complete with bunks, showers, dining contractors, first aid stations. And it would be quite expensive, with costs likely running into the eight figures. These major incidents are known as "campaign fires."

Bromley didn't sleep at all that night. At dawn, the fire jumped over Highway 77 on a trajectory to hit the town of Globe, and that was the cue for Tom Torres to get on the phone with Albuquerque and start the money meter.

—

The decision to call in the cavalry might have seemed an obvious choice for the homeowners of Superior and Globe who stood in the path of the inferno. But the decision was surprisingly fraught. Vigorous suppression of fires can end up doing more lasting damage than a posture of letting the fire chew up as much dead fuel as it likes.

More than a hundred years of conflicting policy is behind these decisions, on which the fate of some Arizona towns can rest, and whose urgency grows as the wildfire season—once contained to the hottest months of summer—now lasts half the year or more. Average annual temperatures in the state have gone up two degrees since 1900 and are expected to rise between two and ten degrees more by 2100. Saguaros are retreating up the mountain slopes. Portions of what used to be desert are taking more of a grasslands character, with a gasoline-like weed called buffelgrass taking the place of more flame-resistant scrub.

In the old days, Torres and Bromley never would have hesitated. American forest rangers had been conditioned to believe fire was the enemy and had to be snuffed on sight. Observation towers went up on mountain peaks, creating lonely vigils for introverts. Old combat aircraft were refitted to rain down water and retardants as well as elite corps of parachuting firefighters called smokejumpers that formed the core of the later Hotshot program. Managers implemented the "10 a.m. rule," indicating the time by the next morning that a blaze had to be out—or there would be hell to pay.

A bear cub rescued from a fire near Capitan, New Mexico, got nicknamed Smokey by his ranger keepers, then turned into the cartoon face of the fire suppression program with the memorable phrase: "only you can prevent forest fires." He got so much fan mail the U.S. Postal Service had to create the 20252 zip code just for him. The Ad Council got the country music singer Eddie Arnold to do a television jingle in 1952; it became an elementary school and summer camp standard.

Smokey the Bear, Smokey the Bear.
Prowlin' and a growlin' and a sniffin' the air.
He can find a fire before it starts to flare.

The U.S. Forest Service also wasn't wrong that discarded cigarettes and careless campfires touched off blazes. But putting the onus on ordinary Americans covered up a more persistent cause.

Fire suppression had stacked increasingly unhealthy forests with waiting fuel, just waiting for a spark. In the early 1970s, ecological thinking started favoring natural burns to cleanse deadwood. The ideal state of the forests, scientists argued, would be like in the time prior to European settlement in the sixteenth century, when there were roughly a tenth of the trees and the forests were like spacious parks and not claustrophobic mazes.

The romantic and anticolonial idea led to a "let it burn" doctrine that stopped traditional firefighting unless people or structures were threatened. Loggers were instructed to stop cutting off tree crowns and limit "slash," or wasted wood. But the Reagan administration stepped back from this practice after fires chewed up Yellowstone National Park and grabbed headlines for weeks in the summer of 1988. Incident commanders were told they could let nature take over only if they had brigades of firefighters and aircraft ready to attack any fire that might misbehave. "Let it burn" turned into "not so much."

And this is the policy justification for today's multimillion-dollar fire encampments, with D-Day-style personnel, infrastructure, and frontline equipment. Traveling Hotshot crews stand ready to be deployed anywhere within a thousand miles to join the interagency strike forces in instant villages of tents and trailers with guys they haven't seen since the previous summer. Entrepreneurs print up souvenir T-shirts at the first sign of a Big One, parking their sales vans at a new camp like Deadheads following a concert tour. "Fire tourism," some call it.

The camps keep getting bigger as expensive new houses keep pushing into the forest outside Arizona towns like Prescott, Flagstaff, and Sedona. These cowboy fantasy haciendas, most of them worth seven figures, attain part of their value from the proximity to the trees, a commune with nature that can put the ponderosa branches within inches of their eaves.

At the first hint that property—especially rich people's property—may stand in the path of a new fire, heavy political pressure comes down on the interagency command to hit it with everything available. Should a small blaze whip up into a large one, the agency is on the hook for a raft of liability lawsuits. There is little incentive then for a commander to play the long game. Nobody but the scientists will cry when a fire is extinguished. "There's a blank checkbook at that point, and an order: do what you need to do to protect the town," said Mitch Tobin, director of the Water Desk at the University of Colorado. "There's not going to be a budget hearing."

The real fight isn't at the heart of the forest but near the streets where flames lick roofs. Geographers call these expanding combat zones the "wildland-urban interface." The best preventive measure for homeowners is time-consuming, expensive, and a never-ending project, which is to get rid of all vegetation within the ignition zone of two hundred feet in all directions. Landscapers make quite a lot of money on it every spring. The resulting defensible space often looks ugly and makes the house look lonely. So not everyone can be persuaded to do it. And it's the Smokey Bear problem once again. Putting the responsibility on individual people takes the heat off the larger problem: local governments zoning these areas for houses, and custom homebuilders pushing as far into the beautiful trees as they can. Mountain living is gorgeous, after all, even if it's the equivalent of living next to a bomb.

Firefighters call these forested enclaves "suicide subdivisions." What's healthiest for the forest, in pure terms, is to let them all go to embers. But conspicuous enjoyment of land and lifestyle has been a perpetual temptation for Arizona. Try talking about the ecological benefits of "let it burn" policies to someone whose dream house is about to get torched.

Costs will keep going up as temperatures rise. Shorter winters mean less snowpack and drier forests. Fire season is already three months longer than it was in 1970, with seven times the number of houses going up in smoke each year. After each catastrophic fire, sorrowful after-action reports call for "better management" of the forests—this language might as well be cut and pasted. Cleaning the forests of deadwood every five years is like sweeping out the Augean Stables, an impossible task. Logging companies find it difficult to harvest every third tree. Hauling out the slash is impossible in the deep brush where no vehicles go. And the poaching of the oldest trees means what's left is more prone to canopy fires, ripping across the treetops like divine judgment instead of cleaning up the garbage on the forest floor.

All the traffic in western fire camps—an estimated $5 billion annually—amounts to an oddball version of rural economic development, a charred Keynesianism. Helicopter rental runs $35,000 per day, even if the bird stays waiting on the ground. Feeding a big crew that day is another $100,000 to the caterer; each hungry firefighter sitting at the tables is getting paid $168 per diem. And so on. And even if an Arizona town gets flattened, nearby homebuilders and construction supply are certain to boom.

Fire is a racket. But the worst part is that all the money showering down like water from a tanker plane will leave nothing behind. The Civilian Conservation Corps of the 1930s plowed tax money into the economy as a stimulus and put a lot of young people to work, just like the new disaster marketplace of fire. But they left hard resources in the western forests: trails, picnic grounds, new roads, bridges, wildlife refuges, lasting gifts that created tourist revenue for generations and the unquantifiable enjoyment of millions. Wildfire spending goes into trouser pockets with no legacy except bulldozed fire roads, invasive buffelgrass, mudslides, and debris-choked creeks. The beautiful land, so seductive in the real estate brochures, looks like the Ardennes after World War I.

Perhaps this is why fire officials and reporters fall back on the language of just war theory when they describe suppression efforts: *fight, attack, battle, save, rescue, extinguish*. But as the author Douglas Gantenbein has noted: "Fire is simply fire. It has no sense of morality, has no persona, does not wish to do good or bad, is neither deliberately enemy nor friend."

Fire Camp is now a permanent city in Arizona, reconstituting itself each summer. We just don't know where.

—

The Telegraph Fire had chewed its way through 41,106 acres by the time several hundred Hotshots from New Mexico arrived at fire camp. Almost all the damage was on isolated state land, but Adam Bromley calculated it was still blasting through more than a thousand acres an hour as wind blew in from the east and temperatures hovered at ninety-seven degrees. Bad fire weather.

Incident commanders drew up evacuation plans for towns that could be in the path. The biggest one was the linear conurbation of Globe-Miami, an old copper boomtown strung out through hills and canyons with a spill of wooden bungalows on the slopes and tailings piles in the valley that looked like a lunar surface.

A handful of Douglas DC-10s were assigned to drop loads of red slurry, and they made confetti-like shows over the Pinal Mountains. As the sun set on June 6 and nighttime security lights winked on over the Good-2-Go gas station in Superior, the hills seemed to sway in the distance like burning charcoal embers floating on a lake, making no sound.

A massive plume of smoke drifted over the eastern part of the state the next morning, turning skies hazy and fragrant with the smoke of vanished oaks and dropping visibility to less than a mile. The Gila County sheriff told people in Superior they should pack their keepsakes and get ready to leave.

There was another problem: a second fire south of Globe had been burning for four days, consuming brush and grass at a steady pace. Cause unknown with a footprint of eighty-two square miles, a bigger area than the city of Baltimore. Tonto officials called it the Mescal Fire. The borders between it and Telegraph were shrinking rapidly; it seemed probable they would merge. The post offices in Globe shut down. Huey helicopters dunked buckets into the Superior municipal swimming pool to spread chlorinated water over the flames—these water drops are often about as effective as squirting an eyedropper into a roaring hearth.

Type 1 firefighters, meanwhile, streamed into the area. School superintendent Glen Lineberry shut down summer school classes at Miami High School and turned the campus into an improvised barracks. Young men bunked down in classrooms; daily briefings were held in the auditorium; the caterers commandeered the school cafeteria and filled it with the scent of chicken fried steak. At night, the football field was lit up by an eerie vermilion glow—the fire devouring the scrub on the eastern slope of the Pinals.

By June 17 the ranching settlement called El Capitan off Highway 77 had been completely engulfed. A vacation cabin owned by Arizona House Speaker Rusty Bowers went to ash. The governor came up for a look and called a special session of the legislature to appropriate more funds. Altogether about 2,500 people evacuated their homes, while fire crews used bulldozers and chainsaws to carve break lines in the desert scrub, trying to rob fuel.

Engaging a wildfire is less like military combat and more like coal mining: hard physical labor, blackened faces, and sweat. Unlike city fires, where pressurized water is the primary weapon, firefighters go after the target by digging and chopping organic material in its path. Heat stroke is a constant danger; the body's internal temperature spirals out of control and drinking water loses its cooling effect. Fainting on the line is not uncommon.

The incident commanders treated U.S. 60—the main route from Phoenix to Globe—the same way the Chinese army viewed the Yalu River, a line to be defended at all costs. The bulldozer tracks were throwing out sparks and creating little sub-fires that then had to be extinguished, wasting time and creating more threats. Fire managers wondered whether the all-out strategy was a good idea. But the Telegraph Fire had now made national news, upping the stakes. The wall of smoke was visible all over Phoenix. Politicians were paying close attention, and acre by acre, the moving orange wall crept closer to one of Arizona's oddball curiosities: the Boyce Thompson Arboretum.

William Boyce Thompson was a blueblood son of a mine manager, a product of New England boarding schools who had been one of the capital movers behind the copper operations in Morenci, Globe, and Superior in the early twentieth century. The scruffy towns in the path of the fire were a part of his legacy, but not as much as the 392-acre garden of exotic plants he founded on Queen Creek, a teeming reserve of succulents, agaves, cacti, boojums, and the largest red gum eucalyptus grove in the country.

Like many rich men of then and now, Thompson thought of his philanthropy as world-saving. "I have in mind far more than mere botanical propagation," he wrote in 1930. "I hope to benefit the State and the Southwest by the addition of new products. A plant collection will be assembled which will be of interest not only to the nature lover and the plant student, but which will stress the practical side, as well to see if we cannot make these mesas, hillsides, and canyons far more productive and of more benefit to mankind." Believing the Arizona climate to be the most healthful in the world, he built a stone mansion clinging to a cliff, overlooking the riot of phyla. It became a state park in 1976. Helicopters with dangling buckets had already made abundant use of the water in its scenic ponds.

With the flames just three hundred feet away from rare international plants, the Incident Command took panicked phone calls from Arizona lawmakers as well as citizens in Superior who feared the loss of their prime tourist draw. An assistant to director Lynn Namath called her to say: "The fire is coming over the ridge, it's cresting the ridge." She put her head in her hands. But hours later, an intense airshow unfolded on that same ridge; DC-10s dumped slurry and two helicopters showered water, halting the line and saving the arboretum's holdings. The Incident Command spread over the ridge more than one million gallons of chemical slurry that looked like powered tomato soup.

That same day, one of the fire commanders told people in Superior they had "a pretty good idea" of how the fire started—the National Guard jets and their practice flares. Brigadier General Jerry Butler confirmed the mock dogfights around the time of the ignition, but he also denied responsibility. "According to a recent U.S. Air Force inquiry and review of radar tapes in the area, the lowest altitude observed was 11,700 feet," he wrote. "Any flares expended during these maneuvers would have been released in accordance with regulations and would have burned out 3,000 feet above ground level."

This explanation didn't impress Superior mayor Mila Besich, who called it a "cover-your-ass statement" and pointed out that almost nobody ever ventures into the part of the canyon where the blaze first kicked up. No roads go there. The skies were cloudless that day; lightning was not a factor. Plus General Butler would have no way of knowing if a flare had malfunctioned and perhaps still been sputtering on its twenty-five-second fall down to the dry brush.

But if the air force conceded fault, it could result in a multimillion-dollar liability claim and a legal mess that could drag on for years. "I don't expect them to own up," said the mayor.

———

Nature wheels and spins around all her citizens at all times but settles on strange ignition points for her forests. Fires can start for the dumbest of reasons.

A U.S. Border Patrol agent celebrated the birth of his son in 2017 with a "gender reveal" party for which he mixed up a batch of blue-colored powdered chalk with explosive Tannerite. Then he set up the target in dry grass and shot at it for the amusement of his friends. The resulting blaze torched a good portion of the west side of the Santa Rita Mountains and cost $8.2 million to extinguish.

Unremarkable acts of turpitude, barely worth noticing on any other day, can mete biblical destruction onto Arizona. Wildfires are powerful visual symbols of a changing planet, but they also open windows onto people's hearts.

On the morning of June 18, 2002, on the Fort Apache Reservation, a twenty-nine-year-old man named Leonard Gregg went off by himself into the woods. He had endured a rotten childhood. Both his parents had been alcoholics, and his mother was fond of a foul-tasting homebrewed wine made from raisins, potatoes, and rice. She had been routinely drunk during her pregnancy and Leonard, as a result, had fetal alcohol syndrome. He couldn't do basic math, had a hard time reading, wrote his letters in clumsy script, and seemed to live only in the moment.

Yet he was cheerful and well liked and had a heart for others. He told people, for example, he felt morally obliged to give what little money he could earn to his girlfriend, Pearlita Haven, to help her six kids have a better childhood than he had.

Gregg lived—along with 1,700 others—in the town of Cibecue down a dead-end highway in the White Mountains, one of the only places in the United States where the dominant language is Apache. The name comes from a Spanish mangling of the Apache word for "valley with green trees." The U.S. Army showed up uninvited near here in 1881 to break up an outlawed Ghost Dance ceremony and a battle erupted after their scouts mutinied. Apaches were proud of their history of resistance and independence, but jobs were scarce. The unemployment rate hovered around 60 percent, and some of the only real work available was manual labor at the tribal sawmill or fighting fires on contract for the Bureau of Indian Affairs. Gregg had a coveted seasonal job there that paid eight dollars per hour.

He lit a match, touched it to some branches, hustled away and then answered the call on his cell phone that arrived minutes later for him to report to the front lines. In the western U.S. tradition of naming fires for nearby geographical features, the crew chief called it—unimaginatively—the Pine Fire. It was put out fast; Gregg was paid less than fifty dollars for his efforts at extinguishing the flames that had spread less than an acre. He would need more cash.

At about 4 p.m., he moved two miles north to the deserted Rodeo Fairgrounds, a place he felt comfortable. He had competed there himself in bronco riding competitions and fancied cowboy hats and boots. He struck another match. Dry branches began to burn. Part of him likely enjoyed the sight: fires had entranced him since he was a child. When he was four, he almost burned a house down by spreading a small cooking fire to the grass in the backyard.

On some of the bigger forest fires Gregg had seen in central Arizona, he reveled in the sight of airplanes dumping red-colored retardant above the flames, and he would reenact it in his playtime by dumping dust from his hands onto wooden blocks that he pretended were burning buildings. This was a make-believe he took into adulthood; the damage done to him in the womb ensured that part of him would always be stuck in childhood. Becoming a firefighter was therefore a dream come true.

Leaving his boot prints all over the site, Gregg went back to his girl-friend's house but told her he couldn't stay long because he would soon be responding to another fire.

A pillar of smoke soon towered over Cibecue. The BIA crew chief called it the Rodeo Fire and assumed it would be as small as the previous blaze. He declined offers of help from other agencies, even as the wind picked up. By the next morning, it had jumped the banks of Carrizo Creek and found the equivalent of a nuclear weapon: up to five hundred thousand acres of dense forest to the west, much of it logging turf full of fallen dead branches and other fuel that had not been cleaned out for decades.

At least seven towns were immediately threatened by the roaring wall, hot enough to boil the sap in the pine trees on its front edge and explode them into fragments before flame even touched them. Propane tanks at rural cabins went up like bundles of dynamite. The governor ordered an evacuation. State troopers shut down the crucial link of Highway 260.

Two distinct and separate Arizona cultures—blue-collar Native and blue-collar Anglo—then intersected, through different kinds of misjudgment.

A thirty-one-year-old white woman named Valinda Jo Elliott from the scruffy Phoenix suburb of Tolleson had been riding up to the Mogollon Rim with a friend named Ransford K. Olmsted. He did a little side work servicing vending machines and arcade games and had a call to fix a coin-operated pool table at the Antler Bar, the one tavern in the isolated ranching town of Young. Hearing news about road closures on the radio, Olmsted made the bad decision not to buy gas at a remote convenience store because the prices were too high, and also to exit the main road onto tribal highway 12A. He soon ran out of gas as a blanket of smoke crept near. Their phones were with Sprint; the only coverage out here was Verizon.

The two slept that night in the bed of Olmsted's pickup truck under pool table blankets. Whether he was dating Elliott has never been disclosed. She left him at the truck and walked down the road to look for a hill high enough where she might find cell phone reception. Elliott wore only the city summer uniform of a tank top, shorts, and flip-flops. She promptly got lost on Cibecue Ridge and spent the night shivering on a flat rock. While wandering around the forest before sunrise, she figured she was going to die. Then she hit upon the idea of setting fire to a dry bush with her cigarette lighter to attract somebody's attention.

A news helicopter from KPHO Channel 5, the CBS affiliate in Phoenix, had been getting video of the nearby Rodeo Fire and spotted the smoke. The crew landed near Elliott, tried to douse her fire with a bottle of purified water, and flew her to the hospital in Payson. She told them she'd been wandering alone for three days—it was actually less than one.

Her signal fire caught an unfortunate breeze and roared out of control on the ridge near Chediski Peak. It soon merged with the Rodeo Fire to become a superinferno that would destroy nearly a half million acres of forest.

A megafire this size makes for arresting television visuals: barreling flames, ashed buildings, tanker planes dumping red retardant slurry down on trees—what firefighters call "the air show." A federal spokesman named Jim Paxon who immodestly described himself as "a humble hay farmer from New Mexico" dominated network coverage with campy expressions delivered like a cowboy balladeer. "The monster reared its head today, and the dragon blew its fire," was one. The firefighters thought him a showboat and shunned him in the camp.

I was in this same fire camp for the *Republic* on the night of June 29 when I received a tipoff: the Bureau of Indian Affairs was about to arrest an Apache firefighter over in Cibecue, near where the blaze started. The winds had blown northeast from the Rodeo Fairgrounds, sparing the town of origin; it hadn't even been evacuated.

Trying not to run to my truck so as not to draw attention from any of the other reporters, I immediately began hauling ass in a nearly hundred-mile loop around the massive blaze, which cast an eerie ocher glow in the sky. Lightning flashed at the edges. Hot updrafts of air in that area nearly the size of Rhode Island contained enough moisture to form pyrocumulonimbus clouds—"fire storm clouds"—that sprinkle a tiny bit of water and whip up engines of airborne electricity. In some cases, tornados form at the heart of the fire.

I arrived in Cibecue after midnight and buttonholed the only people I could find still awake—a couple of weary Type 2 firefighters brought in from out of state—who had heard the same rumor but had no information I didn't. Not that it would have surprised them: current or retired firefighters are notorious for starting blazes out of revenge or pyromania. They know how to do it and how to hide it. It was after the press deadline by that point and we couldn't print an anonymous tip, so there was nothing I could do but sleep in my car and wait for the sun to shine weak light through the smoke.

Before sunrise, I approached an elderly man on the road who spoke only Apache. He gave me a warning hiss and one of the angriest faces I've ever seen. I apologized and got back into my Jeep, feeling like an interloper, which I was. Gregg's name was out on the street by 8 a.m., and folks in the town were deeply embarrassed. Eventually, I found an adoptive brother named Wilson Gregg in the family house on Another World Drive. "Whenever my mother would cook, he would watch the flames," he told me. "It fascinated him."

The massive bonfire Gregg started was dying down. The interagency command had gained the advantage on the night of June 24 by setting a backfire to rob the tree fuel just a half mile in front of the highway junction town called Show Low. The town had been named for a legend about two ranchers who settled an ownership dispute with a cut of playing cards. Now the town got lucky again. Families who had time to evacuate their horses were sent to a special equine camp outside the town of Saint Johns where temporary corrals had been thrown up. Those who had landlines back in their houses dialed their numbers several times a day to hear if the answering machine picked up. If it did, that meant their house was still standing.

Others on the Mogollon Rim told the feds to shove it and refused to obey the evacuation order. After the Incident Command gave up the largely Mormon town of Clay Springs to destruction, a band of renegade residents fought the fire on their own with garden hoses and chainsaws. The town's fire chief deputized people on the spot. I sat in the living room of a welder named Coman Garvin who had bulldozed a seven-mile lane through the ponderosas to create an effective firebreak that saved the town. He took me out to his porch and pointed at a spiky island of remaining trees. His neighbors had taken to calling it Mohawk Ridge, after the shaved punk rock hairstyle.

Professional firefighters scorned what he did. They call it "self-dispatch" or "freelancing." Civilian help is never welcome in a federal attack brigade; they get in the way and may require the distraction of rescue. "In an emergency situation, it can't be a democracy," complained Roy Hall, operations chief of the incident management team.

The town didn't care what anyone thought. Their houses were safe, and they would have certainly been ruined had nobody made a stand. The rest of the rim looked like the morning after Hiroshima. Roots of vanished pine trees still smoldered underground. Rubber bicycle tires had evaporated off their rims. Children's swing sets had melted into Salvador Dalí abstractions. Visitors to the reopened hellscape puzzled over the nails they felt in the ash underfoot before realizing they were all that had survived from a structure that had once stood there.

In Phoenix Leonard Gregg was taken before a magistrate and blurted, out of nowhere, in open court: "Can I just say I'm sorry for what I did?" The magistrate shushed him fast. The case was open-shut anyway. He was eventually sentenced to ten years in prison and ordered to pay an impossible $28 million in restitution. His Apache neighbors would bear the brunt of the resulting prejudice. They heard the insults and felt the angry stares in rim towns for years to come.

Federal prosecutors were less sure what to do with the white side of the catastrophe. They argued privately over whether Valinda Jo Elliott had displayed reckless negligence by lighting a signal fire after just one night alone in the woods. U.S. Attorney Paul Charlton made the odd decision to call a town meeting at the high school gym in Heber-Overgaard to announce to burned-out refugees that he wouldn't be filing charges against her. Catcalls and boos rained down. One man threw a burned log onto the parquet in a sign of displeasure. They looked past the structural causes of the fire—years of poor logging management and the negligence of defensible space—to focus rage on the two hapless human triggers. Gregg and Elliott were merely the sparks, not the fuel.

But logging and suppression policies are frustratingly vague—even boring. The hunger to make sense of catastrophe requires a moral arc where personal flaws may be acknowledged and redeemed in a public forum. The tabloid show *Inside Edition* flew Elliott and her attorney to New York City and filmed B-roll of her strolling through Central Park gesturing to reporter Paul Boyd as she described her ill-prepared walk in the woods. The camera lingered on her black plastic flip-flops.

Then the television crew joined her back in Arizona on a staged visit to the ash-covered foundation of a burned home, where Wanda Clark led a tearful Elliott on a tour of what she had lost. "This was my favorite room because I hung all my plants here." More tears. Hugs were exchanged. A bearded man declared: "Yes, we're hurting, but I think it's time for this community to say we love you."

Inside Edition did not broadcast an encounter two days later that didn't go as well. Someone told Elliott "talk is cheap." Another threw a shovel and gloves at her feet and told her to get to work. Elliott reached her limit of apology. She wrote a defiant letter to the *Republic* insisting she hadn't done anything wrong. "You know I have been beating myself up inside and blaming myself—for what?" she wrote, claiming that the Channel 5 helicopter pilot and the Department of Public Safety should have done more to put out her signal fire.

Her letter closed with a thought for those who had lost their homes: "May God have mercy on your lying souls."

———

Human failings in wildfire country became even more glaring when lightning hit a field of dry grass on the afternoon of June 28, 2013, outside the old mining town of Yarnell on the western edge of the rim.

A small fire took root in the brush, and it would be little remembered today if it hadn't been for a sudden shift of wind that surprised a team of nineteen firefighters in a basin loaded with fuel.

The Granite Mountain Hotshots died horribly seeking protection in foil tents they struggled to pull out of their backpacks as a wind-driven wall of fire came at them at twenty-five miles per hour, four times as hot as an oven broiler at top setting. Granite boulders cracked in half. Wood handles on the crew's tools went to ash, their fiberglass face shields were melted into threads, and the engines on their chainsaws melted into puddles. Nothing alive had a chance. A single inhalation of breath at that temperature would have pulverized any set of lungs within seconds.

Newspapers brimmed with quasi-religious encomiums. They were deemed the Saints of Prescott in a memorial service attended by Joe Biden.

The whiskery bard of the Rodeo-Chediski fire, Jim Paxon, now working for the Arizona Forestry Division, was on hand to lead reporters into the charred basin. "We are going to hallowed ground," he declared, asking reporters to touch a Granite Mountain T-shirt laid over a cactus "in reverence to the loss."

The city of Prescott has always been the most picturesque of Arizona's county seats, with a handsome courthouse looking as though it had been imported from New England surrounded by a square of storefronts and bars, earning it the booster motto "Everyone's Hometown." The public grief for the Granite Mountain Hotshots dominated the national news for a week. But it also obscured the miscalculations that contributed to the disaster.

Prescott made money when the Hotshots were deployed to other western fires but gave them poor funding and had even been considering disbanding the unit. "It is challenging to run a nationally recognized program with minimum standards and requirements that I am unable to meet," wrote crew chief Eric Marsh in an annual review. His boss told him to "make the best of the situation." Possibly because of this, Marsh did not sign off on the certification of his own unit.

Another question: was it smart to form a wildfire unit within a traditional red-truck pumper department whose mission had always been saving buildings? Prescott was the only city in the United States that had tried this hybrid model. Some experts thought the awkward composite was like sending a baseball squad to play on a hockey rink.

The Arizona Forestry Division made an initial decision to fight the fire with prison crews and flame retardant drops. When it began to spin out of control the next morning, they sent in the Hotshots from just up U.S. Highway 89. They were exhausted from an earlier fire but would never turn away from a blaze in their own territory. This move saved money for the Arizona state government, then deeply in debt, but it was done over the objection of the federal Southwest Coordination Center.

Finally, and most devastatingly, Eric Marsh may have led the crew to their unnecessary end. For reasons that have never been convincingly explained, he ordered his men to leave a ridge that had already been cleared by a backfire—an intentional fire to consume wood and grass that might have otherwise fueled the main fire. This is called a black zone, generally seen as safe. But at 4:04 p.m. on June 30, the Granite Mountain Hotshots climbed down into the basin loaded with chaparral and oak, some of it over ten feet high—a perfect fireplace stacked with wood that had not been cleaned out since 1967. When the wind shifted south at approximately 4:30 p.m., a furnace roared. Within twenty minutes, everyone was dead except for twenty-one-year-old Brendan McDonough, who had been left behind as a lookout.

Fire agencies often try to cover up their mistakes; they're like any other government outfit in this regard. Supervisors never want to reveal incompetence. Acknowledging misjudgments invites big lawsuits. But self-correction often comes only through embarrassment. The first to break some of the skeptical stories, John Dougherty of *Phoenix New Times*, had most of his public records requests ignored.

McDonough cooperated with a hagiographic movie about the event called *Only the Brave* and co-wrote a book called *My Lost Brothers*. But he eventually went to the Prescott city attorney to tell him about some disturbing radio traffic he'd overheard that day. Marsh had told his deputy Jesse Steed to take the crew out of the safe zone and down into the basin to pick their way through game trails and faint washes toward a set of buildings called Not Mucheva Ranch. The two had argued until Marsh gave him a direct order. Steed told him it was a bad idea but complied. Then the wind shifted.

"We're not going to make it!" Steed said over the radio. Listeners at the command post heard chainsaws in the background—a sign that the fire was rushing toward them and the crew was frantically trying to create a perimeter. Marsh made a radio call at 4:42 p.m. to report their escape route had been cut off and they were preparing to climb into their thermal cocoons—a dire measure. That was the last transmission.

The strongest theory around Marsh's reasoning was that he wanted his crew to defend the sheds of Not Mucheva Ranch in light of a darkening thundercloud—the same one that kicked up the winds on the nineteen men in the low-lying tinderbox. When he left his post, he also lost visual contact with the fire. He died trying to fulfill a gallant imperative of city firefighters: rescuing buildings. But this is not the aim of wildfire teams, which seek managed containment.

The martyrdom narrative for the Hotshots held for a few months until money got in the way. The city of Prescott became reluctant to pay full benefits to some of the families, who had already received a collective $4 million in private donations. "This is big bucks when it's all over, big bucks," the mayor complained to the *Prescott Courier*.

The Hotshots may have been heroes, but a potential tax hike on their behalf wasn't going over well in a community with an inbred suspicion of government, even though federal fire protection had saved the town on numerous occasions. Various conspiracy theories got thrown around, the most popular one that the state had let the fire burn out of control to make more money on per diems, a grand version of Leonard Gregg's scam gone awry. Friendships ended; lawsuits were filed; a few of the widows left town rather than be accused of greed and be faced with more psychological punishment.

By then, it was clear that the Hotshots had indeed been martyrs, but less to the sudden turn of a wind and more to the equally impersonal and dangerous forces of organizational confusion.

—

The airshow on the Telegraph Fire had been a qualified success. The retardant coating the oaks and grass kept the flames away from Superior and Globe, and it let the Hotshots stay away from the dangerous heart of the conflagration. The lessons of Yarnell Hill were on everyone's minds. "We're trying not to kill more firefighters, to be honest," said Bromley.

When the Telegraph encroached on land already burned to a crisp by the Mescal Fire, it began to slow down. Then it halted almost entirely when it hit a region burned by a previous blaze called the Pinal Fire, which managers had opted to let burn four years ago in the logic that consumption of idle fuel was a good thing. They were right. The ash had made the hilly country look like a heath of the damned back then, but it made the remaining vegetation about as flammable as a concrete sidewalk. The Telegraph "fell flat on its face," said Bromley. "It tried to break through and it just couldn't do it. There wasn't anything but duff and some burned logs in the Pinal Fire scar. To see it go from raging to something behaving quite nicely was incredible."

The only fuel now lay to the south, some fresh red broom and thin Mediterranean grass. Crews could maneuver easily within it to carve out trenches and make a natural cage. With nowhere else to go, the Telegraph suffocated. Evacuation orders lifted. Crew strength dropped by half as Hotshots left to go fight other western fires. By the end of June, the Telegraph was declared dead and scored as the ninth-largest fire ever to hit Arizona by acreage. There were no fatalities or major injuries, and fifty-two structures were lost, mainly sheds and vacation cabins. It cost $23.1 million to extinguish.

Bromley went to Texas for a wedding on his wife's side of the family around this time and met people there who had seen the fearsome images on television. He found himself unable to be eloquent because such events had ceased to be unusual to him. "I don't know what you want me to say," he told them. "Big flames and a lot of smoke. That's about it."

Monsoon rains came in mid-July and again in August, causing mudslides and floods in Miami where the hills had been cleansed of brush. A few cars and pieces of large furniture floated away down the creeks. But the rains also brought a riot of thistle, grama grasses, and wildflowers, making it hard to see—ten weeks later—that a fire had recently swept through.

Most of the damage from the Telegraph Fire was surface level, said Molly Hunter of the University of Arizona's biology department. The soil did not caramelize enough to prevent fresh growth. Manzanita bushes were scarred but not killed. "There's some char on it and some ash, but the bark is still there," she said. "Once you get a little bit of moisture, it'll start producing new leaves. The grasses, in particular, are going to love this fire."

Memories of the Telegraph Fire started to fade. The Forest Service stalled on releasing the investigation into the potential cause from an air force flare. People in Superior resigned themselves to the idea they would never know for sure what caused the ninth-biggest fire in Arizona history. Adam Bromley moved onto other fire management duties. The rains of July had spurred a bounty of weeping lovegrass in the backcountry that would soon be ripe for burning. The shrub-grass ecosystem in the Pinal foothills had shifted from one that burned every two centuries to becoming like gunpowder at the beginning of every summer.

"I hate to say it's 'nothing' to us anymore, but it's gotten to be the new normal," Bromley said. "We've gotten desensitized. We have short lifespans and so we expect the land to stay in its current state forever. And it'll still be there. Just changed."

T HE IGNEOUS HULK OF THE SUPERSTITION range to the east of Phoenix is best known for a piece of fiction that counts as Arizona's most enduring canards, and one far more widely believed than that of the Mogollon Monster. No description of this range can be complete without it, so here goes.

In 1892 a woman named Julia Thomas told the *Arizona Enterprise* newspaper she was in possession of map to a gold mine in the Superstitions that had been drawn by her friend Jacob Waltz on his deathbed. She was selling hand-drawn copies of it for seven dollars each.

Waltz was a Swiss-born farmer who had been in Arizona since the end of the Civil War and had contracted pneumonia in his final days. Like many German-speaking immigrants, he acquired the familiar term Dutch, mangled from Deutsche. Little is known about him or what he may have seen in the Superstitions on one of his occasional prospecting expeditions, other than that he died in poverty and that Thomas's account closely tracked another popular story involving a vanished mine owned by a nonexistent Spanish family named Peralta. These lost treasure yarns became more numerous as the era of the big gold and silver strikes was on the decline and civilian prospectors were muscled aside by corporations.

The story of the Lost Dutchman Mine would have vanished itself were it not for the 1931 homicide of Adolph Ruth, who was found on the east slope of Black Top Mesa with two bullets in his skull. Newspapers ran with the irresistible theory he had been killed by bandits or Apache scouts immediately after finding the Lost Dutchman. The story spread around the nation, along with hundreds of theories on the location, even though the magma origins of the Superstitions makes auriferous veins nearly impossible. Up to nine thousand gold-seekers every year still hike into the Superstitions to poke around the brush, looking for suspicious rock piles. One of them might have accidentally set the 2019 Woodbury fire by flicking a cigarette into the weeds.

Successful myths catch on because they contain a kernel of truth. In this case, the Lost Dutchman Mine underlines the narrative of Arizona—lively ever since Bernardo de Urrea's valley first provided its name—as a place for seekers who want to get rich fast. You could see it in my great-great-grandfather Franklin Larue, who fled here from his medical practice in Idaho to cash in on cotton. You could see it in the builders of Orangedale Estates, who slammed concrete foundations onto what had been his irrigated fields. You could see it in the generic housing clusters that still march to the horizons.

Up and down a few canyon drainages and I came to the site where Elisha Reavis made his ranch headquarters in 1873. Big oaks and sycamores lined a creek with a healthy flow of water. I paused to fill my bottles and wander around. There's a slab where a sandstone house used to stand, wild grass in barely discernable farrows choking the scraps of rusted farm equipment. The circle of a now-fenceless corral contained a deep layer of dark powder—the manure of long-dead livestock. A few apple trees still grew on the flat-bottomed plain of the stream.

Reavis had made a shrewd choice of ground in his isolation, long before the territorial pattern of wagon roads hardened into asphalt. He rode into the mining town of Globe every now and then with a load of vegetables for sale, and a newspaper took note of his "Samsonian locks and Aaronic whiskers," in addition to his fondness for quaffing mezcal. He likely looked more like a classical prospector than Jacob Waltz.

Up the canyon named for him, then, and to the streambed parallel to the trail where Elisha Reavis died in an 1896 ambush by unknown killers. The chaparral on both sides had been blackened and crisped by the furnace of the summer's fire, and the whole valley looked like a blasted heath out of H. P. Lovecraft. And from the pass, it was a dizzying march in the afternoon sun into Rogers Canyon on the other side, where a dry stream led past a thirteenth-century cliff dwelling made by the Salado people. More than a hundred people once lived in these mud-and-pole apartments, secure from the military danger posed by the canal-building Hohokam not far away.

The path eventually led to a trailhead and another dirt road, and I bushwhacked to the top of a nearby peak at the southernmost edge of the range for a truly spectacular view: the whale's hump of the Santa Catalina range far to the south, the copper-bearing folds of the Pinal Mountains to the east, and the bejeweled carpet of the Phoenix basin spread out to the west, porch lights winking on in the dusk as people sat down for their suppers. Planes overhead nosed down toward the mini-city of Sky Harbor International Airport—was there ever a better or more evocative name for an airport?

I knew this would be one of the last good looks I got on this trail of the economic and political crankcase of Arizona, and I wanted to make it last. The sheer size of the "make-believe city, with exotic palms and golf course lawns," as western water historian Marc Reisner once called it, was enough to inspire forgetfulness of the ocher desert that lay all around like a subdued prey in watch.

The decisions that guide modern Arizona have been hatched in Phoenix since the beginning of the twentieth century. How those verdicts come to us is often hidden.

THE PRIZE

Winning a state capitol was a juicy prize for any American city—it brought a battalion of state employees, the important presence of the governor, a militia barracks, lots of cash to the hotels, the prestige that comes from a status as the state's First City, as well as a handsome Capitoline seat of government designed to impress all visitors with the majesty of the state.

But Arizona's early attempts at a capitol had impressed nobody. The first one had been a rectangular log cabin in the mining town of Prescott, chosen in 1864 to stay close to the U.S. Cavalry at Fort Whipple. Tucson merchants then paid the right kind of bribes for the legislature to meet in the back of the Congress Hall Saloon, the only structure that could hold more than thirty people.

The prize then went to the Belvedere Hotel in Prescott for its thirteenth session—the infamous "Thieving Thirteenth" that handed out the jackpots of the university, the asylum, bridges, levees, the normal school, and the prison, while members drank heavily, inflated their traveling expenses, and got into multiple fistfights, one of which was settled with a bullwhip and a monkey wrench.

A fresh start for the capitol in the central farming village of Phoenix in 1889 promised a departure from these embarrassing frontier accommodations. A new neoclassical capitol building would be a way of telling the rest of the country Arizona was ready for membership in the club of the United States. "The old adobe is fast melting away before the march of civilization," boasted a letter writer to the *Yuma Sentinel*.

But then things got messy. The territorial legislature chopped the original budget down by more than two-thirds, meaning that architect James Riely Gordon had to scrap plans for two wings and a grand exterior staircase. Mining corporations refused to donate any copper for the dome. "These companies are denuding Arizona of her natural wealth and they ought to contribute this mite to the territory," fumed the *Arizona Gazette*, to no effect. Gordon had to settle for copper-painted steel sheets.

The ineptitude got worse. A mosaic of the state seal displaying the famous five C's of Arizona's economy mentioned copper, climate, and cotton but inexplicably forgot cattle and citrus. The cornerstone was eliminated because it would have cost a few hundred dollars more. Gordon's men had to find the cheapest carpet available for the interiors. He visited the state only once and returned to his home in Texas before the disappointing Ionic-Grecian vision was finished. His middle name was misspelled as "Reilly" on the dedication plaque the next year.

Though the fake copper dome was more rinky-dink than intended, it still was graced with a Winged Victory statue, cast in zinc, that cost $160. The garlanded maiden was mounted so she could turn with the wind, which newspaper wits took as a metaphor for the politics practiced beneath it. She became a favorite target for pistol-wielding drunks on the trolley line outside, which made a sharp turn right in front of the capitol entrance, pausing just long enough for passengers to get off a few shots. When she was taken down for repairs many years later, restorationists found more than twenty bullets inside her.

The territorial governor George Wiley Paul Hunt, a political chameleon with a walrus mustache, kept three telephones on his desk. He answered all of them himself; one number was listed in the local phone directory. Portraits of all the previous territorial governors went up in the hallways, and sharp-eyed visitors noticed they bore an odd resemblance to one another. In those days the governorship was a short-lived federal appointment and the men often didn't stay long enough in Arizona to sit for a painting, or even a photograph. Artist William Vincent Besser had guessed at their appearances, then covered their features with beards.

The capitol was no bigger than an average Texas county courthouse, and the tight accommodations wore thin. Those who visited for the first time often professed shock that state employees worked inside such a dingy building. "The present capitol is a shame and a disgrace to the state of Arizona," the *Republic* complained in 1955. "It is outmoded, outdated, impossible to properly heat or cool. It leaks in every pore. And it is ugly."

The legislature let it be known they would entertain proposals for an expansion. But they did not anticipate the lobbying blitz they received from eighty-nine-year-old Frank Lloyd Wright, who had chosen a piece of land at the far edge of Scottsdale to build Taliesin West, his winter home and studio.

Wright had already been railing against the postwar Arizona tradition of ignoring Native and Mexican architectural styles in favor of a bland look imported from Los Angeles using blank surfaces, shunning the desert landscape and the past. Wright designed a bold horizontal capitol that resembled a spider, shielded with a lacework and topped with two modernist spires to be built among the red rock boulders of Papago Park in Tempe.

Bypassing traditional lobbying methods, Wright distributed a brochure of his drawings to high school students around the state, in hopes of creating a youthful groundswell of idealism against what he called the "parrot and monkey politics" of the "pole and wire men" who ran the show in Arizona. "A new freedom—this—that would stand in modern times for Arizona as the Alhambra once stood in Spain before our continent was discovered."

Skeptics pointed out this fabulous Alhambra contained room for only thirty-seven offices. The *Republic* derided it as an "Arabian nights fantasy adorned with radio and television antennas." An insulted lawmaker went further and said it looked like "an oriental whorehouse." The state constitution had an inconvenient clause that the capitol needed to be in Phoenix. And the legislature—true to form—thought it too expensive. So that was the end of the Wright plan.

Legislators were more interested in erecting a plain twenty-story executive tower looming behind the original capitol, a modernist obelisk of governance similar to the interwar Art Deco capitols of Louisiana, North Dakota, and Nebraska (the last having earned the nickname "Penis of the Prairies"). Wright ridiculed the plan as "a hat on a pole." And it, too, was eventually deemed too grandiose a statement. So the legislature settled for new chambers for the House and Senate built as wings in front of the old capitol and forming a portico.

Unlike in assembly chambers in other American states, in which members come forward to a central well to deliver their speeches, each desk was equipped with a microphone with a retractable cord so Arizona's politicians could stand up and give their orations—a holdover from frontier tradition, though it gave them the vague appearance of Las Vegas lounge singers. Freight trains on the nearby Nineteenth Avenue tracks rattled the marble facades.

The governor and the swelling executive branch still needed new quarters, so in 1973 Governor Jack Williams authorized a scaled-down version of the skyscraper going up just nine stories, with L-shaped exterior lines propping up the governor's ninth-floor office like an entrée on a platter. Others compared it to a castle parapet from which boiling oil might be poured onto the rabble below. Riely's dinky capitol out front was converted into a museum, and its painted steel roof was finally replaced with a dome of real copper. The catch, however, was that the copper did not come from the rich copper-producing state of Arizona but from a mill in Pennsylvania, and it had to be chemically coated to keep it from turning dull brown in the sun.

The total impression of this jumbled campus was of a medical-dental plaza behind a dumpy-looking courthouse and two rectangles of dehydrating grass. "We ought to be ashamed of ourselves the way we pieced these things together," said former House speaker Jake Flake. When the state faced bankruptcy after the real estate meltdown of 2008, few objected when the legislature voted to sell off its own capitol complex and other assets to a private consortium, then lease them back. It was either that or raise income taxes, which has been as popular here as cancer, and it could be argued that Arizona never felt much ownership in its signature building anyway.

In the midst of all this, the most permanent class of the legislature—the lobbyists—labored on. They carried the true institutional knowledge of the capitol and stood immune to the winds of elections that partly cleaned house every two years. The state has records of approximately 1,100 individuals who attempt to influence the fortunes of bills each year on behalf of their clients, though only about a hundred are consistently present at the capitol. And only thirty or so are said to really matter. One of them is Jonathan Paton.

Paton is from Tucson, light haired and solidly built, a middle-class kid who went to a high school where the parking lot was full of BMWs. Teenage jobs as a busboy and serving up bratwursts had given him an education in dealing with irate customers. A stint as an intern at the Arizona senate gave him a taste for more polite forms of argument, and he started lobbying early for the powerful Southern Arizona Homebuilders Association, which was the local equivalent of what it must have been like to get in with the railroads in the nineteenth century. Builders had juice.

Paton learned who was who in a hurry and started his own lobbying firm. Then he ran successfully for the Arizona House and served two terms before switching to the state senate in what seemed to be an unstoppable trajectory of ambition. He took the inevitable next step of running for U.S. Congress in 2010.

Paton had served in Operation Iraqi Freedom and had an easygoing temperament that allowed him to have unforced conversations with Democrats. He made noteworthy gestures like driving a Toyota Prius, writing a novel in his spare time, being chummy with liberal journalists, and frequenting Tucson's bohemian Epic Café in the Birkenstock-thick Fourth Avenue neighborhood. But he lost to an extremist in the Republican primary and then lost a second bid in the general election two years later.

Losing twice tends to dry up donor money. Paton tried to be at peace with never making it to Washington. He'd nearly destroyed his car after putting a hundred thousand miles on it and felt like he'd been beat with a shovel, in addition to the psychological dreariness of constantly asking people for money, treating old friends like ATMs. The logical choice was to go back to lobbying, his career as a politician sidetracked, perhaps permanently. He married an attorney and bought a house.

Then the firm of Paton & Associates was offered a deal that didn't look great on the surface: helping to save Rio Nuevo, a project to help rejuvenate downtown Tucson that had turned into a catastrophe. Bad enough that the FBI had gotten involved in Arizona politics yet again, and bad enough that Rio Nuevo had become a dark joke—a synonym for Arizona corruption.

This assignment would put Jonathan Paton in the position of having to explain the worst policy failure in the recent history of his own hometown, then trying to aim the hose of taxpayer money back into the smoking hole.

—

The fiasco of Rio Nuevo began when southern Arizona voters approved a proposition in 1999 to put a Band-Aid on Tucson's worst historical design error—namely, abandoning its downtown after World War II in favor of shopping malls and office parks.

The plan involved stitching together the two sides of the dried-out Santa Cruz River, roughly paralleled by the concrete slash of Interstate 10, that had separated the traditionally Hispanic suburb of Barrio Hollywood from the city core that had been built in 1776 around a garrison to defend the interests of the king of Spain. Whoever wanted to build there could be helped out with a $73 million property tax diversion.

The promised basket of goodies had something for every Tucsonan to love: a new convention hotel, better streetscapes, a children's museum, a restoration of the theater where John Wayne used to have a dedicated seat, a university science center, an aquarium, a trade center, improvements to the art museum, a cultural center at the base of A Mountain. It seemed like a great deal on paper.

Years went by and nothing got built. The board of directors spent $230 million of taxpayer money on consultants' reports, master plans, and blueprints without a single brick being laid. The FBI started interviewing witnesses amid charges of bribes and kickbacks and seized nearly three hundred thousand pages of documents that had to be kept in a double-locked room in the convention center for fear that somebody would alter or destroy them.

After three years of interrogating people whose memories were suspiciously faulty, the Arizona attorney general's office put out an unusual decline-to-prosecute memo stating that while they had found plenty of evidence of incompetence and mismanagement, they didn't find any criminal offenses that would likely end in a successful prosecution.

Rio Nuevo's reputation was beyond salvation; it seemed like the bastards had gotten away with it. There was nothing to do now but fold the tent. Except that the structure created by the voters was hard to dissolve. Rio Nuevo was a TIF—technocratic slang for "tax-increment financing district," a device popular in the 1950s for wrecking historic buildings in the name of slum clearance.

The legislature put Rio Nuevo under a custodial board, as if it were a flailing school district or broken water works in preparation to suffocate it. But it refused to die.

The president of the state senate, Steve Pearce, appointed Fletcher McCusker, a graduate of the University of Arizona who had made a fortune providing mental health care services to low-income clients, to get some tangible property erected that people could see and touch. McCusker started by moving the Greyhound bus station—never a gem of any city—out of the way to make room for a Marriott hotel.

They then bought up and demolished businesses on Broadway Road, including a beloved Mexican restaurant named Lerua's, and prepared to widen the street by two lanes, calling it Cactus Corridor. Then came a new division headquarters for Caterpillar not far from the base of A Mountain and the gouge in its side called the Bishop's Hole for the lava rocks quarried out of it to build Saint Augustine's Cathedral. Eight years after the FBI started asking questions, Rio Nuevo was beginning to look like a turnaround story.

The closest thing to eternal life, said Ronald Reagan, is a government program. Enemies of Rio Nuevo turned to the Arizona legislature in hopes of killing it for good. The legal authorization for the district was set to expire and it needed a reauthorization. All they had to do was smother that bill in committee and the game would be over. The nasty reputation of Rio Nuevo, combined with the general allergy to taxes in the legislature, should have been enough.

But Jonathan Paton thought he could play this hand of cards. At heart, lobbying is the art of storytelling, and Rio Nuevo could be framed as a resurrection story with the legislature in the role of hero. He also held a genteel threat over people's heads. Rio Nuevo was still $68 million in debt, a cost the state would have to eat if they let the district expire.

Now somebody had to run this bill, and it had to be a Republican. Democrats had been only a supporting cast in the legislature for twenty years, and Rio Nuevo was perceived to be a classic liberal screwup.

A ridiculous guy like Mark Finchem seemed like the last guy you'd want—a far-right-wing software technician with a cowboy mustache, a Michigan accent, a collection of Western silk string ties and the representation of an overwhelmingly white and conservative district north of Tucson that included the master-planned retirement fortress of Saddlebrooke. He occasionally made the news through his embrace of fringe conspiracy theories. After the white supremacist Charlottesville protest of 2017, he wrote on his campaign website that the chaos and violence had been fomented by Democrats and "deep-state" actors. He introduced bills to punish public schoolteachers who raise "any controversial issue" in classrooms. And he would eventually be among the faces in the angry crowd outside the U.S. Capitol on January 6, 2021.

But here was an "only Nixon could go to China" move—people could call Finchem lots of nasty names, but nobody was ever going to call him a dupe of big-government spending. While his credibility on most other matters might be dubious, his name on the bill would be a signal to the Phoenix budget hawks there were cracks in the local conservative opposition to Rio Nuevo. Paton thought he'd be the weirdly perfect mule for the sponsorship of what became House Bill 2456 (stadium district; extension; Rio Nuevo), prolonging the life of the district for an astounding seventeen years.

Finchem was taken on a VIP tour of downtown—one of the only times he ever visited the center of his own metropolis. He did not disappoint; the fiscal hatchetman spoke of tax districts in glowing terms during the bill's hearing at the House Ways and Means Committee. "Five years ago you couldn't pay me to go to downtown Tucson," he said, contrasting it with the brand-name hotels and construction cranes that he saw in what he had assumed was a hellscape.

The hearing had been chaired by Michelle Ugenti-Rita, a real estate agent from the tony suburb of Scottsdale who would soon play a pivotal role in another of the embarrassments that periodically ripple through the capitol. A gravel-voiced Tea Party Republican from Yuma named Don Shooter had once shown up at her hotel room door at a conference bearing a six-pack of beer and an implicit invitation of romance. He was said to have previously asked if her breasts were real or fake and told her he was in love with her.

Shooter had been a swaggering time bomb for some time. He tried to pay himself twenty thousand dollars in campaign funds for "gas and mileage costs" for driving himself around Arizona five years before and returned half the money when challenged. But the accusation of sexual harassment was more serious; an investigation uncovered multiple alleged come-ons, including one in which he fondled his own crotch.

Forces gathered not merely to censure him but expel him—the nuclear option in the constitution, used only three other times since statehood. Shooter greeted several colleagues that morning with the menacing salutation "It's a great day for a hanging," and some worried he would react with violence. The House Speaker personally confiscated a handgun from his office shortly before a successful vote to expel him for "dishonorable" conduct. "I've been thrown out of better places," he huffed to the *Republic* after security officers escorted him outside—the ultimate professional humiliation.

Ugenti-Rita was hailed as a #MeToo hero for coming forward. But then she was accused of sexual harassment herself in 2020, when a twenty-six-year-old woman lobbyist testified in a deposition that Ugenti-Rita and her boyfriend, an assistant to the governor, had tried to invite her into a threesome. This was preceded by an episode in which Ugenti-Rita reportedly lay on top of a bar and cajoled the lobbyist to slurp tequila out of her belly button, lick salt off her stomach, and bite a lime away from her puckered lips.

The Rio Nuevo hearing came off before this peccadillo broke loose, however, and the debate went forward in orderly fashion. McCusker testified from the witness podium about how state oversight had created "a model district." Then came Jim Click, a Ford dealer with an Oklahoma drawl who had moved to Tucson in 1971 and managed to have a line into almost every major charitable endeavor in the city. He was also a respected Republican kingmaker.

"I helped pass Rio Nuevo, and I'm sorry I did that," he said into the mic. "I gotta tell you it was a disaster." Perhaps realizing this was not an effective sales pitch, he pivoted into praise of the reborn project and admitted that Tucson was still not as economically juiced as Phoenix, "but we're pretty damn close." Paton watched silently as the committee passed the extension bill with almost no debate; Ugenti-Rita voted no in the minority but did not explain why.

The Senate proved a rougher ride. Some of the anti-tax hardliners in Tucson—Paton called them "the flying monkeys"—chartered a bus to take witnesses up for the hearing and made ample use of public comment time to trash Rio Nuevo. Burglar alarm salesman Roger D. Score called it "an open wound in Pima County that oozes dollars" and "the biggest fleece of the taxpayer that's ever gone on in this state." Former congressional candidate

Gabby Mercer complained that "a hole in the ground" was all there was to brag about. "All I see is bunch of cronyism going on here at its best."

The committee seemed unmoved by any of it, and Paton already knew that he had Bob Worsley in his corner, a powerful Mormon from Mesa with a boyish face and a pile of money he'd made from founding *SkyMall*, the glossy catalog full of junkola inside airline seatbacks. Worsley offered his own scorn for the endless production of blueprints and the big consultant payouts. But he also echoed the redemption story that Paton had been telling. "We have saved the original mission somewhat from the disaster that preceded it," he said before voting yes with the majority.

Roger D. Score followed Jim Click around with a cellphone camera trying to catch him in Lord knows what, but it all seemed like so much irrelevant circus. Passage by both houses, now virtually assured, would send the bill to the governor's desk for the anticipated signature. Rio was one step closer to gaining seventeen more years of life.

Then came a sidewinder missile. Paton had been driving back to Tucson on Interstate 10 when his cell phone rang—the caller ID showed a contact of his he'd known for years who worked in the governor's office. Paton pulled over. Just outside his passenger window was the brown volcanic core of Picacho Peak, the site of the westernmost battle of the Civil War, fought here in 1863.

The news wasn't good. In fact, it was awful. "We have a problem with one sentence," said the inside source. The governor was afraid the bill as written could be interpreted to mean Rio Nuevo could take on even more debt than the $68 million it was carrying. Paton felt like vomiting. There was no legal way to pull back the bill to add clarifying language.

The governor was clearly worried about looking bad—one of the true motivating factors in politics—should Rio Nuevo really turn out to be a drunkard on a spree, as its critics had been saying. And if the governor couldn't be placated, all the effort and strategizing had been for nothing.

"Just do it next year," his contact suggested.

"Are you fucking kidding me?" Paton shot back. "If we have to bring it back, it's going to be bad." The anti-tax forces would know they had found a way to get under the governor's skin. Should the Arizona economy take a downturn, as some economists were predicting, nobody at the capitol except some hardcore Democrats would be in the mood to keep raising taxes.

Paton hung up and stared at the freeway. He'd have to report the dismal news to McCusker, but he wanted to do it with some options on the table. The best one was a bit of a trick play, a sneak across the endzone, but it would require almost total secrecy. The tactic was called a "trailer bill." What he had to do was find an innocuous piece of unrelated legislation, bury a non-sequitur sentence about Rio Nuevo debt deep within the legalese, and get it through third readings in both House and Senate and to the governor's desk all without Bob Thorpe or the flying monkeys finding out. And it all had to be done within five days. The 2018 session was almost over.

Paton found his secret cargo ship in the form of an inoffensive bill requiring online lodging websites like Airbnb to register with the Department of Revenue for a license. He persuaded a backbencher Republican named Todd Clodfelter to quietly add a floor amendment prohibiting Rio Nuevo "from incurring any new debt through bonds or contractual obligations."

To anyone who didn't know what was really going on at the governor's office, it looked like fiscal prudence and even a hostile move toward Rio Nuevo. But what it was really doing was ensuring the survival of the machine that created the biggest tax waste Tucson had seen in decades.

The unknown factor was whether this Airbnb bill would actually get approval. If it stalled out for any reason—if somebody got indigestion over creating more paperwork at the Revenue Department—Rio Nuevo would be dead. Paton tried to survey the vote landscape as discreetly as he could and found no hint of opposition.

His friend at the governor's office called him again. The governor had been briefed on the plan and was prepared to sign the Rio Nuevo bill ahead of the trailer bill, which would effectively leave his ass hanging out in the wind.

"Are you sure this is going to pass?" he asked.

"Yes," said Paton.

"Would you stake your reputation on this?"

Paton paused. His future credibility with the governor's office now depended on some dipshit Airbnb bill. "Yes," he said.

The governor signed the Rio Nuevo bill on April 6 amid newspaper stories and a few jubilant press releases in Tucson. Four days later, the Airbnb bill arrived on his desk and he signed it without any notice whatsoever. Only a handful of people knew what really happened.

Paton had long been fond of homebrewing German beer, and that night he had several pilsners from his own keg.

———

The architects of the House and Senate had left an open space between the chambers, a small park of crunchy Bermuda grass known as "the portico." Bleachers are set up around it whenever a governor is inaugurated. When the legislature is in session, and it becomes a de facto meeting place for lawmakers and the smiling, besuited, skirted, and high-heeled circle of lobbyists who come here pushing various causes, from the simple to the hopelessly arcane.

They don't wear their clients' names on their chests, yet they embody the interlocking structure of cities, small businesses, nonprofits, banks, law firms, utilities, Fortune 500 companies, public agencies, and interest groups that give Arizona its vitality and keep it growing.

Disguised in expensive clothes on the portico on any given day are Boeing, Lyft, Blue Cross, Motorola, Cardinal Health, the Professional Golf Association, Freeport-McMoRan, Prudential, Pfizer, and the Prescott Chamber of Commerce. Johnson & Johnson are here, along with Intel, the Petroleum Marketers Association, the Navajo Nation, and 1,200 other interests, many of them represented by some of the same superlobbyists alternatively pushing and trying to stomp on multiple bills and amendments. The worth of their contracts is dependent on the influential friends they can charm.

Of all the interests elbowing for power at the capitol, almost none rivals the muscle of Pinnacle West, the holding company for the utility behemoth Arizona Public Service (APS), which keeps the lights on for most of the state's counties. During the 2014 elections, they reportedly spent $10.7 million in donations to dark money groups in hopes of influencing elections. The FBI called the ensuing investigation Operation High Grid.

In its own way, the APS corruption scandal was perfectly in line with the spirit of the famous Thieving Thirteenth legislature of 1885, one of whose most powerful members was a lawyer for the Southern Pacific Railroad. A century later, Evan Mecham complained about a semi-mythical body called the Phoenix 40, a group of country-clubbers that was supposed to have called the shots from behind the scenes, much like the Rio Nuevo crowd in Tucson. Whether they even existed as a coherent group was a matter of debate, yet the aura of a group of mercantile forces gaming the legislature had durable storytelling power.

Jonathan Paton made an unlikely embodiment. He was not the flashiest, richest, or loudest of those in lobbyist corps; his U.S. Army background lent him a spit-shine demeanor that made his conversations more like tactical briefings than sales pitches. He kept four rules for himself: show up to the capitol, understand the process, never lie, and always be nice to everyone, especially the interns. He had been one of them once, and just ten years after that, he was an elected member of the House who remembered who had treated him badly. And habitual liars soon acquired a reputation that sullied their currency.

"There are sixty legislators here," Paton liked to say. "That's basically your high school class. If you make promises you can't keep, you're screwed."

When he was in the House, he learned an important lesson. One of his bills had gotten stuck in a committee chaired by Carolyn Allen, a Republican from Scottsdale who had been raised in Hannibal, Missouri, and took from there a mid-South accent and an unwillingness to suffer fools. "If you screw with me, I will bite back," she liked to say.

Paton had kept a respectful distance from Allen but grew so irritated with her unwillingness to calendar his own bill that he cast a committee vote against a breast cancer screening bill that she had championed. A few minutes later, she came charging up to him and another Republican on the brown portico grass.

"Y'all are trying to give me payback!" she said, and proceeded to ream out Paton's companion, who struggled to deny there had been any ulterior motives. Then she leveled a long, bony finger at Paton.

"And as for *yew*," she demanded. "I suppose you think this isn't some kind of *payback*?"

Paton decided to take a calculated risk. "You're damn right it's *payback*," he told her. "And I'd do it again."

Allen spun around on her heel and stalked away. Within the week, Paton's bill was on the committee calendar. He had seen her correctly—as a realist who appreciated honesty and didn't hold grudges.

Honeyed charm went a long way too. One of the most affable people at the capitol liked to introduce himself as "Jim Norton, lobbyist extraordinaire." Among his many clients was a water utility seeking business in the San Tan Valley, an explosion of forty thousand recently built ranch homes on the extreme southeast edge of metropolitan Phoenix, and Norton wanted to curry the favor of a corporation commissioner named Gary Pierce.

According to court testimony, Norton persuaded his wife to hire Pierce's wife for a fictitious job at a consulting firm that paid $3,500 a month. The scheme came out when Jim Norton's wife started cooperating with prosecutors and divorced her husband for purportedly having multiple affairs—a common pitfall at any state capitol, a fragrant hive of charismatic and energetic people whose moral sensibilities may become all too flexible in the heat of the job.

The no-show job or vaguely worded "consulting contract" was also a common trap at the Arizona capitol, and it was notoriously hard to prove that anything was legally wrong with it. No legislator was ever going to say their public affairs consulting for an ambulance contractor was in exchange for votes. And yet the practice was rampant. "What pisses me off most is the pettiness of the corruption," said one longtime observer. "They feel they're owed something because they're only paid $24,000 a year."

Yet another irony of the design of the Arizona capitol is that it happens to be surrounded on three sides by some of the worst poverty the state has on display. Down Washington Avenue eastbound are soup kitchens with grimy tents pitched outside; the houses in the blocks north and west are shabby bungalows dating from the 1910s and long since gone to seed; train tracks and warehouses complete the scene. In the middle of it all is the dome of Pennsylvania copper and the hum of legislation that seems deaf to the squalor outside. "The problems there are almost never discussed in the capitol," said former lawmaker Tom Prezelski. "That's because the lobbyists want to make their issues the center of conversation."

For Paton, the 2020 session presented a different challenge: how to make Rio Nuevo not a part of *any* conversation, how to keep it in the shadows. The seventeen-year extension had been passed. The Republican expectation of low-impact government meant that state oversight was only a factor when the time came for a renewal vote; until then, it was assumed that nobody cared. But Paton had heard that Representative Bob Thorpe—a Flagstaff Republican who had once worked as a Walt Disney Imagineer—was taking some cues from the flying monkeys to make another attempt to kill Rio Nuevo.

"I can guarantee you it won't end in thirty years," Thorpe had complained. "This extension will add another quarter billion to the amount of tax dollars that go to this project." And sure enough, a few weeks before the opening of the legislature, four bills were dropped into the Senate hopper and given the numbers S1006, S1007, S1008, and S1009. Taken together, they proposed to eliminate the district's ability to take on long-term debt, bring in a joint committee to oversee spending decisions, and, for good measure, prevent Rio Nuevo from hiring a lobbyist.

That last bill was a personal insult aimed directly at Paton and his $65,000 annual contract. "I guess I did a good job," he thought sardonically. Now it was his mission to suffocate these quadruplets in their crib. There were many ways to do it, but one of the best was to make sure they were turned over to committees with hostile or indifferent chairpersons who wouldn't put them on the docket.

The Fifty-Fourth Arizona Legislature was gaveled to order on January 13, 2020, with a speech from Governor Doug Ducey called "Welcome to the Crackling Energy of Booming Arizona." The governor had always been a hard man to pin down; never much of an orator or a gladhandler, he preferred to do his business outside the watch of the public. Part of his appeal was the Arizona cult of the businessman: he was known as a master marketer when he ran a storefront confectionary franchise called Cold Stone Creamery, an ice cream parlor with a performative twist—the customer's selection would be mixed with sprinkles on an electrically cooled slab of granite.

Ducey sold the business in 2007 for a massive profit, but the buyers later accused him of fluffing up the value by opening franchises at a breakneck pace without due diligence and handing the keys to unqualified partners. Failures started piling up. "Serving ice cream isn't exactly like serving in state government, but what I learned guides me today," he said in a campaign video.

Ducey's speech was no more memorable than his other pronouncements. He called himself "a kid from Toledo" and emphasized that 70 percent of the adults in Arizona weren't born here. He praised veterans, denounced taxes, excoriated cities that wouldn't turn in undocumented immigrants to federal officers, and promoted his pet issue of charter school vouchers. Then he announced the state had gotten free of the embarrassing lease arrangement of 2008 that had sold off the Arizona capitol.

"We prioritize fiscal responsibility," he said. "We've learned from the mistakes of the past. This building? We now own the deed."

Watching from one of the lobbies off the House floor, an official from Prescott shook his head. "Yeah, I don't know if you want to be bragging about that one," he murmured.

—

The guy running the bills in the Senate was a genial sixty-eight-year-old from Mesa named David Farnsworth, known for his conviction that the state Department of Child Safety was shielding a child sex-trafficking ring within its bureaucracy—an idea with roots in the QAnon theory that a liberal deep state is running a pedophile network.

"You might know these bills better than I do," he told a visitor, gesturing to a tall stack of unread legislation on his desk. Around his office were totems that broadcast a specific East Valley political habitat: a Book of Mormon on the window shelf, a tin sculpture of a windmill on a side table, a photo of himself in the White House Gold Room standing next to the forty-fifth president alongside certificates from the National Rifle Association. Outside the window of his office, a marching band from Eastern Arizona College in Thatcher rehearsed anthems in preparation for the legislature's opening.

He acknowledged he had sponsored the bills in the belief Rio Nuevo always had the flavor of something sinister along the lines of what might be happening with missing children in the DFS system. "See, these all are connected," he said. "It seems like there's invisible hands promoting it—what the right word?—propelling it, and you don't know who's behind it. Washington, D.C., has a swamp and Arizona has a swamp and both need draining. We don't know who the swamp creatures are because they're all wearing suits and ties." He might as well have been back in the 1980s railing about the Phoenix 40, or in the 1880s talking about the Southern Pacific Railroad.

If Senate President Karen Fann assigned the bills to Farnsworth's Government Committee, he could turn the hearing into a kangaroo court to intone the word "corruption" over and over. And Fann could make it happen because the actual content of a bill often has no clear relationship to its committee assignment.

The answer came on January 13. The bill would be going to the Finance Committee. Paton cheered up almost immediately. Finance was the domain of J. D. Mesnard, a former legislative intern (always be nice to the interns) who helped found Voices of the World, an evangelical food relief charity. He had a youngish face, a straightforward demeanor, and a careful guard on his tongue.

Paton called him on January 16 and made his five classic arguments. What was rotten about Rio Nuevo had become good; the bills would essentially shut it down; the state would have to eat $68 million in historic debt; the anti-tax platoons in Tucson had not shown up to renew their attack; and the governor had already demonstrated a willingness to let it continue. Mesnard didn't give away a position. But then again, a smart legislator never wanted to close unnecessary doors.

Twelve days later, Paton was watching an Education Committee hearing on the capitol's closed circuit TV network. It was a farce. One of the body's reliable culture war extremists, Senator Sylvia Allen, had introduced a bill to require abstinence-only sex ed courses in public schools. Outraged pressure groups packed the room. The chairman of the Vail School District had been lobbying against the matter for six months and rallied a group of protestors to intimidate the senators into thinking they'd commit the one mistake everyone dreads: looking bad in public.

Paton once again marveled at the power ordinary citizens had in Arizona. If the flying monkeys really wanted to kick Rio Nuevo in the teeth, he thought, they'd do something like this. It's what he would have encouraged himself if he had been on a contract for the other side. They had lots of juicy dirt: missing money, an FBI raid, big taxes. Killing Rio Nuevo ought to have been easy. But thanks to the random collisions of politics, it would live on for more than a decade.

He went into the men's room to take a leak and passed none other than J. D. Mesnard at the sinks without recognizing him at first; the thirty-nine-year-old Finance Committee chairman had shaved his winter beard and looked even younger. Not one to let a chance meeting go to waste, Paton off-handedly asked him if anything had changed on Rio Nuevo, and mentioned with a touch of calculated disapproval that he hadn't yet been able to talk to David Farnsworth about why this initiative was happening in the first place.

"Yeah, I'd like to meet with him, too," said Mesnard, wiping his hands on a paper towel.

As non-answers went, it was a pretty encouraging one. Farnsworth hadn't even bothered to lobby the chairman. He was either too wrapped up in nonexistent sex-trafficking conspiracies or working another bill of his to cap the interest rates on title pawn loans. Paton was able to do more in a quick phone conversation and a chance encounter in the men's room than the flying monkeys had been able to do in two years.

Lobbying involves fewer dark arts than many suppose. Delivering a message to Mesnard hadn't been like arranging an audience with the pope. And that turned out to be the last word for Rio Nuevo in the Fifty-Fourth Legislature. Mesnard let the bills die without fanfare before the adjournment.

Political victories often come in the form of secret fizzles. What doesn't happen can just as consequential as what does. All it takes to stop an idea from becoming law is one act of sabotage on the conveyor belt up to the governor's office. Paton liked to conjure an image for his clients: a turtle lays dozens of eggs on a beach while groups of people try to stomp the eggs into goo. The one egg that survives is the law that gets passed. For all its faults and follies, the Arizona legislature is designed as a filtration system for bad ideas.

Farnsworth didn't overtly mourn the death of his bills, but neither did he indicate that the knives were sheathed. If Rio Nuevo kept collecting taxes, it would be for the same reason: a perception that the public didn't care. Most Arizona citizens didn't know they could come down to the capitol and help swing an issue by their very presence. Lawmakers were too vulnerable to elections and term limits to be a stabilizing force. The real power center of the Arizona legislature was the lobbyist corps.

Power is sweet to those who wield it. But to be an Arizona lobbyist is to do it without prestige or recognition. Nobody will play a band for you. But the capitol cannot function without this invisible society.

Farnsworth got his first glimpse of their hidden clout when he was elected on a write-in ballot a quarter century ago. Then he sold cars for twenty years before retaking a Senate seat. He was shocked to recognize the same familiar faces on the portico, slightly more aged, certainly, but still yapping about the same issues, out to promote or kill every springtime.

"I used to think they were the devil reincarnated," he said. "But I don't anymore. The lobbyists provide continuity and stability. The citizens don't understand their power."

THE PATH DOWN THE SOUTHERN edge of the Superstitions switchbacks toward a place called Mud Spring, through chaparral thick with burrs. I was tempted to save time by bushwhacking down the incline, but that risked ankle damage, and I had been told that rattlesnakes aren't uncommon here late in the season. Backpacking contains one essential rule: do not lose the trail. This is good advice in many dimensions.

"In philosophy, where truth seems double-faced, there is no man more paradoxical than myself," wrote medieval doctor Sir Thomas Browne, "but in divinity I love to keep the road; and though not in an implicit, yet a humble faith, follow the great wheel of the Church, by which I move, not reserving any proper poles or motion from the epicycle of my own brain: by these means I leave no gap for heresy, schisms, or errors."

Free-thinking is not always the best course because orthodoxy isn't always wrong. And it serves its purpose on this maddeningly twisty path down the Superstitions, set here by nameless ancestors and geology. Would it be a great idea, in the name of independence, to choose my own path here in the darkness, though burrs? No thanks. Eventually I came to the valley floor, a dried stream, and a huge slab of flat granite, elongated and white in the moon. I pitched my tent upon the rock. No snakes in sight. And not the worst feeling on my aching back.

The canyon was silent, and the moon was a hazy coin beyond the vinyl walls. There were a few novels loaded on my Kindle, and I resumed my slow rereading of *Moby-Dick*, Ishmael explaining the migrations of leviathans in the Indian Ocean. I could manage only a few paragraphs before blinking myself to sleep.

Gray half light filtered in and the canyon was still quiet as I folded up the tent, now down to a four-minute operation as methodical as packing a parachute. No need to change clothes: I'd been wearing the same synthetic top and beige pants since the Grand Canyon and there was nobody out there to pass judgment. My shoes—non-waterproof Moab 2s—were holding up nicely. Blisters were an annoyance of the past. Silent morning chill pervaded the canyon and I could see my breath in front of me. After about an hour, orange light started to crawl on the west walls. The streambed widened and twisted through patches of scrubby mesquite.

I paused at a massive reef of reddish granite, tipped up like a sailing ship sinking to unknown fathoms, frozen in time. The geologic layers—each representing thousands of years—were in clear relief on the side, crowned here and there with little green wigs of hackberry. I wondered who herded cattle in here a hundred years ago and whether that cowboy had a private name for this landmark, which does not show up on the map. And before him: the Salado people. Perhaps this was a favorite resting spot for someone who gave it a name and perceived the energy of the universe to be embodied within it in a particular wordless way.

I'm not sure what arrested me about this reef, as the lower Superstitions are full of rock formations just such as this. They're a dime a dozen, topographically speaking. And yet I paused and wondered before moving on, southward, toward the highway that was still a five-hour march away.

My aunt Diane picked me up around noon in her dented Lincoln Town Car at the base of Picket Post Mountain, a gigantic multicolored colossus at the southern edge of U.S. Highway 60, which leads to the eastern suburbs of metropolitan Phoenix. In a car for the first time in weeks, I marveled at the speed at which the landscape flickered by and how much gets missed by an average motorist. The dirt seemed less like a painting and more of a movie. Passing through here on this same highway more than sixty years ago, photographer Esther Henderson made the following observation:

Wherever you go in the state of Arizona there is always a scene, a story, an incident. Though little may remain of the physical structures at each location, the atmosphere of legend encompasses them all. Mountain snows have buried, then disintegrated cabin scenes of pioneer excitement; desert winds and rains have covered and melted the adobe structures of pioneer activity; massacres, feuds, battles, captures, surrenders—the most stirring events are today located often by only a pile of rocks, a mountain spur, a desert spring. To know them all would take a lifetime; to know a few will at least make a portion of that lifetime more interesting.

I craved chain-store comforts: a grocery, a coin-op laundromat, and a Mexican restaurant. We accomplished the last at a generic dive in Apache Junction called Los Gringos Locos. A plate of red chili enchiladas and a salt-rocks margarita in a goblet the size of a desk globe hit my calorie-deprived stomach like a cannonball of toxins.

I excused myself and staggered toward the bathroom but didn't make it as far as outside the front door, where I vomited the whole lunch into a decorative planter. A few people in the parking lot stared at this spectacle, and I sheepishly went back inside: not the best advertisement for this restaurant. Diane had remarked earlier on how emaciated I looked after three weeks on the trail. Perhaps I should have listened.

But I felt a little better after changing into freshly washed clothes and brushing my teeth in the bathroom of Superstition Express Laundry. Aunt Diane really is a good soul for helping me with power errands with the intensity of a silver miner's binge during a monthly provisioning trip.

Apache Junction used to be known as one of the least diverse towns in Arizona, which is perhaps why a restaurant with a name that means "crazy white people" had a certain local appeal. But its Latino population had been growing steadily over the last twenty years, mirroring an increase statewide.

This profound demographic shift had a permanent effect on its politics, especially since a mean streak in state government helped bring out a spirit of activism even greater than the Chicano awakening of the 1960s, creating a challenge to the power structure like no other force in Arizona the last seventy years.

EL REY

Raquel Teran experienced a jolt of life-changing electricity a few seconds after she put her hands on an object on March 24, 2006.

She had never much cared about politics—she had studied to be a schoolteacher—until some friends persuaded her to join a march in Phoenix against an anti-immigration bill on a long, hot day. Teran was ready to go home after a few hours, but she paused at a folding table that had been set up by the nonprofit group Mi Familia Vota ("my family votes").

A strange feeling came over her as she inspected the clipboard stacked with blank forms. Within moments, without fully understanding what she was doing, Teran raised the clipboard over her head like a torch and yelled to the crowd: "Who wants to register to vote?"

That was the beginning of a journey that soon found Teran working long hours trying to stop Arizona's quest to punish Mexican American immigrants. She made door-knocking a regular hobby, then a full-time job, then a full-blown crusade. And within a few years, Teran made an audacious bid to run for the state legislature.

Her new visibility brought trouble. A conservative activist named Alice Novoa brought a lawsuit alleging Teran was an illegal immigrant. "This is not her country, and it's never going to be her country," said Novoa. "She should've kept herself quiet *y no andar corriendo en dónde no le importa*" (and not run around where she doesn't matter).

That statement was both dishonest and insulting. But far-right conspiracy theorists had sensed a threat in Raquel Teran's upward trajectory, and they latched onto a footnote in her biography that would have been no big deal in nearly any other political environment: she had grown up in the twin cities of Douglas, Arizona, and Agua Prieta, Sonora.

Her mother gave birth to her in 1977 in the Copper Queen Community Hospital on the U.S. side, making her an American citizen, but she went to school on the Mexican side, where her father owned a lumberyard. Her identity, as she put it, was *ni esto ni que*, "neither this nor that," an entirely normal state of being for the town divided by an international fence.

Arizona border towns are collisions of ethnicities, languages, currencies, and national attitudes. Flags fly on towering staffs, cops proliferate, boxes get ticked, transactions are sealed with inky stamps. Asymmetrical laws create plentiful opportunities for smuggling and vice; differing economies conjure desire as surely as the wind blows toward lower air pressure. Languages pidgin themselves into a third tongue. Families have members on both sides. Crossing is a yawn.

To a child's eyes, the fortified border didn't seem unusual; it was just the way the world worked. Teran crossed over it every day, learning the names of the immigration officials and greeting them by name. She would often see green vans with metal mesh on the windows taking sullen passengers into Mexico. Somebody explained to her these were deportees who had been caught trying to cross illegally and it made her feel weird.

She could sense the difference between the two sides: the angular lines of Douglas versus the freewheeling spirit of Agua Prieta, where the Terans had been an old-line mercantile family since the nineteenth century. They imported Arizona pine wood for home construction at their lumberyard. Her father, Jesus, was a well-liked leader of the youth group at Guadalupe Catholic Church, where he talked to teenagers in a blunt style laced with humor. He was able to have a good laugh at himself, too. His brothers never let him forget the time he managed to get his head stuck in a gap in a chain-link fence.

Jesus Teran stayed away from politics, knowing the bite of local corruption could be hazardous to one's health. One of his relatives, Bernardino Meza Ortiz, had been chased away from a burning city hall in 1985 in a riot started by a mob from a rival party who claimed he had stolen the office through ballot box stuffing. Another member of the extended family, Vicente Teran, was an establishment politician widely suspected to be in league with drug cartels.

Douglas was three-quarters Latino, but the spirit felt different there than in Mexico, where Raquel understood you had a specific place in the universe prepared for you, defined by faith and family. But the Mexican economy was sclerotic, the jobs were low-paying, and the schools were bad. The American side was where you found opportunities. That meant spending time in Douglas, a town every bit as contrived as Fountain Hills had been, though the money came not from lifestyle haciendas but from an older form of industrial capitalism.

The shareholders of the Phelps Dodge Corporation had purchased this flat chunk of the Sulphur Springs Valley in 1900, erected a hasty town named for its president, and built a smelter to process copper. Puffballs of smoke blotted out the sun on the days when the wind wasn't blowing into Mexico. The stench burned noses and throats. White-collared shirts could turn dingy within minutes. When ranchers on the U.S. side found sulfur dioxide dusting their gardens, they complained to the general manager, who laughed and told them he'd heard it was a form of fertilizer, so they should instead pay Phelps Dodge for the courtesy of the gunk.

When Raquel was in elementary school, the Douglas Reduction Works had deteriorated to the point where experts were calling it the filthiest smelter on the continent. Phelps Dodge knew it was malfunctioning but insisted the pollutants weren't harmful. They put out the story that the stack's local nickname was "Old Reliable," but people actually called it "Old Smokey," as it flung out green-gray smoke around the clock, towering like a sundial over the working-class bungalows below. Her uncle would make the same joke whenever they drove by. "Santa Claus doesn't work there," he said. Meaning that it was not a toy factory, or a particularly magical place.

The jet-powered geyser in Fountain Hills could send a stream of water 560 feet into the air. The stack in Douglas stood higher at 719 feet.

The jobs it brought made Douglas more prosperous than its counterpart of Agua Prieta across the Mexican border, but it had its own form of instability. City hall was captive to a political machine run by a police chief and judge named Joe Borane, who became the county's biggest landowner through Democratic Party patronage and amassed a net worth of $5.9 million. If you passed through his courtroom, you could get your tickets dismissed. He was eventually charged with racketeering and money laundering.

A new form of prosperity had come to town in the mid-1980s, just as Phelps Dodge was decommissioning its smelter. The Sinaloa Cartel built a marvel of engineering: a secret tunnel with a two-hundred-foot track where workers could move bricks of cocaine in handcarts. Nine tons a month went over the border this way. Customers at Keoki Skinner's juice bar in Agua Prieta started paying in U.S. twenty-dollar bills. New black SUVs prowled the streets.

The Mexican end of the tunnel was hidden inside a mansion built by a Sinaloa cowboy named Rafael Camarena, who could flick a switch designed as a water spigot and raise a billiard table on hydraulic pillars. Underneath was the tunnel that led to a warehouse on the U.S. side bearing the sign "Douglas Redi-Mix Concrete," a sham business. Judge Borane had sold this strategic parcel of land to his friend Camarena at a profit of 500 percent. The scheme was uncovered in May 1990 when Raquel was ten years old. "It was as dark and dank as the hold of an old seagoing cargo freighter," reported the first federal agent in the tunnel.

Whispers gave way to laughter. Entrepreneurs sold T-shirts with dwarves singing *hi-ho, hi-ho, it's off to work we go* inside a drug tunnel. Local wits suggested that Arizona's five C's of economic pillars that included cattle, copper, citrus, cotton, and climate ought to add cocaine to the list. The Douglas City Council entertained serious proposals to turn the tunnel into a tourist attraction. A local troubadour recorded a song called "The Ballad of Joe Cocaine," and bootleg copies were played on Douglas jukeboxes and on Mexican radio.

But Joe Borane never faced charges in the tunnel case, protesting "the guy didn't march up to me with a goddamn sign saying he was a drug smuggler." He pleaded guilty to lesser offenses in the earlier corruption case. The U.S. Border Patrol beefed up its presence in town, though agents learned the hard way to be careful around the abandoned smelter, where lead and arsenic made some of them sick.

Raquel's father told her he'd once heard clanking sounds coming from the Camarena house and didn't want to know anything more about it. The wisdom of this hands-off philosophy—a way of life in Agua Prieta—kept Raquel away from politics through her years majoring in social work at Arizona State University and then working as a children's advocate. But after her awakening with the clipboard at the protest march, she knew it was time to stand up and be visible.

Then came her first campaign, in a neighborhood she barely knew. South Phoenix was the most impoverished legislative district in the state outside the Indian reservations: a sun-washed jumble of auto junkyards, fabrication plants, old Japanese flower gardens, cheap strip malls, inconvenient bus connections, and underfunded public schools. The largely Mexican American population had put roots here south of the Southern Pacific tracks and stockyards in the 1890s because restrictive covenants stopped them from buying homes anywhere else.

The "clean" defense industries so coveted by Barry Goldwater and the *Republic* did absolutely nothing for South Phoenix; they offered none of the unskilled high-wage jobs that lifted people out of poverty. When Interstate 17 came through in the Goldwater era, the asphalt slash did even more to isolate the neighborhood. Warehouses and bad apartments sprouted over the citrus orchards that stretched to the mummy-like hump of South Mountain.

The Republicans have long been afraid of a unified South Phoenix. An ambitious conservative reformer named William Rehnquist—the future chief justice of the U.S. Supreme Court—headed up a vote suppression project here in the 1950s called Operation Eagle Eye designed for pure intimidation effect, forcing Spanish-speaking voters to read words from a white card to prove their literacy. South Phoenix still carried the scars and had only one polling place. But even through this narrow bottleneck, the upstart newcomer Raquel Teran came within 113 votes of unseating her opponent.

Change now seemed possible. South Phoenix politics ran dynastic and clubby; officeholders had tended to view their seats as a lifetime sinecure. But Teran had learned to play the game. When she came back for another try in 2018, she came armed with a pocketful of endorsements from all the right people—Mary Rose Wilcox, Alfredo Gutierrez, Ruben Gallego, the crowds of minor politicos who hung out at El Portal restaurant—as well as a lunch-bucket message of safe streets and better education.

The canvassing paid further dividends. One of the houses she hit was that of Eddie Barron, a shy man in his late thirties who had been charmed by her direct way of talking. On New Year's Eve 2018, they were both at a party thrown by a mutual friend who was getting all her single friends together so nobody would feel lonely. In an uncharacteristically jubilant mood near the stroke of midnight, Eddie danced over to Raquel and—without saying anything—moved in for a kiss that she welcomed. They got married and had a son, E.J.

It was partly due to his new daughter-in-law's urging that Eddie's father, Rodolfo Barron, changed his mind about an important issue. He was a great believer in the promise of America and raised his children to have, as he put it, *manos de computadora*, "computer hands," hands that would be left unscarred by the crops he himself had labored to pick when he migrated to Arizona. He was a news junkie and an avid observer of state and national politics. But he thought the game was crooked. As he bluntly told Raquel when she asked him about his preferences, "Lady, in this house we do not vote and that is the end of the discussion."

Raquel persuaded him to cast his very first ballot for Joe Biden and Kamala Harris in 2020. When he dropped it off, a mariachi band outside played his favorite song for him: "El Rey," the king. He spread his arms wide and sang along with them.

"I know I didn't do the right thing in my life, not voting, not trusting, I know that," he told a reporter for the *Republic* who had been tipped off. "I apologize for that. But from now on, I hope I can convince some of my friends, like me, who don't believe in politics."

———

If Raquel Teran found new direction in her life by laying hold of a clipboard stacked with registration forms, one of the main beneficiaries of Arizona's turn toward right-wing populism had found his own magic in seeing what a newspaper could do.

Joe Arpaio was a drug enforcement agent from Springfield, Massachusetts, who retired to Fountain Hills and won election as Maricopa County sheriff in 1993. He then turned the office into a freak show and bottomless source of publicity, branding himself "America's Toughest Sheriff" and showing off a grotesque concentration camp outdoor jail called Tent City, where pre-trial inmates were made to wear pink underwear and denied minor comforts like coffee, television, pillows, and salt. Elderly white voters saw these antics as an effective crime-fighting strategy and kept reelecting him.

I covered him for the *Republic* for a brief time and there was never a conversation with him that didn't quickly swing around to his favorite subject—the glories of Joe Arpaio. Pathos lay not far from the surface. He once told me that the first time he felt his distant father was proud of him was in 1963 after he made a dope bust overseas. "Ton of opium seized in Turkey," read the wire story in the Springfield *Times-Union*, where dour old Ciro Arpaio happened to see it, clipped the story, and showed off the headline around town. Joe never forgot the lesson. Publicity means love.

To any reasonable observer, it was apparent Sheriff Joe brought a prime case of narcissism with him into public office. He possessed immense reserves of self-pity, obsessing about whoever he felt was "blasting" him, even when he brought the trouble on himself. He couldn't have cared less about data showing his cruel jail policies had no benefit on recidivism. Worst of all, I never got the sense he understood the pointless suffering he caused.

The pathology came wrapped in charisma. He could be charming, putting on a gruff Italian grandpa act, and he would occasionally give you a tiny signal that he knew he was slinging bullshit, rolling his eyes a millimeter at some of his own pronouncements. And when he found out I had a great-uncle who had died in the line of duty as a Maricopa County sheriff's deputy (Warren La Rue, 1971), he took an interest and made sure my family knew about the dedication of a memorial statue to fallen deputies outside the courthouse.

He didn't have a mean face. If anything, he looked like the friendly headwater at a slightly dowdy restaurant: a bulbous nose, molasses-colored suits, dyed hair damp with Brylcreem. Though he rarely carried a gun, he always wore a tie clip in the shape of a pistol. "I go back to the cowboy days," he said. "I always said I wanted everybody to know who their sheriff was. I'm not walking down a dusty street with a six-gun, but that's the concept."

Arpaio came to epitomize, for me, a certain quality of loneliness in Arizona's soul. "I don't know what that means, 'friendship,'" he told me during one marathon conversation in his office atop the downtown Wells Fargo building. Other than his close family, and reporters, nobody ever got close to him. His only validation came from faceless crowds. When a former chief deputy told him he loved him like a father, the sheriff replied: "Jerry, I never had any friends. I never looked at any of you as my friends in the sheriff's office." He had peculiar self-awareness—even a tragic honesty—in this regard, a trait common in those with narcissistic personality disorder. "I have no friends, as far as I'm concerned," Donald Trump once told a packed audience at a rally. "You know who my friends are? You're my friends."

Joe Arpaio could not be ignored: his power had consequences. He was an unavoidable force in Arizona politics. But I came to conclude that every story I wrote, even the critical ones, was just providing him what psychologists call "narcissistic supply," making me complicit in the whole mess. The only metrics he cited for his job performance were his approval rating in pre-election polls, and the hundreds of journalists from around the world who made the tour of Tent City and did stories about this piece of American ugliness. The walls of his townhouse in Fountain Hills were lined with framed newspaper headlines proclaiming his exploits.

But he soon found another way to bring attention to himself. He had been a moderate on immigration; he liked to tell people he was the son of an Italian immigrant who would not be locking up undocumented workers just because they crossed the border for a job. But by 2006 he could sense the winds blowing in a certain direction.

His chief deputy, Russell Pearce, who insisted Tent City had been his idea, won election to the state House on an anti-immigration message, championing a ballot initiative that required citizenship documents for voter registration and public benefits. Arizona Latinos had doubled in population since 1990, adding to a generational presence dating to the seventeenth century. The rise of supermarket-level agriculture had been shrinking the white majority in Arizona, bringing anxiety that pricked the subconscious.

When state schools superintendent Tom Horne learned that Tucson public schools were running a successful Mexican American studies program, he sought to kill it by promoting a law banning classes "designed primarily for students of a particular ethnic group." All immigration law is federal, but Arizona demagogues found a way to play it out locally, devising punitive initiatives against immigrants that resembled Arpaio's jail policies: showy cruelty with little other benefit.

There had always been an Old South streak in Arizona politics. Now it emerged in full magnolia bloom. Joe Arpaio used a new law against human smuggling to arrest not just coyotes but entire vanloads of migrants on conspiracy charges. He had run a frivolous "threat assessment unit" of deputies commissioned to investigate people who phoned in death threats against him, usually about one call per week. Now he set up another special division: a human smuggling unit charged with making as many arrests as possible. And he called—of course—a press conference to announce he was setting up a twenty-four-hour hotline for snitchers to call in tips on people who looked like they didn't belong.

His deputies felt relentless pressure to round up migrants and diverted their attention from other crimes. The police chief of El Mirage complained the sheriff wasn't bothering to investigate rapes; up to four hundred were simply ignored. Arpaio still cruised to victory in the 2008 election. Observers took note: a conspicuous stand on the "problem" of Mexican immigrants was a political winner.

Pearce rammed a bill through the legislature that would forever be known by its indexing number: Senate Bill 1070, which gave agencies like Arpaio's the authority to check immigration papers and even required them to do so lest they face lawsuits. The murder of rancher Douglas Krentz near the border that year—a crime that went unsolved but one widely blamed on a Mexican migrant—persuaded Governor Jan Brewer to sign it, even as more than a thousand people jammed the portico of the capitol to protest. "Our law enforcement agencies have found bodies in the desert, either buried or just lying out there, that have been beheaded," she said two days later, an untrue statement she had to retract. Brewer's popularity skyrocketed, and she set herself on a glide path toward reelection.

Arizona paid a national price in ways not seen since the tenure of Evan Mecham. Comedian Jon Stewart branded the state "the meth lab of democracy." Musical acts lined up to say they wouldn't be booking any shows here: Pitbull, Los Tigres de Norte, Rage against the Machine, Tenacious D, Maroon 5. Conventions canceled. The Phoenix Suns basketball team started wearing jerseys labeled *Los Suns* in acknowledgment of their huge Latino fan base. Representative Raul Grijalva called for a boycott against his own state.

A delighted Arpaio ripped off a press release that he would be opening a new section of Tent City to handle all the prisoners. "Citizens here sincerely hope that SB 1070 will result in large numbers of illegal aliens being captured and arrested by local law enforcement officers," he said.

When Donald Trump began to pick up momentum after his Phoenix rally in 2015 and his words were broadcast at length, I recognized him immediately: the self-regard, the neediness, the weird charm, the obliviousness to real-world impacts, the guy-from-the-neighborhood earthiness, the dog-whistle racism. He had emerged in Arizona first—carrying a gun and a badge.

—

Arizona's cities grew up by the measuring stick of the automobile's gas tank, so it should not have been a surprise that cars were a primary theater of its racism and that many of the new generation of activists first found their voice after a roadside humiliation.

The interrogations ordered by Arpaio were usually conducted during traffic stops, many of them at the point of a flashlight with "probable cause" coming from bent license frames, failure to signal a turn, or various other picayune reasons. Tomas Robles still gets angry when he tells the story of an incident on the side of Interstate 10 outside Marana.

His family had blown two tires on their drive to Phoenix from the border town of Naco. They had no cell phone. A Department of Public Safety officer rolled up and, instead of helping them, conducted an illegal search of the car. Robles said he never forgot the cop's eyes covered with aviator sunglasses, the clothes scattered on the side of the road, his father's angry face, and that the officer just drove away after failing to locate any drugs, without even helping them call for a tow truck.

As popular disgust over SB 1070 grew, Robles joined with Alejandra Gomez to start up a pressure group: Living United for Change in Arizona, or Lucha. The acronym is the same word for "struggle" in Spanish, and its aim is to build the firewalls against laws that punish ethnicity. Raquel Teran became an enthusiastic supporter. "If we don't build a structure, we're going to get a lot more SB 1070s," she told people.

Teran already had reason for hope of a better future. The dark lord of the state senate, Russell Pearce, had been targeted by Arizona's fed-up Latino activists. Former labor organizer Randy Parraz and a team of volunteers took a chance and forced a special election by gathering approximately eighteen thousand signatures in Pearce's heavily Mormon district in Mesa. The Democratic establishment in the legislature hated Pearce, but they weren't happy about the recall: they thought it a waste of time and money. Some of them, notably future U.S. senator Kyrsten Sinema, worried that angering "her boss," as she called Pearce, would sink her chances of getting any bills passed.

Parraz plunged forward anyhow. The door-knocking was methodical and sometimes discouraging; one woman told a volunteer Pearce was "going to take all that Mexican trash out of here." Against long odds, the recall got onto the ballot, and Pearce lost decisively to one of his moderate coreligionists, school administrator Jerry Lewis, who viewed the mass deportations as a crime against families.

Groups like Lucha are also known to use street theater to get a point across. Robles got sent to Arpaio's Madison Street Jail after conducting a sit-in protesting labor conditions at the McDonald's outside the Arizona State Hospital in 2014. They paraded an inflatable blow-up figure of Joe Arpaio wearing jail stripes and handcuffs. Most spectacularly, state troopers evicted Gomez from a Senate Judiciary Committee during a 2020 debate over a constitutional amendment to outlaw "sanctuary cities," in which local police are forbidden to conduct immigration enforcements. One of Lucha's witnesses said the measure embodied the same "racism, divisiveness and hate" of SB 1070, incensing chairman Eddie Farnsworth, who ordered him to sit down. Alejandra Gomez took the podium to lead a chant of "Whose house? Our house!" before Farnsworth ordered her tossed.

"We will be back, they should count on it," she said afterward.

Gomez is haunted by childhood memories of seeing workers in the California strawberry fields running away from enforcement agents after voters passed the 1994 Save Our State initiative that established a "citizen screening" system. But she also takes heart that the law spelled catastrophe for the California Republican Party, thanks to the wave of Latino activism and mobilization that followed. Gomez hopes the work of the SB 1070 generation may also result in the permanent decline of the Arizona GOP and the growth of a more reasonable political culture.

Her interests go beyond immigration into New Deal–style reforms for the working class. Lucha's support was viewed as crucial for the passage of the Fair Wages and Healthy Families Act of 2017 boosting the minimum wage to twelve dollars and creating mandatory sick time. A few sympathetic Republican officials agreed to one-on-one meetings, which seemed like a miracle, but they usually gave her a version of the classic dodge that she describes as a gut punch—*my heart is with you but I can't buck my party*. Senator Jeff Flake told her that himself before he got hounded out of the Senate anyway by Trump's mean tweets.

Arizona Latinos used to get the same shrug from white liberals who occasionally got their hands on the levers of power, epitomized by former Phoenix mayor Terry Goddard, a preppy intellectual who never quite connected with this side of the state. An observer summed up their attitude thus: "We don't care about your issues, we care about your turnout." Which gave rise to one of the most enduring political clichés of the state: the sleeping giant of the Latino vote—nearly a third of the state and forever rising—which was always just about to wake up each election cycle and never did. Democrats lamented this endlessly. An effective liberal-Latino coalition could deliver a knockout punch to the state GOP.

Why didn't they vote? There were certainly some historical factors at work. Decades of government neglect fostered cynicism and a perception of brokenness. Suppression efforts like Operation Eagle Eye had taken their toll. White liberals showed up only at election time and disappeared shortly thereafter. Sprawling residential patterns—an old Arizona tradition—meant a lack of tight neighborhoods where ethnic interest groups could build lasting clout; nothing existed here like the cooperative networks in Harlem, South Boston, Little Havana, or any number of Chinatowns in major cities.

Perhaps most profoundly, the chaos of the Mexican Revolution had left psychological scars on a founding generation of immigrants, even after it ended in 1920. Politics in Mexico was blood sport back then. Holding the wrong beliefs or even attempting to vote for change could get a whole family massacred. Those who made it to safety in the United States chose nonparticipation as a survival strategy, and the agnostic custom held among children and grandchildren. Immigrants of the twentieth century could share their own stories of corruption and rigged elections by the omnipresent Institutional Revolutionary Party, or PRI. Idealists who dared to cross the political arms of the drug cartels risked their lives for the sake of a gesture that wouldn't mean anything in the end.

The turnout battles in South Phoenix and other Latino precincts must still be fought every cycle. "You don't have to convince them of the issues—they've lived them. You have to convince them on patience," said Luis Heredia, the former executive director of the state Democratic Party. The activists at Lucha join an older set of interest groups like Chicanos Por La Causa in trying to put a blowtorch to the Republican power structure, which gets its own boost from conservative Latinos who can't stomach abortion and respond to an American Dream prosperity message. The group Latinos for Trump carpeted Yuma County lawns with signs touting the now-former president, and he easily carried the region, populated by many Spanish-speaking agricultural laborers.

Latinos steadily captured local offices. Regina Romero from the industrial farm town of Somerton won election as the mayor of Tucson. A former chambermaid named Betty Guardado joined the Phoenix City Council where Barry Goldwater once held court. And the rising clout of Latinos even achieved what had once seemed impossible: Joe Arpaio went down to electoral defeat.

America's Toughest Sheriff lost his fifth attempt at reelection in 2016 after Lucha and Raquel Teran's group Somos Arizona mobilized voters in record numbers, a remarkable blow at the heart of racist Arizona power. "This is proof that our community can move mountains," said organizer Carlos Garcia. He had been one of the organizers of the roadblock outside of Trump's infamous Fountain Hills rally. Less than four years later, he would win election to the Phoenix City Council.

Arpaio had hung a portrait of Donald Trump in his office, telling visitors he'd been waiting all his life for a hero and finally found one. "We seem to be traveling the same highway," he told people, riffing on his favorite song, Frank Sinatra's "My Way." The lavish praise may have come along with an expectation Trump could save him from going to prison. A federal judge had found him in contempt of court for violating an order to cease the traffic sweeps.

The president teased the crowd at a rally in Phoenix on August 22, 2017. "You know what, I'll make a prediction: I think he's going to be just fine.

OK? But I won't do it tonight, because I don't want to cause any controversy. But Sheriff Joe should feel good." Three days later, a pardon was hand-delivered to the sheriff's door in Fountain Hills. "He is loved in Arizona," the president told reporters.

The pardon didn't make Arpaio feel good for long. Nothing really could. The essential pathos of the man came out again, the inability to see the world beyond his own nose. "I've got two new titles now," he complained. "'The Disgraced Sheriff,' that's everywhere. And the other one is 'Racist.' So I've got two new titles. I lost my 'America's Toughest Sheriff' title." Hungering for the twisted form of love that comes from media coverage, even at the age of eighty-nine and unable to climb stairs, he filed to run for an open U.S. Senate seat and finished last in a five-candidate primary.

Arpaio's need for constant adulation could never be satisfied, just as Trump's imperial misery was not soothed by the presidency. Ethno-populist movements are a lot like narcissistic personality disorder in that way: they require endless stoking with no hope of resolution. The movement always demands an internal enemy; the grievance can never be allowed to mellow into acceptance. The wolves must always be at the gates to maintain the reason for existing.

Such inquiries into Arpaio's soul are of little interest to Gomez and Robles. They look instead at the families he ripped apart and the lives he's ruined. They were determined to prevent it from happening again. And they have been steadily effective at eroding Republican dominance. In the 2020 election, even in the midst of the pandemic, they went out with Teran's Somos Arizona and three other groups to knock on more than a million doors. That helped boost Latino turnout by a factor of 20 percent, meaning that half on the rolls followed through with a vote: an impossible dream not a decade ago.

"The irony of Russell Pearce's legacy was a lot of Latinos who got into politics because of him turned out to be some of the most assertive and outspoken politicians in our state," Rebecca Rios, the minority leader of the state senate told me. "These were kids who were terrified their parents would be deported."

There was more irony to the pushback against racism. Arizona may have been where Trump's national momentum first became undeniable, but Arizona was also where his reign symbolically ended at 9:20 p.m. local time on November 8, 2020, when Fox News announced that Arizona's electoral votes would go to his opponent—putting the presidency out of his reach, though the final outcome would not be clear for several more days.

Many factors had been at play: the steady influx of Californians with Democratic preferences, the nausea in the suburbs over Trump's vulgarity, the outspokenness of a few determined Mormon women who pointed out how far the values of the president were from their church. But the most crucial factor of all was the success of Latino organizing, even more so than the rising population of Mexican Americans.

Gomez takes nothing for granted. More Arpaios and Trumps are out there, waiting for a chance.

"Demography is not destiny," she told me. "We need to put in the work year-round. If a seat at the table is not offered to us, we're going to take one."

I WOKE UP TO A SUNRISE blocked by the wall of Picket Post Mountain, a hunk of volcanic material shaped like a yurt. The gaining light threw shades of ocher, buff, coral, and cantaloupe on the southern cliffs—each representative of magma blasts separated by thousands of years—and I paused several times to marvel at how a solid-colored rock can appear so prismatic.

Picket Post takes its name from the military. The U.S. Army set up one of its many forts against the Apaches at its base in 1870, and a mining town named Pinal later sprung up in its shadow. Celia Ann Blaylock, the Iowa-born girlfriend of Wyatt Earp, died of an overdose of opiates mixed with booze and was buried here. She had been depressed that he left her for another woman and had returned to her former job as a prostitute without finding much in the way of business. We know of her today only because Earp, who jilted her, was a crack storyteller who met some movie people in L.A. near the end of his life. That same gunslinger mystique that drew her to Wyatt is why her grave in the Pinal cemetery is often decorated with flowers.

All history is made of publicity, and the patterns of Blaylock's misery are transhistorical. The mythic figures of the past were no better than you or me. The same virtues and sins coursed through their consciousness, and they chased the pleasures rediscovered by every generation as though they were pioneers coming into undiscovered territory: money, fame, fleeting friendship, casual sex, the vanity of looks, the relaxation of alcohol, the awe of the land, the hope of a second chance, the red heat of revenge, the wages of excess. I'm sure they also gorged on enchiladas and tequila with unfortunate gastronomic consequences. If they'd had smartphones, they would have posted barroom selfies as promiscuously as any Arizona State University undergraduate. And in wartime, they traveled to darker places.

Picket Post served as the staging base for a vigilante party that confronted a group of suspected Apache raiders taking refuge on top of a nearby mesa in the 1870s. As the unverified part of the story goes, the vigilantes opened fire into the crowd, driving the Apache survivors toward the edge of the cliff until they were forced to leap. Blobs of volcanic glass later found at the site took on the nickname "Apache tears" and, after a polish, were sold as trinkets in Phoenix rockhound shops and ticky-tacky emporiums. I had one myself as a Cub Scout, never thinking much about what it symbolized.

The Apache War in Arizona was, in fact, a dirty quagmire that dragged on longer than America's twenty-first-century experience in Afghanistan. Leaders like Geronimo, Cochise, and Eskiminzin were canny tacticians who used the boulder-choked mountains as fortified bunkers and governed their citizens as a loose confederacy that could not be pacified with a decisive punch. The Apaches may not have been in Arizona even as long as the Spanish—some evidence indicates they migrated here from the plains at some point after Francisco Vasquez de Coronado's 1540 expedition—but they commanded the high ground with Viking-like prowess and lived off choreographed raids against their Tohono O'odham neighbors and anyone else who set up housekeeping on the flats. They called it "searching enemy property," a term with a note of military bureaucracy. Anglos or Mexicans trying to ranch or hunt for gold outside the range of a U.S. Army post were asking for trouble. After Charles Poston persuaded Abraham Lincoln to split off Arizona Territory from New Mexico, he kept a running list of Americans killed by the Apaches, showing it around to justify the expensive military presence.

American soldiers dreaded a posting to the Department of Arizona, thinking it a snake-bitten griddle between civilization and California where the only people content with the hostilities were the merchants getting rich by selling provisions to army quartermasters. The 1849–86 guerilla conflict seemed an endless racket for the sake of a restive outback the nation had acquired almost by accident in the Treaty of Guadalupe Hidalgo. "We had one war with Mexico to take Arizona and we should have another to make her take it back," complained General William T. Sherman. "The cost of the military establishment in Arizona is out of all proportion to its value as a part of the public domain."

Bad feelings lingered long after the Apache leadership was deported to Oklahoma and most of the population herded onto three awkwardly shaped reservations. The architecture of the war can still be perceived in the ruins of some of the old posts, like Fort Lowell and Fort Bowie, the continuing big footprint and generous subsidies of the military, and in legends like that of Apache Leap.

To live anywhere in the United States, of course, is to sleep unwittingly near a place of historic violence against the continent's first people, the blood effaced from memory except for scattered place-names. History is tyrannical and pitiless that way: the quantities of love and heroism spilled on the earth can never be charted; they sleep with human vessels in unvisited graves.

The miles south of here are the most hazardous on the entire trail; it's a waterless thirty-mile trek to the Gila River, and the sheriff's search-and-rescue teams spend a lot of time here answering calls. Alamo Canyon presents a series of ups and downs through washes and over ridges lined with cholla—basin and range foothill country. Rain comes here infrequently, just eighteen inches a year, not enough to remain in pools or seep up though the secret underground rivulets that create springs. This desolate valley soon opens to another canyon, a truly spectacular chasm with two-thousand-foot walls and peach-colored spires: Martinez Canyon, a gorgeous place I never knew existed—new and ancient at the same time.

English writer J. B. Priestley spent a few winters at a dude ranch on the shores of the Hassayampa River in the 1930s and made an observation that I think apt for most of central Arizona. "It seemed to me the oldest country I had ever seen, the real antique land, first cousin to the moon. Brown, bony, sapless, like an old man's hand. . . . This country is geology by day and astronomy at night."

In an hour, I was up at a gunsight gap in the southern wall and could see from the view outward that I'd been looking at the edge of this canyon for most of my life without realizing it. Fields of Pinal County cotton lay upturned to the sun and grew fuzzy with agricultural soot and humidity at the far horizons.

There's a road out there that I know.

THE LOVE SONG OF INTERSTATE 10

Journeys take place in the mind as much as they do in physical space, and I have noticed a recurring thought pattern that unspools every time I travel Interstate 10 between Phoenix and Tucson.

Lots of people are joining me out there: this is the state's most traveled piece of rural asphalt, according to the Arizona Department of Transportation. But the state's busiest freeway is also its most reviled, crossing what many consider swathes of unattractive scrublands and cheerless little off-ramp villages. "At night and with a six-pack" is how one historian friend of mine—a great lover of this state—described his preferred way to travel I-10.

Nobody writes a poem to this section of expressway, completed in the heyday of the optimism of the Kennedy-Johnson New Frontier between 1961 and 1971. I have lived in both Phoenix and Tucson off and on and have probably traversed this road more than eight hundred times, looking at the same sunbaked landmarks and thinking the same reliable thoughts each time: about old friends, old happenings, old mysteries of my life here. How many others mark their I-10 journeys with a mental libretto of musings on the roadside spectacle?

My sequential reverie doesn't really start until I-10 breaks free from metro Phoenix at the buckle of viaducts that connect to the Santan Freeway and the road bends into the beige expanse of the Gila River Indian Community. The twelve-story hotel at the Wild Horse Pass Hotel & Casino is the second-to-last tall building a motorist sees until Tucson, and I wonder: "Wild Horse Pass?" Is that an actual place-name or just a faux-western branding tool?

I imagine the smell of bath soap and linens inside the rooms, the universal aroma of hotels. And I think of Ira Hayes of the Gila River Pimas, whose people *farmed the Phoenix Valley in Arizona land*, in the geographically fanciful words of Johnny Cash. The shy U.S. Marine was among the crew that raised the U.S. flag on Mount Suribachi at Iwo Jima, and he died consumed with survivor guilt and alcoholism ten years after the war.

You'd hardly know this was an Indian reservation, however, as we pass the infinity loop of Firebird International Raceway and then the earthen bowl of what used to be called Compton Terrace—a big concert venue in the 1980s when DJs on the hard rock station KLPX talked about it constantly and kids in my high school talked in reverential terms about getting high and drunk after hearing Def Leppard. The venue now lies unsigned and abandoned, looking like a ruined Roman amphitheater on the coast of the Mediterranean. Much of what lies on the edge of I-10, in fact, falls into the category of relics: castoffs of a modern era, their bones bleaching in the sun.

On its brief path through the reservation, the highway passes a small mountain to the east. The gnarly stump of a mesquite tree used to be out here, and some joker painted the top appendage bright red, giving it the appearance of a turkey. It stood watch here for many years and was a small family joke to us. I will never know who else noticed it or came to regard it with affection, a bit of levity in what was otherwise an uninviting landscape. The "turkey" is long gone. But I remember it.

We come up to the offramp to Arizona Highway 347, widened to four lanes in 2004 to make room for Maricopa, an uncontrolled thermonuclear explosion of baked red tile houses that qualified it as the fastest-growing city in the nation until the foreclosure crisis hollowed it out. Though the maze of curving streets cannot be seen from the interstate, I invariably think of the mortgage economy: the desert chewed up for families on the move. The detached air-conditioned rancher is Arizona's coal, its steel, its bushels of wheat.

Before long, we pass the ruined museum and visitor's center at the exit for the tribal village of Sacaton as we move into a ragged stretch of Upper Sonoran hardpan and the first showings of another kind of boom: the swathes of ragged land that have never really recovered from the mania for cotton that swept Arizona in the 1910s. Big chunks of land near the rivers were scraped bare and planted with a long-staple variety called Pima cotton, a primary component in tires and airplane wings. My great-great-grandfather

Franklin La Rue got caught up in the craze and planted cotton himself on the edge of Phoenix. Little vegetable farms vanished and fruit trees were cut and burned as three-quarters of the agricultural land in the state went to cotton. Demand collapsed after World War I and most of the desert fields went fallow. They still look hard-used and wasted. In a few places, you can see the ghost lines of long-vanished furrows.

Over a slight rise and we're now into the basin, dominated by shabby cotton fields and the sun-worn jumble of Casa Grande, where my old Jeep overheated twenty years ago and I had it fixed at a desert garage that seemed ripped from a Cormac McCarthy novel. The left side of the freeway here has been barricaded with a grim concrete wall with a stylized bas-relief of crop furrows radiating away from mountains. The wall shields a Sam's Club store and a beige cluster of starter homes thrown up by the mega-builder D. R. Horton—an architectural vernacular as integral to twenty-first-century Arizona as the brick townhouse was to Victorian London.

But soon we come upon the highly visible corpse of the Tanger Factory Outlet mall off Jimmie Kerr Boulevard, which opened in 1991 and devolved into a husk twenty years later when newer outlet malls opened in Phoenix. Few monuments to capitalism look more pathetic than a dead mall. The empty shells of Guess and Izod and the blank cube that was once a Wendy's out front announce their victimhood, as well as the pitilessness of the rural Arizona economy.

Just south of here I-10 and I-8 split, and I-8 bends off to the west toward San Diego—the ocean a fantasy abstraction here in the midst of the Sonoran Desert. In the crotch between the two is a lonely wooden sign for Campground Tierra Buena, "good land," which seems to have vanished years ago along with so many other failed projects clinging to this midcentury desert arterial. But travelers still need to eat, sleep, defecate, and buy gasoline at regular intervals, and very soon we spot the cheap plastic stalks of commerce that grow alongside every freeway in America as reliably as wooden water towers used to mark distances on early railroad lines.

Here is the franchise village of Sunland Gin Road: Love's Travel Stop, Motel 6, Arby's. And a curiosity: Blue Beacon Truck Wash—formerly known as Red Baron—which has a second-story tower with strange portholes looking outward. What's in that roasting attic, I wonder. What does it smell like in there? Who thought a medieval-nautical truck wash was a good idea?

The interstate now takes another bend, and we're up against another dreary strip of the quick life: hamburgers, gas, an RV resort. This exit is called Toltec Road, and it seems to have been the response of the depressed cotton town of Eloy to the economic stink bomb of the freeway. Eloy had made its life from transportation—its name comes from a 1902 Southern Pacific Railroad acronym for East Line of Yuma—and it stood to die by the same forces unless it could suck a little sales tax off the asphalt. The city annexed the interchange in 1971, meaning they get a cut of every bacon cheeseburger sold at the Carl's Jr. I recall playing basketball in junior high school against a tough team from Eloy, a long-distance trip that then seemed magical.

It isn't long before we pass another dingy I-10 ruin, this one a set of weird-looking birdcages on poles and truck tires half-buried in the dirt—the lone remnants of an amusement park and drive-through zoo called Family Fun World that lost its financing in the late 1990s. I can recall a ferocious metal dinosaur that used to stand out there; it's now as extinct as its prehistoric avatars. The big hole was a clay quarry used for the construction of this very interstate.

The property is within sight of one of the only verdant patches on the journey: a huge stand of pecan trees. Half of them are now gone—chopped away by the Arizona Department of Transportation for a road-widening project, along with nearly the entire town of Picacho and its funky little motel with a giant sign with an oval on top that could be seen for miles. Air-conditioning units encased in brown-painted slats hung from the back windows. What did it smell like in those rooms? What little family dramas and road romances happened in there?

My childhood friend Sheldon Fowler and I used to gaze at the threadbare town of Picacho from the windows of my mother's car, wondering how anybody lived there, and what the kids did for fun. "I'll bet they play some kind of desert game," Sheldon had volunteered, and I imagined an improvised combat scenario with low-power BB guns and rocks as weapons. It didn't sound terribly appealing. Picacho's now gone, sacrificed to new road. The interstate giveth and the interstate taketh away.

From here you can spot the volcanic saddle of Picacho Peak, whose name is a tortured combination of Spanish and English—literally, "little peak peak"—and the strongest visual symbol of this drive, looking like a frozen sloth rising from a vanished swamp. It's a bit of a spiritual halfway mark. Tucson used to be represented at the state capitol by Andy Nichols, who made countless trips on this road. On the front of his memorial marker, he has a metal plate with an etching of a car trundling past Picacho Peak.

A little dash of highway commerce is scattered at the base: a Dairy Queen, a sex toy store called Lion's Den, a Shell station. Up a side road lies the barely existent ruins of a Nickerson Farms restaurant that closed in the early 1980s and spent the next three decades falling apart. After the roof collapsed, I photographed the spindled chaos of the beams. Eventually only the ramada over the driveway was standing. Now even that is gone, along with the vanished sign for Furrer's Truck Stop that bore a model of an antique truck at least 150 feet up over the baked plains.

We're almost two-thirds home now and getting close to an APS power plant, which is when, driving here on my way back from college in the late 1980s, I was able to pick up the signal of my hometown pop radio station, KRQ, on the radio of my old Ford and feel a flood of gratitude, familiarity, and dread at coming home. The feeling increases as we pass a railroad water tower for the jerkwater stop of Red Rocks, where my pal Sheldon and I—older by then—once drove out to because he had heard of this tiny bar where they served mini-pitchers of beer and were not particular about carding minors. We arrived after 10 p.m. to find the bar closed. Another adventure foiled. Story of my youth.

Not too much farther and I can see the turnoff for Pinal Air Park and a jumble of tailfins of parked planes, mainly scrapped 747s, looking like the upright necks of pigeons. Guards used to turn visitors away from the gates of this obscure airport back in the Reagan era, though the story eventually leaked out: it was a staging ground for the CIA, which used it to retrofit planes that ferried guns to Nicaragua. Another mystery of I-10, highly visible and extremely concealed all at once.

Upon us is the edge of Marana, a cotton town whose heart was destroyed by this freeway in 1962, just as Picacho had been sacrificed more recently. Perhaps in revenge, Marana became one of the truly greedy jurisdictions of the state during the 1990s, annexing and developing great gobs of empty caliche. Now it has forty-four thousand people, a burgeoning school district, and a whole lot of boxy tract homes. Some of the prior character remains, though—the remnants of Miller's Market in the dot village of Rillito, where I once thirty years ago glimpsed a young girl standing outside near a gaunt older man who looked like her father, a scene right out of a Walker Evans photograph from the Great Depression. And nearby the desert gothic kilns and furnaces of the Portland Cement Company are tucked into a grove of eucalyptus trees against a hillside.

A truck that used to be parked here assured passersby *Jesus Is the Answer* with a big placard. It was near this spot in the year 1980, when my family was finishing its move from Phoenix to Tucson—a move I hated—transporting a final load of household knickknacks and two reluctant cats in a Volvo station wagon, that we passed through a brief squall and came over a viaduct to see a double rainbow shining between us and the green-gray hump of the Santa Catalina Mountains off to the west. My mother describes it as a near-religious moment: a signal to her that a better future awaited in Tucson. I can remember a few caterpillars crawling across the asphalt of I-10 and being not so convinced.

This moment turned out to be a kind of hinge: I was about to experience the horrors of new classrooms with strange people in a new town, leaving childhood behind. The rainbow was gone within minutes but the viaduct still there and I am now thinking about it still, in middle age, still traveling this most essential of Arizona's rural arteries.

To the right, I can see the Santa Cruz River, which Father Eusebio Kino had used as his own version of I-10, planting missions four hundred years ago under the authority of the king of Spain. To the left, I can see the faraway fold of Pima Canyon, where Indigenous rebels against that reign were said to have taken refuge in 1751. Near it flows the alluvial wash called Canyon del Oro, which means "Valley of Gold" and gave its name to my high school. My first real girlfriend lived in a tract home right beside it, and we had a first kiss in her driveway under a cauldron of stars when I was eighteen and the world was new. Past and present mingle in a carburetor of thought.

And then here comes Orange Grove Road, a name I always loved, an exit from the freeway, and the way that leads toward home.

HERE'S A THEORY ONLY GEOGRAPHY nerds could love: Arizona is defined by five scars across its midsection. The furthest one north is the hockey stick of the Colorado River that created the Grand Canyon.

Then comes the Interstate 40 corridor closely tracking the route of the Atlantic & Pacific Railroad and the necklace of towns across the northern tier born as division points: Holbrook, Winslow, Flagstaff, Ash Fork, Seligman, Kingman, the fabled cast of Route 66 towns, which, except for a few white-knuckle miles near the mining town of Oatman, was generally a smooth road out to the dreamland of the West Coast.

The third iconic lash across Arizona is the Mogollon Rim, the set of cliffs dividing the piney volcanic plateau from the basin and range country.

Then comes the Gila River, originating as snowmelt from the Continental Divide and flowing through high-walled canyons before getting bled away for agriculture.

The fifth and last is the Interstate 10 corridor that roughly follows the route of the Southern Pacific Railroad.

But I was thinking that day about the Gila, the most haunted line on the map, a once vibrant river that's been turned off as firmly as a sink faucet before it reaches the flat expanses of Pinal County traversed by I-10. The doomed river was my goal, even as thirst crept up on me in the droning furnace of the afternoon. A line from an old country song reverberates just as monotonously. *All day I've faced a barren waste. Without the taste of water. Cool water.*

That one was from the *Gunfighter Ballads and Trail Songs* album by Marty Robbins, the kid from Glendale, Arizona, who wore immaculate black vests and who my Aunt Doris always claimed to have dated in the early 1950s before she married my uncle, Evan Wilson, a Phoenix police detective. Robbins was a master balladeer known for cowboy twangers like "El Paso" and "Big Iron." And in his own way, he was a pioneer of a certain Arizona style of music—a loose regional category, but one I'd argue is a distinct category defined by a reinterpretation of classic American droving songs and norteño military brass from Mexico, with some spaghetti Western melodrama thrown in.

Arizona was a natural home for the music that lionized the cowboy and his wide lonesome spaces and stoic heartbreak, a twist on the Appalachian folk song and its fiddles, valorizing a disappearing way of life. A young man named Stan Jones growing up in the 1930s on a cattle ranch near Douglas was fixing a broken gear atop a windmill when an older cowhand told him an approaching storm cloud looked like "the devil's herd" composed of "red-eyed cows." Jones recalled the image years later when he was working as a park ranger in Death Valley and wrote the supernatural cowboy ballad "Ghost Riders in the Sky." Another Cochise County ranch kid, Rex Allen, grew up in Mud Springs Canyon south of Willcox and gained his fame as a television cowboy who sang covers like "Riding Down the Canyon" and "Partners of the Saddle."

Waylon Jennings put an outlaw lash on this sound when he performed at the Gallopin' Goose in the Texas-like cotton farming town of Coolidge and later on the upper floor of JD's nightclub in Tempe. He had found a squeezebox of creativity at the AM radio station KCKY in Coolidge under disc jockey Lee Hazlewood, who developed a lively morning show from a second-floor office at the Studio Theater, nurturing a crazed cowboy aesthetic in the 1950s with other artists like Duane Eddy, Buck Owens, Al Casey, and other masters of twang who pressed their vinyl at Ramsey's Audio Recorders on Seventh Street and Weldon Avenue in Phoenix.

Western balladry was in for another modern twist of lime: a brass-based Latin shimmy. Few bands epitomized a specific Arizona touch more than Calexico, who channeled scorpions and painted saints in the 1990s with albums like *Feast of Wire* and *Garden Ruin*. They saw their trail paved by Tucson's eclectic KXCI radio station, as well as the godfather of Tucson's shabby-cool ecology, Howe Gelb, who helped make the Hotel Congress a thumping hive with his band Giant Sand. The relative hollowness of downtown in the 1990s only added to the ambiance. Some of Gelb's associates took up with a steel guitar and a violin to form Friends of Dean Martinez, a hybrid of jazz, alt-country, and lounge.

Their languid notes reached Aaron Gilbreath when he was an undergraduate at the University of Arizona, evoking for him "all the colors that the desert painted across my sensitive tearful heart, all the atmospheric magic of this enchanting rattlesnake land, amplified and audible for the first time and made concrete in a way that I could never articulate when I described southern Arizona to people."

Phoenix had its own musical herbarium—slicker, faster, more L.A., more urgent in its alienations. The Meat Puppets started as a conventional punk band but moved into a unique artillery barrage of druggy anger. A more family-friendly act, Mr. Mister, found pop radio traction in the 1980s, but not until moving to California. The guitarist Doug Hopkins turned his own misery into art, and then got kicked out of his band Gin Blossoms for misbehavior. His friend Brian Jabas Smith came to visit him in a squalid Tempe apartment shortly before this happened and found him eager to get drunk in the dark. The electricity had been cut; a girlfriend had just dumped him after blackening one of his eyes. He turned the event into the megahit "Found Out About You." Gin Blossoms songs had been mainly nonfiction.

"Doug took in beauty everywhere," wrote Smith. "It'd sometimes freeze him in his tracks. He'd stare over the cinderblock wall in someone's backyard, with beer in hand, at an Arizona sunset that'd descend over acres of suburban rooftops repeating to the horizon."

Despite all this musical richness, Arizona never had a national recording studio to promote a cluster of distinct musical identity, in the same way that Sun Records made Memphis in the national consciousness, or Sub-Pop enshrined Seattle. Arizona's indigenous sounds grew on hot afternoons in clubs, backyards, teen dances, and roadhouses. An aunt of my high school friend Mindy Ronstadt, Linda Ronstadt, is from a German Mexican family that owned a downtown Tucson hardware store in the 1930s and produced a battalion of local musicians. Paul McCartney and his wife Linda owned a ranch east of town. Neko Case lived and recorded here for a while.

And there are those who came of age here before migrating someplace else—usually Los Angeles—to refine their music and find their audience: Stevie Nicks, Lalo Guererro, The Tubes, Alice Cooper. In this sense, the Arizona sound is as in motion and wandering as the narrator of Glen Campbell's ode to a man driving away from his ex-girlfriend. *By the time I get to Phoenix, she'll be rising.*

The trail leads down a graveled slope from the lip of Martinez Canyon, past an old mining settlement, and then to a thick grove of mesquite amid a powdery black soil that signifies the presence of many years of cattle run through this country. I fought my way through the trees to stand at last next to the Gila River—a marvelous living thing, flowing at an impressive speed, looking at least ten feet deep and twenty feet wide, bearing no resemblance to the dried-up corpse under the I-10 bridge.

I was also intensely grateful for it because I was down to my last swallows of water after a ten-hour march. This kind of thirst feels like an invisible hand from deep within your body pulling you down into a grave.

The water I drew from the Gila River into my bottles was thick with mud and agricultural runoff, and had the appearance of weak cocoa. I filtered it twice, dumped in extra lemonade flavoring, and hoped for the best. And then I drank and drank.

WHITE BONES

The mayor of Casa Grande urged the whole city to shut down on May 10, 1922, so that the crowds could be as impressive as possible at the dedication of the Hayden-Ashurst Diversion Dam. Women were encouraged to clip flowers from their gardens to be loaded into a special baggage car of the Arizona Eastern Railway taking visitors uphill to the spot where an immense load of concrete had been poured between a pair of granite outcroppings.

The water diverted from the Gila River was certain to create, in the words of one enthusiast, a "great inland empire" in the central part of Arizona, spurring the sandy earth to life and remaking it into verdant fields of cotton and melons.

Crowds picnicked on barbecue in front of the new gray wedge in the canyon and listened to the governor and the secretary of the interior make speeches. President Warren Harding sent a congratulatory telegram. An official pulled a lever and the waters of the Gila River, called by newspaper poets "one of the most erratic and torrential streams in America," sloughed dutifully into a canal and toward sixty-two thousand acres of the brittle soil.

Thousands of new settlers soon flooded into central Arizona, primarily from Texas and Oklahoma—those who knew a thing or two about cotton farming and breaking sod. The population of Casa Grande quadrupled. Baptist churches and cotton gins popped up on dirt road corners all around the valley. An entrepreneur named R. J. Jones founded a farming town called Coolidge, named after the thirtieth president, that looked like a panhandle town on the southern plains, with wide avenues, compact bungalows, and commercial blocks painted white under a downpour of year-round sunshine.

Pima cotton blossomed in every direction around the jagged remnants of a multistory mud dwelling built by the Hohokam around 1350 and then abandoned because of crop failures. Nicknamed "The Big House," the ruin had given the town of Casa Grande its name. As the water from the Gila River's natural course dried up and the aquifer sank, the mesquite trees around the ruins withered and died. A river that was perhaps three million years old had been switched off, just like that.

A hopeful migrant from Texas named Lewis Storey liked what he saw and signed a contract with the San Carlos Irrigation District in 1930 to receive a guaranteed supply of water from the diversion dam, in exchange for an annual fee and his promise not to drill a well on his property.

Storey was a pragmatic man who had fought for his country against the German kaiser in World War I, and what he valued about his new acreage on Eleven Mile Road was the brilliant reliability of the water. There wouldn't be any gambling on the weather like there had been back home in the Dust Bowl. And there was also a cheap source of labor: some impoverished Tohono O'odham up from the nearby reservation, who lived in a row of concrete houses he built next to one of his canals.

Some ecologists had wondered whether it made sense to build a new Midwest in the midst of Arizona's hardpan desert that receives less than nine inches of rainfall per year, to grow a crop that drinks six times as much water as a comparable field of lettuce. But the money didn't lie.

Droughts came and went through the years, but most cotton farmers stayed in business until the rainfall in the high country took a dramatic fall around the turn of the twenty-first century and never truly came back. Scientists called this prolonged aridity a megadrought, and it threatened to set records on a thousand-year timescale.

In 2021 the granddaughter of Lewis Storey received a letter in the mail from the San Carlos Irrigation District informing her of "delivery constraints." That meant that Nancy Caywood wouldn't be getting a drop of Gila River water that year. And she was still on the hook for a maintenance bill of $22,000.

Caywood took me out for a walk on her dehydrated farm and showed me the cracked earth where lush stands of alfalfa should be growing. Only a few struggling plants with tiny purple flowers had managed to stay alive in the 110-degree heat. All water had been cut off in April. Now all her fields were lying clodded and bare, showing only little patches of Bermuda grass whose seeds were blown here from faraway golf courses. "You look at this and it makes you want to cry," she told me. "It was green until May. Now it's just crunchy. We're getting sucked dry. All our fields are out of production."

These were conditions Lewis Storey might have recognized from the 1930s. When high winds pick up across fallow farmland such as this, it tends to create dust storms that the Phoenix television meteorologists call haboobs—an Arabic word describing the massive brown walls that rain dirt and debris over valley cities on summer evenings. Whether Pinal County's "great inland empire" of cotton could be sustainable had always been an open question. Now the threat seemed existential.

The new Dust Bowl also opened the broader question of whether Arizona's quest to reengineer itself was coming up on a breaking point.

———

The lowest point in Arizona by elevation lies not in a desert basin like California's Death Valley but in the bed of the Colorado River as it exits the nation.

This spot is seventy-two feet above sea level, cut off from public view by a high fence along the east bank to foil migrant workers, so I had to cross into Mexico at the town of San Luis de Colorado, catch a taxi to the highway bridge, and hike up the drainage until my GPS showed that I was standing on the U.S. side. The spot amounts to a low point in many senses of the term.

Sand. Weeds. Tire tracks. A few salt cedars. The border fence high up on the banks.

No water anywhere in sight.

The Colorado River Delta that once lay here had been one of the world's most beautiful estuaries. Naturalist Aldo Leopold paddled through lush lagoons in 1922. "The still waters were of a deep emerald hue, colored by algae, I suppose, but no less green for all that," he wrote. "A verdant wall of mesquite and willow separated the channel from the thorny desert beyond. At each bend we saw egrets standing in the pools ahead, each white statue matched by its white reflection." Clam beds grew in the sun-flickered shallows and jaguars prowled the shores.

Standing here in the melancholy wastes of a once-flourishing magnificent river delta, it was possible to imagine the Laguna Diversion Dam twenty miles upstream, which sluiced water away from the river in 1908, making possible the corporate empire of perishable food around the city of Yuma that today supplies 90 percent of the nation's leafy vegetables, plus huge amounts of lemons, alfalfa, dates, melons, wheat, and corn.

"I am told," wrote Leopold, "that the green lagoons now raise cantaloupes. If so, they should not lack flavor. Man always kills the thing he loves, and so we pioneers have killed the wilderness. Some say we had to."

The Laguna was only the beginning of the Colorado River's transformation into a plumbing pipe of twenty-eight large dams that provide water for the lawns and golf courses of every metropolis in the Southwest; four major artificial lakes; three coal-fired generating stations; a chain of Jet-Ski resorts with names like Pirate Cove, Havasu Landing, and Hidden Shores; enough hydropower to light up all of Phoenix; and, most impressively, a 336-mile aqueduct bearing an oceanic tranche of water into the interior of Arizona—the Central Arizona Project.

The CAP's planners had relied on the same euphoric rainfall projections of the 1920s that made the diversion dam above Nancy Caywood's farm seem like a good idea. After a period of fighting over which western states could divert water and how much, representatives from Colorado, Wyoming, Nevada, New Mexico, Utah, California, and Arizona met around a conference table at the Bishop's Lodge resort in Santa Fe in 1922, the same year Leopold paddled the green lagoons in the delta. They agreed the river's water should be divided between upper and lower basin states in specific numerical allotments. But they were working from grossly exaggerated figures. The previous decade's rainfall had been uncommonly and deceptively generous.

Lawyers like to make a distinction between "paper water," which exists in theory, and "wet water," which exists in physical form. The difference between paper and wet in this case was at least four million acre-feet. The Colorado River Compact was a flattering mathematical portrait of a Southwest that would never exist again. Experts called it and the resulting court cases, without irony, the Law of the River.

As the numbers became plain, Arizona looked at California with distrust that festered into paranoia. It refused to ratify the compact, pointing out that its tributaries fed a majority of water to the lower river while California gave almost nothing from its own mountains. When the U.S. Bureau of Reclamation started construction on Parker Dam in 1934, Governor Benjamin Moeur saw it as a sweetheart deal for Los Angeles and sent a detachment of the Arizona National Guard to the eastern banks to "stop an invasion," he said, and prevent any concrete from being attached to state soil. Two wooden boats were requisitioned, named the Arizona Navy, and sent upriver on patrol. One ran aground, and its crews had to be rescued by the dam builders. Courts weren't on Moeur's side; the dam got built, but Arizona found revenge in filing the longest court case ever adjudicated, *Arizona v. California*, which took twelve years. Then they set to create facts on the ground with the most expensive water transfer project of the century.

A powerful figure was ready to pave the way. Carl Hayden grew up in Tempe on the banks of the Salt River before it stopped flowing. He realized young that politics was the great love of his life and won election to Congress five days after statehood. A pint-sized infighter with oversized eyeglasses and a nurser of grudges, Hayden clawed his way to the chairmanship of the Senate Appropriations Committee and thus became, in the words of Lyndon Johnson, "the third senator from every state," able to trade vast sums of federal money for what he wanted for Arizona—namely the CAP. "Arizona is doomed to wither away to the point of disaster," he warned.

Other Arizona politicians behaved like this when it came to water, whether they were tax-loathing archconservatives or big-spending New Dealers. "I cannot understand how anyone living in a desert can turn down any water, regardless of what it costs," said the otherwise tightfisted mayor of Phoenix, Jack Williams, perhaps proving author Mary Austin's observation that "rain falls on radical and conservative alike, but the mother ditch makes communists of them all."

The state's newspapers raged against California and used birthright language: "our water." For decades, it was said, the sole imperative for an Arizonan in Congress was to come back to the state every month with assurances CAP money was on its way. In 1968 it arrived, and the digging began. "Colorado River water will someday flow to the fertile valleys of central

Arizona where, before the time of Christ, the Hohokam Indians established an extensive irrigation civilization," enthused the editor of *Arizona Farmer*, with a dose of arrogance. "Had these primitive people known how to build storage dams and drainage systems as does man today, they might not be called Hohokam—'the people who are gone.'"

Mountains blocked Phoenix to the east and west—this natural framing was the reason why the city was never a stop on transcontinental rail routes. The same geological inconvenience required some hydrological creativity. From a mouth at Lake Havasu, an electric pump lifts water 824 feet to a portal in the Buckskin Mountains and thence toward central Arizona on a zigzagging path. This is the rough equivalent of streaming twenty-two thousand gallons per second over a skyscraper twice as high as the Chase Tower in downtown Phoenix. But as an old western saying holds, water flows uphill toward money and power.

After two decades of digging and sealing, the project delivered its first drinking water to Tucson with minerals that wreaked havoc on pipes. The city was forced to build a set of recharge basins that let CAP water seep into the aquifer where it could be pumped out as groundwater. Seen from the air, the basins wink in the sunshine like a giant set of solar reflectors.

The problem for the CAP today is no different from the time bomb wedged inside the original Colorado River Compact. There is simply not enough water there to satisfy the supercharged growth machine of Arizona's cities. Hotter summers in an era of climate change reduce the winter snowpack and evaporate more of the canal water before it can get to central Arizona: nearly 5.2 billion gallons of it disappears each year. And the problem is only going to get worse. Western U.S. mountains could begin to see entire winters pass without any snow as early as 2040. This doesn't just spell doom for ski resorts. Melted snowpack represents almost three-quarters of Arizona's water consumption.

The megadrought that dried up Nancy Caywood's field of alfalfa also shrank the two greatest artificial lakes on the river, Lake Mead and Lake Powell, down to alarming levels—near the status of "dead pools" that can no longer be tapped even by the lowest pumps. Lake Powell has dropped 140 feet in the last two decades, leaving mineral stains on the cliffs. Submerged rock formations are rising back into view as the turquoise water sinks lower and gets dirtier. Writer Elizabeth Kolbert went out for a look and reported the following sight:

> In front of us stood a grove of dead cottonwoods. Several of the trees were festooned with plastic jugs. The empty jugs had served as buoys when the trees first started to re-emerge from the lake, presumably to prevent boats from getting snagged on them. The jugs now dangled twenty-five or thirty feet off the ground.

Images like this tend to arrive with tracings of sin and apocalypse. We have demanded too much of the earth, taken far more than our fair share, robbed from our descendants, and will die off like the Hohokam, whose fields went to salt.

But such prophecies are hyperbolic. The reality is more complicated. The state's major rivers were engineered into ghosts to prop up the horizon of lights and bluegrass that drives Arizona's economy. Our modern technological civilization and our ability to make a home in the desert depends on these dams: supersized village wells. They aren't evil in themselves. The sheer force and ambition of them should inspire as much admiration as dread.

Bringing arid lands into life is an urge that lies close to humanity's collective unconsciousness: the need to find fresh territories and new horizons. "The desert will rejoice, and flowers will bloom in the wilderness," proclaims the Book of Isaiah. "The desert will sing and shout for joy." The libido for raising crops is buried deep in the cerebral soil. Iowa psychologist Mike Rosmann has described what he calls the Agrarian Imperative: the atavistic urge to cultivate that prompts Congress to keep passing ridiculous subsidies to prop up family farms in an era of corporate agribusiness.

Perhaps we sense what kept us alive in the Mesopotamian valleys of twelve thousand years ago. Organized hydrology is not merely an arranging device of civilization: it is civilization itself. "Any people who, for the first time, managed to divert a river and seduce a crop out of wasted land had tweaked the majestic indifference of the universe," wrote Marc Reisner. "To bring off the feat demanded tremendous collective will: discipline, planning, a sense of shared goals. To sustain it required order, which led to the creation of powerful priesthoods, of bureaucracies." Ancient peoples like the Sumerians and the Hohokam, liberated from the uncertainty of hunting, could build battlements and food storage bins and develop higher pursuits like writing, astronomy, and law.

In the case of modern Arizona, the Agrarian Imperative had allowed civic dreamers to deform three rivers and build the nation's fifth-biggest city in a totally unsuitable region. Had the lower Colorado River not been muscled over here, Arizona would have been much less populated, perhaps saner, and more conscious of its place within an arid ecosystem. Instead, said historian Jack August, we believe in boundless growth, acting as though we have a rich grandfather who will pay the bills.

There is no going back. The rivers will not return. So long as mega-droughts continue, Arizona's urban planners will find ways to keep piping the daily average of 120 gallons into every house for showering, cooking, and gardening. Housing comes first; that pecuniary engine cannot go unfed. Agriculture gobbles nearly three-quarters of the state's water, and it will pay the price when the shortage becomes unmanageable. The end for cotton and pecans is near, perhaps even the luxurious green salad bowl outside Yuma. Water flows uphill.

———

The main branch of the CAP canal is conspicuous enough to be visible from outer space, twisting in a snakelike path toward the money of Phoenix through the unsettled portions of western Arizona, a place that used to inspire a special dread for those who traveled across it. Few ever came to plant roots, then and now.

Martha Summerhayes, the wife of an army officer, deplored the "miles of dust and burning heat" in 1874, the year she crossed the region of dead cinder cones and lonely plains of greasewood that would one day be the home for the biggest American aqueduct ever built. "The dry white dust of this desert country boiled and surged up and around us in suffocating clouds," she wrote. "I did not see much to admire in the desolate waste lands through which we were travelling."

A few unique personalities found comfort in western Arizona. A raw-boned jokester who called himself Dick Wick Hall opened a filling station on the dirt road from Phoenix to Los Angeles in the 1910s. He reflected on how travelers in their Tin Lizzies must have felt pity for that gas jockey in that lonely wasteland, but the secret was he felt sorry for *them*. The dried-out country provided a solitude "where I can get acquainted with myself and maybe find the Something which every man in his own Soul is consciously or unconsciously Searching for—Himself."

Drive what is now U.S. Highway 60 through the McMullen Valley and you can see the spirit of Hall's gentle misanthropy in what tourist brochures tout as "Arizona's Outback." The road through the low rises of the Harquahala Mountains is speckled with RV and trailer parks, some scruffier than others, populated by desert rats, low-income seniors, quail hunters, no-frills winter visitors, and those who want to be left alone. They cling to the highway as the Quechans and Mohaves clung to the Gila River. The dry bones of the landscape that so horrified Martha Summerhayes—"so white, so bare, so endless, and so still"—still yawn in all directions.

But if a motorist turns at a place called Vicksburg Junction and goes five miles south, crossing the CAP canal on the way, a different landscape materializes: luxuriant and sensual fields of green grass, watered by center pivots the length of an airport concourse. A sign announces this unanticipated slice of Nebraska as Fondomonte Farms. The scent of manure wafts over from a nearby feedlot.

All this grass is attributable to an astonishing hydrological savings account under the McMullen Valley: land that looks worthless on the crust but conceals a treasure chest of subterranean water, three times as much as the state takes from the Colorado River every year. Scientists call it fossil water: it's been here since the retreat of glaciers fifteen thousand years ago.

This water reserve under Arizona's Outback is at the center of a *Chinatown*-like conspiracy story. Evidence is circumstantial and key players deny it. But events came together in a way that illustrates the power of cities to manipulate water politics for their own ends.

In January of 1982, folks in the sunbaked towns of Salome and Parker watched as men dressed in tailored suits handed out leaflets calling for the secession of the northern part of Yuma County. *It's Time to Draw the Line!* they thundered, playing on themes of grievances about the delayed build of a fire station and having to pay for care for migrant farmworkers at the county hospital.

A twenty-nine-year-old attorney named Don Moon was one of those well-tailored interlopers who drove out to the line of boating resorts and honky-tonks along the cheesy highway promenade called the Parker Strip. This was a true Redneck Riviera in the 1980s, with wet T-shirt contests at 3 p.m. each day at the waterfront Sundance Saloon. Deputy sheriffs wrote hundreds of DUI tickets in the winter months. As a popular local saying had it, "come on vacation, leave on probation." Moon set out, as he put it later, to "register every California transplant drunk in every bar along the Colorado River. They never voted before, and they'll probably never vote again."

Moon understood the tiny local power structure. He had grown up in Parker, the son of a federal game ranger, and he spent his weekend nights with the rest of the secessionists in a big Winnebago owned by Mayor Wally Davis. They rode out to desert hamlets to ply the locals with libations from a well-stocked bar, making a political raid on a region the size of Connecticut with just 5,323 registered voters—marbles rattling around an enormous box. "They were no doubt doing it for their own economic benefit," mused local businessman Jim Downing, "because why else does anyone do anything?"

The measure passed by just thirty-two votes. Rumors circulated of typewriter correction fluid applied to some of the ballots, but the whispers of fraud in the whisker-thin contest didn't get in the way of the need to form a baby government on the fly. They named it La Paz after a mining settlement on the river where Barry Goldwater's grandfather had once operated a general store. It had once been the primary port for goods shipped up the Colorado River; it had long since gone to ruins.

Moon took over as county attorney, just a decade removed from his graduation from the local high school. A hamburger stand was converted into arm of the Arizona Superior Court; at one point a judge had to tell a carpenter to quit sawing boards so he could sentence a defendant to prison for second-degree murder. The instant county was declared open on January 1, 1983, a few days after Governor Bruce Babbitt said at a ceremony: "You are sitting astride some of the most important and dynamic future-oriented real estate and beachfront in the Southwest." Within months, the county was in serious financial trouble. The legislature had to raise sales taxes to keep it from immediate bankruptcy.

But more cash was on the way. Paranoid cities were soon buying up big parcels of La Paz County desert. The Groundwater Management Act required developers in urban areas to prove a hundred-year supply of water for any new housing. The centurial measurement was beyond capacity for Phoenix, Mesa, and Scottsdale, which had yet to receive CAP water. So just as clandestine agents from Los Angeles had gone out to the Owens Valley to buy up farmland for the water rights in 1905, Arizona's cities sought to grab "water ranches" in weakly governed La Paz County, where the big agricultural interests in Yuma no longer had a voice.

Scottsdale bought a gorgeous spread called Planet Ranch in the watershed of the Bill Williams River; Mesa acquired a bunch of cotton farms not far from Nancy Caywood's place; and Tucson bought up so much land in Avra Valley that it had to take some out of production. Tumbleweeds grew on the derelict land and dust storms kicked up where cotton used to grow. The Phoenix financier Charles Keating acquired property near a jumble of trailers called Vicksburg, with the idea of transferring the underground water via the CAP main canal. Moving water this way is a bit like sending natural gas through a pipeline, a hydrological maneuver known as wheeling.

No speculation about water politics appeared in the press during the run-up to secession. Babbitt told me he could recall no discussions along those lines. Don Moon had a reputation as a private man, but he surprised me with an invitation to come meet on the porch of his retirement house in Prescott. He puffed a cigar and denied La Paz County had ever been set up as a water bank.

"That's a bunch of bullshit," he told me. "It's not like we all got together in a secret room and said, 'hey, we could become water czars.'"

But he did, in fact, go into the water business after resigning as county attorney, partnering with superlobbyist Ron Ober in a firm called AgriCom Management to buy up lots in a bleak-looking basin called Ranegras Plain. The Groundwater Management Act didn't apply out in the countryside; they could pump it all down to dust if they liked.

Legalized dehydrations had happened in other parts of Arizona. Some of the big cotton operations near Nancy Caywood's farm had taken so much groundwater that the town of Eloy dropped seven feet in elevation in the space of two decades and opened fissures in the earth—some of them large enough to swallow a car. A group called Citizens for Water Fairness pressured the legislature to limit interbasin transfers, which they eventually did, even as Moon complained of "widows and orphans" being trotted out to sway public opinion. AgriCom went bankrupt. Arizona's cities never got a drop from La Paz County.

"Water is a visceral subject," lamented Moon. "It's hard to get people to be rational about it."

Then the situation got even weirder. Phoenix sold its 12,900 acres to the International Farming Corporation of North Carolina, which leased part of it to Al Dahra of the United Arab Emirates. They grow tens of thousands of tons of hay, compress it for packing in plastic wrapping, load it onto rails for transportation to the Port of Long Beach and then ship it halfway around the world on box boats to be fed to cows on the Arabian Peninsula.

A similar alfalfa operation is underway at Fondomonte Farms, which is really owned by the Saudi Arabian company Al Almari, which tried and failed to grow the livestock feed in its own country during a food independence program. The next best place to do that, it turns out, is Arizona. This is a mass exportation of the state's water resources to the Middle East in the form of grass—a version of laundering that happens to be completely legal and unregulated.

That's not the only problem. Ranchers nearby have complained the well levels around the Arabian properties have sunk precipitously. Aquifers that used to be tapped at three hundred feet have sunk to seven hundred feet. The city of Salome had to cut off water to its high school football field, which turned into a patchwork of dirt and dead grass. Some residents have barely enough pressure to take a shower. "They've sucked us dry," a rancher named Brad Mead told me. Some of the wells on his property in Vicksburg are now unusable. "We used to grow everything around here, onions, melons, peppers," said Maria Burris in the nearby hamlet of Wenden. "Now it's just hay, hay, hay everywhere."

Other water-rich places in Arizona have seen this type of speculation in the new global marketplace for laundered water. Peacock Nuts grows pistachios—a high-moisture crop—on more than 125,000 trees outside Kingman. Thirsty vineyards around Willcox require pumps that go nearly a half mile deep, which have bled residential wells dry and forced people to haul water in buckets to their trailers. Corporate interests can pump and spray as much groundwater as they like, with no limits, even though they take it away at a rate four times faster than what the ground can recharge. It as if these megafarms occupy a small lily pad on top of a pond—with the power to drink up the entire pond. Private investors took notice of the loophole, and New York hedge funds have made investments in Arizona land in anticipation of upcoming water shortages.

The underground drought became alarming enough for conservative state representative Regina Cobb to swallow her misgivings about government interference in the market and push bills that would have set up "irrigation non-expansion areas" in parts of rural Arizona. But she couldn't get a hearing in the 2021 session. "Whoever has the longest straw and the biggest well is going to get that water," she told me. "As I've seen things in the past, we don't want anything to be regulated until people from elsewhere take advantage—Saudi interests or hedge funds. That's when these conservative residents start getting their hair up. They could kill La Paz County."

She faced a formidable—and unexpected—opponent in her crusade: the Arizona Farm Bureau, whose chief executive officer wrote an op-ed in the *Republic* that tried to paint the foreign water lords as though they had arrived in a covered wagon with a horse-drawn plow and a team of mules in a heroic mission of altruism. "It was the farmers who pledged their land as collateral to make the Salt River Project a reality," wrote Phillip Bashaw. "It was farmers who developed the infrastructure in Pinal County that has made the population growth in those communities possible over the years. And it was agriculture that put its allocation of Colorado River water to use when we feared it would be taken by other water-thirsty states."

How much groundwater remains is a mystery. Studies are few and surrounded with controversy. There are some hydrologists with a poetic streak who talk about aquifers with a quality near awe, like a Beethoven sonata, for instance, or a *La Pietà* sculpture, a sponge of life from a prehistoric time. But water is a hard resource with mathematical limits. What Mark Twain is supposed to have said about land—"they ain't making any more of it"—is also true of water: there is an equal amount of it on and under the planet now as there was since the earth was formed four billion years ago. Water can only be moved, not destroyed. At some point, the wells of La Paz County will turn to mud, and then dust, if not allowed to recharge. The gifts of the ice age won't last.

Even since its questionable founding, La Paz County has struggled economically, with an anemic growth rate far out of sync with the rest of the state. Unemployment is high; wages are low; most of the groundwater leaves the nation in the form of grass to be eaten by Arabian dairy cows. Though he retired long ago and spends half the year at a villa in Tuscany, Don Moon told me he'd talked to officials in Mohave County to consider a possible merger four decades after La Paz's split-off. That would make him the obstetrician and then the potential mortician of America's most awkward county.

The public isn't allowed on the Fondomonte Farms property to see the transoceanic hay-growing operation, but I was able to talk to a representative of the company on a background basis.

"Agriculture is global," this person said. "Eat a banana and it likely came from Ecuador. Everybody is stealing everyone's water and taking it somewhere else, right? That's just how it is in the West."

—

The state's three major rivers—the Colorado, the Salt, and the Gila—are all dead before they hit their natural ends, diverted and sucked away, yielding only pebbles and sand in their last miles.

The city of Tempe celebrates the corpse of the Salt River with an artificial lake stoppered at both ends with rubber curtains. Glassy office towers and loft apartments cast a romantic smear of lights on the dark rectangle at night. The Colorado's tumble through the Grand Canyon is an evergreen tourist draw that sees five million visitors a year. The least known of these, the Gila, begins as snowmelt on the slopes of New Mexico's Black Mountains and carves a route through a gorgeous high-walled strait called the Gila Box on the way to its cottony doom at Florence.

The Spanish didn't think much of this river when they first saw it wild in the 1540s, calling it reedy and irregular, and not bothering to name it for a saint. They marked it as Xila—corrupted from the Apache word for "mountain." Boats could occasionally make it upriver as far as the junction with the Salt, fifteen miles west of Phoenix, but the Gila's transportation potential could be found mainly on its banks: a highway stomped through groves of mesquite and willow that could be used as a military or settlement road. Travelers thought it miserable. "One day march on the river is so much like unto another that one description will do for all that is to say," wrote John S. Griffin in 1848, "sand, dust & black stone, so blistered from the effects of heat that they look like they hardly got cool—no grass, nothing but weeds & cactus."

Dreams flourished along this unlikely corridor. Arizona's first Anglo boomtown sprouted up near its junction with the Colorado, a wild place called Gila City that had billiard tables, card games, whiskey, and lots of petty crime. Prospectors had found chips of gold in the river bluffs, and rumors of more drew in a wave of settlement. One of those strivers was Michel "Big Mike" Goldwater, a tailor from Poland who up bought a whole store's worth of goods on credit in Los Angeles, bumped his way toward the outpost, and made a tidy profit.

When the easy placer deposits were gone, the Gila City miners turned their attention to some lower-grade claims about a mile away from the river. But dry-washing this ore was not an option—the muckers needed river water that only a steam pump could deliver. They formed a company and ordered just such a machine to be taken to Yuma by schooner. But the *Arno* hit a sandbar in the Colorado River Delta and sank, her cargo a total loss. Big Mike drifted to the new mining camp of La Paz and eventually to the territorial capital of Prescott, where he founded a regional empire of department stores. Another busted-out resident, Jack Swilling, moved on to the site of the vanished Hohokam settlements on the Salt River and started digging out the old canals for what he hoped would become a Venice of the Southwest. The ungovernable river overflowed its banks in 1862, wiping out most of Gila City. Scavengers had it practically scraped bare by the time J. Ross Browne camped there the following year and found only ruins. Today the site lies partly under the Wellton-Mohawk irrigation canal.

Another vanished folly on the Gila: the settlement of Arizola, not far from the present-day I-10 bridge, where the "Baron of Arizona," a sharpie named James Addison Reavis, set up shop in the 1870s as a potentate after he presented land grant documents from Old Spain that seemed to give him title to millions of acres south of the river. A territorial court deemed them genuine, and Reavis made a fortune by shaking down homesteaders and mine owners for quitclaim deeds before an editor for the *Florence Enterprise* discovered a watermark from a Wisconsin paper mill on the supposed 1748 grant from King Charles III, which was also rendered in schoolboy Spanish. Reavis spent two years in federal prison for the stunt—not the first nor the last figure to run an Arizona land swindle.

Mormon settlers filtered down from Utah the following decade, following their prophet Brigham Young's command to "make the desert blossom as a rose," and set up a chain of irrigated settlements. Contraptions made of wooden boards, one for each family, sluiced away at the river as it emerged from Gila Box, a foretaste of what was to come. By that day in 1922 when most of the town of Casa Grande took the day off for a picnic at their new diversion dam, federal officials were calling it Hayden-Ashurst in tribute of the two U.S. senators from Arizona who had secured the funding.

The dam did its job well; within two years, it and the Coolidge Dam had erased the western end of the Gila River. For those fields outside the irrigation district—especially on the nearby reservations—dehydration and soil exhaustion soon left the earth spent and dead, crusted with salts, crisp as a burned cracker.

"It took a long time for that dam to fill up and when it did, the water no longer came down the Gila," wrote a Native famer named George Webb in 1959. "The Pimas were left without any water at all to irrigate their farms or water their stock or even to drink. They dug wells. The wells dried up. The stock began to die. The sun burned up the farms. Where everything used to be green, there were acres of desert, miles of dust, and the Pima Indians were suddenly desperately poor." Trees turned to "white bones." Red-winged blackbirds flew off, never to return. Weeds grew on murdered furrows.

A team of German prisoners from World War II staged a breakout from Camp Papago Park on the eastern side of Phoenix on the night of December 23, 1944. Armed with a makeshift kayak and a filched highway map of Arizona that showed the blue line of the Gila, they made their way down to its shores only to find a bed of sand. "I can laugh about it now but at the time it was very disheartening," one of the escapees told a historian. Another complained that Americans shouldn't be putting rivers that didn't exist onto their roadmaps.

"Some mapmakers acknowledge this truth by marking the lower Gila with dot-and-dash blue lines, cartographic code for the dead," wrote Gregory McNamee in his book *Gila: The Life and Death of an American River*, "but most atlases continue the tragic fiction that great waters still lace the intermountain West, awaiting millions of new conquistadores."

I went to go see the Hayden-Ashurst Diversion Dam on the same broiling day in July when I had visited Nancy Caywood's dying farm. It lies seven miles east of Florence, a former cotton boomtown with a handsome 1891 brick courthouse in the Second Empire style. Pinal County ran out of money before it was finished and had to forgo a working clock in the belfry. They instead mounted a painted simulacrum with the hands perpetually frozen at 11:44. Florence's main income now comes from the wages paid by eleven public and private prison facilities ringing the town, including a major lockup for undocumented migrants who sought jobs picking crops.

As the igneous foothill lumps of the Pinal Mountains grew more pronounced east of Florence, the Gila Valley grew more indented; saguaros poked up from the slopes. Then I came to a low fence barring the road and had to stop the car. *No Trespassing*, said the sign. Fortifications like this were thrown up around federal dam facilities after 9/11, even if there was nothing of military value about most of them. It would take a stupid terrorist indeed to attack a wall on a dead river. My map indicated it was about two miles from this spot.

I decided to chance an illegal walk along the levee. Sun poured down on the Gila Valley, a dry, hot day. After twenty minutes or so of walking, I hit a more serious barrier: a fence with barbed wire and more dire warnings against interlopers. I figured they meant business this time, accepted defeat, and turned around. After five minutes, I saw a white truck coming toward me on the levee, billowing dust, traveling at a purposeful government speed.

I braced myself for an official scolding and perhaps a court summons, but the guy behind the wheel barely slowed as he passed me on his way to the second fence. The plates on the truck were federal—he was clearly with the U.S. Bureau of Reclamation but didn't seem to care about my presence. I trotted over to the truck as he was unlocking the second fence. Could I see the dam, I asked, blabbering something about Arizona history.

He was a middle-aged Pima guy with a ponytail, here on an inspection mission. Sure, he shrugged, gesturing to the bed of the pickup. I climbed on top of a spare tire and rode the last mile in the open air as some Diet Coke empties rolled around on the floor.

We rounded a bend and there it was: a modest thirty-foot wall shaped like an L with nine rusted metal gates. The balustrade had been painted bone white. A retaining wall made of river stones on the south bank marked the spot of a long-gone dam tender's house. This is also where—ninety-nine years ago—barbecue grills smoked, bands had played, and the president had sent a telegram from the White House to announce a bountiful future in central Arizona.

There was nothing to be seen of the Gila River upstream or down; the diversion dam had all the purpose of an Egyptian pyramid tomb. The district official leaned over the railing to take pictures of the empty containment basin for his flow report. He told me the situation was almost as bleak at Coolidge Dam, where fish were suffocating in deoxygenated puddles.

I remarked on the lack of water, and he only shook his head. "We can always hope for rain," he said, looking at the sky.

THE TRAIL PARALLELED THE GILA RIVER through a valley almost tight enough to be a canyon, and I walked along its banks as the sun turned the nearby mountains pink fading to purple, then stopped to build a campfire that flickered against a sandstone wall perhaps two hundred million years old.

The next day brought me eight miles, over a railroad trestle and up to a Pinal County maintenance yard where a kind soul had set up a ratty old patio chair next to a public water spigot, underneath sunlight filtered through the toothpick branches of a palo verde. To me this spot looked like a cabana on the beach in Saint Croix. I hydrated gloriously for the next half hour before hitching a ride into the town of Kearny, one of the state's handful of unambiguous company towns—designed, built, and managed by the mighty Kennecott Corporation as a bedroom community for its copper-mining army.

I paused to look at a rock monument near the railroad tracks that commemorates the army of General Stephen Watts Kearny that passed by this spot in the fall of 1846 to go fight in the Mexican-American War, a forgettable non-incident flagged by a Phoenix real estate lawyer more than a century later as a romantic name for what the company called their "New West" settlement. The main street looks like a strip mall gone to seed under chipped white paint.

But I liked this place. There's an IGA grocery store run by Norm Warren, who started here as a sixteen-year-old stockboy and later bought the place. There's the General Kearny Inn arranged around a weedy courtyard like a midcentury Howard Johnson's. A pizza parlor, a liquor store, curved residential streets spreading out like a Chinese fan, a model of one of the steam locomotives that used to pull the ore on the Copper Belt Railroad toward the smelter. The natural frame of the Dripping Springs and Tortilla Mountains makes the valley feel protected and secure, even if the fortunes here are tied to the global price of copper and the labor whims of the mine owner, now a foreign conglomerate called Grupo Mexico.

The trail out of town passes over a high point in the Tortillas called Big Hill, which affords a view of the astounding gash of the Ray Mine, still pouring out a red flood of copper as steadily as it had since the administration of Rutherford B. Hayes. And to the west lay a set of bald bumps as stark as the Judean Hills and beyond it, a scrubby plain crisscrossed by a few unused Jeep trails.

Here's land too distant from the Gila River to farm cotton and too high above the groundwater to do much of anything useful: the Arizona nobody wanted. Once I made it down from the Tortillas, the path flattened out into an unattractive hardpan basin flecked with ocotillo and creosote that makes the walking go easy, one of the real moments of tranquility on the journey.

This was early ranch country but since abandoned: no house ruins, few fences, almost no signs of human intervention at all except for a marching line of electrical pylons on the horizon, zinging megawatts from the APS Saguaro gas-fired power plant at Red Rock some twenty miles away. They look like giant Hopi Kachina dolls with stubby arms raised to the sky, holding wrapped cables fifty feet above the desert floor. And when I found a sandy spot in a wash to sleep in as the sun went down, the horizons glowed in multiple directions, the lamps of central Arizona cities ablaze: Casa Grande, Winkelman, Phoenix, Marana, the northeast edge of Tucson.

A particularly strong luminosity to the northeast represented the unseen poles loaded with LEDs at the Ray Mine, bathing the pit in light so the ore loaders can run around the clock and feed copper into the markets to make electrical wiring. I almost expected to hear the crackle of the grid, but all was quiet. This unwanted and seldom visited portion of the state, pancake-flat and featureless, is ringed by soundless fire.

A rougher patch to the south called the Black Hills didn't have much to mine in the early twentieth century; small patches of gold and silver hid within the mafic lavas and rhyolite. Those patches played out years ago, and the lonely country is crisscrossed with faded wagon roads and arroyos cut channels full of rounded stones and the memoires of ten thousand seasonal floods from the alluvial fan of the Galiuro Mountains. One of these sandy riverbeds that I cross, Camp Grant Wash, traces to a canyon twenty miles away where one of the most shameful episodes of the nineteenth-century Southwest unfolded in the early morning hours of April 30, 1871.

A gang of Anglo and Hispanic vigilantes from Tucson—some of the most prominent men in town—crept in with a band of Tohono O'odham allies and within a half hour shot, clubbed, and mutilated more than a hundred Apaches under the protection of the U.S. Army. The merchant grandees of Tucson, led by Jesus Maria Elias, had genocide on their minds: they viewed the Natives and their raiding culture as threats to progress and had vowed at an earlier meeting to "eat up blood raw every Apache in the land."

President Ulysses S. Grant demanded the killers be brought to justice, but the conspirators were acquitted in pro forma trials and resumed their commercial activities, mostly in freighting and dry goods. The Camp Grant massacre marked another defeat, psychological and otherwise, for the various bands of Apaches herded to reservations after Geronimo's surrender. A few defiant stragglers hid out in the Sierra Madre Occidental range in Mexico and emerged to steal horses and raise hell as late as 1924.

The word "wash" in relation to Camp Grant seems appropriate enough. Memories of the slaughter were wiped from Tucson's historical memory just as surely as rocks swept down the channel. Few here today have any clue it happened. I went to high school just forty miles down the road and was never told about it. The collective amnesia had been a deliberate act: the elite ring of conspirators went on to found the Society of Arizona Pioneers that created a sanitized account of just another conflict during the Apache roundup—regrettable but necessary. This mutual aid group morphed into the Arizona Historical Society, the official guardian of the letters and the documents that promulgated the first draft of history: noble settlers, dashing cavalrymen, stoic ranch wives, savage Indians, a "tamed" West.

"Behold now the happy results immediately following that episode," wrote William Oury, one of the leaders of the massacre, in an apologia published in an 1885 edition of the *Florence Enterprise*. "The farmers of the San Pedro returned with their wives and babes to gather their abandoned crops. On the Sonoita, Santa Cruz and all other settlements in southern Arizona, new life springs up, confidences restored and industry bounds forward with an impetus that has known no check in the fourteen years that have elapsed since that occurrence."

The tools of history themselves were deployed in a type of violence against the reality of the Camp Grant. And as Arizona matured into an era of railroads, telegraphs, and highways, a layer of forgetful asphalt accumulated over the blood. No marker commemorates the spot.

The trail winds out of the dead mining country and skirts the town of Oracle by way of a former territorial post office called American Flag. And once it passes a ranch once owned by the showman Buffalo Bill Cody, who hoped to find gold there, it begins a relentless ten-mile ascent up the lengthy eastern ridge of Samaniego Canyon toward the summit of the mountain that captivated a generation of Tucson's leadership that came fifty years after the Camp Grant murders.

They also wanted to bend history to their desires, and they also had a plentiful supply of asphalt.

WINDY POINT

Take the Catalina Highway up from the desert floor of Tucson and feel the magic: a serpentine ascent around 206 road curves unveiling delicious vistas of stone and sky in nine distinct zones of southwestern flora and fauna until you terminate after twenty-five resplendent miles at the log cabin village of Summerhaven, a mini Saint Moritz for the middle class, serving the nation's southernmost ski resort.

Going up this two-lane blacktop seems close to flying in spots, especially in the earlier miles, when glorious pictures unfold in front of the windshield like a motion picture, and the bulges in the mountain part like a curtain to display the head-spinning lattice of the Tucson metropolitan sprawl. A road to the snowy pines so close to a desert city: it all seems improbable.

In fact, it was. The Catalina Highway, statistically the most dangerous road in Arizona, is there because of a confluence of factors. An enigmatic Republican operative who made a retirement project out of a Tucson newspaper in the 1920s. His friendship with an unpopular U.S. president. The desire of the business class to make Tucson a "four-season town." A national mania for blazing roads to the tops of mountains. And a willingness to force prisoners to do the hard labor for this road to Mount Lemmon, a granite hump the Tohono O'odham had called Babad Do'ag, or Frog Mountain.

The new name came from the wife of John Gill Lemmon, a botanist who had fought in the Civil War and been imprisoned in horrific conditions in a Confederate prison camp at Andersonville, Georgia. The trauma left him "nervous and excitable," though he found tranquility in looking for new plants, falsely calling himself a professor. He married a bookseller named Sara Plummer and took her on a honeymoon trip to Tucson via the brand-new Southern Pacific Railroad in November 1881 so that he could, in his words, "make a grand botanical raid into Arizona and try to touch the heart of Santa Catalina."

The Lemmons convinced a rancher named Emerson Oliver Stratton to take them up the northern slope to the summit via horseback, where, he recalled in his memoirs, "I chopped the bark off a great pine tree and we all carved our names." Stratton fancifully named the peak for Sara Lemmon, and the Pima County surveyor, George Roskruge, solidified the appellation when he put it on the county's official map in 1893, consigning Babad Do'ag to the memory heap. Such was the randomness of a western place-name—a blend of fancifulness, ego, colonialism, and the fickle whims of popular acceptance.

The range's local esteem got a boost from romantic fiction. Harold Bell Wright, a minister turned best-selling author who lived in a pueblo-style house off the east end of Speedway, crafted a 1923 buried-treasure mystery called *The Mine with the Iron Door*, which contained this passage in its opening:

> But of all the peaks and ranges that keep their sentinel posts around this old pueblo there are none so bold in the outlines of their granite heights and rugged canons, so exquisitely beautiful in their soft colors of red and blue and purple, or so luring in the call of their remote and hidden fastness, as the Santa Catalinas. Every morning there they are—looking down on our little city in the desert with a brooding Godlike tolerance—remote yet very near.

Tucson's boosters sought to correct that remoteness. They wanted to make Mount Lemmon not a distant watchtower but an actual extension of town. The *Citizen* quoted a Roman Catholic bishop in favor of the road under the grim headline: "Tucson Doomed to Be 8 Month Town unless Mountain Road Built." The editors of the *Star*, more fanciful on the subject, opined on July 20, 1927, that the automobile would likely be obsolete within two decades, so the government should just plow an airstrip into the mountaintop so vacationers could fly in.

One unique personality then put his clout behind the project: Frank Hitchcock, the former postmaster general and a powerful fixer in the Republican Party who had bought the *Tucson Daily Citizen*.

Liberals viewed his influence with conspiratorial awe. "He is inscrutable, imperturbable, impenetrable and notably closed-mouthed," wrote Edward G. Lowry of the *New Republic* in 1920. "He offers no more inviting avenue of approach for scrutiny and communication than a well-made billiard ball." Hitchcock never seemed to sweat, was always impeccably dressed, and looked like he had stepped out of a magazine advertisement for shirt collars. *Real America* magazine was even more colorful, calling him a "steely, blue eyed maharajah" and a "tall white haired sage" who did lobbying work for DuPont Chemical on the side. "He dresses immaculately, walks like a West Point cadet, talks like a British lord," wrote correspondent George Max. He insisted people call him "General," even though his title was civilian and not military.

Hitchcock kept a diary in the form of loose-leafed pages covered in neat script describing his activities of the day. These piles of paper, stuffed into business-sized envelopes, came embossed with the logos of the various hotels in which he stayed and the institutions with which he dealt. His stationery paints a picture of a man in constant oscillation about the exclusive zones of the nation: the Willard Hotel in Washington, D.C., the Pioneer Hotel in Tucson, the U.S. Senate, the Old Pueblo Club in Tucson, the Multnomah Hotel in Portland, Oregon. Hitchcock's entry for June 8, 1930, is typical: "S.F.—plane landed at Bakersfield en route to oil motors and reached L.A. at 8 p.m., 9 p.m., reached St. Francis Hotel (room 9323), 9:30 p.m., Mr. Fred Thompson called and remained until 1 a.m. discussing settlement with Spoor Thompson Co."

Hitchcock instituted a pro-business editorial policy at the *Citizen*, eliminating any news of labor union successes. Coverage of airplane crashes was also discouraged because Hitchcock was an aviation enthusiast and did not want to create a negative association around air travel in the mind of the public. He also became known as a skinflint, paying his reporters and copyeditors less than fifteen dollars a week. "You ought to be glad you have a job," he told them. "I am keeping you out of the breadline. The only reason I am running this newspaper is because I hate to see you starve."

After he seized on the Mount Lemmon highway idea, he talked with Sanford Bates, the director of the Bureau of Prisons, about compelling prisoners to do the blasting and the grading. On February 27, 1933, Hitchcock sent the governor of Arizona a telegram from Washington, D.C., to announce successful funding in his usual laconic terms. "Instructions have been already issued for prompt completion of preliminary arrangement incidental to construction of proposed Catalina Highway." His journal for that same day is typically brief, and indicates he met with his friend President Herbert Hoover, though he offers no details on what was discussed. "1 p.m., lunch with Osborne Wood at the club, 2:30, with Mr. MacDonald re Catalina Highway, 5:30, went to the White House to call on the Pres."

This was one of Herbert Hoover's last days in office at the end of his catastrophic term; Franklin D. Roosevelt was sworn in on March 4, 1933. It seems reasonable to conclude that Hitchcock knew that his influence would diminish once Roosevelt was inaugurated and felt an urgency to get his Tucson highway project approved by Hoover while a Republican president was still in office.

The use of prison inmates to build highways already had a dismal history, particularly in the American South. "When negro convicts are put upon the public roads in the free, pure air, I do not know of a more humane way of handling these unfortunate men who must be held in confinement," said Georgia Governor John Slaton in 1915. Sheriffs touted jail labor as a progressive version of ancient practices used by Romans and Egyptians. And now Arizona was about to host to its own experience with convict road-building, thanks to the potent combination of local boosterism, federal intervention, and manpower shortages.

The first laborers arrived at the Catalina Federal Honor Camp in June 1933, having been convicted on various offenses from the minor to the serious: immigration violations, bank robbery, and selling liquor to Native Americans, which was illegal at the time. Inmates dumped their garbage and leftover dinners over a rock ledge, where skunks and javelina feasted on the slop. Escape attempts began almost immediately: two Mexican immigrants tried to walk away on a Sunday afternoon, but guards tracked them down quickly. When three others tried it, guards turned dogs on them.

The men spent their days hand-drilling holes in granite reefs, blowing them apart with gunpowder, using sledgehammers to break down chunks to manageable sizes and wheelbarrows to haul the debris away. The broken rock was eventually loaded into mine cars on a railway that Hitchcock named the Catalina Short Line.

The first several miles of the highway crossed several canyons and smaller culverts, which presented an engineering problem: how to keep water from gushing over the road during the frequent summer monsoons? The solution came in the form of a series of masonry arch culverts, some with wingwalls on the discharge end to facilitate the anticipated wash of water, rocks, displaced plants, and other debris. The Works Progress Administration donated a Cat 60 tractor with a bulldozer, a few International dump trucks, an end loader, and some worn-out grease trucks that had been judged too unreliable to be used on the building of the Alaska Highway. One inmate who helped fix the Cat 60 painted the legend "Methuselah" on its side.

Frank Hitchcock died unexpectedly on August 5, 1935, at the Desert Sanatorium on Grant Road. Almost nobody had known he was sick. An initial report in the *New York Times* repeated a rumor that he had broken his ribs in an aviation accident that had been censored from the *Citizen*, but the *Phoenix Gazette* clarified that he died from pneumonia and "a general breakdown after an injury suffered while moving a heavy piece of furniture in his newspaper office." Governor Mouer ordered the flags at the state capitol to be flown at half-staff.

The following year, the *Star* called for the road to be named for the former owner of its rival paper, a request that was not honored for another twelve years. "When Frank Hitchcock originated the idea, Prohibition was in effect and the federal prisons were overflowing with convicted bootleggers," the paper editorialized. "Either the federal government had to build more prisons or find some other way of caring for their prisoners. What could be more simple and what could be better than to put these men to building roads!"

The inmates moved into a prison camp of two barracks, a kitchen, a dining hall, a heating plant, a laundry, a septic tank, an administration building, and several higher-quality granite cabins for the officers and guards. A local contractor, Ralph A. Wetmore, whose family had graded Tucson's Wetmore Road, found a water source after drilling through granite. Nine miles of road opened to the public the next year. "Dynamite—and lots of it—is building up the new Catalina highway up the southern slope of the Santa Catalina range," wrote J. Robert Burns of the *Star*, who had been invited up to watch a blast that pulverized four thousand cubic yards of granite. "Clouds of dust, mottled with colors ranging from ochre to white, reared up into the air, to drift away with the breeze," he observed.

About forty men of Japanese ancestry wound up shoveling asphalt in the Santa Catalinas after refusing to be transported to one of the internment camps or refusing induction into the military. Among them was a University of Washington student and practicing Quaker named Gordon Hirabayashi, who served two ninety-day sentences at the Catalina Federal Honor Camp, forming a special friendship with a group of Hopi Indians who had also refused to fight what they called "the white man's war" in Europe. They had been permitted to build a wooden ramada on a nearby hillside for religious reasons and invited Hirabayashi to their ceremonies. "Gave me a hair wash with soap weeds, all natural you know, and tea, they brewed some tea and gave it to me, and just treated me like a brother," he recalled. Hirabayashi's fellow prisoners at the Catalina camp described him as a low-key personality who spoke like a college professor.

After his release, the U.S. Supreme Court heard his case challenging his incarceration, *Hirabayashi v. United States*, and upheld the government's view that it was legal. But he would later recall the Catalina Highway project as "a fairly liberal camp"—better than being sent to Manzanar, Heart Mountain, or any of the other desolate internment centers. The guards generally did not abuse the inmates, and a few even expressed sympathy for their position. Noboru Taguma recalled a Latino guard telling him: "You know, I feel really sorry for you people, because you were chased out of California."

Ken Yoshida learned how to weave belts from the Hopi inmates, who taught him the skill on the condition he not reveal it to anyone else. His friend Susumu Yenokida had taken some metal shop classes in high school and was assigned to the blacksmith shop. "And I kind of enjoyed it," he recalled in 1999. "I did my own thing, whatever I could do, I did for the day, and I went home." Inmates warded off boredom by playing games of mah-jongg, as well as softball. They recalled an incident involving a skittish guard named Murphy who was doing a bed check one evening in a darkened barracks. One of the inmates suddenly yelled the Japanese military cry *ban-*

zai and the guard "took off like a bunny rabbit on TV," recalled an amused Harry Yoshikawa.

The front edge of the highway reached the top of the range in the fall of 1947, and approximately five hundred cars were soon making the trip every Sunday. Customers swamped the Mount Lemmon Realty Company with bids on cabin sites and forest lots. Forest Service officials, meanwhile, found an excellent site for a ski resort—the broad north slope of Mount Lemmon where winter snow lingered long after it had melted elsewhere. The crews began working in March 1950 on a steep road to access the site at approximately 8,500 feet above sea level, where trees were leveled for a parking area, a lodge, and a restaurant whose name contained a flourish: The Iron Door, after Harold Bell Wright's saccharine novel about the Catalinas.

The highway punched into high country that had been viewed before only by Tohono O'odham and Apaches and their ancestors, along with a few Anglo soldiers and prospectors. The *Star* wrote about its progress into this territory with overheated rhetoric, but a grain of truth: "It is a spectacle that inspires comparison between the days when those who did invade the deep canyons won every step by stout perseverance, and today, when a party of business men can leave their work, climb into shiny automobiles and go zipping along the mountainside with almost as much ease as buzzing along Speedway."

The dark side to this convenience remained unquiet. Project chief G. L. McLane was so satisfied with the work of Mexican border crossers on the pick-and-shovel crew that he recommended using them for other hard-labor projects without pay. In short: a constant source of slave labor. And on their crash course to the top of Mount Lemmon, Lane and the rest of the designers had paid little heed to the land's natural contours. "Boulders, trees, cactuses—and anything else that got in the way of the mountain road—were shoved aside with little thought of preserving the landscape," wrote Phil Hamilton of the *Citizen*.

All those curves—when combined with winter ice and the fecklessness of boozy picnickers—conspired to make the road the most dangerous thoroughfare in the state. Cars wrecked there at a rate ten times above average. In the view of Mary Ellen Barnes, who had watched its construction as a little girl, the road had "a lot more turns in it than there needed to be. It could have been shortened quite a bit, but they wanted to show off Tucson."

The road to the ski area was only one of a rosacea of secondary roads on which vacation cabins would stand: Willow Canyon, Marshall Gulch, Upper Sabino, Rose Canyon, Bear Wallow, and Loma Linda Extension. The Tucson Chamber of Commerce, meanwhile, built a memorial to the enigmatic operative who had conjured these riches. The General Frank H. Hitchcock Memorial featured a bronze plaque with Hitchcock's likeness mounted on a granite boulder at a panoramic pullout the builders had named Windy Point. Hitchcock's old newspaper, the *Citizen*, said his bust "looks out over the great valley of the Santa Cruz as lasting as time itself."

The valley may be timeless, but the city is not. From Windy Point, it is possible to contemplate the astonishing growth of what 1920s Tucson boosters had decided should be called the Old Pueblo, a nod to the romantic Spanish fantasy aesthetic then popular: the flamboyant architectural style that erected Moorish turrets on the El Conquistador resort, threw pink arcades around the new courthouse, and rammed exposed beams into the roofs of hundreds of new desert haciendas.

But the original village core of Tucson—with a genuine colonial Spanish character—hadn't always been so celebrated. In fact, most newcomers considered it ugly. Writer J. Ross Browne, on an 1854 trip across the region with mine promoter Charles Poston, wrote a withering passage about the general disorder he perceived:

A city of mud boxes, dingy and dilapidated, cracked and baked into a composite of dust and filth; littered about with broken corrals, sheds, bake-ovens, carcasses of dead animals, and broken pottery; barren of verdure, parched, naked, and grimly desolate in the glare of a southern sun.

How different, then, the profusion of lights and the spreading municipal quilt seen from Windy Point: the interlocking jumble of Circle Ks, Walmart Supercenters, Safeways, Casa Molina Mexican Restaurants, self-contained neighborhoods with atavistically meaningless names like Loma Verde and Old Spanish Trail Estates. The twentieth-century embrace of the white-bread Spanish Mission aesthetic, along with the effacing of the real barrio, was a prime example of the Arizona ethos. Reality must be defeated, and a more comforting vision set in its place.

I knew nothing about the quasi-slave labor or the dangerous road conditions when growing up. For me and my high school friends, the Catalina Highway was a route to summer camping and beer drinking up at Bear Wallow, and an easy way to get in a day of skiing without driving more than ninety minutes, even if Mount Lemmon Ski Valley—with its logo of a vertical lemon crusted with snow on top—offered only three good runs and a lot of tree stumps when the base was low, which it usually was.

The highway was beautiful and somewhat magical. "General *Bitch* Cock," said my friend Brian Lawver with contemptuous glee as we passed the sign for his memorial. Neither of us had a clue who he was. I assumed, dimly, that he was a Civil War general. In those days, the ruins of the labor camp went unmarked and neglected. The highway was just there, as if it had always been there.

But isn't this the case with so much that lies around us in Arizona? In a state where so much of the legacy has been the gift of now-anonymous armies of Mexican and Indigenous labor, we easily look past our status as guests of the most recent kind. A forgetfulness about the origins of the Catalina Highway descended almost as soon as the first ski lifts started operating. As Carl Sandburg wrote of European battlefields:

> *Two years, ten years, and passengers ask the conductor:*
> *What place is this?*
> *Where are we now?*
> *I am the grass.*
> *Let me work.*

The Japanese inmates called themselves "the Tucsonians" and vowed to stay in touch with each other, and they did until almost none of them were left. At one of the last gatherings in 2002, Ken Yoshida recalled that he had never experienced a winter storm before his sentence to the labor camp. He got his first look at snow when four inches of it lay on the dirt of what would become the Catalina Highway, some five thousand feet above sea level.

"It's beautiful up there," he said. "Isn't it beautiful up there?"

A GRANITE MAZE CALLED WILDERNESS OF Rocks near the top of the Santa Catalinas is a study of weathered granite. Bulbs of crumbling rock squat like starlings on a wire or hard-boiled eggs standing en pointe. Others hunch over the soil like Russian babushkas or elderly monks.

They had formed in the Cretaceous period when soft igneous rock withered underneath a hard rock cap that kept the figure from disappearing entirely. Years of winter frost cycles—the constant freezing and thawing of droplets in the cracks—worried and pulled the stone away from itself as the sculptures patiently carved themselves.

The curious pillars are called hoodoos, and they can be seen in certain other places around the mountain West, most famously in Bryce Canyon, Utah, and the Badlands of South Dakota. Their unusual name is a transformation story in itself—as wonderful a lesson in the flexibility of language as the hoodoos are a picture of malleable geology.

Folk etymology holds that hoodoo is a variation of Vodou, the Caribbean religious practice whose name from the Kwa languages of West Africa has been appropriated by U.S. pop culture to signify grotesque magic. This seems plausible enough, and some park rangers still spread this version around. But it isn't true.

The name is more probably derivative of the neighboring African language of Hausa, spoken in the Sahel Desert, in which the word *hu'du'ba* means "misfortune." Enslaved people who spoke Hausa brought the word to southern U.S. port cities like New Orleans and Mobile in the early nineteenth century where, in the linguistic stew of what had recently been New France, the multiracial working class started using "hoodoo" as slang to mean anything of malign origin. Some scholars think it was also a chance cognate of the Gaelic phrase *uath dubh*, meaning roughly the same thing and in common use by Irish immigrants to New Orleans who worked on the docks alongside free people of color and shared their curse words.

Those French creoles who set out from the Gulf Coast to strike it rich on beaver pelts had been familiar with the semi-humorous phrase that signified the type of exasperation they encountered on a daily basis. They likely used it in casual banter with some of their Native trading partners, especially the Lakota Sioux, who had been familiar with the sterile moonscape of the Badlands for centuries and invested its pillared forms with spiritual resonance.

Other words for these rocks contain their own poetry: *cheminées de fees*—"fairy chimneys"—was a descriptive term of French explorers. Settlers to Quebec in the seventeenth century also used *demoiselles* or "young ladies." Mormons old-timers sent by Brigham Young into the weird red-rock landscape of southern Utah called them "goblins." But as an evocative term in any language, *hoodoo* is nearly perfect with its internal rhyme and shades of the mystical. Anglo settlers across the West picked it up for their descriptions of the unlucky sentinels who watched over land that couldn't be farmed.

So from Hausa in Africa, into French (with a Gaelic twist) in colonial New Orleans, to pidgin English on the plains, into a Sioux borrow word, and into its final form as an English academic term comes the complicated but wonderful word *hoodoo* to describe the granite forms of the Wilderness of Rocks, shining here under the sun as they had for seventy-five million years.

I walked through it marveling at the variety of forms and the way that stone globes seem to be balanced precariously on slender stems. One could almost look for shapes in them as though they were clouds.

As it happened, this hidden garden on the southern slope of Mount Lemmon had a spectacular view of Tucson some 6,500 feet below, sprawling toward Mexico in a massive hashtag of streets cut through with the brown veins of arroyos—"like a palm stretched out for a fortuneteller to read," wrote Barbara Kingsolver of one character's first view of town, "with its mounds and hillocks, its life lines and heart lines of dry stream beds." I stopped for a water break in a sunny place and looked at my hometown through the viewfinder of a boulder and two pine trees. The city is itself a work in progress, like the hoodoos that overlook it, and its identity also a result of many international cultures in unlikely collision.

The Tohono O'odham had been farming the valley since at least the sixteenth century and possibly longer, using the *ak-chin* method of planting seeds at the mouth of a dry arroyo right before one of the desert's brief bursts of monsoon rains. This ingenious technique was one of the only reliable methods of capturing enough agricultural moisture to support a community. Soldiers and priests loyal to the king of Spain marched here and in 1776, built a garrison, central *plaza major*, straight streets, and "buildings all of one type for the sake of the beauty of the town," prescribed by the Law of the Indies.

When Anglo Americans began to take over government, they brought wider streets, more parks, and differentiated homes in the way of English manors: the ideal brought to colonial America by William Penn in 1683. The twentieth-century paradigm of automobiles, freeways, and low-interest home loans blasted this prodigious Philadelphia vision for miles in every direction, and it still creeps outward.

But Tucson remains wrapped around the vanished Tohono O'odham farming settlements and the hard cap of a Spanish colonial core, a district called Barrio Nuevo hit hard by "slum clearance" mistakes of the last century and now overrun with homebuyers looking for cheaper Santa Fe–style charm that can be rehabbed. Such is the frost-and-thaw cycle of the Tucson urban hoodoo—an ice-wedging process unfolding every day.

I descended from the Wilderness of Rocks down to Romero Pass and then into West Canyon, a lengthy slog that drops from the subalpine forest of pines down into the canyon woodland zone of oak trees, bluegrass, and sideoats that decorates the topmost level of Sabino Canyon. Another campsite, another sunrise, and I walked past the dead pool of the abandoned Sycamore Reservoir and the foundations of the aqueduct that had sucked water over to the camp that housed the inmates who built the Catalina Highway. And then up a tall ridge and to the ruins of the camp itself, consisting of stark concrete foundations and a stone staircase. The site is now called the Gordon Hirabayashi Campground, after its most famous inmate.

I paused for a water break and settled in for the trudge through a working cattle ranch north of Redington Pass, where livestock have grazed for centuries, and not far from where a spread operated by the Redfield brothers was raided by a posse led by Wyatt Earp in search of stagecoach robbers in 1881. Then as now, the Rincon Mountains veer up from a seismic rift at the bottom of a wash and watch like an indifferent Greek god over the valley.

The Rincons are another of the sky island ranges of the Southwest that host a multiplicity of plant and wildlife zones at differing elevations, like a layered wedding cake. Geographers have counted sixty-five of them on both sides of the U.S.-Mexico border, solitary forms on the cordillera like islands in an open sea. Another name is *huérfano*, "orphan." As you climb them, you ascend through distinct expressions of western aridity, greener with every thousand feet. The spot where I made camp for the night was typical of the high Sonoran Desert with its spawn of pencil cholla and leafless palo verde.

The next day's climb sailed nearly five thousand feet through a layer of mixed hardwood forest of juniper and pinon and into a ponderosa zone where a gurgle of water called Italian Trap—in memory of a nineteenth-century immigrant goatherder—was so clear that I didn't bother to filter it. From here a brief hike took me over the hump of Mica Mountain, which has the arboreal character of a Canadian forest and the flatness of a runway. I was now at the highest point of the range, but it offered a view of little other than more trees and a concrete platform for a now-vanished fire tower.

Not for nothing are the Rincon Mountains among the least known of the ranges that form the walls of the Tucson valley. Their name, spiritlessly enough, is Spanish for "inside corner." They can be seen from most everywhere in town, but they rarely catch the eye; they elude visual apprehension. Perhaps the only times they are ever noticed by Tucsonans is as a frame for dramatic rises of a full moon, or during a westbound flight into the airport, a path that goes directly over the knob of Rincon Peak (elev. 8,664 feet) at an alarming clearance that seems near enough to scratch the underside of the fuselage. This is as close as most locals will ever get.

"Even people who have lived next door to them for years know nothing more of these mountains than their name," wrote botanist Janice Bowers. "On a map or from the air, the Rincon Mountains are shaped like an L, but from the city, the three major ridges line up on the horizon like goods in a bakery display case, two lumpy loaves of French bread and a brioche, prosaic as toast, unromantic as an electric oven."

Few ever make it up to the summit; it's just too difficult. An *Arizona Daily Star* reporter named Levi Manning bushwhacked his way up here in 1905 and, with the help of his family and a team of mules, built a six-room stone cabin as a summer retreat, complete with his wife's piano. But he had to give it up when the U.S. Forest Service claimed the mountain. Manning only shrugged and went on to build Tucson's trolley system.

A more serious threat emerged in 1933, when General Frank H. Hitchcock tried to plow an asphalt road up here just as he had conquered Mount Lemmon. A map of the never-built highway was later found in the files of the superintendent of nearby Saguaro National Monument. But bureaucratic inertia rendered the verdict: the Rincons would remain obscure. There are those who would not have it any other way.

My long descent into Saguaro National Park—another federal creation spurred by General Hitchcock—was fired into brilliance by lightning in a twilight monsoon that mingled and danced with the evening ocher of the sunset. The rain came shortly thereafter and fell on the roof of my tent, the smell of releasing petrichor and creosote perfuming the night. And the scent remained into the late morning as I walked on flat country past the remnants of a wind-mill and mud-walled corral on the old X-9 Ranch.

The lumpy massif of the Rincons was off to the left, and in the clarity of the rain-fresh morning I saw that the chaotic field of boul-ders I'd navigated the previous evening was ordered in layers: a distinct band of striation visible only from far away. It was like one of those tricks of a drone camera in which a ground view widens into a vista of the entire landscape. You see how it all fits together, how a small element has a greater logic, a place in the design.

The stratification that resembles wavy lines on a Navajo blanket is the result of a geological process called tilted block faulting. The plates of the earth stretched apart and thrust folds of metamor-phic rock thousands of feet into the air, old sediments that had once been lying flat, a bit like a table turned on its side. The earth exposed its secret basement. This was the same dull range my eyes had been sliding over all my life; I had never noticed this before.

The trail spooled onward, and the painted wall of the Rincons receded. I slogged on past a ranch called La Posta Quemada (the burned station) and crested a rise to see a line of cars on Inter-state 10 about five miles away, traffic bound for Los Angeles and El Paso. Not far away was a long rural road called Old Spanish Trail that I used to drive at high speeds as a teenager full of inarticulate passions and a need to shout. Today a train whistle sighed over the low hills and after a few more hours through the prickly pear and creosote I passed under the Union Pacific tracks in Cienega Creek past birches turning tawny autumn colors. Right through here the Butterfield Overland Mail route delivered packages from Saint Louis to the Pacific.

And I came to the roadside parking lot anchored by a display: a tile mosaic of a dark-haired young man, barely out of his boyhood, with a pack on his back and a permanent smile on his face.

I lowered my own pack and read the legend once more.

Gabe (1981–2011) loved Tucson, its desert, its people and its unique
spirit. A Tucson native, he hiked and mountain biked throughout

the mountains and canyons that you see from here. Gabe was a dedicated public servant who died serving the community he loved. He brought people together, encouraged us to respect one another and appreciate the place we call home. Gabe lived a life of exuberance. You should, too. Enjoy this special area.

Gabe Zimmerman had been a friend of mine. I had worked alongside him on one of the most gratifying things I ever tried to do for Arizona. He stuck with it after I left. He was standing at the boss's side when a man in a hoodie walked up.

I wish to God this parking lot were not named for Gabe.

GABRIELLE, THEN AND NOW

The laugh: her eyes in a squint, head cocked in mocking recoil, mouth open. Her whole bearing telegraphed: *this is funny, this is too much, you're ridiculous, I like being with you.* Gabrielle's giggles lasted two seconds; they were warm as a campfire.

Brightness seemed to emanate from an inner hearth. Some lucky few are born that way, imbued with the biological magic of charisma. With the right amount of intelligence and ambition, they often find their way to public authority. Character is destiny, said Heraclitus. Gabrielle Giffords knew where she was going.

I met her near the beginning of her career, at a policy conference at the Grand Canyon, after she had first been elected to the state legislature. A delicate gold necklace sparkled under a starched white shirt. We walked around in the dark, the canyon yawning open beside us, telling stories to each other. She laughed and laughed.

We went out for about a month, in the way of fumbling young adults in a world of click-through relationships. But I was diffident and hurt her feelings with my emotional distance. I came to regret it. She forgave me for my stupidity. But much more interesting than that early foundation was the resulting friendship. We talked and emailed often after I moved away.

Then a question came—she was going to declare a run for U.S. Congress in an open seat in southern Arizona. Would I be able to help her in the campaign? I was living in New York City with two roommates, struggling to pay rent as a freelancer, cut off from the world of dependable wages. This offer sounded appealing, though. It felt like a call to public service of a sort I'd never experienced. What convinced me to move back to Arizona, I suppose, was the thought that if good-hearted and competent people like Gabrielle could be set next to the levers of power, we'd be a whole lot better off as a country. Somebody I knew well, and trusted, could join the roll call of Arizona federal representatives like Udall, Goldwater, McFarland, Greenway—historic figures I had only read about but never met. They were as austere as faces engraved on coins.

I moved to the funky town of Bisbee, encircled by rough hills, and organized volunteers for three months on a pro bono basis, not really knowing what I was doing. But those were the days before big Washington money and consultants got involved, and it felt like a bunch of kids building a treehouse.

I reported to Gabe Zimmerman in the Tucson office. He was a few years younger, and far more capable at retail politics. He talked about public service in the reverential way others talked about bands or video games. It seemed impossible a guy his age could be so earnest and free of detached irony; it was as though he'd stepped in from a wormhole in time from the civil rights movement. I watched him listen to bark-skinned progressives, nodding along where he could find comity, gently demurring when the campaign couldn't be pushed leftward. It was a swing district and Gabrielle was no starry-eyed radical.

We won. She went to Congress. But we ask too much magic of individual politicians. There's only so much they can do, especially as legislative backbenchers. True influence takes decades to build. And with repeating elections every two years, survival is never guaranteed.

I came back for both efforts, knocking on doors and writing little bullet-pointed speeches for her to deliver to small gatherings. Another volunteer and I muttered about the seeming futility of it all—the grind of money-driven democracy, the disappointments of compromise, the growing ugliness of the dialogue. But what else is a citizen supposed to do? Algerian French philosopher Albert Camus said your best hope was to find meaning in the struggle itself, hopeless as it may be, and not set up a desired outcome as a silver chalice. You make your rebellion against an absurd universe wherever you can.

She twice faced an opponent who said awful things about her; cradled a gun in his advertisements; and later become a right-wing commentator calling for the breakup of the United States to stop a "liberal utopian nightmare," describing for his audience the imagined thrill of carving off the skull of an enemy on the battlefield and carrying away the scalp "of somebody you hated and who hated you back."

That kind of apocalypse talk had been gathering in Arizona; the scent of oncoming Trumpism. Gabrielle got shouted down at town hall meetings. Talk radio savaged her; the internet was worse. A vandal broke out the windows in her office. National conservatives drew target marks on her district map. An unemployed former restaurant busboy from the west side of Tucson had been listening to the chatter and filtered it through his growing case of paranoid schizophrenia. He began to see her at the center of a conspiracy.

On the morning of January 8, 2011, he brought a Glock semiautomatic handgun to one of her meet-and-greets in front of a Safeway grocery store. Gabe died instantly, his formidable intelligence and kindness blown out like a candle. Gabrielle barely survived, left without ability to form words without struggle. Five others died; eighteen others were wounded. It was as if the worst parts of Arizona had risen up from the ground to eat them.

When I learned the pathetic biography of the shooter and met some of those who had known him, I recognized a piece of my own upbringing: the sad streets with no sidewalks or character, the air of vague suspicion, feeling drowned in all the pricey elbow room, the lack of human connection. All the good parts of American society had been pulled apart until they were out of sight from each other.

The story dominated the news for weeks. Those who never knew Gabrielle spent a lot of time talking about *tragedy*, a syrupy newscaster word that enraged me. It implied a set of circumstances that couldn't be helped, a regrettable outcome. But this atrocity was entirely preventable. The same social malignities she had been working against had exploded in her face that morning. The *whys* weren't a part of the story; instead it was all being mutated into an inspirational smoothie fit for *People* magazine. A collective decision had been made that this story was about heroes, not about causes.

That the country's latent violence could have been brought to her—of all people—and to Gabe, who was the best human being I ever met in the tawdry game of politics, one of the rare ones who got involved for all the right reasons. Five others dead, eighteen others injured. Why? Such a profane joke, absurd to the core, Camus's idea coming home to roost.

The day after I was allowed to hold Gabrielle's hand in the intensive care unit and saw life in her eyes, I resolved to write a book that tried to explain the winds at the back of the twenty-two-year-old who went to the Safeway to kill: the permissive gun laws that allowed an obviously dangerous person to obtain a gun and ammunition; the climate of fear whipped up by partisan media; the lack of concern for one's neighbors that let a paranoid schizophrenic fall into a private hell. Reporting was the only contribution I knew how to make; it felt like a mandate.

Her husband didn't care for this prospect. He was a navy pilot from top to bottom. My project fell outside the chain of command and he wanted to write his own book. She was still unable to form words at that point in mid-January and had barely opened her eyes, but he told me she was "disappointed in me." I would not be allowed to be around her, he said, or talk with anybody associated with her. The old campaign staff surrounding her had come to feel like a church. I would be excommunicated.

There was nothing to do but write the explanatory book as best I could, without cooperation, immersed in a fog of sadness. There is only so much to say about a moral outrage. It felt a bit like the hopeless quest in Thornton Wilder's novel *The Bridge of San Luis Rey*, the story of the monk Brother Juniper who conducts hundreds of interviews trying to understand why five people died in the collapse of a rope bridge. Why did God choose those people and not others? What sort of divine justice must have been at work? Was there any point to it at all? Brother Juniper is declared a heretic for even asking. No answers are forthcoming. Except one, revealed at the conclusion:

> Soon we shall die and all memory of those five will have left earth, and we ourselves shall be loved for a while and forgotten. But the love will have been enough; all those impulses of love return to the love that made them. Even memory is not necessary for love. There is a land of the living and a land of the dead and the bridge is love, the only survival, the only meaning.

Gabrielle appears on television every now and then, a representation of what was lost, as laconic as a Buddha, inscrutable and distant, a figure of reverence for those who never knew her. Her most magical gift—making hope seem possible through words—has been immutably changed.

I miss the laughter most of all.

She is a face on a coin.

M Y PARENTS HAD ARRANGED TO pick me up for a temporary break from the trail. I hugged them both; my mom fussed over my weight and I discovered when I got on a scale that I'd lost nearly thirty pounds. My frame now had the aspect of a walking twig.

They've lived in this same house since we moved here from Phoenix when I was an awkward pre-adolescent. This arrangement of custom-built and tract homes, uncreatively named Shadow Hills, had been just carved out of a large chunk of alluvial sediment that had cascaded down from the Santa Catalina Mountains some ten million years prior. The region is now called, with some self-consciousness, the Foothills, a local byword for the wealthier side of town.

How it took on its character is an instructive story of image-making. A go-getting student at the University of Arizona in the 1910s named John Murphey bought up a parcel of worthless desert hillsides some twelve miles to the north of downtown's railroad core. People thought he was foolish, but he perceived two important things: the automobile's growing ability to make distance meaningless, and the sensual abundance of classic Upper Sonoran flora all over the hills—saguaro, ocotillo, paloverde, cholla, prickly pear—as abundant here as the bluestem prairie grasses in Illinois, and extremely appealing to newcomers seeking their own piece of southwestern sublime.

Murphey partnered up with the Swiss immigrant architect Josias Joesler to help him turn the Foothills into a little Santa Barbara, with romantic Mexican street names and Mission-style manors that rambled on big acreage, with mixed cacti in the front and horse stables, an emerald lawn, and a swimming pool out back. Privacy and isolation were key selling points. With the right kind of home loan, a petit bourgeois engineer for Hughes Aircraft could live in a cowboy manor fantasy with a view of city lights below.

The U.S. Home Corporation of Houston, Texas, bought a large section of unused Murphey land in 1979 and put down a warren of streets for considerably less-stylized homes that had no pretenses toward Old Money. Many of them were made of cheap materials and aimed at first-time buyers. My dad had been fleeing a bad job with a high-flying Phoenix bank and bought one of the first homes in Shadow Hills: a three-bedroom rancher with cinderblocks stained maroon to look like adobe and an inside that smelled of caulking.

The streets had the same kind of faux-Spanish names that Murphey had loved. Ours was called Camino Padre Isidoro for no discernable reason. I learned years later it was a possible reference to the friar Isidro Ordóñez, who seized power from the governor of New Mexico in 1613 during a labor dispute. "Trust me," he wrote, "that I can arrest, cast into irons, and punish any person without exception who is not obedient to the commandments of the church and mine." The padre got recalled to Mexico City and censured for his arrogance in this minor incident, not knowing that his misspelled name would one day grace a green reflective street sign in an instant neighborhood.

Whenever I come back to see my folks—who actually lived out their thirty-year mortgage—I'm reminded of the lonely days of my childhood, even though Shadow Hills has filled in a bit. Our house has the same thin wallboard and the same dark-bottomed swimming pool. If I want to go anywhere, I have to borrow the car. Claustrophobia inevitably sets in. And yet I find myself acutely aware of the Santa Catalinas looming over the city—that "brooding Godlike tolerance," as author Harold Bell Wright once put it. My awareness of raw topography seems to be an effect of walking two-thirds of Arizona.

After a week of slamming calories in an attempt to regain lost weight, we drove back out to the Gabe Zimmerman trailhead and

I hugged my parents goodbye again. I'd see them again soon—the Mexican border was just six days away if kept up a good pace.

The trail took me through a concrete drainage culvert, a jumbo version of the kind I used to play in, designed to funnel water from Cienega Creek under Interstate 10. Trucks bound for unknown warehouses rumbled above, and I walked south for another half hour through the scrub until I heard another rattling sound: gunfire.

Bullets cracked vaguely from the east. I couldn't see a shooter. Somebody was out here banging away at targets, or rabbits. It's not an uncommon sound on the edges of Arizona cities but I couldn't be sure about this person's target discipline. Affixing two orange bandannas to my pack, I headed in the opposite direction from the reports and, before long, was at the borders of a stucco subdivision within the unincorporated community of Vail, near Sahuarita Road—the road's name an invented word that's a portmanteau of saguaro and Santa Rita.

These former pecan groves exploded with dwellings after the turn of the century when MDC Holdings of Denver discovered them and added one master-planned neighborhood after another. Twenty thousand people flooded in to buy formula houses with design names like Moonstone, Coral, and Onyx not far off the $150,000 mark. It's a common enough insta-barrio story, similar to that of Shadow Hills.

To live in Arizona for any length of time is to see the land molt and morph in front of your eyes. There aren't many old families in the state; the newcomers run the show, just as they have since the first wagon bearing territorial officials showed up at Navajo Springs in 1863 and swore in the governor. The Natives didn't have a lot of say in the matter. I paused for water in the shade of a mesquite tree and then strode away from Sahuarita Road, as fast I had from the gunfire.

Perhaps it was the recharging effect of the weeklong rest, but I felt energetic enough to keep going after sundown, ridge after ridge, as the Santa Rita Mountains got closer. The full moon helped, casting gray illumination on the road. Scrub oaks threw shadows of their branches into the grass, and at the top of the rises I could see the fires from hunters' distant camps.

At around 11 p.m., another cattle gate presented itself over the footpath. Beyond it was a tureen-shaped valley studded with knolls and unseen hollows, and I could see how gorgeous it must look in daylight spilling away from the western escarpment of the Santa Ritas.

Under the floor of this place called Rosemont, deep beneath the ricegrass, lay a treasure that many want to dig out.

THE RED EMBRACE

As so many Arizona stories do, this one begins with picks and shovels.

Miners started poking around the lower reaches of the Santa Ritas in 1876, a few years before the Southern Pacific Railroad arrived in a tornado of blasting and hammering to usher in the future to southern Arizona.

A canny twenty-four-year-old striver from Canada named Walter Vail had foreseen the riches this could bring—a railhead meant that Arizona beef could be shipped to Chicago for high prices. He gathered some rich British partners to buy a property they called the Empire Ranch. Vail first slept on the ground with his saddle for a pillow, cradling his revolver in case of Apache assault. Then he built an adobe house for his aristocratic wife from New Jersey, complete with linen tablecloths and tea sets. In old photographs, he looks every inch the portly gentleman rancher with trimmed whiskers under a sombrero.

In time, the Empire Ranch would stretch out over a million acres, abutting the hilly territory to the west where prospectors were digging shallow pits in hopes of seeing a wink of gold.

They, too, saw how advantageous it would be to haul their ore to the railhead at the settlement of Vail, which the ranching boss had named for himself. "I saw gold mining and washing for the first time," wrote one of Vail's British partners. "It seems precious hard work. This man was making two pounds a day at it and the night before he had just lost £100–200 at gambling but did not seem to mind it at all."

The hills around the Rosemont valley proved much richer in copper, a metal that had previously been used in kitchen tools and cathedral roofs. But just as fast as railroad tracks were knitting America together, electricity was hustling the world into a modern age. Arc lamps cast brilliant yellow light onto streets in Paris, London, and New York. Telegraph stations connected the coasts, and Thomas Edison was conducting his first experiments on central generating stations.

All of these innovations demanded copper, the metal with a high level of conductivity thanks to its atoms, which had a relatively empty outer layer of electrons and thus an ability to pass charges without interference. Copper prices boomed as lamps went up in major cities around the globe.

Native Americans in Arizona had occasionally used the reddish mineral as a textile pigment and the gold-hungry Spanish settlers had ignored it entirely. But the American miners soon became passionate for the new metal of progress. They sunk copper shafts in the high country over the Empire Ranch on claims with names like Backbone, Sweet Bye Bye, Old Pap, and Narragansett.

L. J. Rose and his partner William McCleary founded a little town they called Rosemont with twenty-seven canvas-roofed houses, a hotel with a dance hall, and a store that sold bacon, chili, potatoes, gunpowder, coffee, soap, and tobacco. The road to Vail was jammed with wagons bearing copper ore hacked out from underground, destined for Europe. Walter Vail got into the game, founding a settlement nearby that everyone called Total Wreck for the proliferation of boulders on the hillside.

The good times wouldn't last. Rose and McCleary sold out to the Lewisohn brothers of New York City. The Empire's boss, Walter Vail, died when he got hit by a streetcar in downtown Los Angeles. The industrial depression of 1908 soon turned Rosemont into a ghost town. The hotel faded away in the sun, a target for wood thieves and vandals until only sticks were left.

A New Mexico outfit called Banner Mining bought the claim in 1961. Their president, Allan B. Bowman, the descendant of Mormon pioneers, had always told his employees to "get beyond the obvious" and think of creative ways to exploit old deposits. He also liked to quote a philosophy learned from a friend in China: educate yourself as much as possible before deciding, but always be aware that you're taking a chance. Bowman had been hiking the eastern slope of the Santa Ritas since 1949, and he harbored a hunch that more copper oxide lay beneath the granite. But there was no free method to peel back the ground for a look.

Bowman researched the history, weighed the costs, took the risk, and paid for a series of exploratory drills near the place where the town of Rosemont had stood. Most turned out useless dirt. But hole G-33 disclosed an astonishing find: a thousand-foot intercept that showed copper at just under 1 percent purity. This oxidized sea under the Santa Ritas would have been worthless just fifty years prior, but it wasn't anymore. Modern purification methods made it exploitable. Rosemont was richer than anyone could have dreamed.

It soon triggered a fight whose ending still isn't clear and raised a vital question. Does Arizona still need copper?

—

The fever that drove the first Rosemont miners made a permanent mark on the young state of Arizona. Copper money dictated the founding of its first major towns, the routes of its railroads, its banking, its political culture, its constitution, and its ties to the rest of the nation.

Arizona copper is mostly porphyry copper, the kind that appears in grains about a tenth of an inch across, sweated out of magma rocks about seventy million years ago and brought closer to the surface by uplift and erosion. Perhaps it was a joke of providence that hunger for what had been a tertiary mineral should have dawned across the globe at the same time that Anglos were trickling into Arizona. As the eventual state motto averred: "God will provide."

A down-and-outer named George Warren was hanging around the U.S. Army post at Fort Bowie one day in 1877 when a pair of soldiers offered him a deal. They had found some promising outcrops in a high valley of the Mule Mountains. But their unit had been called up to go chase Apaches, so Warren could put his name on the claim forms if he filed them at the courthouse, plus be allowed to poke around the site. He staked out a few spots, including the site of the Copper Queen, one of the richest mines in the world.

Warren then got into an argument about the speed of horses and wagered his share in the mine that he could beat one in a hundred-yard race; he lost. He was forced to take a job cleaning floors and spittoons in the offices of the Copper Queen mine, whose ownership he had pissed away. Tombstone photographer C. S. Fly, who owned the studio in front of the O.K. Corral, once took a photo of Warren leaning on a pick and shovel;

the image was used as a model for the grizzled prospector who stands as the lone human figure on the Arizona state seal. Some thought it appropriate that a dimwitted gambler with whipsawing luck should be held up as a symbol of the state.

The Copper Queen started out crude and rinky-dink, with an adobe smelter and a hoist works with a whistle on top. When four blasts sounded, it meant Apache raiding parties were coming near and that everyone should take refuge in the underground tunnels. But soon the magnificent town of Bisbee formed outside the gates, with all-night saloons, red-wallpapered bordellos, restaurants that served imported seafood, a San Francisco–like spillage of gabled cottages on the slopes, Queen Anne mansions for the mine managers, a trolley network, Greco-Roman public buildings, the same type of arc lamps that hung over the Rue de Rivoli in Paris, a Goldwater's department store, breweries, ballfields, and a commercial block winding up Tombstone Canyon that looked like it belonged in a fairytale village in the Pyrenees. Clouds of sulfurous gas rolling out from the smelter hung over the peaks at all hours. Every green plant on the slopes died, and summer thunderstorms sent cascades of water down the slopes, washing the streets of garbage and manure. And workers flooded in from all over the globe to get a crack at the high wages: Czechs, Serbs, Cornish, Italians, Chinese, and Irish joined a mostly Mexican workforce, and those from the nation that neighbored Arizona and occupied the land for hundreds of years often found themselves at the bottom of a racial pecking order. They could supplement their wages on the sly by packing out the nuggets of turquoise that showed up in the copper ore—"lunchbox turquoise," they called it, sold on the black market and hung from the ears of society ladies in Boston and New York.

Over this fiefdom stood Walter Douglas, who ran the local arm of the Phelps Dodge Corporation with a patrician's white glove over a metal fist. His chemist father, James, had built the Copper Queen hotel with Italian marble pillars and a Tiffany glass ceiling to project wealth and power from the center of town before handing over the reins to his son in 1917. Walter Douglas commuted to Bisbee every now and then in a private railcar from his home in New York. He kept the labor unions docile by exhorting patriotism and cracking down on suspected agitators with the help of the Cochise County sheriff. And he concealed the true extent of his influence with a culture of secrecy. The *Bisbee Daily Review* barely ever mentioned the name of the most powerful man in town.

This autocratic style repeated itself in those pockets of Arizona where lodes of porphyry copper had mineralized in the Cretaceous era. A single company usually ran the mine and controlled the city council, the stores, the churches, the newspaper, all in the name of forging a "corporate colonial order." Their power hardened like ingots in such towns as Superior, Ajo, Ray, Bagdad, Jerome, and Globe. Copper outposts circled the capital of Phoenix in bright electron paths.

Over in the San Francisco River valley on the far eastern side of the state, the Arizona Copper Company went even further to protect its kitty and led a drive to splinter off its operations into the state's smallest county, which it could run with unchallenged might. A legislative committee named it Greenlee County after well-liked rancher Mason Greenlee, but it came within a whisker of being named Colquhoun County after the company president. Metallurgists on his staff had developed a processing technique that could make lower-grade sulfide ore profitable even when the purity got as low as 1 percent.

The tunnels at their Morenci mine got deeper even as spurs for copper hauling sprouted off the transcontinental railroads like snakes from Medusa's scalp: forty-six of them in all. The grandest of them may have been the vertiginous short line to Jerome on the slopes of Mingus Mountain, financed by Montana kingpin William A. Clark, who paid $600,000 cash for it and also built a smelter in a town he called Clarkdale, linked to the Santa Fe, Prescott and Phoenix Railroad. Everyone called this link the Peavine. All that copper wealth gave him the ability to bully state officials. In 1900 the mines owned an estimated $100 million in physical capital that was mysteriously valued for taxes at just $2 million.

The influence was both obvious and obnoxious. A wagon driver from Globe named George Wiley Paul Hunt had complained that dirty copper money could buy a territorial governor's veto for two thousand dollars, and he played on that resentment to win a seat on the committee charged with writing the state's constitution in 1911—a bush-league Philadelphia-style convention of regional burghers gathering for one of the last times in American history when such a consequential document would be penned.

Hunt exuded perspiration and charisma. A whiskered man who resembled the Uncle Pennybags mascot of the board game Monopoly, he encouraged people to call him "The Old Walrus." He campaigned in shabby clothes, and favored open-top Packard automobiles on his parade marshal rides through downtown Phoenix, loving the attention. But he was canny about showing his cards—another delegate called him a "behind-the-scenes manipulator who presided in the manner of a stoic, benign Buddha—if one can picture Buddha with a splendid handlebar mustache."

Hunt understood how Big Copper operated, and how it might be checked. He never ceased reminding voters that he had shoveled ore himself as a young man at Globe's rapacious Old Dominion mine. With some backroom arm-twisting, he pulled together a coalition of laborers and farmers to give Arizona one of the most progressive state constitutions ever seen. They secured an eight-hour workday, a ban on child labor, a workman's compensation program, and an independent state mine inspector who could shut down hazardous pits. As a reward for himself, Hunt got elected Arizona's first governor, styling himself the champion of the commoners.

But what he and the labor unions couldn't do was limit the number of immigrant Mexicans who worked in the mines. Viewing them as scabs and wage-depressors, the white miners ran racist ballot initiatives to require all employees to be "native-born citizens" that passed with overwhelming support. A federal court tossed the law out within a year. Though copper barons had promoted segregated housing policies designed to discourage solidarity, they came out of the "native-born" debacle looking like enlightened progressives.

The colonial order took further revenge when the price of copper soared in 1917 as the War Department grew ravenous for the metal to build airplanes, tanks, telephone wire, and all the accouterments of combat, even as the International Workers of the World pressed for higher wages. The IWW had a tiny presence in Arizona, but copper lords treated them as a threat equal to the modern boogeyman of Antifa. The newspapers hinted German saboteurs were hiding in the labor pool. Walter Douglas made a rare public appearance and gave a speech in Globe in which he thundered: "you cannot compromise with a rattlesnake."

Two days later, the Cochise County sheriff and a posse of deputized men off the street went door to door and rounded up approximately two thousand suspected union workers while the sheriff rode around in an open-topped car with a swivel machine gun mounted on the seat. The unlucky were herded to the baseball field in Warren, a neighborhood named for the prospector with a gambling problem. Those who refused to swear a loyalty oath were herded into boxcars of the Phelps Dodge–owned railroad and taken to the New Mexico desert, where they were dumped off at 3 a.m. without food or water.

One man died in what came to be called the Bisbee Deportation, and officials in Washington hit the ceiling. A federal grand jury handed down indictments for Walter Douglas and twenty others. In an eerie replay of the judicial outcome of the Camp Grant massacre forty years before, all charges resulted either in dismissal or acquittal. As Sheridan noted later, frontier justice won the day even when "the frontier was a company town." Unions would never again challenge the power structure so directly. And Arizona continued to produce as much as two-thirds of the nation's copper supply. A hole in the power structure had opened for six years, then closed again.

The victory of the copper lords would also blaze a path for the future dominance of the Arizona economy by out-of-state corporations, from the postwar technology boom created by Motorola, then IBM, then Intel; to the munitions plant outside Tucson operated by Hughes Aircraft and now Raytheon; and to the bank mergers of the 1990s that swept lending institutions like Valley National Bank into the JPMorgan Chase bank leviathan.

The state's most cherished money-machine today—homebuilding—also has a distinct copper flavor. Builders such as KB Homes, D.R. Horton, Shea Homes, and PulteGroup are all based far away but stride knee-deep into Arizona sawdust and mortgages, creating seas of clay-tile roofs that when viewed from above have the same uniformity as company towns, the same reddish scars as an open-pit mine.

The mighty Phelps Dodge Corporation, once so crucial to the growth of Arizona's economic culture, faded into history in 2007 when it was purchased by a New Orleans petroleum giant with a name resembling a chemical formula: Freeport-McMoRan. Unlike other absentee companies, however, it chose to move to Phoenix, where it erected a twenty-six-story headquarters in 2009, the first skyscraper to be built downtown in years.

The fin-covered office slab stands as a monument—or a reminder—of the red metal that remains lodged like a splinter in the Arizona consciousness.

———

All that copper hiding below the Rosemont site was enough to string electric wire through every house in Dallas with plenty left over for the suburbs. The trick would be getting it out of the ground.

The best time to have built the Rosemont Mine would have been just after its discovery in the 1960s when the ordeal of securing permits was considerably easier. But copper prices were comparatively low back then, and nobody could find the capital or the right timing.

The discoverers at Banner made a fast deal with the gargantuan Montana player Anaconda to form a joint venture called Amax. They drilled 113 more holes to get a better picture of the deposit, but then sold it to Tucson-based Asarco, which Grupo Mexico bought in a 1999 merger. Their engineers hatched a stupendous vision: an excavation deeper than the abandoned moon crater called the Lavender Pit that had split the town of Bisbee in half. But the promised mine didn't materialize; the willpower wasn't there. "They thought it would be a lot of work and bad P.R.," observed Gayle Harrison Hartman, one of the founders of the opposition group Save the Scenic Santa Ritas.

Then came an unexpected twist: Asarco unloaded the whole property to a real estate development company called Triangle Ventures. One of the principals there was Yoram Levy, who happened to be the son-in-law of Don Diamond, a mega-rich former Wall Street trader who retired to Tucson in his mid-forties but never stopped working. He became the bête noire of local environmentalists for his massive planned communities like The Canyons, Rocking K Ranch, and Pima Canyon Estates and his penchant for finding creative angles to get around regulations.

Environmentalists now had a golden opportunity to shut down Rosemont forever. Levy told people his company had no intention of finding a mining partner but instead aimed to do what they did best: build a lot of tract homes on the site. Whether this was a negotiating tactic or not remains murky, but Pima County was soon talking to Triangle about a deal. The nononsense administrator Chuck Huckleberry offered $10.5 million. But the county—hurting for cash after the mortgage debacle—couldn't match Triangle's higher counteroffer, and it was sold off to a tiny Canadian company called Augusta Resources.

Matters grew more serious in 2006 when a construction boom in China pushed the price of copper up to $3.05 per pound. Now Rosemont was looking not just possible, but economically logical—even inevitable. Augusta launched a charm offensive. The mine would bring jobs, the company promised: 430 of them, with the high average salary of sixty thousand dollars. They did not clarify that the managers would come from out of state. Nor did they rush to point out the meagerness of the number of promised jobs: less than one-tenth of one percent of all the jobs in southern Arizona.

Augusta's extraction plan was modest by global market standards but horrific to U.S. environmentalists: a terraced pit more than a mile in diameter and half as deep, into which the entire campus of the University of Arizona could fit easily. At the side of the hole, a molybdenum-copper concentrator would chuff twenty-four hours a day, an updated version of the old mud smelters that had been there in the 1870s. Unlike the copper overlords of the past, Augusta wouldn't build a railroad to haul out the ore but move it down Highway 83 in a parade of trucks carrying a daily load of ninety thousand tons.

Another thing Augusta didn't say was that it had about as much intention of mining Rosemont as it did colonizing the moon. It was a junior company that emerged in the specific context of the metals exchange in Vancouver, in which the entire point is to pump up a claim until it can be acquired by a big multinational that has the money to build an extractive infrastructure. Promises from a junior might as well be written on tissue paper.

Hartman's activist group circulated outraged petitions; the Center for Biological Diversity revved up its legal team for an upcoming cannonade of lawsuits; and the drama shifted to a paper war, waged in the endless pages of the impact statements required by five agencies: the U.S. Forest Service, the Environmental Protection Agency, the Arizona Department of Environmental Quality, the U.S. Army Corps of Engineers, and the U.S. Fish and Wildlife Service. And to further complicate matters, an endangered jaguar showed himself on wilderness cameras secreted in the brush. Scientists nicknamed the savior cat El Jefe, and he was surely given less flattering names by the would-be developers.

A consistent pattern emerged and dragged on for fifteen years. The lower-level staff of these public agencies—composed mainly of PhD scientists—spent years gathering data that led them to negative conclusions and informed reports that were gently withering in their appraisals of Rosemont. They all agreed the mine would suck out precious groundwater, pollute the San Pedro River, kill El Jefe, dry up Cienega Creek, doom the Chiricahua leopard frog, and leave an ugly gash that would never heal. They sent their painstaking reports to political appointees at the top, who overruled the recommendations. *Arizona Daily Star* reporter Tony Davis remarked that the clear driver of events was big money, not what was best for people who actually lived in Arizona.

That didn't stop his newspaper—itself an out-of-state concern, owned by Lee Enterprises of Davenport, Iowa—from publishing one of the most poorly reasoned editorials in the history of Arizona newspapers, on January 19, 2014. Titled "It's Time to Move Ahead and Build the Rosemont Mine," the first definitive statement from the local newspaper on the biggest story in its backyard basically shrugged: "Well, it's legal so it should happen."

Though the *Star* acknowledged the mine was "unwise," it offered up its resigned conclusion in the first paragraph, which had the stench of a diktat from an Iowa boardroom, spun as best as could be managed by embarrassed hostages:

> Rosemont Copper has met extensive government requirements to improve its mine proposal, and so it is time to accept that the mine will be built. We respect the laws, though flawed, that permit mining in a national forest in a region with limited water.

What the *Star* and its new best friend Augusta Resources didn't mention, yet again, was copper's tendency to move in boom-and-bust cycles, albeit slower ones. Just as rising prices signal investor confidence in manufacturing, news of a big new mine brings a chill wind. Because of its bulk and weight, rolled copper can't be easily stockpiled, so it must be purchased on an as-needed basis and therefore tends to be immune to speculative bubbles. But recessions also create a long hangover. Copper mines closed all over the world, from Chile to Congo, during the COVID-19 recession, for example, and the price sank back down to $1.85 a pound. There could be no guarantee that another unanticipated market shock could close down Rosemont, leaving the mountains plowed down and groundwater permanently tainted.

My friend Bill Carter lived in a miner's cottage in the played-out town of Bisbee for seven years before planting a garden of lettuce, tomatoes, and peppers in his backyard. After his salads made him sick, he investigated and found the lead and arsenic levels in the soil were off the charts. He and his family had been living atop a pile of waste from the nearby Copper Queen mine, which investors were eyeing as revived property in case the price shot up higher. These factors helped drive him out of a town he loved.

"It is almost impossible for me to imagine mining companies walking away from known sources of copper," he wrote later in his book *Boom, Bust, Boom*. "And I can't travel around the pit without thinking of sulfuric plume leaking toward the town's aquifer."

As if to offer a living demonstration of the instability of the business—and the worthlessness of corporate promises—Augusta Resources was acquired in 2014 by HudBay Minerals, another Canadian company with no ties to the area except for possession of the lease.

Did Arizona need copper any longer? The mineral had laid down the state's modern foundations, but was the cost worth it anymore? Rosemont wasn't the only place this question was playing out in the second decade of the twenty-first century. A deposit four times as rich was under a spot called Oak Flat off the highway from Phoenix to Globe. Corruption has dogged the project for years. Many Apaches consider the spot sacred, and it includes the site of the Apache Leap. Much of it sits on Tonto National Forest land, and the company had to trade private land to claim it.

Critics noted that Resolution Copper (a joint venture of the British giant Rio Tinto and the Australian giant BHP-Billiton) was given land worth $7 million for a parcel worth $112 billion: a laughable valuation of 1 to 784,000. The exchange received federal approval, but not before former "family values" congressman Rick Renzi had told a Resolution vice president he'd sign on if they would also include an alfalfa field near Sierra Vista owned by a business associate. The mining boss was so alarmed by this corrupt proposition he wrote down an account of it and mailed it to himself so the postmark would show what he knew when he knew it. Renzi went to jail for extortion and fraud. On top of this sleaze, Oak Flat had been caught in the same dynamic as Rosemont: blistering federal environmental assessments overturned by political appointees.

The copper companies held a powerful card. In 1872 the U.S. Congress had passed the Mining Act with an eye toward luring new residents out west into what had been Indian territory with a promise that if they found minerals on public land, they could exploit them for free. Foreign mining companies could get away with plundering American metal, as long as they played the paperwork game correctly.

Then another plot twist. One of the lawsuits brought by Save the Scenic Santa Ritas and other plaintiffs landed in U.S. District Court, where Judge James Soto ruled on a fuzzy point of grammar in the 1872 law as well as an immutable principle of physics: when you dig a hole in the ground, the dirt must go somewhere. Rosemont's plan was to create a tailings pile on two thousand public acres adjacent to the site, but Soto ruled that was not covered in the nineteenth-century definition of a spot where minerals could be "extracted, removed and marketed at a profit." This put a revolutionary spin on the dusty law, with dramatic implications. For many in southern Arizona, the permanent sacrifice of the Santa Rita Mountains and the risk to the water table is too high a price to pay.

"It's sad and kind of horrifying," said Hartman. "It's all about money, and they never seem to have enough money. They seem to live in a different world than I do."

Most Arizona stories end this way: with no real end. The world still hungers for more wiring. Electric cars that reduce the carbon load on the atmosphere need at least eighty pounds of copper in their guts versus the twenty required for a gasoline vehicle. Where is that metal supposed to come from? No freeze on mine development can be truly permanent. The mammoth blob of copper under the Santa Ritas has been there twenty million years; laws cannot make it spontaneously dissolve.

Arizona had a long run with copper. But its economy matured and veered away, no longer depending on the quasi-colonial metal any longer. In its time, it provided high-wage jobs, a railroad infrastructure, ethnic diversity, and a sense of purpose and order.

Whether it would wise to return to the red embrace is a question well worth asking. Whether Arizona can ever escape its natural copper inheritance, however, is not a question at all. Because it can't.

NOT FAR FROM THE ROSEMONT SITE is Kentucky Camp, a wealth scheme from a different era. A dice-throw of old wooden houses stands near a field littered with odd-looking humps, as if a blanket of dirt had been tossed over a herd of giant toads. Shallow pits lie agape to the sun. Here are the abandoned diggings of Kentucky Camp, the scene of a gold rush in the 1870s in the same decade when the silver boomtown of Tombstone offered a full menu of sin and entertainment forty miles to the east.

They didn't have long to enjoy Kentucky Camp; the good times came to an end because of a lack of water to wash the ore. Mules had to haul it in bags from the San Pedro River. The frightful expense of three cents per gallon meant only the easiest and purest gold could be harvested from a dry stream everyone called Boston Gulch, the venue for more exuberance and petty violence than ever was recorded.

I cooked a lunch of dehydrated food on my stove just outside the office of the old Santa Rita Water and Mining Company, founded in 1902 on a second wave of gold fever. Such is the nature of western mining. If you want to find a new mine, look next to an old mine.

An engineer named James Stetson thought he could defeat nature with an aqueduct to pipe in water from perennial streams in Big Casa Blanca Canyon seven miles away. He raised money from some California speculators and hired teams of Mexican laborers—the backbone of most Arizona construction projects, then and today—to level out a flat path and lay twenty-four-inch-diameter steel pipe through a series of dams, valves, tunnels, and stone penstocks. They worked fast. Within two years, Stetson's crews were blasting the water at the humps of Boston Gulch, "tearing up the ground with splendid results," according to a man from the *Arizona Daily Star*.

Then came a murder mystery. On May 20, 1905, Stetson went up to the Santa Rita Hotel on Broadway in Tucson for a meeting of the board of directors. Some important people from California were coming in to ask questions about money. At four o'clock, an observer from Ronstadt's Hardware across the street reported Stetson was sitting on the window ledge of Room 319 in his underwear, looking drunk or disoriented. A maid cleaning the room directly beneath him then heard a loud bang on the windowsill as Stetson bounced off it and tumbled to the street below. The coroner's report came back inconclusive, so the question of whether it was accident or foul play was never answered. The water company went bust shortly thereafter, and the remaining buildings and some rusted equipment are now in the hands of the U.S. Forest Service, which maintains them as a ghost town.

Near the end of my lunch, I started talking with two other long-distance hikers, both considerably more accomplished than I. Balto was a laconic veteran of the U.S. Army with a wife and kids back home in Florida. He'd done at least five long-distance trails, some of them in the company of his friend Eric, a PhD candidate from Wisconsin who looked a bit like Santa Claus, except with black hair. We exchanged the standard questions with each other. Their base weights, thanks to a more monkish approach toward extended deprivation, put mine to shame.

As we fell in together in a temporary alliance and started hiking south, it became clear their constitutions were tougher too. I lagged because I couldn't keep up, but also because I wanted to look at the remnants of James Stetson's hydraulic masterpiece of 1904: broken lengths of steel pipe embedded in the ground, stone supports here and there, cuts and fills in strategic places. Balto and Eric cruised onward, also not looking at this, or the mountains, or seemingly anything else around them.

The Arizona Trail isn't as long as any of the triple crown of national trails—the Appalachian, the Continental Divide, and the Pacific Crest—and it's also a lot less crowded, but it still attracts at least four dozen through-hikers per season. They can be a funny breed: obsessive, masochistic, prone to addiction, junkies for the endorphins squirted out during physical stress, the so-called runner's high of natural opioid peptides. The most ambitious among them seek to achieve the FKT or fastest known time on these various trails—in fact, earlier that year, a man named Jeff "Legend" Garmire had finished the Arizona Trail in an unbelievable fifteen days, eating while running, sleeping in four-hour bursts, and fighting hallucinations and searing pain near the end.

Some of the lesser trail Olympians take the time to move their gaze around and appreciate the surroundings. For others, the landscape is mere wallpaper, and their eyes remained glued to the dirt tightrope in front of them. I had joined up with the latter kind. But I am not one to judge. One of the most repeated tenets among this subculture is "hike your own hike." Nobody gets to lay down doctrine for anyone else.

I ambled along the path of the pipeline as it wound around the bulges of peaks and retreated into the folds of canyons with all the pitch of a dining room table. The anonymous labor teams of the water company had done tremendous work. This was their physical legacy. It was hard not to wonder what other backbreaking achievements had been pulled off in Arizona with no remnants to tell the story: mine tunnels, wooden houses, railroad tracks, telephone wires, storefronts, earthen dams, schools—lovingly built objects ripped out to make way for new seedlings of civilization, or simply abandoned to decay and disappear. How many cathedrals where people had worshiped with their hands and sweat had since vanished?

I caught up with Balto and Eric in the near-dark at a place called Bear Spring not far from the terminus of the pipeline. There was a stream where we could wash up and refill and a flat place with room for three tents. We talked for a bit over our dehydrated suppers as the temperature dropped to shivering. And at the usual time of "hiker midnight," 8 p.m., we retreated into our respective tents. After dark on the trail, there simply isn't much else to do but sleep.

They outpaced me again the next morning, after about an hour in the predawn, and I caught up at the saddle as a pink alpenglow illuminated the conical summit of Mount Wrightson a few thousand feet above us, a mountain named for a mining engineer chased down and killed by a band of Apaches in 1865. Charles Poston had looked on this pyramid-shaped massif every day, before it was named, when he served as the mayor of the little village of Tubac near the base. "We had no law but love and no occupation but labor, no government, no taxes, no public debt, no politics," he wrote later. "It was a community in a perfect state of nature." The reality was certainly different from how he presented it; the bishop of Santa Fe had to dissolve all the illegal marriages Poston performed, and Apaches raided the town several times before it was abandoned.

It was another three hours or so down Temporal Gulch to the town of Patagonia. As the footpath turned into a Forest Service road and the town bobbed into view, its low skyline and an arrow-like church steeple made it look like an oil painting of a New England village nestled amid wooded hills, only with a leathery southwestern edge. Its exotic name accurately portends a funky mix of cattle ranchers, U.S. Border Patrol agents, leftist nonprofit employees, retirees, cyclists, artists, and hard-drinking writers, in the tradition of former winter resident Jim Harrison, a man of huge appetites.

A mingling place for all of them is a café called Wagon Wheel that's been there since 1933 and qualifies as a state institution. You don't come here for the food unless deep-fried is your preferred school of cuisine. But to me, it felt like a five-star bistro. As I wolfed, a woman in the next booth took note of my pack and asked me where I'm headed, and I told her Mexico, a three-day walk away. We talked about the border and then the Rosemont mine project for a bit, the two evergreen subjects in Patagonia.

She was a relocated Bostonian with a *pakh-the-cah* nonrhotic accent to prove it, and she'd chosen southern Arizona for her retirement to let the sun and the isolation wash away memories of hard city winters. She lived on a ranch outside a retirement town about an hour away. Had I heard of this place, she wanted to know?

I told her I had.

THE GREEN VALLEY GRIN

Betty Chadwick wakes up at 5:30 most mornings, and she opens her living room curtains for a panoramic view of the Santa Rita Mountains some twenty miles to the east. These peaks have never looked quite real to her—so impossibly steep and beautiful as though they were affixed to the sky like a plywood backdrop to a movie set.

Some mornings she wonders: *how did I wind up here?*

The only piece of furniture she brought with her from Canton, New York, is a rocking chair coated with black lacquer that sits next to the couch, which has pastel lines in the fashion of a Navajo rug. A lamp perches atop a metal Kokopelli figure. A family of Gambel quail made of brass sits on an end table.

Chadwick is eighty-four years old, long retired from a career as a secretary. She had never given the state of Arizona much thought until her husband, Al, took her on a vacation here when their two daughters left for college. They peered into the Grand Canyon, saw red bluffs at Sedona, then came down here to the active senior community of Green Valley to visit some older friends.

Al was smitten with the town at first sight. There were plenty of dry arroyos all around where he could set up targets and shoot them with his pistol—a favorite hobby that he rarely got to enjoy in New York, with its tighter gun laws and population density. Before they left Green Valley, and without telling her, he signed a mortgage on an $80,000 casita in anticipation of the time when he could quit as the athletic director of the State University of New York at Canton and join the other seniors in one of Arizona's premier retirement towns.

He died six years ago, in a hospice bed set up next to the breakfast nook. The oncologist had told him in June he had six months, and he passed at the end of December as internal organs failed. In his last days, he spent a lot of time on the patio looking at the Santa Rita Mountains. From behind the glass door, Betty could see his lips moving, and she knew that he was praying and that he had faith. "I know, my dear, that you'll be just fine because you're tough," he told her.

Betty Chadwick isn't sure she lives up to that flattering judgment, but—after the initial pain and shock faded—she resolved not to wallow in sadness. It was a mistake she had seen her mother make time and again during the Great Depression when the family lived on a vineyard near the Finger Lakes. All that worrying was futile, Chadwick thought, and she decided when she was a teenager to make the optimistic best of her circumstances. "You're not going to talk me into worrying about this," she once told her mother. It was a lesson that proved useful when she became widowed.

Chadwick signed up as a volunteer at the White Elephant Thrift Shop, where she spends most mornings, but not until after a set routine: coffee, cereal, *Good Morning America*, the newspaper, a few laps in the pool over at Desert Hills recreation center. She doesn't swim but walks through water that goes up to her chin. The resistance is good for her shoulders. After her shift, it's an afternoon nap and—more likely than not—taking one of several phone calls from her younger sister, who unfortunately inherited their mother's habit of worrying. Chadwick tries to be a good listener but doesn't love the daily hit of negative energy because she is bracing herself for more sadness, one that Green Valley residents know too well.

Fourteen years ago, she met a kind and gentle man who had been a regional manager of F. W. Woolworth stores in the Pacific Northwest. Chadwick thought that was amazing—she'd had a childhood fascination with Woolworth's. They both loved ballroom dancing. Al had never been much of a dancer, but this man was liquid grace on the hardwood. They began going to dinner together at the Elks Club.

Chadwick resists the term "boyfriend" in the classic sense—they were never precisely romantic and she was pretty clear to herself that a second marriage was out of the question because she would lose Al's SUNY pension. And it wouldn't have felt right. So the subject never came up, even though she heard from a friend that he would have been open to it. The question is moot, though, because the kind man is in hospice care. He has diabetes. The doctors aren't hopeful.

At night sometimes, especially when the moon is full, Chadwick walks in her nightgown to the place near the rocking chair where she saw Al praying in front of the Santa Ritas. The gray light creates its own kind of shadowy beauty on the slopes. Again she marvels at the strangeness of it all. To wind up in the twilight of life, in a place that never occurred to her until she was forty-nine. The mountains look painted.

A friend once asked her if she was afraid to die herself.

"I'm not going there," she said. "No, no, no."

—

A major part of Arizona's economy is dedicated to the retirement-industrial complex. Speckled through the state, usually clinging to the edges of cities, 137 master-planned communities explicitly reserved for older adults do a robust business, even if heavy on turnover.

Hundreds of other wildcat subdivisions and trailer parks dedicated to gray-haired migrants fly under the statistical radar. The highway town of Quartzsite booms in the winter months, as senior citizens piloting RVs flock to the government land south of the interstate and spend their days playing cards, rockhounding, and taking dance lessons.

Together with their more affluent cohort, who own homes in places like Green Valley, they make Arizona the twelfth-oldest state in the country, with 1.1 million people over sixty-five who comprise 16 percent of the population. Seniors are expected to make up about a quarter of all Arizonans by the middle of the century. Dr. Elisabeth Kubler-Ross, who popularized the "five stages of grief"—denial, anger, bargaining, depression, and acceptance—made her retirement home in Scottsdale in her mid-seventies after a series of strokes. She went through the five stages herself and then grew impatient. "I told God last night he's a damned procrastinator," she said in a 2002 interview with the *Republic*.

The hot, thorny, and isolated territory of Arizona wasn't a friendly place to the elderly through most of the nineteenth century—"no country for old men," in Alfred, Lord Tennyson's phrase. But that changed when doctors began preaching the benefits of warm, dry air for their patients who suffered from tuberculosis, then the second-leading cause of death. In 1882 bacteriologist Robert Koch discovered the bacillus that caused the disease and concluded that sleeping outdoors would be therapeutic. A railroad ticket to Arizona was considered excellent medicine. Among those who took the hint was the gunfighter Doc Holliday.

The gasping migrants, called "lungers" by unkind locals, helped Arizona Territory get enough population to be eligible for statehood. Not all of them were of retirement age, but almost none of them were healthy enough to hold a job, and they spent their days quietly in tents or shacks in slum neighborhoods like Sunnyslope north of Phoenix, or near the corner of Stone and Speedway in Tucson. "The nights were heartbreaking," said Dick Hall of one such camp, "and as one walked along the dark streets, he heard coughing from every tent. It was truly a place of lost souls and lingering death."

These first climate tourists—generally unwanted and even despised—provided an eventual payback because they paved the way for a more high-class desert retreat. Hoteliers cashed in on the health-seeking crazes of the 1920s with golf resorts like Jokake Inn, El Conquistador, the Wigwam, and the Arizona Biltmore. Older and wealthier people marveled at the reliable sunshine and lack of snow; some bought property and moved here.

Arizona's geriatric side became industrialized on January 1, 1960, when contractor Del Webb opened the first five model homes of Sun City, the first dedicated "retirement community" in America. He built it on the Levittown model: curving streets, detached homes on a quarter-acre, a retail zone on a feeder street. But he completed the golf course and recreation centers first so that people could envision themselves happy and active there before they signed a mortgage. It was then separated from Phoenix by twelve empty miles and announced itself from a distance with crisscrossing palm trees spiking in proud X's and W's, an island amid the sea of dirt.

Webb had initially thought central Arizona "a primitive, under-developed desert and hot as hell." His new fantasyland for seniors would be a direct rebellion against the realities not just of Arizona heat but of aging itself.

More than a hundred thousand potential buyers turned out the first weekend, and Webb was soon on the cover of *Time*. No longer did the unpleasantness of aging have to be hidden away in a nursing home. Now it could be hidden away in a mimicry of every other America suburb, except in the hardpan of the Upper Sonoran Desert where the warmth felt good on the old bones and they could put thoughts of death aside for a bit. "Sure, it's going to happen," one resident told Jack Tucker in 1985. "But death is not as frightening to me out here. I suspect it might have been different back in St. Louis."

Other developers followed Webb's lead, and the fifty-five-plus communities became an Arizona staple, from affluent gated labyrinths down to small mobile home parks: Leisure World, Sun Lakes, Lamplighter Village, Dove Mountain, Whispering Palms, Desert Pueblo, Saddlebrooke Ranch, Quail Creek, Casa del Sol, Pebble Creek.

Most of them had a single corporate owner who enforced codes of appearance, conduct, and minimum age through a powerful homeowner's association. The buyers were also overwhelmingly white, as most Arizona retirement communities remain today. "Let's face it, a Negro would be miserable in Sun City," said Webb's vice president, Thomas Breen, in 1964. They also became known, if not notorious, for their consistent political opposition to any new taxes, especially those funding nearby school districts.

A pair of Chicago developers named Don Maxon and Lee Chilcote came up with a different idea when Congress added a provision to the Federal Housing Administration Act that guaranteed loans for multiunit dwellings for the elderly. They envisioned a cheaper and smaller version of Sun City. People could simply rent small casitas rather than go through the hassle of buying another house in their old age.

They scouted out unproductive farmland in Hawaii and California before settling on a spread of cotton fields wedged between a pyramid of terraced mine waste and the dramatic rounded peak of Mount Wrightson south of Tucson. The Chicago partners called it Green Valley, laid out streets, and hired architects to design apartments and public buildings based on the whitewashed eighteenth-century plaza of Álamos, Mexico.

Green Valley was a flop out of the gate. An apartment boom in Tucson in the early 1960s sent the occupancy rate plunging. But when the developers agreed to open the golf course to all residents—a premium perk—a wave of Greatest Generation retirees took an interest. The energetic builder Del

Webb, regarded as a wizard for such things, signed on as a consultant and moved away from the rented casita idea.

Fairfield Homes bladed ground for a new subdivision for the elderly and hired a local adman named Jay Taylor to run a 1980s television campaign with images of golf, sun, card games, and smiling retirees with the tagline: "The Green Valley Grin comes from living good again!" Home sales took off. Here was a mortgage that came with the cherished American idea of a reboot—a fresh start—applied to the last chapters of life.

Some even found this to be true. The sociology of retirement towns like Green Valley tends to be a lot like high school. Charisma and sunny personalities can bring popularity and a set of friends. But introversion, thoughtfulness, or a different personality can result in unwanted loneliness. Once the high of new freedom and endless golf starts to get wearisome, a certain depression sets in.

Dave Shepherd has managed retirement accounts in Green Valley for more than a quarter century and sometimes hears clients tell him that he— their financial advisor—is their most meaningful social connection. The isolation becomes far worse if a spouse dies, especially if the spouse was the more social of the two. Dinner invitations dry up after the condolence casseroles go cool. Grieving spouses frequently sell the house and move back east. "I can't tell you the number of widows who have told me, 'I can't wait to die and be with my husband again,'" said Shepherd.

As one local joke has it, the Green Valley Grin can fade to a Green Valley Grimace. Heavy drinking sometimes results. Sunset is a customary starting gun. As one local saying goes, "when the mountain is pink, it's time to drink." Cashiers at the chain drugstores tell stories of vodka handles purchased along with arthritis medication. Those who have lost spouses figure *what the hell*, and there's nobody around to object. One study of census data showed that 40 percent of elderly Americans drink more than their younger counterparts; the golden years sometimes bring hazy afternoons.

Another common character is what some here call the FIP, or "formerly important person," who seems to talk about nothing more than past exploits. Serving in a public function with an FIP can be exhausting. At Desert Hills Golf Club, some of the members of the landscaping committee are retired lawyers who show up to meetings carrying briefcases. The fish stories and one-upmanship at some of the more crowded lunch tables marks yet another point of convergence with high school. Self-confident egos command the room, and distinct social food chains emerge, as well as a class system and some downright bad manners. Who you were, it seems, is who you remain.

Not everyone gets older equally. There are stories of people getting kicked out of their bridge clubs as they start to lose their ability to keep the cards straight. Posada Life Community Services offers a daily community lunch for those with modest incomes at the early-bird time of 11 a.m. It is not unheard of for a client to collapse in the line, and coordinator Regina Ford has watched as others step over the fallen person. "They weren't going to going to miss out on their mac and cheese," she said.

A city of twenty-one thousand built around the hard fact of aging brings its own set of particular hazards. Drivers sometimes lose control of their vehicles in parking lots, confusing the gas with the brake, and come hurtling through plate glass windows. The Safeway grocery in the Continental Shopping Plaza is said to be especially prone to this mishap. During one two-day period in December 2014, window-crashing happened three times across town. The local charity Friends In Deed had to erect metal stanchions in front of its entrance to stop runaway cars.

There are also the novel acts of violence that occasionally liven the pages of the *Green Valley News*. A jilted lover once fired gunshots at a woman's house and took off on a golf cart—the nation's first drive-by shooting by golf cart. And in a 2019 incident that might be described as Peak Green Valley, two men got into an argument at Anamax Park after their dogs started chasing the same tennis ball. The seventy-five-year-old used his walking cane to whap his eighty-nine-year-old antagonist, who responded by snatching away the cane and using it to administer a reciprocal beating on its owner. Neither were injured enough to go to the hospital, but police charged both with disorderly conduct.

———

I got into a car with Joyce Finkelstein, a member of the Rotary Club and just about every other civic organization in the directory. She is a petite and dynamic woman who moved here in her late forties—practically an infant by Green Valley standards—because her husband had a job procuring materials for garage door openers and they wanted to live close to his wholesalers across the Mexican border thirty miles away.

Finkelstein is proud of her town, likes to show it off, and took me on a driving tour of the major sights.

We went past the corner of Esperanza and Abrego, anchored by one of the oldest structures in town, the Green Valley Recreation Center, with white Spanish arcades built in 1962, the first of what would become a chain of health clubs and a reliable source of local squabbles. Everyone who moves here is automatically made a member and charged a fee whether they use it or not. And nobody is ever completely happy with the board of directors.

We next went down to a county park where two people with oxygen tanks sat together on a bench overlooking a pond. Huge fields of cotton and guayule shrubs watered by the Santa Cruz River used to grow here, first planted in 1916 as an emergency tire-material project during World War I. Nearby is the food bank, the new regional medical center (*We're in the ready position. Surgery 24/7*), and the stucco headquarters of Valley Assistive Services, a charity that helps struggling seniors with rent payments and trips to the grocery store.

"Among the things I love about this community," said Joyce, "is the way we take care of one another." Beyond the surface of graying desert gentility, she told me, there are many behind the doors of ranch houses, especially women, whose spouses died in ways that ate up nest eggs, and whose Social Security checks are not enough to pay the bills. Poverty here is much more invisible than in almost any other town in Arizona.

So, too, can be hidden depression. Joan Browning was a beloved figure here—a people connector just as good as Finkelstein—who served on a long list of boards. In 2010 she drove out to the Sahuarita Road viaduct over Interstate 19 and leaped off, to the utter shock of everyone who knew her.

To live in Green Valley is not just to understand that surfaces can conceal tough realities but also to be more attuned to the omnipresence of death. Making friends and then losing them is an unspoken reality, part of the arrangement, but it doesn't mean the Supreme Mystery is any less of a puzzle or a slightly rude subject to bring up in polite conversation. There is no human experience of death, said Albert Camus, and that's just as true in Green Valley as anywhere else.

"I buy sympathy cards by the bulk package," Joyce told me. "It's not funny, but it sort of is."

Then she switched topics immediately to the next sight out the car window.

"And this is our fire station," she said. "We have wonderful firefighters. We rarely have fires, thankfully, and they go out on a lot of medical calls. Most of them are paramedics. They don't just resolve the issues; they try to find the underlying problem. They get a lot of calls for slip and fall with chairs on smooth tile. So they cut up a rubber mat for the person."

We came up on the Animal League of Green Valley, a shelter where pets go when their owners die, and just a bit down La Cañada Drive, the Green Valley Mortuary and Cemetery, dotted with plastic flowers in inlaid metal vases. The cemetery is surprisingly small for a town of twenty-seven thousand; as it turns out, few residents want to be buried here.

When she first moved here, Finkelstein remarked on this curiosity, and the manager told her that almost everybody chooses to have their remains shipped to the family plot back in Ohio or Massachusetts or wherever their home ground might be. The old joke that this town is "God's waiting room" turns out not to be true. Green Valley is generally a second-to-last station stop: a door leading to the foyer, an airlock with dry and pleasant oxygen and sunshine that feels comforting on wrinkled skin.

Finkelstein's husband, Mike, is at the cemetery more often than most people: he's a member of a group called Buglers across America, and if a military veteran chooses to be buried in Green Valley, Mike will come out to play "Taps," out of a belief that anyone who served should have a live performance of the soldier's elegy instead of a tape recording. Relatives don't always make it out from back east. Mike is sometimes part of a very small graveside cluster.

"Nobody is 'from' here, so our friends become our family," said Finkelstein. "Very few people here have family in Tucson or even in Arizona."

A certain population in Green Valley does, however, have more of a connection to Arizona: the extremely old and infirm who live in memory care facilities scattered unobtrusively around metropolitan areas, barely noticeable. One example, the Villas at Green Valley, is tucked down a nondescript cul-de-sac near the freeway. It would be invisible to anyone who didn't know it was there. Eight rectangular sand-colored buildings share the same design: a common room with high ceilings and a kitchen, surrounded by a ring of bedrooms with polished laminate flooring, minimal furniture, and a slight odor of cleaning fluid.

The co-owner is Bobby Larson, a former baseball coach and athletic director from Catalina Foothills High School, who got into the business after a lawyer friend presented him with what seemed like a safe business model: buy ten acres of some undistinguished real estate, get it zoned residential, secure a construction loan, build the cookie-cutter units, give them a country-rustic interior design, hire a team of semi-skilled caregivers, take out some ads, charge about $3,600 a month.

Larson maxed out his credit cards and leveraged himself into a corner before the first project in Tucson filled up to capacity on opening day, an outcome as successful as Del Webb's Sun City. Nature's pitiless movement ensured a stream of business: nothing can stop people from aging and becoming unable to take care of themselves.

The Villas at Green Valley caters mainly to those in some stage of dementia. The clients come mostly from other Arizona cities, though some are from the midwestern country club set next door. Once at the Villas, nobody is allowed to leave the campus without the accompaniment of a family member or a caregiver. The walkaways suffering from Alzheimer's are the biggest legal challenge for a memory care facility.

"How are you doing, darling?" said Larson, bestowing a courtly kiss on top of the head of one of the residents sitting at the dining table in one of the units. She offered a smile but no other response. The smell of lunch wafted over from the oven in the nearby open kitchen.

Two caregivers are here at all times, watching over a rotating cast of residents living in the geriatric version of a college share home. Larson hasn't coached baseball in a decade but he retains the deliberate and semi-stern manner of a no-nonsense PE teacher as he relates the story of his grandparents being confined to a poorly managed corporate nursing home back in Paxton, Illinois—basically a warehouse of the nearly dead that smelled of diapers and despair.

The Villas are different: lots of natural light, non-cafeteria food, a one-to-five staffing ratio, activities to keep the withering mind active. "They get to live in a nice house; they get to know their caregiver instead of somebody dropping in who doesn't even know their name," said Larson.

He and his partner have had to make some structural adjustments through trial and error. They welded an extra three feet on top of the six-foot perimeter fence after a farmer from Canada kept successfully climbing it in the belief that he had to go milk the cows. And while exit doors must necessarily be at a minimum to foil potential walkaways, the architects suggested a discreet side door so that residents who die can be taken out without creating an upsetting spectacle. And this is never done during mealtimes.

Assisted living facilities like the Villas are like the graduate program for the cinderblock country club homes. On the other side of Interstate 19 from the Villas is a mammoth one-story spaceship called Silver Springs, whose carpeted hallways seem to go on and on. The approximate center is a café with padded chairs and pitchers of iced tea and lemonade on side tables. Glenn Lundell, who helped do the materials contracting for the hydrogen bomb explosions at Bikini and Eniwetok, has lunch here on most days. He's ninety-four but his hearing and thinking are as good as they ever were.

"You learn lessons in humanity living here," he told me over a 5 p.m. dinner. "There are those who fight aging and those who accept it. You learn to tell the difference."

On a long winter afternoon, I sat with Dick Coler, a ninety-two-year-old rancher, in the octagon-shaped atrium in his apartment at Silver Springs. His case was classified as hospice, and his pulmonary fibrosis was then bad enough that he needed constant oxygen, but he kept up a stream of stories and jokes as the sun-shadows lengthened across the walls and the upright cactus ribs in the corner.

"I'm pretty well blessed with a family," he said. "Married sixty years. I have no regrets. I had a good business. Sold that. Made money in real estate, did ranching with Frank Moson. Rode professional rodeo in Red Lodge, Montana."

Totems from his life are all around the room. There are two volumes of cowboy poetry that he wrote, and several Western novels of his authorship. Many cowboy hats. Oil paintings of horses, canyons, and the Taos pueblo. The taxidermy of a bonefish he caught on a trip to the Bahamas with the golf pro Jack Nicklaus in 1978. Pictures of him and his wife, Scottie, when they both had full, round faces. A balsa wood oar carved for him by a Native guide named Eph Shilling on a long-ago trip to Canada. The inscription reads: "May his trip through the happy hunting grounds be more enjoyable than his life in the northwoods."

Ten green bottles of oxygen sit at his side, and the machine makes a low hiss.

Dick has enjoyed his time at Silver Springs as best he can. He used to play in a band with a guitarist, a piano player, and a guy on the trumpet. But one by one, they all died. "We kind of broke up," he said.

He still has many friends. People around here call him "The Cowboy," and he obliges the image by peppering his speech with words like *pardner* and *dadgum*. A few weeks before, six men from the local American Legion came by and pinned a medal on him honoring his time as a U.S. Marine master sergeant.

He has faith in a painless transition for whatever comes next. "The Lord and I have a special meeting every once in a while," he tells me. And also: "When you're dead you don't know you're dead, just like when you're stupid you're not aware of it."

By any measurement, Dick Coler has lived a happy and successful life. He has lived to be ninety-two years old and retired into more comfortable surroundings than most other nonagenarians, with a cheerful attitude, good finances, no anxiety, and almost no regrets.

So why should this be so sad?

Memory comes to Dick in flickers and fragments: playing linebacker for Purdue, acting a bit part in a movie with Spencer Tracy, his father on the farm back in Ohio, the sight of dogs coffled by the neck so they wouldn't bite the hamstrings of the cows. They are like the same series of photographs on a repeated shuffle: two-dimensional and frozen, predictable, lacking the sensuality of earlier recollections.

And one particular image from an otherwise forgettable day on the Moson ranch over in Santa Cruz County back in the 1950s. Dick was out riding with a hand named Les Parker who amazed him by drawing his pistol and dropping a rattlesnake at twenty yards. Dick thought he'd just witnessed an act of supreme marksmanship until Les told him he'd loaded his pistol with birdshot. It was a good gag, funny at the time.

Dick thinks about that day, over and over.

—

A common Green Valley ritual when someone dies is for their children to show up in town, take the last pet into the shelter, pick through their possessions, and donate the unwanted stuff to the White Elephant Thrift Store, where Betty Chadwick is one of 640 volunteers who accept the goods, arrange them by department, and put sticky price tags on them.

The store is a giant arched building looking like a mausoleum, with a polished concrete retail floor the size of a high school gym. The volunteers here receive a lot of formal suits on hangers, a sign the owner has either died or gone to an assisted living center. Service medals get sent back to the Department of Defense. Wedding photos—the names of the guests no longer known—must be thrown away. Two dumpsters on the loading dock get emptied of memories three times a week.

In the holiday section, an eighty-two-year-old volunteer from New Hampshire was helping arrange Santa and snowman figurines and a ceramic mouse dressed as Mrs. Claus in a painted red jacket. The volunteer asked me not to use her name, so I'll call her Sarah.

Sarah told me she felt numb and paralyzed when her second husband died six years ago. He had loved her in ways she didn't know were possible after she suffered an abusive first marriage. She had grown up an outcast, with big Coke-bottle glasses, and went through high school without ever going on a date. Losing her husband right after their move to Green Valley was an uncomfortable flashback to that social isolation.

But Sarah decided not to wither, forcing herself into making new friends, first through a grief support group and then by working multiple shifts at White Elephant. She was determined to avoid the dull noonday blanket of loneliness by throwing herself into activities. "The whole thing is you're not alone," she told me. "This town is full of people who have had horrible things happen in their lives. But you don't need to be alone if you don't want to be."

And indeed, a booklet published by the *Green Valley News* shows the meeting times and places for a dizzying array of clubs: mah-jongg, billiards, investments, weight loss, writing, quilting, radio, choirs, genealogy, ballroom dance, astronomy, tango, acting, wood carving, politics, twenty-three churches of various denominations, tennis, volleyball, twelve-stepping, hiking, pickleball. It is possible to be even busier here than during the parenting and career phase of life.

Sarah tries to keep thoughts of death at bay, as do most in Green Valley when contemplating the transition from existence to nonexistence, or to a different existence that cannot be fathomed. When she got a knee replaced not long ago, the CAT scan showed an enlarged heart. *Oh dear, I'm on my way out*, she thought, but then forced it away. Though she isn't happy with the Catholic church of her girlhood faith, she considers herself a follower of Jesus.

"I hope I go quiet," she said. But for now, she has achieved one of the hardest lessons of her life—the trick of late-stage reinvention and the full gratitude of what she had been given. As she said of the amazing happiness that she had with her second husband: "I never would have found out if it hadn't happened."

Sarah is asking an existential question, one for the young and the old: the same question asked by Betsy Chadwick when she looks at the moon over the mountains, and the same that the rest of the world outside the gates of retirement would do well to bear in mind. *How can I make the most of what time I have remaining?*

At the regular meeting of the Green Valley Rotary Club at Canoa Ranch Golf Resort, the members held a moment of silence for one of their members, Andie Grantham, a retired histologist who had died of cancer that week after lingering in a coma. She had been the president of another nearby Rotary Club and was one of those people on whose shoulders the whole town seems to have rested.

Before the country club staff brought out a lunch of beef Wellington, a retired military chaplain, Eugene Freisen, stood up to deliver the benediction. Everybody stood. A quartet of golfers was holing out on the green in full view of the picture window, a pastoral oil painting in motion.

Eugene was ninety-one years old and had lived an amazingly full life, one that seemed improbable for a Mennonite farm boy from Nebraska. He had served as army chaplain, a paratrooper, a missionary to the Indigenous people in Suriname, a psychologist, a hospital administrator, and a Methodist minister. He had traveled the world and made thousands of friends before coming to a place of rest as a widower in a country club villa in his tenth decade.

"Oh Lord," said Eugene, his head bowed. "How ludicrous it for us, who number into the billions of inhabitants on this speck of cosmic dust called earth, in the mystery of millions of galaxies, to invoke the presence of a creator of a vast universe that we cannot began to comprehend. It brings thoughts of mortality and immortality. Let us remember who we are and where we're going. We often forget who really we are."

ONWARD FROM PATAGONIA, DOWN SOME unhappy miles on an asphalt road, and then blissfully back into the juniper hills. I was now headed for the Huachuca Mountains, the last sky island to get over before the border. Step by step, range by range, this is how Arizona is put together: canyons, peaks, deserts, plateaus, all clicked together in a complex pattern that can never be fully grasped in a single lifetime.

What I thought had been so simple—a dull place full of corporate chains I only wanted to escape—proved more beguiling than I ever appreciated. There were times I arrogantly thought I "knew" Arizona when I was younger, but I now realize I'll never understand it beyond the tiny portion of its existence that I was privileged to live in, or see even a fraction of the secret forces and hidden histories that assembled the state. All the corners of it I'll never see; all the people I'll never know; all the actors whose names I will never learn.

Such is the nature of a lifelong dialogue with a geography. There are colors in the spectrum that cannot be perceived by the weak human eye, red-greens and blue-yellows that swim outside sight. Arizona's natural hues are the most painterly among the states. Its dazzling landscape is the subject of uncounted watercolors and oils, plus more annual photographs snapped than there are stars in the galaxy.

The most powerful recruitment tool for newcomers in the previous century—beyond the famous low taxes and hostility to unions—were the color images of mountains and canyons depicted in *Arizona Highways*, the most influential state-sponsored magazine in American history. The red and yellow hues of our sunsets are the central design elements of the state flag. But even more important to Arizona's deepest character are the sightless colors that transcend time and history that nobody can really see.

This section of the trail goes through the Canelo Hills, classic ranching country, tawny brown, and named by Spanish settlers for "cinnamon." The land is pockmarked with stock tanks and windmill basins that make water no problem for a long-distance trekker with a strong stomach. I used a filter on the brownish liquid laced with mud and cow spittle and then dosed it with an iodine tablet. Something else this walk has taught me: a new relationship with water. I now understand its crucial role in the body, how it is both motor oil and gasoline.

Cows with plastic tags on their ears stared at me as I walked through a crowd of them near sunset at a place called Down Under Spring. Their eyes glistened and looked vaguely sinister, though I knew they meant me no harm. This is grass-fed Red Angus country, and I imagined some of these steers were bound for the packing plant in the next few months. It was tempting to feel sorry for these gentle creatures.

Ranching is an enormous client industry for public land in Arizona, and the renegotiation of federal grazing leases is a reliable source of contention. But what drives the business for many of its modern practitioners is a sense of aesthetics and mythology, a fun retirement project for the wealthy. The beef industry—once a giant of the nineteenth-century economy—is today an economic skull. Beef sales make up just 0.5 percent of total gross domestic product in any given year. Our Stetson hats are sold almost exclusively to tourists.

The greenish trickle in some of these creeks is a reminder of the paucity of water in the Canelos that confronted the first ranchers who came here from Texas in the 1870s in hopes of getting rich by selling their beef to the hungry cavalry over at Fort Crittenden and Fort Huachuca. They shoveled together dams made out of dirt to conserve what water they could, often leaving ghost humps on the landscape that marked the spot of a now-vanished spring or river-bed. Capturing even a thin flow could mean the difference between solvency and bankruptcy.

The physical artifacts belie the essential kinetic nature of ranching. It's agriculture in motion. Money on the hoof, as the saying went. To raise cattle for sale is to keep them rotating: from winter to summer forage, from the fields to the feedlot to the railhead. Not for nothing is the cattle drive an essential ritual of the business that turned into an American parable for adventure and transformation.

I made a camp in a melancholy little notch at the base of Sunshine Canyon, a funnel that leads up into the Huachuca Mountains. The weather was looking sketchy when I started climbing early in the morning up the drainage, scaling a layer of red sandstone over pumice and past hand-built stone walls that stand as a tombstone to a prior settlement. Bushes turning autumn colors enhanced the feel of chilliness in the morning shade. It's not uncommon for the higher parts of the range to get snow in odd months and as I got up to the first crest, I could see dark clouds dumping water into the San Rafael Valley over in Mexico, a potential lightning hazard if the cataract drifted closer. The center of the squall shimmered in the late morning light. A Tohono O'odham song has these lines:

> And somewhere along the way I stopped again
> And it was my cloud that reached me
> And it was sprinkling wetly
> And here I reached your rainhouse and looked in
> There lay many winds, there lay many clouds
> There lay many seeded things.

The promising storm broke apart after a half hour without having granted a drop to this side of the border. Another Arizona psalm: *The Lord giveth water. But the Lord mainly withholds.*

The final ascent to Miller Peak (elev. 9,465 feet) offers a view of the city of Sierra Vista, the commercial blob that formed around

Fort Huachuca, a military garrison commissioned as a headquarters for fighting Geronimo and his band of Chiricahua Apaches, now a training center for army intelligence and a center for cyber warfare. The orderly network of streets visible from this peak is a shadow of the unseen networks humming with electronic aggression over at the fort, which lies tucked near the mountains next to a stream where the cavalry used to wash up after their expeditions.

All downhill from here. The path winds down the southern slopes, affording a view of the spot where historians think the caravan headed by Francisco Vázquez de Coronado entered the present-day United States for the first time in 1540, chasing wild rumors of Cibola, the seven cities of gold. Some of his men laid eyes on the Grand Canyon, and the clanking parade wandered as far as what is now central Kansas before Coronado quit and retreated to a life of minor officialdom in Mexico City, having seen far more than he pocketed. His epic exuberance and disappointment would be repeated in smaller typography more than two hundred years later when silver-hungry farmers heard stories of riches in Arizona, the place of the good oak tree.

Within three hours I was in a parking lot at a place called Montezuma Pass, just a few miles from the international line. A van from the U.S. Border Patrol had a giant radio mast poking up from its roof and about seven soldiers from Fort Polk, Louisiana, were leaning against a railing nearby, looking bored out of their minds. One of them told me they'd been dispatched here for the "national emergency" on the border declared the year before by presidential fiat. They had caught almost no crossers. The private said nothing bad about his duties but gave his eyes a roll to let me know what he thought. I wished him well.

And then my parents were here in their white truck. I hugged them hard, even though I'd last seen them just six days ago. While I was home in Tucson during that break, I had noticed a small but subtle change: the mountain consciousness. When embraced by the softness of an Arizona city—the air conditioning, the restaurants, the cold drinks, the shaded patios—it is easy to forget the presence of the encircling mountains and the vastness they promise that lies beyond them, just as it is easy to forget our own mortalities or be reminded that we're carbon-based mites clinging to a rock in a sea of unfathomable intergalactic space. "In nature, we never see anything isolated," wrote Johann Wolfgang von Goethe, "but everything in connection with something else before it, beside it, under it, and over it."

I had become aware in a way I hadn't been since late childhood of the high slabs of the Santa Catalinas overlooking our corner of Tucson. How could I have failed to see them for days on end? I had watched clouds cast shadows on them over the roof of a ritzy mall called La Encantada—the haunted—that had been built in front of the elementary school where my mother used to work. From their peaks, you could look north to the Black Hills and Montana Peak in the Superstitions and from there to the Mazatzals, which offered a glimpse of the San Francisco Peaks from which you could see into the Grand Canyon and to the dazzling red malpaís of the Colorado Plateau. Forms beyond forms. Even in its topographical chaos and its human confusions, Arizona was connected to itself in an unbroken chain.

There was one more piece to click in place. An old friend of mine, Adam Skolnick, had brought his wife, April, here to walk the last mile and a half with me down to the iron obelisk that signified the U.S.-Mexico border and the end of the Arizona Trail. We ambled down slowly, laughing as we went.

Here was the moment that I yearned for during the hard moments of weather and fatigue. Now I didn't want the walk to end. It was over all too soon, and here we were walking the last paces toward International Boundary Monument 102 behind a few strands of barbed wire fence, the only barrier at this spot on the international line.

On our side, the monument read: *Boundary of the United States, treaty of 1853, re-established by treaties of 1882–1889*. I went over the barbed wire and read the same message on the south side. *Límite*

*de la Republica Mexicana, tratado de 1853, restablecido por tratados
de 1882–1889.*

Beyond the short pinnacle yawned the flax-colored expanse of
the San Rafael Valley and a few ranch outbuildings under a huge
sky. The air was scented with the morning's rain. I felt my heart take
grateful flight, as the dominant perception from this gorgeous slope
into a different country is one of flying, and of the non-separation
of anything in sight, the unity of all.

Within a year, this area would be sealed off by the Department
of Homeland Security and all the surrounding vegetation bulldozed to make way for a section of thirty-foot steel bollard fence
that obliterates the view and slams down a far more expensive and
brutal monument.

The new border wall is an epitaph. Here at the bottom of Arizona used to stand an unobstructed picture window into the house
next door—the home of a neighbor that has molded us from the
very beginning, and one we still can't embrace and still fail to understand.

LECHUGUILLA

Two days after he almost died in the desert, Daniel stood in front of a charity cafeteria. He held a cheap camouflage bag with a tag on it from the U.S. Border Patrol certifying they'd sorted through all his clothes before they fingerprinted him, photographed him, taken down all his details, and loaded him onto a bus for ejection into Mexico through the port of entry.

There are thorn stubs in his hands he hasn't been able to pry out, another reminder of his failed crossing. Behind him is a weary line of cars and produce trucks on a viaduct, chuffing exhaust, each waiting for their turn at the gates to El Norte. This can take up to eight hours. Daniel is waiting here in Nogales, Sonora, for another coyote to take him several miles along the border fence for another attempt. If he is caught again, he could be sentenced to approximately nineteen months in U.S. federal prison. But he won't be deterred.

Daniel is from the state of Quintana Roo on the Yucatan Peninsula. Work there is hard to find. Though there is a substantial amount of construction, most moneymaking activity is lorded over by cartels. Outfits like the Jalisco New Generation are quick to torture and dismember those who cross them, and few get a paying job without one of the narcos taking a nick. To even get a job, you have to pay a tribute up front, which Daniel could not afford. The murder rate went up 330 percent in two years. Local cops are so corrupt in Quintana Roo that the federal government seized control of eleven agencies. If you were with people you trusted, you could say the cartel boys were leeches. But you never showed open disrespect, unless you were tired of living.

I had to leave my house, Daniel says. My mother has ovarian cancer and I have to make money to take care of her. You never cross the border because you want to stay in the United States. You do it because of your need.

Daniel left his wife and child and caught a bus to Nogales with a friend, and they engaged the services of a coyote for a thousand dollars each. They were given the cheap bags and driven by night to a spot in the desert to the west. Then they were handed water jugs and told to start marching. The goal was a mountain their coyote called El Elefante, which in the United States is known as Elephant Head, a mound of magma on the western edge of the Santa Rita Mountains. A van would pick them up near there.

The trek went slow. They did their best to avoid walking across the dirt roads, where border patrol agents had dragged old tires lashed together to create a blank slate for footprints. They watched the skies for helicopters.

On their left side during the day they could see the ziggurat pinnacle of Baboquivari Peak—a sign they were still going north. They slept at night with the cheap bags under their heads and stayed under bushes during the hottest parts of the day. Daniel hated going through the empty washes—he called them *pozos*, pits. Dryness like this was never seen in the Yucatan. Daniel was a bit fat, out of shape, and lagging behind the others, but nobody made fun of him or threatened him. His feet blistered up. This went on for three days.

They started to run out of water. El Elefante was nowhere in sight. Daniel started to feel like he was creaking inside. He couldn't walk much further. Despite the assurances of his friend and the rest of the crew, he worried they would leave him behind in the cactus-covered hell. He prayed even harder.

The Bible says God gives strength to those who are weak. From a long time ago, Daniel said, I believed He does everything to save you.

Thoughts of being left behind, *dejado atras*, began to plague him, not just as a physical possibility but as a spiritual condition. Even the idea of dying wasn't as terrifying as this. You only had to do that once. You passed through the curtain to the final judgment. Daniel hated the idea of not seeing his mother, wife, and child before that happened, but he was ready to face God. He had lived thirty-six years and not everything had been perfect, but he believed he had done right by the mandate of Jesus.

Getting left behind in this place, though, was an unfathomable terror. He would be forced to stay, *quedarse*, in a place that looked like purgatory. His body would mingle with the dust.

He could feel his throat muscles stretching with thirst. Then he became dizzy. And without anyone in the party realizing what was happening, a green-and-white SUV from the U.S. Border Patrol came bouncing toward them. Nobody bothered to run; Daniel didn't think he would have the strength, anyway. The officers had to drag him toward a waiting vehicle with mesh on the windows. Daniel drank deeply from the water they gave him.

Now he stood on Bulevar Luis Donaldo Colosio, a street named for an assassinated Mexican politician, waiting for his friend to find another coyote. The traffic backed up to the south of Mariposa gate was a line that seemed to have no end. He could get some more money wired up from Quintana Roo for another try at the job that would be waiting for him, one that could pay up to six times as much as he could make back home, with no harassment from the cartels.

People are going through hard times, he says. People are going to keep crossing. What else am I going to do?

—

There is taking on, and there is casting off. To walk along the migrant trails of southeast Arizona is to happen across a succession of emptied black water jugs and cheap vinyl backpacks, such as the one Daniel carried.

I'm out in the Roskruge Mountains west of Tucson on a patrol with a volunteer with the Pima County Office of the Medical Examiner. The purpose of the trip is to monitor the state of the faint trails trodden by the northbound and see if anyone out there needs water or immediate medical aid. Another purpose is to see if any new corpses lie in this quadrant.

We're carrying cell phones loaded with data that pinpoint the locations where others have died, marked by red dots. One of the geotags we walk past bears the following entry, noting the medical examiner's case number, name of the decedent, date of discovery, and the determined cause:

03-00841
Cristobal Candelario, Dionoso
2003-05-23 (C1)
Hyperthermia due to exposure

These coronial notations can help locate other bodies. Ground that was deadly seventeen years ago has a greater chance of indicating where others may have died, their remains secreted under ledges or curled around the trunks of shrubs. But not all who die alone in the desert do so clinging to whatever shade they can find. Some in the last stages of disorientation have been known to simply lie down in the open, limbs akimbo, their faces turned up to the killing sun as if in embrace.

A number of entries in the data set and maps—first compiled by a diligent geosciences professor named Ed McCullough—have no names or causes attached to them. They read only: *unidentified skeletal remains.*

The medical examiner's volunteer and I walk past chunks of volcanic rocks tumbled off the side of a rounded hill. He's a data guy, unemotional, but something inside keeps motivating him to come out here on the grim walkabouts. He can cover perhaps two square miles a day, looking right and left the whole time, a tiny fraction of the aridity rolling away for 1,800 square miles in every direction.

He points to a spot where he had previously come across a body and had to phone it in. "She was fully fleshed," he said. The animals had not yet gotten to her.

We circumnavigate the hill, walking about fifty yards apart. To the southwest, we can see the rounded pinnacle of Baboquivari Park, the holiest mountain in the Tohono O'odham cosmology. The creator god I'itoi lives in a cave near its base. He came to life and taught the people their ways, but they killed him and he came to life again. He stalks the land. It is said he can raise armies and sing his enemies into blindness.

I can see a faint trail through the cholla; there are said to be close to five thousand miles of these migrant tracks in Arizona's southeast desert. I see more black plastic jugs, the basic shape of handled bleach bottles, cracking open after weeks in the sun. Near them, a pair of slippers made from carpet strips to avoid leaving footprints in the sand that could pinpoint their locations.

A faded jug label reads El Manantial, with an address of Altar, Sonora, a farm town an hour south of the border that has turned into a metropolis of border capitalism, a depot where the crossers make their deals with coyotes. The central square of Altar is lined with three-dollar guesthouses;

the open-air market stalls are stuffed with camouflage T-shirts, salt tablets, billed caps, prayer cards, bandages, crackers, electrolytes, and caffeinated sports drinks. For young children, there is Pedialyte. Our Lady of Guadalupe Church is a traditional last stop to light a votive candle and pray for a safe crossing.

Water companies in Altar started bottling their product in black plastic in the belief that it would be tougher to spot from border patrol aircrafts. It doesn't really work, but it provides psychological comfort. The other common artifact from this town are cheap Chinese-made backpacks into which the migrants typically stuff a change of clothes and a few minimal personal items. The packs are supposed to be tossed aside as soon as the pickup van arrives; the immigration cops at the checkpoint known exactly what they signify. The pickup spots on Highway 86 in the Tohono O'odham Reservation are littered with stacks of them.

The volunteer has found curious items inside these discarded packs: cellphones, sprigs of garlic carried in the belief they repel rattlesnakes, photographs of family left far behind, prayer cards bearing the image of the Virgin of Guadalupe. The backpacks are sometimes dropped by accident when border patrol agents do an overhead "dusting" with their helicopters: banking to one side so the rotor wash kicks up big clouds of dirt and scatters the party below in all directions.

GPS indicates another red dot in a clearing:

13-01545
Castano Forero, Liborado
2013-06-11
probable hyperthermia

When the body's internal temperature soars above the body's own ability to control it, hyperthermia results. It's an excruciating way to die. Sweat releases salts and electrolytes and a fatal cascade begins. Muscles begin to cramp. The stomach clenches. Already burned skin gets redder. Without electrolytes to hold in precious water, sweat pours out of the glands like an internal dam has burst; the water might well as be dumped on the ground for all the good it does.

Bodily temperatures start inching north; they can reach 104 degrees within an hour. And thinking gets fuzzy, which is perhaps why many who succumb do so in places of total sun exposure. They simply stop feeling the sun hammering down the way the icebound stop feeling their limbs, a merciful anesthesia that extreme temperatures convey upon the dying. But the feeling of clothes lying on the skin becomes as painful as sandpaper; it is not uncommon to rip off garments in the last moments and die naked. Some of the dead have been found with handfuls of sand stuffed in their mouths. In their last moments, they think they are swimming in cold, clear water.

—

The slant of Arizona's southern border, which gives the state the distinctive shape of a rocking chair, is an afterthought of the Mexican-American War.

The Gadsden Treaty of 1853, signed five years after hostilities ended, put a land dispute to rest by running a surveyor's line along the thirty-first parallel until a spot not far from the present-day city of Nogales. The line then kinks northwest to hit a spot on the Colorado River a comfortable distance south of its confluence with the Gila. This was a compromise designed to leave Mexico with an intact land bridge to the Baja peninsula while granting the United States what was then thought to be a strategic river junction, which is now useless.

Nobody gave this arbitrary border much credibility for decades. Citizens of both nations crossed it as a matter of daily business. It was marked at wide intervals with cairns of white-painted rocks, sometimes knocked over in the night. Only in 1924, in the midst of national paranoia over Chinese immigration, did anyone start treating it as a domestic threat. The Labor Appropriation Act established the U.S. Border Patrol. Horse-mounted agents rode the line watching for Asians crossing the desert in hopes of finding menial labor.

The modern cult of death around the Arizona desert, however, began in 1994 with a national mood swing that turned against Mexican immigrants. A policy change called Operation Gatekeeper put the emphasis on urban crossing spots in San Diego, Nogales, and El Paso, armoring them up with high walls, barbed-wire forests, and surveillance equipment. The intent was to push human traffic into the harshest quarters of the Sonoran Desert, seen as a natural barrier that needed no investment—a deterrent "wall" made of sun and dirt. But it created a killing zone. The Mexican and Central American farmers put out of business by NAFTA and its flood of cheap corn were not going to let the Arizona desert become an impediment. Family and food, as in Neolithic times, had to come first.

At an evening meeting at the Southside Presbyterian Church in Tucson, a bearded man named John Fife stood up to speak. I hadn't seen him since I interviewed him for my high school newspaper back in the mid-1980s when he was active in the movement to hide people fleeing the civil war in El Salvador. Now he was active in the Humane Borders movement, helping teams of volunteers set out jugs of water near the secret killing paths. Fife looked a bit more weathered from the time I last saw him but still had the same buoyant demeanor, and he told the newbies in the room a bit of the history.

Migrant deaths in southern Arizona had been so rare that nobody bothered to keep statistics on them prior to Operation Gatekeeper. But then bodies began to stack up in the solar abattoir, and the freelance mercy efforts kicked into high gear. Fife struck an agreement with a sector chief of the U.S. Border Patrol: the agents would not conduct surveillance on the humanitarian water drop sites. But in 2005 a new boss came to town and reneged on the agreement. He pressed the point by arresting two twenty-three-year-old volunteers for driving a critically ill migrant to the hospital. "Harboring certain aliens" is a crime punishable by five years in prison, a perverse section of the federal code that does not distinguish humanitarian rescue from human trafficking.

The hostility between the U.S. Border Patrol and Humane Borders (and especially their more radical cousins at a group called No More Deaths) climbed to record highs under the Trump administration. Covert surveillance increased. A pair of agents watching a building called The Barn near the town of Ajo filmed a geography PhD candidate and humanitarian volunteer named Scott Warren pointing at a cleft between hills for two men from Guatemala who needed to know where the highway was in the event they ran out of water.

In the mechanistic language of the border patrol and federal prosecutors, the hills he pointed at were "large terrain features," not the Childs Mountains, and what he had done was not mere good manners but a combination of "harboring" and "conspiracy" that could net him twenty years.

It was practically a foregone conclusion that a federal jury would acquit Warren, which they did in November 2019, but not before the U.S. Attorney's Office wasted thousands of hours chasing the longshot case, probably because somebody wanted to promote themselves as a hardliner within the Trump Justice Department. That same year, 497 people died in the killing fields on the border.

———

Never mind immigrants commit far fewer crimes than U.S. citizens. Never mind they pay extravagant amounts of taxes that go directly into the public treasuries. Never mind that border towns are statistically among the safest in Arizona. Never mind the vast majority of street drugs are smuggled through well-guarded official ports of entry in the middle of cities. Never mind that immigrant labor built Arizona, and never mind that its economy would utterly collapse without it. The cold truth is that an overmilitarized border is profitable for almost everyone who has a stake in it but the migrants themselves.

Congressional immigration hawks benefit from the tough-guy image that comes from bringing big security projects and chests of federal money. Local police departments get grants from a program called Operation Stonegarden that pays them to divert their resources toward capturing the undocumented. Coyotes get to charge $1,700 or more per head, an underground business that reaps an estimated $24 billion for the gangsters who rely on danger to justify the fare.

Most of all, the U.S. Border Patrol thrives on an endless mission that provides secure employment for more than forty-five thousand armed employees. They are difficult to fire, even though the agency's top officials have estimated that one in five agents has engaged in corrupt activity, such as abusing a detainee or taking a bribe to wave through a vehicle that ought to have been searched. Border patrol agents are arrested at twice the rate of their counterparts in city police departments.

The bill for the fortified border with Mexico has cost the United States more than $300 billion in the last three decades—a sum roughly equal to the cost of the entire space shuttle program plus the annual gross domestic product of the city of Philadelphia thrown in. And this for a flimsy screen to prevent a migration that financially benefits the United States far more than it drains away. Why, then, do we do it?

We have been told of an "invasion," a word repeated like an incantation. The brown hordes from the south will rise up and sweep across the land. It doesn't matter that Tucson was mostly a Mexican town until the beginning of the last century; it doesn't matter that Arizona was *all* Mexico not so long ago. The caravans of the South remain primed for an imagined Reconquista—an invasion. Fox News used the word approximately sixty times a month in the fall of 2018. Now it's everywhere.

"This is an invasion. There's no other way to describe it," wrote Glenn Beck. "America cannot allow this invasion," said a Trump ad. "I'm protesting the invasion of the United States by people of foreign countries," said a man from Oracle, Arizona, outside a children's detention facility. "I have noticed a change in people saying 'illegals' that now say 'invaders.' I like this," wrote a man named Robert Bowers. Six days later, he killed eleven people at a Pittsburgh synagogue. A twenty-one-year-old man killed twenty at an El Paso Walmart after posting a note online that said: "This attack is a response to the Hispanic invasion of Texas."

America's border-industrial complex profits from the heated rhetoric. So do the freelance border enforcers who tend to have extreme right-wing views and criminal backgrounds. Customs and border protection agent Lee Morgan II called one band of them "a volatile mix of wannabe vigilante soldier-boys and Southern tobacco-stain-chinned rednecks." And they commit violent crimes at a far higher rate than the migrants they delight in hounding.

Then there is the detention racket. All the crossers who get caught must be detained before their deportation hearings, and an archipelago of 250 federal lockups is stretched along the border, costing taxpayers $5 million a day. Some inmates can wait months or years for their cases to be heard. Juveniles and children separated from their families during the Trump administration's nauseating "zero-tolerance" deterrence experiment in 2018 were held in seven Arizona facilities run by the private company Southwest Key.

The primary lockup for adults is a series of facilities in the town of Florence, home to the stone barn of the old 1908 state penitentiary, a place where guard labor is plentiful and prying eyes are scarce. The biggest unit is known as the Florence Service Processing Center; it gives away nothing to what might be "serviced" or "processed" in the complex that sprawls behind cyclone wire and under klieg lights, as relentless as feeding troughs on an industrial pig farm and just as hopeless. If the penal accouterments were stripped away, it would resemble nothing so much as one of the slaughterhouses that many of those inside had been trying to reach for the privilege of a gruesome minimum-wage job.

Euphemisms abound in this parallel world at the edge of the Arizona consciousness. "They call them detention centers, but they're indistinguishable from prisons," said Daniel Hernandez of the Florence Project, a legal aid group. "People enter and leave in shackles, and the immigrants are made to don jumpsuits like hardened criminals. The buildings are like warehouses and they call each cellblock a 'pod' or 'tank.' The food is often rotten. Solitary confinement is enforced casually. Suicide attempts are common. Medical neglect is atrocious."

A private company called CoreCivic makes $331 million per year from this facility along with its chain of other immigration lockups across the Southwest, most of which are strategically located. Not because of their proximity to the border—Florence is a two-hour drive away—but because of their discretion. "The men and women held behind the perimeter fences are never seen, never discussed," Tom Barry has written. "The prison is treated as a waste dump, similarly placed on the community's edge where property values are low and there are no neighbors."

When seen in satellite photographs, the grid of passageways between the cellblocks at the Florence Service Processing Center looks like the orderly streets at the master-planned jumble of houses just down Hunt Highway called Sun City Anthem at Merrill Ranch.

Between the migrant prison and the subdivision, on a volcanic mound called Poston's Butte, is the grave of Charles Poston, the gold-mining promoter who had plucked the name of the new territory out of the pages of a Spanish travelogue that mentioned Arizona, the place of the good oak tree.

Poston rests underneath a stone pyramid of his own design. The view from up here is panoramic. Poston is known as the "Father of Arizona."

—

One of the easiest places to cross the border unobserved is near the bottom of the Lechuguilla Valley, one of the least-visited places in the entire United States.

The fence here is not bolted into the mountains on either side, so there's lots of room to slip around the edges. Even a limping grandfather could do it. Then it's a forty-mile walk to the asphalt river of Interstate 8, where vans kitted out for a dozen or more passengers can better hide from the border patrol. Despite the snap entry, only the hardy or desperate try to walk up the valley. Veterans of the journey describe it like going to war.

A crosser will need at least three gallons of water, which is twenty-five pounds, and must do most of the walking at night. The Lechuguilla Valley is as flat as a city sidewalk but almost completely devoid of shade or sheltering brush. The average summer daytime high is 110 degrees, with zero precipitation. There are no human settlements: the military claimed nearly two million acres of this patch of the Sonoran Desert as a bombing range. Desertion yawns in all directions. The immigrants from wetter country have not walked in horrifying lunar territory before, this perfect killing griddle.

About five miles into the Lechuguilla Valley, they must walk across a single-lane dirt track called the Camino del Diablo—"the devil's highway"—an insane road blazed by Spanish padres in 1698 as they followed Native trails in search of a route to the Pacific. I'm on this road on a mild day in early March, looking at another black plastic jug cast aside. No telling how many hours it has lain here, or what kind of shape its onetime owner might be in. Soft migrant trails twist off to the north and south, but I don't have the practiced eye to spot them. They braid through the sand and loess in unpredictable patterns, appearing and disappearing over time like tiny channels of water in a river delta.

The Camino twists to the southwest and passes a hill with a rough trail carved into its slope, and I climb to the top to find a crude rock shelter in a semicircle. According to naturalist Bill Broyles, this spot has been used as a lookout post by smugglers to watch the movements of the border patrol, radioing them to their compatriots. The more sophisticated scouts know the times of shift changes and the patrolling habits of individual agents. Some of the lookout crews are known as "rip boys"—they aim to rob the migrants or the dope mules.

A rippling section of desert stretches to the northwest horizon, a basin between the Growler and Granite ranges with deceptive splashes of green that represent clumps of greasewood that would yield not a drinkable drop. Out there in various unmarked spots between May 23 and 24 of 2001, a series of men—many of them teenagers—succumbed to dehydration after wandering in desperate loops.

They had paid $1,400 each to a broker to get them safely into the United States so they could work menial jobs in Florida and Illinois, but the chief of the organization sent them a nineteen-year-old coyote named Jesus Lopez who put on a tough-guy persona but had no idea what he was doing. He let some of the migrants carry bottles of Coca-Cola as their only hydration. One wore black jeans, which absorbed sunlight like a sponge. Lopez started them off too early in the day, lost his bearings, told them to stay put while he went to fetch more water, and then never came back.

The group, many from the tropical state of Veracruz, soon realized their predicament but had no method to find their way. Fourteen of them collapsed and died; border patrol rescued twelve barely able to move, vomiting bile. "Have you ever seen a mummy from ancient Egypt? That gives you an idea," said one of the doctors in Yuma who treated survivors. "They looked shriveled up." A judge sentenced Lopez to sixteen years.

That atrocity, plus the general paranoia following 9/11, persuaded the government to drag three prefab trailers out to the edge of the Barry M. Goldwater Bombing Range and call it Camp Grip, because (it was explained) they were trying to "get a grip" on the influx of migrants. The camp can be disassembled and trucked away in a matter of hours, in the style of an Afghanistan forward operating base, but it has stood here twenty years. A gasoline-powered generator chugs outside.

I knock on the door. There's a barbecue grill outside and a wrought iron sign with barbed wire that says Cocina del Diablo, "the devil's kitchen." Inside I can see fitness equipment and not much else. It might as well be a space station. An agent eventually comes to the door. She's got cop eyes, humorless authority. I ask about road conditions ahead, and she doesn't have much to say. "We've been busy. Change of administration, you know?" She looks at me and ticks her head a bit eastward, and I take her to mean Washington.

And sure enough, a few more miles down the Camino, I come to a new service road bladed into the desert, bending off toward a new section of incomplete thirty-foot "wall" that is really a row of diamond-shaped steel pillars. Unused sections are stacked like dinner plates next to a fuel tanker bearing the logo of Fisher Industries. This is the North Dakota company that won, under opaque circumstances, a $1.3 billion task order from the U.S. Army Corps of Engineers to build forty-two miles of the barrier in the final weeks of the old presidential administration. Now the job sits idled, a mad pharaoh's lost dream.

In other places along Arizona's border, smugglers have sawed out portions of the steel pillars to create hatchways. Whole SUVs can come through holes cut to the size of garage doors and portable two-track ramps. A few enterprising Mexican scrap metal dealers scooped up pieces of older metal barriers and sold them for eight hundred dollars a truckload. The newer sections may one day also go into a drop forge, or perhaps stand here in the sandy desolation as a monument to a war whose purpose has been forgotten, like the foundations of an old Cossack garrison.

Looking down the line of the border fence is like an imperial vision. Here stands the official slash between two civilizations divided by sixteenth-century rivalries long gone to ashes in Europe but still preserved in the herbarium of the New World. One uses a country dialect of Latin formed in the Iberian peninsula in the waning days of the Roman empire, the other an unlikely soup of Old Norse and High French created through the repeated invasions of a cold northern island.

The surveyor's line drawn by the Gadsden Treaty parallels the Camino del Diablo for approximately forty miles past the Agua Dulce Mountains and across a nameless dry lake and the edge of the Pinacate volcanic field. This last-chance road was littered with graves long before the desert hegiras started in the 1990s. A swarm of would-be miners tried to rush into the California gold fields via the fastest means possible in the 1850s, following the old padres' improvised path to the Colorado River through Charles Poston's

Arizona. They had minimal word-of-mouth directions ("travel northwest for a day and then go two hours in the morning toward the second pass under the peak that looks like a big anthill"), and many were badly prepared for the ordeal. An official from the International Boundary Commission counted sixty-five graves in one day and concluded:

> It would be hard to imagine a more desolate or depressing ride. Mile after mile the journey stretches through this land of "silence, solitude and sunshine," with little to distract the eye from the awful surrounding dreariness and desolation except the bleaching skeletons of horses and the painfully frequent crosses which mark the graves of those who perished of thirst.

Today's northbound argonauts—chasing the "gold" of a job offer on a Chicago construction site or a Georgia pig farm—who want to avoid paying a coyote can use a few landscape features by which to navigate. One is the pinnacle of Sheep Peak on the extreme western side of the Growlers. Walking toward it is a reliable pointer to the halfway mark to Interstate 8.

Another is the triangular form of the magma mountain called Cabeza Prieta, or "dark head," some ten miles from the border. As you travel the Camino south of the peak, you can see dust devils rising up from the thirty-foot wall that look like steam leaks from cracks in the earth, signs of a vast underground fire. They puff up from the new service road parallel to fresh stretches of wall. The whirling dust devils common to the Southwest almost never rise up from native soil; they're a result of loose dirt kicked up by the wind around plowed fields of crops, or the earth scraped bare at construction sites.

One of the only semi-reliable sources of water out here—for ancient and modern travelers alike—can be found at a small natural basin called Tule Tank. Geology had to line up exactly right for one of these rainfall holders to even exist: the rock basin had to be partially shaded, made of granite, and under an incline to catch brief summer torrents. Even so, it can evaporate unpredictably. Travelers who counted on it were playing dice with their lives.

I had vague directions to Tule Tank that consisted of "1,600 feet up a narrow canyon" about a half mile from the Camino del Diablo. Without a map, I wandered around a valley that seemed to be right, but I couldn't be sure. Several side canyons branched away from the main channel, and I got tangled up in the acacia while poking around for this bathtub-sized feature. The thorns left bloody scratches on my legs and arms. A wispy smear of high cirrus clouds provided the only shade. Had I been a crosser who got separated or betrayed, my disorientation would have been fatal. Except for the whine of tinnitus in my ears, the silence was complete.

Earlier travelers had remarked on this tomb quality of the region: the disquieting lack of sound, the absence of birds or buzzing insects, the way the air itself acts as a smothering velvet cloak.

Olga Wright Smith, who camped near here for a year in a prospector's camp, later wrote that the persistent "deathlike hush" almost drove her mad, and all but convinced her that there were no other human beings in the universe. Time grows flabby and loses its shape for anyone who stays here for more than a day and feels the assault of the hours in addition to the piercing sun.

Beyond Tule Tank sprawls the Lechuguilla Valley—a flat funnel between mountain ranges that takes its name from the Spanish for "lettuce," but really from the spiky plant *Agave lechuguilla*, which grows best in hostile soils of high calcium carbonate. The ground alternates here between mushy sand and irregular granite pebbles over caliche.

This is the pitiless southwestern edge of the Sonoran Desert, its hardest expression, with tough perennial greens like sand milkweed, pygmy stonecrop, dwarf prickly pear, and a few limberbrush (*Jatropha cuneata*) that look like puffballs from a distance but offer only a maw of slicing thorns. The few plants capable of growing in the valley create a thin illusion of green. Seven miles from this spot, looming like a smaller version of the Teton Range baked down in a kiln, are the Tinajas Altas Mountains. Made primarily of pegmatite granite that shines whiter than bones in the moonlight and with menacing glare in the sun, the range is pockmarked with small cavities called tafone that look like a thousand empty eye sockets.

But as if to prove that even harsh deities can have a quality of mercy, the Tinajas Altas (Spanish for "high tanks") holds a treasure for those who know where to find it. A series of natural punchbowls on the eastern slope can hold stagnant rainwater for months, and that offers a last chance to ward off dehydration.

The Tohono O'odham people, of course, have known about this place for centuries and used it as a camping spot; they called it Oo'oowac, "place where the arrow fell." The Cocopah name is closer to practicality: Xamilk-wilau, "lofty water." There are anywhere from five to fifteen pools of water here at any given time. Only the bottom pool is easy to access; the others are cradled in a high cove and require a difficult scramble up a plane of rock. The water is stinking and nasty, a soup of bacteria, protozoa, giardia parasites, bird corpses, animal droppings—a cauldron loaded with fermenting carbon material. The color is deep green going to black.

"They know it's here," a border patrol agent told me later. "We sometimes find them there in groups. At some point, you'll drink anything."

Almost no evidence of human alteration can be found here, except for a single iron spike about a hundred feet up the incline, as well as several depressions in the stone worn hundreds of years ago where Tohono O'odham and Cocopah women used handheld rocks to grind mesquite beans into paste. Some unfortunate travelers of the 1850s arrived here in a dehydrated panic and found the first pool had gone dry. They died next to it, "their sufferings aggravated," wrote David Du Bose Galliard, "in many cases by the knowledge that the water which they craved could be obtained in one of the tanks but a few yards above them, had they the strength to climb it."

I scrambled up the slope all the way to the fifth pool, looked out across the Lechuguilla Valley going dimmer in the evening sun, and brought some of the water up to my lips. It tasted like a combination of a metal garden hose and a slimy banana.

That night, I slept on the bluff about a quarter mile away from the pools, a spot called "the mesa of the dead" for the number of people who had been buried here since the sixteenth century, those who had found the pools dry. No aboveground traces of these graves remain, but the dead seem unquiet. The sky was crammed with stars until the moon came up and made the peaks luminescent. At 3 a.m., a coyote howled and the sound echoed in the natural amphitheater.

One of the great nature writing clichés about the desert is that a wealth of life lies under the harsh surface, and that a viewer must only pay attention to see the majesty. It is true, for example, that the dirt underfoot often contains a hibernating mush of cyanobacteria, protozoa, and miniscule lichen, and that a cup of spilled water can result in the soil turning greenish with life within hours. But such science class tricks don't concern the person whose tongue is turning black.

The "land of little rain" of the poet's enthusiasms is an obscene griddle, a killer, a torturing instrument. Anybody crossing the Lechuguilla with limited supplies would be an absolute moron to stop for one second to enjoy its subtle beauty. Such aesthetics are the luxury of those with means to survive more than twenty-four hours, those who are not escaping poverty and gangs for the privilege of hard labor in a strange city. The desert is then an enemy, a bully to be avoided at all costs, as sinners shrink from an angry god. A *despoblado*: a vacant place, as empty as outer space.

As it happens, the most deadly place in Arizona is also among the most militarized. Pilots at Luke Air Force Base outside Phoenix, the Marine Air Corps Station Yuma, and the U.S. Army Yuma Proving Ground use it as a range for combat practice. The eerie silence that so disconcerted the early travelers of the Camino del Diablo is occasionally broken by the shriek of A-10s overhead, far disconnected from the killing ground below, and the ground off the dirt trails may be speckled with rusted rocket engines and bomb casings dropped years ago. Visitors are warned never to touch the ancient ordnance lest they trigger a long-dormant fuse and get their hands blown off.

In the predawn, unable to sleep any further, I traveled four miles down to the bottom of the Lechuguilla Valley, at least as far as it goes into the United States. The fence here is not affixed into the mountain rock and I steal into Mexico for fifteen minutes, looking at many hairpin loops of tire tracks. Here's where the innumerable vanloads are dropped off. A few cigarette butts are scattered on the ground, a last smoke before plunging forward. The lights of a ranchero a few miles south flicker and fade as the Tinajas Altas turn milky orange in reflected sun: another day like ten million others, up to fourteen hours of unbroken glare.

The soil here becomes so hot that the spiky *Agave lechuguilla* plant that gave the valley its name must spread its seeds underground just to keep them alive. The tough plant lives for three to twelve years before an extraordinary and never-to-be-repeated event occurs: it flowers. The stalk that rises from the cradle of its knife-sharp leaves can go as high as twelve feet; its colored blossoms of purple, gold, and red can be seen from miles away like a festival banner. But this is all the plant can give, an extravagant and defiant burst of life after years of hoarding every drop of water.

The Lechuguilla always dies after this event, its *petit mort* become final.

Almost nobody leaves the Lechuguilla without visions of negation and eternity. One of the only Anglo people to have ever lived here on a long-term basis, Olga Wright Smith, said that the desert had eventually made her indifferent to thoughts of death, no longer a frightening transition but just a slipping away from one place to another with a sigh breaking apart in the breeze. The air so dry that it made nails fall out of wood would embalm the body after the spirit had left. The interstellar stillness that once seemed so profane would turn to peace.

"You could simply go to sleep under that ironwood tree over there," she wrote, "and with the shining stillness around you, go on through all eternity feeling the sun and the wind and the warmth of life about you."

Not all have found it thus. Most survive their crossing through the Lechuguilla Valley, though they never forget what they have seen in the void. There is a taking on, and there is a casting off. Determined strivers like Daniel from Quintana Roo, and tens of thousands more like him every year, will keep risking it all to cross Arizona's killing grounds. The multibillion-dollar blocking efforts of the U.S. government will never succeed in stemming the tide of ambition, desire, and love that keeps people making a bid for a better life, the tough agave giving up the last bit of itself for the sake of a blossom.

A FEW DAYS AFTER REACHING THE BORDER, I crossed over it at a different place: the city of Nogales. There was one last pilgrimage I needed to make.

I walked over from the international port of entry to the sidewalk out front of the Hotel Fray Marcos de Niza, the only highrise in town, ten stories tall in the sterile International style, with a penthouse level that juts out like the stone cap on top of a cliff. The hotel opened in 1950 "with Americans in mind," noted a travel writer, and it used to be a lively center for betting that would have been illegal in the United States. When I was a teenager coming down here in search of booze—a Tucson rite of passage—the hotel was painted pink and stuffed with televisions showing dozens of baseball games and horse races. A costumed floor show went down each night in the Sky Room.

Now it looked a little scruffier. The exterior had been painted sandy brown and the gambling had been wiped out thanks to the rise of Arizona's Indian casinos. A policeman in a green uniform out on the street gave me a look of mingled curiosity and suspicion as I loitered outside the revolving door.

I was here to meet a man named Alvaro Valencia Maldonado, a son of the family who now owns the old ranch called Arizona. We had talked briefly on the phone and texted a few times. He promised to take me out to the site of the 1736 silver rush, which is behind a series of locked gates far from any paved road. Pretty soon, a black SUV pulled to the curb and I was waved into the front seat by Alvaro, a handsome man in his mid-thirties who introduced me to his friend Ivan in the backseat.

We headed south on Sonora Highway 15 and crested a rise that showed the eastern suburbs spilling over the hills like heather. The people who live here have a saying: *ambos Nogales*, both Nogaleses, a cohesive unit that happens to be cleaved in half by a political and metal slash through the deep ravine in which it sits. But "half" isn't right because the Mexican side has a population of a quarter million and the American side has barely twenty thousand, a snail riding on the back of a husky.

The shared economy of *ambos Nogales* is exemplified by the row of fruit and vegetable cooling houses out on the side of I-19. The northern side has been an entrepot for Mexican produce for more than a hundred years: about seven billion tons of tomatoes, radishes, cucumbers, corn, peppers, mushrooms, and virtually every other kind of supermarket perishable comes through this food keyhole, the highest trafficked on the border. The bigger Nogales to the south, by contrast, earns its living from American manufacturing interests, mainly in the maquiladora factories that make electronics. A strange trade here: motherboards and vegetables.

The perception of drug cartel violence has killed the tourist trade that used to thrive on American vice and the shopping for curios like clay pots, woven blankets, and onyx eggs on Avenida Obregon. The armoring-up of the border hasn't helped, either. What used to be a wall made of corrugated metal sheets left over from the Vietnam War—they had been used as portable helicopter landing pads—is now a spray of concertina wire attached at every level of a thirty-foot row of steel bollards that practically screams *bad neighbor*.

We stopped for a bowl of fish soup at an open-air roadside restaurant where Alvaro knew the owners. He knows a lot of people through his work as a petroleum salesman and also as an emergency management coordinator for the Sonoran state government. Holding down public and private jobs at the same time is not uncommon in Mexico. This dual role means he's personally acquainted with most of the mayors and police brass throughout the state, as well as the gas station owners. It's a pretty good place to be.

After making a second stop at a OXOO convenience store for a case of beer, Alvaro turned off onto Highway 2 and headed west through a flat valley of dun grass and oak trees. He pointed out the racetrack out front of a horse-breeding ranch owned by a wealthy man from Saudi Arabia. Then we pulled off next to a cluster of houses and Alvaro used his keys to open the first locked gate, which leads to a bumpy dirt track through a cleft in steep hills. Two more gates and a half hour later and we arrived at the Esmerelda Ranch, where Alvaro's relatives were busy herding up cattle for slaughter. Plastic tags dangled from their ears. A flat plain of grass lay in front of the corral, and on a hill over the creek, a ten-foot cross painted white had been mounted. The family walks up to it every Easter.

Alvaro's father-in-law fixed a saddle over Napoleon, a brown and white pinto with an easy disposition, and I swung my leg over him to and joined Alvaro and Ivan on their own horses. They led me on a path up the creek called Arroyo Plancha de Plantas. The walls narrowed to the width of a slot canyon in places, and the sharp brush came up to my knees. I wished for a pair of chaps. We paused at a spot where the stream riffles and splashes over a ledge six feet high; this spot is known on the ranch as *el salto*, the jump. A storm the other day had made the creek unusually high for this time of year.

We rode onward. Ahead of me and under the slopes terraced with mesquite trees, Alvaro started singing a popular tune by Antonio Aguilar, "Caballo de Patas Blancas," or "Horse with White Feet."

White-legged horse with steel horseshoes
Today you'll jump the bars before the stars come out
I'll ride you to the woman that I love

The path crossed and recrossed the stream at least six times before the canyon opened up and we emerged into a spacious glen. There's enough constant sunlight here to support a few sycamore trees next to the stream. On the banks, several circular muffins indicated the Esmerelda runs cattle in here from time to time. And carved into the side of a hill, a cave that Alvardo tells me once had bars on it and had been used as a jail by the Spanish authorities. We were getting close.

Another bend in the creek and we came to an extension of the valley with more holes in the valley slopes, except these extend far deeper into the earth, disappearing into darkness. Alvaro called whoa to his horse and dismounted.

"This is where it happened," he said simply.

Besides the horizontal mine shafts on the valley walls, there is not much human archaeology to see at the spot that gave Arizona its name. The remnants of a vaquero's stone cabin and what might have been a water well, now filled in. Though it was running high, the stream flowed only in sections, vanishing at one spot and re-appearing a few hundred feet later: a sign of unseen flow through the sand underfoot.

Yaqui herdsman Antonio Sirumura had wandered into this spot in the autumn of 1736 to prospect for minerals in his free time. As he testified later, he found a huge silver nugget lying next to a yellow rock. His children later helped him dig up a slab of near-pure silver that weighed fifty pounds. The unlikely nature of this find was what had led Juan Bautista de Anza to suspect the "discovery" was a ruse to launder some treasure stolen from the royal supply, and that the wealth of Arizona was a con. He never got to the bottom of the question.

I scrambled up the hill and used Alvaro's cell phone flashlight to walk in about fifty feet. Bat dung crusted the floors. The tunnel corkscrewed off into a new direction; some colonial miner's pursuit of silver through the bulwark of stone. All sunlight eventually faded to a pinpoint.

Here at the obscure valley that gave Arizona's name came a blast of images, imprints of personal memories from half a century: the scent of petrichor arising from my grandmother's front yard, the spaceship-like disk on top of the Hyatt in downtown Phoenix, mourning doves calling *coo-LOO-oo-coo-coo-coo*, the aroma of reclaimed water on a golf course, the windows of the abandoned jail in Clifton keeping watch over the mine traffic, the sun lowering over magma ridges in Kingman, a woman who fastened me with a meaningful look in a dormitory elevator in NAU when I was nineteen, the naked moon on the San Francisco Peaks, the smears of headlights outside the windows of the Pinon Café in Payson, the bite of dust in my mouth in a pinkish rivulet near Echo Cliffs, the concrete tubes on the playground at Lookout Mountain Elementary School, the incomprehensible lines in the cliffs on Shiva Temple.

Love is complicated. Love is rarely clean or explainable. Like a romantic partner whose greatest flaws make them attractive and mysterious, Arizona baffles and beguiles and will never leave my consciousness.

So many travelers with their own narratives have passed through. J. Ross Browne stopped in with Charles Poston, dreaming of their own utopias. Coronado before them, looking for the golden pueblos, and the Diné in search of the place of emergence their Hopi neighbors believed was at a bend in the river in the Grand Canyon.

It may be that the cities will become uninhabitable, that the name of Arizona will disappear, just as the Apache and Papago words for the land have faded from popular use. We are dust on the sandstone. A grain of porphyry copper, heading toward an unknown unity. I know my own narrative of Arizona, this one, will joins Browne's and innumerable others, books locked away in receding corners of basement archives. But while I was here, I tried to live it as best I could, and see it as clearly as I could. And the Arizona land will remain, no matter how we abuse it or fail to stand in awe of its powers.

To the north I could see an afternoon monsoon kicking up, dumping a shimmer of rains several miles away, over both Arizona and Sonora without regard to where the line is drawn. The water would eventually pass through this lazy intermittent stream that washed silver ore in 1736.

I lay on my stomach, bowed my head, and took a drink.

ACKNOWLEDGMENTS

I have many debts. Thanks must begin with Amy Silverman, who assigned me the essay on the Arizona novel for *Phoenix New Times* and gave me the confidence to think big. The University of Arizona School of Geography, Development and Environment granted me a fellowship after I finished the walk. I am grateful to Dr. Diana Liverman for the opportunity. Clara Migoya translated interviews in Nogales, Sonora.

I am in awe of the extensive scholarship of Greg McNamee and Thomas Sheridan; they were gracious enough to read the manuscript and offer suggestions. Geraldo Cadava helped me navigate some political history, and Jon Talton showed me the Phoenix that has always been hiding in plain sight.

At the University of Arizona Press, editors Kristen Buckles and Kathryn Conrad believed in the project from the start. Thanks, too, to Abby Mogollón, Amanda Krause, and Mari Herreras. It was a dream to work with this publisher after so many years of admiring their books.

Erin Dunkerly and Peter Zoellner kept the home fires aglow.

In unconscious ways, I've been "writing" this narrative since I was a six-year-old boy in the Moon Valley neighborhood of North Phoenix, wondering about the surroundings and how they came to be shaped that way. There would be no way to properly list all the people who helped me in the reporting or the trail, or otherwise taught me about Arizona in ways that can't be charted. But here are a few: Greg Cullison, Phil Boas, Alberto Ríos, Ray Stern, Korey Riggs, Ken Western, Kerry Benson, Elvia Diaz, Walt Nett, Greg Burton, Kristin Gilger, Ken Billingsley, Jason Ground, Jennifer Randle, Bonnie Henry, Weldon Schweigert, Jeff Strensrud, Kristen Cook, Joe Salkowski, Deborah Sussman, Mary Martha Miles, Mark Shaffer, Dennis Wagner, Jude Joffe-Block, Sybil Francis, Lattie Coor, Grady Gammage Jr., Paul Bergelin, Margaret Regan, Judd Slivka, Jack August, Lauren Gilger, Peter Corbett, Phil Gordon, Sativa Peterson, Robrt Pela, Jill Anderson,

Austin Aslan, Steve Vendituoli, Mariah Claw, Bruce Babbitt, Mary Tolan, Robin Hoover, John Fife, Dennis Welch, Morgan Loew, Daniel Hernandez, Vanessa Barchfield, Win Bundy, Annette McGivney, Roger Clark, Tom Riggenbach, Lydia Millet, Laura Trujillo, John Faherty, John D'Anna, Brian Jabas Smith, Jason Ground, Pat McMahon, Raul Rodriguez, Ty Coon, Kim Martinetti, Honey Albrecht, Chrysa Robertson, Jody Kent, Luis Alberto Urrea, Bill and Brenda Viner, Pat Flannery, Axel Holm, Cal Lash, Hank Stephenson, Carrie Heinonen, Luis Heredia, Chris Limberis, Matthew Nelson, Jim Nintzel, Tony Davis, M. Scot Skinner, Fenton Johnson, Jill Jorden Spitz, Norma Coile, Tom Spratt, Pat Flannery, Dan Shearer, Betty Reid, Jennifer Jayne Johnson, John Richard Davis, Peter Seidl, Lori Carter, Christa Severns, Steve Meissner, Bob Etter, Tom Beal, Britt Hanson, Jason Rose, Mark Jude Poirier, Tom Prezelski, Ted Prezelski, Terry Greene Sterling, Karl Jacoby, Alison Hawthorne Deming. These families too: Gary and Lori Minor; Anne Marie and Robert Ward; the Kleiners (Rick, Jan, Emma, and Sam); Jack and Jane Chilcott; Paula and Tim Cullison; Jacques-Andre and Felicia Istel; Evan, Doris, and Dan Wilson; Fred von Blume; Anna Marie von Blume; my parents.

I can only hope this list keeps expanding as the years go on. Understanding Arizona will never be a finished work. Nobody knows but their own fraction of it.

NOTES ON SOURCES

Arizona has a tradition of nonfiction that far outstrips the fiction explored in the essay "The Canon." The expansive reality of our ravines, peaks, cities, rivers, and people may need no further embellishment. This book is built on a sprawling bedrock of distinguished journalism, history, memoir, and other truthful accounts of Arizona, a few of which should be given special mention here.

Arizona: A History by Thomas Sheridan is the best general history of this—or any—American state. "The land should make us humble," writes Sheridan, "but it rarely does." I tried to remember that on my walk. A good companion volume, a bit more romantic, is *Arizona: A Panoramic History of a Frontier State* by Marshall Trimble and the wonderfully erudite (even obsessive) *Arizona Place Names* by the cattleman politician Will C. Barnes, a work of love later augmented by Byrd Granger. A delectable sampling of Arizona nonfiction is in the anthology *Named in Stone and Sky*, edited by Gregory McNamee. Librarian and antiquarian Lawrence Clark Powell compiled an essayistic bibliography in *Southwest Classics: The Creative Literature of the Arid Lands* and wrote a brief history of the state for a 1976 bicentennial project by W. W. Norton. I would also like to give credit to Preston Sands, who wrote historical narratives for all forty-three passages of the Arizona Trail. They are unpublished as of this writing but deserve an audience among those who walk this extraordinary route through the state.

Each Arizona town or city is its own human protoplasm. While the base economies might have varied somewhat—mining, farming, military, tourism, housing—the personalities of these places were flavorful and varied. The classic municipal histories are *Phoenix: The History of a Southwestern Metropolis* by Bradford Luckingham and *Tucson: The Life and Times of an American City* by C. L. Sonnichsen. The former has an excellent update in *Phoenix: A Brief History* by Jon Talton, a civic treasure in his own right who exposed the workings of the real estate-industrial complex in his columns for the *Arizona Republic* and in more acerbic form on his independent site Rogue Columnist. Rural Arizona gets loving treatment by the experienced traveler Peter Corbett on his site On the Road Arizona.

Tucson's conventional history is made both humane and heartbreaking in Lydia Otero's extraordinary *La Calle: Spatial Conflict and Urban Renewal in a Southwestern City*, which explains the shape of my hometown better than anything I've read. Sheridan's *Los Tucsonenses: The Mexican Community in Tucson, 1854–1941* charts the rise and fall of Mexican political and economic power.

Charles Bowden was the dark prince of Arizona letters. When I first read *Frog Mountain Blues*, his portrait of the Santa Catalina Mountains, the year I graduated from Canyon del Oro High School, I had no idea that prose in English could burn off the page like that. That was only the start. In a series of first-person narratives that were as hallucinatory as they were clear-eyed—*Mezcal, Blood Orchid, Red Line, Blues for Cannibals*—Bowden created a meta-historical and completely original way of seeing Arizona. These books aren't for everyone. He could be slack and gassy, spinning ridiculous apocalyptic prose out of boring conversations with truck stop customers. But when he was good, he was extraordinary.

The border is a story that never ends, and its chronicles are both detailed and enraging. Jason De León did memorable anthropological work on the physical leavings of migrants in *The Land of Open Graves: Living and Dying on the Migrant Trail*. Former U.S. Border Patrol agent Francisco Cantú tells a unique and horrifying story from the insides of enforcement in *The Line Becomes a River: Dispatches from the Border*. Eric Meeks provides a historical-sociological panorama in *Border Citizens: The Making of Indians, Mexicans and Anglos in Arizona*. Luis Alberto Urrea's *The Devil's Highway* is a masterwork of reconstruction, detailing an event that stands in for thousands of other episodes. Another account of dehydration is *The Death of Josseline: Immigration Stories from the Arizona Borderlands* by Margaret Regan. Bill Broyles's *A Visitor's Guide to El Camino del Diablo* is a rich storehouse of human and natural history.

The Latino activism that arose as a direct result of twenty-first-century anti-immigrant laws—arguably even more influential than the 1960s Chicano movement—is related in *Empowered! Latinos Transforming Arizona Politics* by Lisa Magaña and César S. Silva and *Driving While Brown: Sheriff Joe Arpaio versus the Latino Resistance* by Terry Greene Sterling and Jude Joffe-Block.

An entire library wing could house the books, studies, and photographic albums—mainly from the Anglo point of view—dedicated to the Indigenous peoples of Arizona. Some of these accounts are condescending; others are thoughtful; none have told the complete story because none ever can. A few that I found especially helpful for this narrative were *Weaving a World: Textiles and the Navajo Way of Seeing* by Roseann S. Willink and Paul G. Zolbrod, *Indian Running: Native American History and Tradition* by Peter Nabokov, and *The Navaho* by Clyde Kluckhohn and Dorothea Leighton. Arizona's sensational "captivity narrative" of teenaged kidnap victim Olive Oatman is expertly unpacked by Margot Mifflin in *The Blue Tattoo: The Life of Olive Oatman*. And one of the most shameful local events of the nineteenth century—the slaughter of a band of Apache families in Aravaipa Canyon near the site of Camp Grant—is meticulously examined through four distinct cultural lenses in Karl Jacoby's prizewinning *Shadows at Dawn: A Borderlands Massacre and the Violence of History*.

Arizona's Native people who came of age before the era of typography narrated the world through different means and materials. Their books were etched on sandstone walls, painted on clay, sewn into rugs, and sung to groups: stories about historic figures, battles, expeditions, loves, cosmological mysteries, family sagas, jokes. Features of the landscape—mesas, arroyos, plains, mountains—were also made into books, the atavistic venues of innumerable experiences made to come anew inside the listener through the telling of the story, meant to warn, instruct, and enrich. The Diné word *ajini* appears in many of their stories—it means, roughly, "we have been saying this for a long time." The tradition of nonfiction in Arizona is ten thousand years old; only a fraction of it has been preserved and interpreted beyond its original community of readers. Pueblo writer Leslie Marmon Silko has observed that a written document "is highly suspect because the true feelings of the speaker remain hidden as she reads words that are detached from the occasion and the audience." That said, three conventionally typeset books by Native authors I'd like to cite are the lyrical *A Pima Remembers* by George

Webb; the disconcerting *The Only One Living to Tell: The Autobiography of a Yavapai Indian* by Mike Burns; and Don Talayesva's *Sun Chief: The Autobiography of a Hopi Indian.*

Because so much of the Arizona experience is traveling from place to place in search of various objects of desire—water, silver, new pastures, fresh sights—it should be no surprise that many of its literary contributions are road stories. Martha Summerhayes was a proper resident of Nantucket who was at first appalled and then enchanted by the dry expanses of western Arizona she saw in the 1870s. Her travels are recounted in *Vanished Arizona.* One of the state's finest poets, Richard Shelton, wrote a lovely memoir, *Going Back to Bisbee*, structured as a composite of various trips to the city where he had his first teaching job. Some of the first European American eyes on this part of the North American continent were those of J. Ross Browne, whose sardonic style and bighearted manner were an early influence on Mark Twain. He wrote of his journey along the Gila and Santa Cruz Rivers alongside the fabulist Charles Poston in the mostly true *Adventures in the Apache Country.* Two shorter manuscripts also occupy this category: the unpublished recollections of rancher and stagecoach agent E. O. Stratton, taken down by his daughter as he lay dying, and the fantastical *My Confession: Recollections of a Rogue* by the scalp-hunter Samuel Chamberlain, a document that inspired Cormac McCarthy's hyper-violent novel *Blood Meridian.*

Accounts of Arizona's perennial water struggles are never confined to the state because the element knows no political borders and is intimately connected with the continental neighborhood. General histories that shine light on the domino line of Colorado River dams and the staggering liquid highway of the Central Arizona Project include *Cadillac Desert: The American West and Its Disappearing Water* by Marc Reisner and *A River No More: The Colorado River and the West* by Philip L. Fradkin. One of the best nonfiction books written about a river, anywhere, is *Gila: The Life and Death of an American River* by Gregory McNamee.

In addition to the books and storytelling objects of Arizona, there's the words not entrusted between covers but impressed on flimsy paper that blows away in the wind, intended to last for only a week or a day.

The first printing press wasn't hauled into the territory of Arizona until 1859—an iron Washington Press about the size of an adult mule, equipped with a giant handle that lowered a plate of type onto a sheet of paper in the cradle. It was shipped from Cincinnati via a river barge down the Ohio and Mississippi Rivers, taken through the Panama Canal on a freighter, then moved up to Guaymas, Sonora. From there it was loaded onto an oxcart and taken to Charles Poston's settlement at Tubac, where an editor named Edward Cross started printing the weekly *Arizonian*, mainly as a promotional tool for the Santa Rita Silver Mining Company.

Cross's public needling of Sylvester Mowry, a rival in the mining business, led to a duel in the streets. Shots were fired but neither man wounded. Mowry would later be detained at Fort Yuma by the U.S. Army on charges of selling ammunition to the Confederates and for espionage. Cross died fighting for the Union at Gettysburg. His modest Washington Press, meanwhile, was hauled in a wagon up to Tucson, where it would go on to produce the first issues of the *Arizona Citizen*, the rival *Arizona Star*, and the *Tombstone Epitaph*—a vivid example of how the means of literary production were rare in the period of Anglo frontier settlement. Mexican readers were informed by *El Fronterizo*, whose founding editor, Carlos Ygnacio Velasco, encouraged a proud Hispanic identity.

Up in Prescott, meanwhile, editor Tisdale A. Hand started the *Arizona Miner* in 1864. In the view of historian Budge Ruffner, it was "fat on flowery phrases, woefully thin on factual presentation." This was about average. Arizona's territorial newspapers were in business mainly to secure government contracts for printing official documents and legal notices. Advertising for dry goods, livestock, and sundry items brought in some additional dollars. An editor had to run propaganda articles for either the Republicans or Democrats, depending on his business posture. As Marshall Trimble has observed, Arizona had politics written into its DNA because of the representational prize the state offered for tangling political parties. This heated context was never better shown than in the bareknuckle nature of its first printed material. Whatever time might be left in the week was devoted to rounding up a mixture of letters, trivia, gossip, innuendo, courtroom tidbits, rumblings from the telegraph office, rhetoric against the Apaches, items cribbed from rival papers, and acrimony directed at rival editors—a jumble of words corralled under the category of "news."

The editors who narrated Arizona in the nineteenth century were the bloggers of their era, quasi-celebrities, followed and hated in equal measure. John Marion of the *Miner* was an atheist and open bigot. William J. Berry of the *Yuma Sentinel* was a roly-poly comedian. John Clum of the *Epitaph* was laughably fabulist, comparing the dingy mining settlement of Tombstone to the glories of ancient Rome even as he ran off his paper from under a canvas tent. Future surveyor John Wasson of the *Citizen* was more interested in touting his territorial delegate friend Richard McCormick than he was in news. The most reliable paper in the territory was, for a time, the Globe *Silver Belt*, published by Aaron Hackney. Their feuds and deeds are chronicled in the excellent cultural history *Those Old Yellow Dog Days: Frontier Journalism in Arizona, 1859–1912* by William Henry Lyon. A curated selection of articles can be found in *The Arizona Story*, edited by Joseph Miller.

Arizona's rowdy newspapers came under more stable governance soon enough. Copper companies seeking to control their own message and ward off state taxes started to buy them up for propaganda reasons. By 1905 they owned at least nine Arizona dailies, leading James McClintock to observe: "idealism and good business rarely go hand in hand." Still, the *Phoenix Republican* had proclaimed itself "first, last and all the time a newspaper" in explaining its decision to write about a Salt River flood that some business interests wanted to cover up because they thought it harmful to the territory's image. Philanthropist Dwight Heard made it the biggest paper in Arizona when he bought it in 1912. Its name was shortened to the more ecumenical *Republic* in 1929.

Today the gravitational pull of the internet and the disconnection of the *Republic*'s outside corporate ownership from the community has—as with almost every other newspaper in Arizona—shrunk it in size and ambition from its late twentieth-century heights. Yet the thousands of journalists who passed through those bustling open rooms, hustling out the first account of history, fostered an understanding of place, people, and purpose that broadened readers' understanding of their beguiling southwestern home.

Surviving editions of Arizona's newspapers—in printed bound editions and on two hundred thousand rolls of microfilm—are kept in the climate-controlled basement of the State of Arizona Research Library in Phoenix at Nineteenth Avenue and Madison Street, just to the southwest of the capitol. Manager Sativa Peterson endeavored to transfer all of them—more than seven hundred titles, most out of print—to a lasting digital format.

Many of the newspapers, printed on cheap material, are tattered and crumbling. They tell of long-dead events, the doings of those now vanished: school board meetings, road-building, Indigenous wars, political campaigns, dinner visits, localized heroism and cowardice, marriage notices, tax increases, obituaries, sales, council contretemps, droughts, plantings, animal migrations, rumors, store openings and closings—the stuff of public life, long past but still a part of the invisible foundation on which we play out our present dramas that will also have their sensual moment and then disappear.

The name Arizona—that good oak tree of the silver mines—may one day not appear in any atlas, and the United States itself may fade away and be replaced as a country with different labeling, but the Vishnu Basement Rocks at the bottom of the Grand Canyon will still be here, marking time. So too will the words that made Arizona. The words survive us.

NOTES

---

3 *Anza interviewed... pieces for easier carrying*: Patricia Roche Herring, "The Silver of El Real De Arizona," *Arizona and the West* 20 (Autumn 1978). See also Donald T. Garate, "Who Named Arizona: The Basque Connection," *Journal of Arizona History* 40 (Spring 1999).

The Glittering World

12 *"So you go into your womanhood..."*: Schwarz, *Molded in the Image*, 200.

13 *The newspapers heaped coverage*: "Are Moqui Runners World Beaters," *San Francisco Chronicle*, October 5, 1902, quoted in *Hopi Runners*, 171. See also Talayesva, *Sun Chief*, 11. According to historian Thomas Sheridan, when Tewanima and another Hopi runner came home from London, two older men challenged them to a race and beat them soundly.

13 *"Because water is so scarce..."*: McNamee, *Gila*, 144. A Yavapai named Charley A. Behm witnessed boys running with bells strapped around their waists to scare away evil spirits in 1869.

15 *When a boy came of age...*: Kelley and Francis, *A Diné History*, 65–83. The elder was Arnold Paddock.

16 *More than sixty clan groups were spread out on a rugged plateau...*: Underhill, *The Navajos*, 63–64. The traditional view of a thirteenth-century Athapaskan migration has been recently challenged by some archaeologists. Some have hypothesized the Diné were an "autochthonous development in the Southwest"—a hybrid culture descendant from Puebloan groups in the Four Corners region who mingled and intermarried with some migrants from the Pacific Northwest. See Wade Campbell, Kerry F. Thompson, and Richard M. Begay, "*Naasgo*: Moving Forward—Diné Archaeology in the Twenty-First Century," *Kiva: Journal of Southwestern Anthropology and History* 87, no. 3 (2021): 253–67. See also Kelley and Francis, *A Diné History*, 33–45.

16 *... she learned from a benevolent animal called Spider Woman...*: Kluckhohn and Leighton, *The Navaho*, 183. See also Thybony, *Burntwater*, 15.

17 *in a place that could least afford to have its water turned into dark gunk and piped away*: Years later, scholars discovered a horrible fact: the Hopi's trusted attorney,

John Sterling Boyden, was also on the payroll of Peabody Western Coal Company, even as he negotiated a strikingly unfair deal for his Indigenous clients. See John Dougherty, "A People Betrayed," *Phoenix New Times*, May 1, 1997.

17 *"When you look over it . . . you have come upon eternity"*: Quoted in McNamee, *Named in Stone and Sky*, 117.

18 *"the spirit-way-out"*: Kluckhohn and Leighton, *The Navaho*, 201.

—

Heidegger at the Grand Canyon

24 *"When a writer has tackled everything . . ."*: Quoted in Schullery, *Grand Canyon*, 127.

25 *"A combination of regions infernal and celestial . . ."*: Quoted in Lummis, *Mesa, Canon and Pueblo*, 516.

25 *"It is understood that in a time long before this one . . ."*: "Native Peoples of the Colorado Plateau," Museum of Northern Arizona, Flagstaff, April 2018.

25 *"Man is a living lie . . ."*: Van Dyke, *The Grand Canyon*, 65.

26 *"It seemed to me as if it were the burying ground . . ."*: Quoted in Higgins, *The Grand Canyon of Arizona*, 113.

26 *"It flashes instant communication . . ."*: Quoted in Higgins, 9.

26 *"You can feel the energy coming off it . . ."*: Melissa Sevigny, "'Not Your Playground': Indigenous Voices on Grand Canyon's Centennial," KNAU, February 16, 2019.

26 *"One's powers of articulation are paralyzed . . ."*: Quoted in Kinsey, *The Majesty of the Grand Canyon*, 1.

26 *"Men of rigid exterior . . ."*: Quoted in Higgins, *The Grand Canyon of Arizona*, 115.

26 *"Full of sunken mountains . . ."*: Quoted in Engel-Pearson, *Writing Arizona*, 48.

26 *"There is a sadness in the canyon . . ."*: Quoted in Higgins, *The Grand Canyon of Arizona*, 115.

27 *"This face-to-face meeting . . ."*: Quoted in Marder, *The Philosopher's Plant*, 174.

29 *"When thinking of these rocks . . ."*: Powell, *Exploration of the Colorado River*, 55.

29 *"the most sublime and awe-inspiring spectacle in the world"*: Dutton, *Tertiary History*, 142.

30 *"The lover of nature . . ."*: Dutton, 143.

30 *"the forms which seemed grotesque"*: Dutton, 144.

30 *"I have always said . . ."*: Albright, *Creating the National Parks Service*, 266. See also Hal Rothman, "Second-Class Sites: National Monuments and the Growth of the National Park System," *Environmental Review* 10, no. 1 (Spring 1986): 44–56.

30 *Using frivolous mining claims . . .*: The best account of this lengthy scam can be found in Douglas H. Strong, "Ralph H. Cameron and the Grand Canyon," *Arizona and the West* 20, no. 2 (Summer 1978): 155–72.

32 *When you take a map at the entry booth of a national park, you're looking at Mather's vision*: Albright, *Creating the National Park Service*.

32 *"I got lost in the geology for a moment . . ."*: Laura Trujillo, "Stepping Back from the Edge," *USA Today*, November 28, 2018.

33 *Easier not to think of it much*: Dillard, *Teaching a Stone to Talk*, 24.

—

38 *"frequent forays of drunken cowhands, . . ."*: Ashworth, *Biography of a Small Mountain*, 27.

—

Enchiladas and Whiskey

40 *Enchiladas and Whiskey*: Portions of this essay are taken from two pieces I wrote for the *Phoenix New Times*: "10 Iconic Arizona Restaurants Worth Traveling For," June 14, 2017; "Arizona's 16 Most Iconic Bars," June 2, 2018.

41 *"for me these fruits"*: Niethammer, *A Desert Feast*, 45.

41 *"an entire worldview complete with proven strategies for survival"*: Silko, *Yellow Woman*, 25.

41 *"Lost travelers and lost pinon-nut gatherers"*: "Landscape, History, and the Pueblo Imagination," in Glotfelty and Fromm, *The Ecocriticism Reader*, 264–75.

42 *tortillas with the diameter of dinner plates . . .* : Arellano, *Taco USA*, 13–19.

42 *"Homemade white cheese sizzling in a pan, . . ."*: Anzaldúa, *Borderlands*, 83.

43 *African American cooks in the cowboy wagons brought a distinctively Deep South taste . . .* : Gregory McNamee, "Southwestern Food, Southern Food: Portrait of a Marriage," *Journal of Arizona History* 64, no. 3 (Autumn 2022). See also McNamee, *Tortillas, Tiswin, and T-Bones*, 99.

43 *Not until 1973, in fact, did an Arizona restaurant win four stars from the Mobil Travel Guide*: McNamee, 101.

44 *Other signature dishes include the* caldo de queso *and the* carne seca . . . : Torres, *Notitas*, 23.

44 *"Anything you stuck in the ground would grow, . . ."*: Niethammer, *A Desert Feast*, 51.

45 *"an overly large platter of mixed messes . . . and greasy fried chips"*: Arellano, *Taco USA*, 125.

45 *"alluring and fun, dangerous yet irresistible"*: Arellano, 233.

45 *Tequila Sunrise*: Katie Johnson, "The Biltmore Original Tequila Sunrise," *Phoenix New Times*, June 28, 2012.

48 *late night taco joints like Nico's, Losbeto's, Alberto's, and Filberto's . . .* : Tim Steller, "Multiplying Mexican Restaurants with 'Berto' Names Derive from Common Ancestor," *Arizona Daily Star*, August 6, 2020.

48 *"There are some things that cannot be described accurately . . ."*: Torres, *Notitas*, 26.

—

49 *"After a million wordless years . . ."*: Ashworth, *Biography of a Small Mountain*, 19.

50 *"What disorients most of us . . ."*: Yetman, *Natural Landmarks of Arizona*, 16.

Hellsgate

53   *Hellsgate*: Some material has been revised and adapted from my M.A. thesis entitled "This Is the Place," submitted August 2011 at Dartmouth College.

54   *"Mary Fisher was shot . . . law enforcement sources said Friday"*: Tom Zoellner and Judd Slivka, "Family in Blaze Slashed, Shot," *Arizona Republic*, April 14, 2001.

55   *Judd covered the funeral for Mary and her two children . . .* : Judd Slivka and Tom Zoellner, "Dark Side of Fisher Described," *Arizona Republic*, June 8, 2001.

57   *And that was the beginning of the end of the search*: Tom Zoellner, "Fisher Search Fruitless," *Arizona Republic*, April 23, 2001.

60   *But what of the deeper caverns . . .* : For other expeditions in Club 41 cave more probing than mine, see Adam Klawonn, "Where in the World Is Robert Fisher," *Phoenix*, March 2011; and Anne Ryman, "Robert Fisher: The Clues He Left Behind," *Arizona Republic*, April 11, 2021.

63   *"Strangers who went into the valley . . . in a lonely wilderness"*: Forrest, *Arizona's Dark and Bloody Ground*.

63   *"Innocent and unoffending men were shot down . . ."*: Cremony, *Life among the Apaches*, 117.

64   *Valley police reporters consequently have a lot of material*: D. T. Kenrick and S. W. MacFarlane, "Ambient Temperature and Horn Honking: A Field Study of the Heat/Aggression Relationship," *Environment and Behavior* 18, no. 2 (1986), 179–91.

65   *He hired washed-up actor Cesar Romero . . .* : Lazar, *Evening's Empire*.

66   *Gary Tison told one of his sons . . .* : Clarke, *Last Rampage*, 125.

66   *"A sorry goddamned mess, this town"*: Jon Talton, "Bolles: A Player's Guide," *Rogue Columnist*, May 31, 2016.

67   *"it was just a kind of rangelands justice"*: Robert Lindsey, "Vengeance Suggested as Motive in Slaying of Arizona Reporter," *New York Times*, July 9, 1976.

67   *In 1984 it was classified a federal wilderness*: "Hells Gate Wilderness, Recreation Opportunity Guide, Tonto National Forest," undated pamphlet published by the U.S. Forest Service Southwestern Region.

68   *"Jensen, if you've hurt that lion . . ."*: "Rescue Party to Aid Lion," *New York Times*, September 20, 1927; Gail Hearne, "Tale of Lion Rescue Made for Movies," *Arizona Republic*, September 30, 2007.

70   *"No one had ever thrown a line . . ."*: Gillette, *Pleasant Valley*.

71   *the harrowing experience of one I. W. Stevens . . .* : Lamberton, *Chasing Arizona*, 203.

73   *it set off immediate speculative thoughts among Poston's friends . . .* : Goff, *Charles Poston*, 7. See also William A. Douglass, "On the Naming of Arizona," *Names: A Journal of Onoastics* 27, no. 4 (1979): 217–34.

74   *"Old Spanish history was ransacked . . . and covered by forests primeval"*: Charles Poston, "Building a State in Apache Land," *Overland Monthly*, July 1894, 88.

74   *"From these reports . . . were forced to abandon the country"*: Adlai Feather, "Origin of the Name Arizona," *New Mexico Historical Review* 34, no. 2 (April 1964): 89–95.

75   *"For years the very word 'Arizona' has had a gruesome sound to the Easterner . . ."*: Black, *Arizona*, 4.

———

The Canon

77   *Arizona yearns for a good novel . . .* : This essay is revised and adapted from my article "Why Is There No Great Arizona Novel," *Phoenix New Times*, August 3, 2015.

79   *It was a best-selling contributor to defective Arizona myth-making*: Adapted from my contribution to a group-authored article, "40 Essential Arizona Books," *Tucson Weekly*, February 28, 2019.

———

The Fountain

89   *"It's not enough just to sell land . . ."*: "New Cities Seen as Population Solution," United Press International, July 16, 1975.

90   *Then he laid into the "total disaster" of the national budget*: A portion of this essay is adapted from my article "Proto-Trump," *Phoenix New Times*, September 14, 2016.

90   *a quasi-religion of romantic individualism*: Kevin D. Williamson, "The American Right Hits Its Hippie Phase," *National Review*, July 23, 2021.

90   *at his packed anti-immigration rally at the Phoenix Convention Center*: Philip Bump, "Trump Returns to Phoenix, the Place His Campaign Truly Began," *Washington Post*, August 22, 2017.

90   *"This has become a movement . . ."*: Roy Carroll, "'I'm, Like, a Really Smart Person': Donald Trump Exults in Outsider Status," *The Guardian*, July 12, 2015.

91   *"Planes could be flown and tested every day of the year"*: Shermer, *Sunbelt Capitalism*, 74; Douglas C. Towne, "Throwback Thursday: 'Valley of the Sun' Motto," *Arizona Republic*, December 31, 2015; Sheridan, *Arizona*, 240.

91   *a streak of booster aggression written into its character*: Shermer, *Sunbelt Capitalism*, 27; Needham, *Power Lines*, 40.

91   *the slopes of Camelback Mountain*: Yetman, *Natural Landmarks of Arizona*, 53.

92   *When that enterprise failed, he turned to Arizona . . .* : Perlstein, *Before the Storm*, 19.

92   *Big Mike Goldwater's grandson Barry . . .* : Stephen Lemons, "Goldwater Uncut," *Phoenix New Times*, October 19, 2006.

92   *"I was one of the lucky few . . ."*: Iverson, *Barry Goldwater*, 66.

93   *"a young merchant prince . . ."*: Perlstein, *Before the Storm*, 23.

93   *"stand up and be counted . . ."*: Shermer, *Sunbelt Capitalism*, 68.

93 *"Make loans ... to put money in people's hands"*: Shermer, 56.

93 *"The city can regenerate itself..."*: Shermer, 308.

93 *"With refrigeration came Republicans"*: Iverson, *Barry Goldwater*, 73.

93 *"If you'd dropped a five-dollar bill..."*: Stewart Alsop, "Can Goldwater Win in '64?" *Saturday Evening Post*, August 24, 1963. See also Perlstein, *Before the Storm*, 19.

94 *"a step upward toward the fulfillment of the American Dream"*: Edward Abbey, "The Blob Comes to Arizona," *New York Times Magazine*, May 16, 1976.

94 *One of Barry Goldwater's personal contributions...*: George Henhoeffer, "Arizona Industry Moves In," *Business Week*, December 13, 1952.

95 *he lost to Lyndon Johnson in a drubbing*: Alsop, "Can Goldwater Win in '64?"

95 *moved away from business-friendly optimism into suspicion of any government initiative*: Geraldo L. Cadava, "Barry and Beyond: Conservatism in Arizona before, during, and after Its Most Famous Representative," *Journal of Arizona History* 61, nos. 3 and 4 (Autumn/Winter 2020): 582.

95 *"Frankenstein's monster... that any step forward is suspect"*: Andrew Kopkind, "Modern Times in Phoenix: A City at the Mercy of Its Myths," *New Republic*, November 6, 1965.

95 *treated it as an outrage on the level of Yalta*: Shermer, *Sunbelt Capitalism*, 308.

96 *"constructed new plants, ... cars, radios, refrigerators"*: Shermer, 279.

96 *the populist voices wielding the power of anger*: Pat Flannery and Amanda J. Crawford, "Former Ariz. Gov. Evan Mecham Dies at 83," *Arizona Republic*, February 22, 2008.

96 *"a community of strangers"*: Paul Dean, "In a State of Disarray," *Los Angeles Times*, March 15, 1992.

97 *"Within such a population..."*: Dean.

97 *"Perhaps it is the splendid isolation ... over the lights of Phoenix"*: Barry Goldwater, *With No Apologies*, 17.

98 *"I say it's ... happy people in their little trailers"*: "Land for Sale," *Look*, October 8, 1963.

98 *"There is nothing ... on a huge tan rug"*: Robert A. Caro, "Misery Acres," *Newsday*, 1963; See also the report from the U.S. Senate Committee on Aging, "Frauds and Quackery Affecting the Older Citizen," Washington, D.C., January 16, 1963, 141–264.

99 *"Co-existence is a lot of baloney..."*: *Arizona Republic*, September 9, 1962.

100 *dependence on government benefits*: Tom Zoellner, "Polygamy on the Dole," *Salt Lake Tribune*, June 28, 1998.

101 *Golden Valley may vote en bloc in presidential elections...*: Another of the brightest rubies within Red Arizona is Prescott Valley (pop. 44,311), which also got its start as a 1960s scam. The hustler Ned Warren set up a network of shell companies selling lots here for sixty-five dollars down, promising paradise and delivering no water. None other than Barry Goldwater had written a letter of endorsement. He later denied knowing the nature of what was going on, but the damage was done. Prescott Valley spit on its wounds, threw up a jumble of businesses along Highway 69 and

lurched forward into an uncontrolled spasm of growth. Today Prescott Valley is laced with streets with names like Tuscany Way, Santa Fe Loop, and Florentine Road and resembles North Scottsdale in its bourgeoisie look, white population, and rock-ribbed conservatism. See Catherine Reagor, "After Don Bolles," *Arizona Republic*, December 23, 2019.

102 *It was in that trailer where McVeigh . . .* : Mark Shaffer, "Did Arizona Militia Leader Aid Bomber," *Arizona Republic*, June 10, 2001. In the days right before he left for Oklahoma, he stayed in room 119 of the Hill-Top Motel and then at the Imperial Motel across a part of Route 66 that bends through coffee-colored buttes.

103 *McSally is a native of Rhode Island . . .* : The next several paragraphs are adapted from my article "Trumpism Ate Martha McSally's Brain," *New Republic*, October 12, 2020.

104 *"You flew your Warthog to the dark side"*: David Fitzsimmons, "Martha McSally Has Some Questions to Answer from This Liberal," *Arizona Daily Star*, January 18, 2020.

105 *"Martha, just come up fast . . . Let's go"*: Laurie Roberts, "Trump's Disrespect of Sen. Martha McSally Was Painful to Watch," *Arizona Republic*, October 28, 2020.

105 *"the only goddamn thing I've done in the Senate that's worth a damn"*: Bart Barnes, "Barry Goldwater, GOP Hero, Dies," *Washington Post*, May 30, 1998.

106 *"I don't think it would be proper . . ."*: Asa Bushnell, "Barry Wasn't Asked Advice on Quitting," *Tucson Citizen*, August 8, 1974.

107 *"Not everybody wants to vote . . ."*: E.J. Montini, "Arizona Republican Lawmaker Unwittingly Exposes Election Reform Scam," *Arizona Republic*, April 27, 2021.

---

110 *Whatever "Old World charm" resides in Tucson . . .* : Gammage, *Phoenix in Perspective*, 146. Credit to Thomas Sheridan for the insight.

Monotony Rules

115 *"surprised it would ever amount to much"*: Palmer, *The City of Surprise*, 25. Her second husband, Homer Ludden, came from Surprise, Nebraska, which likely also influenced the choice.

115 *Statler and her husband sold three-hundred-dollar lots . . .* : The first marshal found a used pink Plymouth and painted it beige to make it look like a real police vehicle; the first fire truck didn't arrive for seven more years. Without garbage hauling services, residents dumped household waste in arroyos or burned it in their backyards. See Palmer, *The City of Surprise*, 57.

116 *John F. Long bought up some cabbage farms west of Phoenix . . .* : Gammage, *Phoenix in Perspective*, 46.

116 *Rumors of shoddy construction did nothing to staunch the sales*: At one point he signed an order for twelve million fireproof concrete blocks—the largest ever re-

corded. See "1958: A 'Heavy' Order of Superlite Blocks," *Arizona Contractor and Community*, July/August 2021. See also Talton, *A Brief History of Phoenix*, 84–87.

117   *The average home in Surprise lost half its value*: Palmer, *The City of Surprise*, 95.

117   *until there were only nine left in the Phoenix metropolitan area*: "History Repeated Itself in a Big Way with the Great Recession," *Phoenix Business Journal*, November 2, 2015.

118   *nearly 40 percent cheaper than masonry*: In 1943 architect Walter Field praised this form as "a simple cage" that reflects "those twin conditions that underlie all that is American in our building arts: the chronic shortage of skilled labor, and the almost universal use of wood." See Justin Fox, "Why America's New Apartment Building All Look the Same," *Bloomberg Businessweek*, February 13, 2019.

118   *radiates the sun in dull hues with manufacturer's names like Almond Mocha . . .*: Gammage, *Phoenix in Perspective*, 104.

121   *created a new kind of American civilization*: Gammage, 46.

121   *Arizona comes in last in the country when it comes to spending time with neighbors*: Joanna Allhands, "Loneliness Is a Public Health Issue," *Arizona Republic*, January 17, 2020. See also U.S. Census Current Population Survey, September Volunteering/ Civic Engagement Supplement, 2019.

———

Flashpoint

128   *"It's pretty much kindling at this point"*: Alyssa Marksz, "Arizona's Current Historic Drought May Be 'Baseline for the Future,'" Cronkite News Service, June 1, 2021.

132   *seven times the number of houses going up in smoke each year*: "The Climate Change Link to More and Bigger Wildfires," National Public Radio, July 27, 2021.

132   *instead of cleaning up the garbage on the forest floor*: Tobin, *Endangered*, 164.

133   *"Fire is . . . neither deliberately enemy nor friend"*: Gantenbein, *A Season of Fire*, 279.

134   *about 2,500 people evacuated their homes . . . trying to rob fuel*: Dale Bales, "Telegraph Fire 2021: Executive Summary," Tonto National Forest, June 19, 2021.

135   *Incident Command spread over the ridge more than one million gallons of chemical slurry*: "Arizona Arboretum Saved from Wildfire," *Here and Now*, National Public Radio, June 10, 2021.

135   *"According to a recent U.S. Air Force inquiry . . . burned out 3,000 feet above ground level"*: Brahm Resnik, "Did Fighter Jets Cause Arizona Wildfire? Here's What We Know," *12News*, June 29, 2021.

136   *cost $8.2 million to extinguish*: Bill Gabbert, "Forest Service Releases Video of Explosion That Started 46,000-Acre Fire," *Wildfire Today*, November 27, 2018.

139   *"The monster reared its head today, and the dragon blew its fire"*: Judd Slivka et al., "Two Towns Burn," *Arizona Republic*, June 23, 2002.

140   *"Whenever my mother would cook . . . It fascinated him"*: Tom Zoellner, "Fires 'Fascinated' Subject; Situation Got Out of Hand," *Arizona Republic*, July 1, 2002.

141　*The rest of the rim looked like the morning after Hiroshima*: Tom Zoellner, "Defiant Firefighters Snub Feds," *Arizona Republic*, July 14, 2002.

141　*Gregg and Elliott were merely the sparks*: Dennis Wagner, Mark Shaffer, and Brent Whiting, "No Charge Filed; Fire Victims Irate," *Arizona Republic*, July 19, 2002.

142　*"May God have mercy on your lying souls"*: Valinda Jo Elliott, "You Would Have Done the Same Thing I Did," *Arizona Republic*, August 4, 2002.

143　*"We are going to hallowed ground, . . . in reverence to the loss"*: John Dougherty, "Yarnell Hill Fire: The Granite Mountain Hotshots Never Should've Been Dispatched, Mounting Evidence Shows," *Phoenix New Times*, August 13, 2013.

143　*Marsh did not sign off on the certification of his own unit*: Dougherty.

144　*Brendan McDonough, who had been left behind as a lookout*: The most complete version can be found in Santos, *The Fire Line*.

144　*this is not the aim of wildfire teams, which seek managed containment*: Anne Ryman, "What We Learned about Yarnell Hill Fire," *Arizona Republic*, July 24, 2018. The ranch would likely would have been spared because it was surrounded by a sixty-foot perimeter of dirt, a place the owner said he used to "park my junk."

145　*"This is big bucks . . ."*: "City Won't Budge on Ashcraft Status: Widow Takes Her Plea to Courthouse Plaza," *Prescott Daily Courier*, August 8, 2013. See also Santos, *The Fire Line*, 201–6.

146　*It cost $23.1 million to extinguish*: Bales, "Telegraph Fire 2021."

146　*"There's some char . . . to love this fire"*: Gianluca D'Elia, "As Telegraph Fire Nears Containment, a First Look at the Damages," Cronkite News Service, June 24, 2021.

The Prize

151　*"These companies are denuding Arizona . . . for copper-painted steel sheets"*: Roberta Graham, "Fit for a Goddess: The Capitol's Copper Dome," *Arizona Contractor & Community*, Summer 2014; *Arizona Gazette*, June 22, 1900; *Under the Copper Dome: The Arizona Capitol, 1898–1974*, Archives and Public Records, Museum Division of Arizona State Library, Phoenix, 2001.

151　*restorationists found more than twenty bullets inside her*: Moore, *Too Tough to Tame*, 93.

152　*they would entertain proposals for an expansion*: "A New Capitol," *Arizona Republic*, February 21, 1955; Clairborne Nuckolls, "Shabby Arizona Capitol Shocks Touring Planners," *Arizona Republic*, December 17, 1955.

152　*So that was the end of the Wright plan*: Lloyd Clark, "Frank Lloyd Wright and the Arizona Capitol," *Journal of Arizona History* 55, no. 1 (Spring 2014).

155　*for fear that somebody would alter or destroy them*: Rob O'Dell, "City Sees Errors in Scathing Audit," *Arizona Daily Star*, November 17, 2010; Rob O'Dell, "City Criticizes Joint FBI-AG Probe over Rio Nuevo," *Arizona Daily Star*, April 13, 2011.

155   *any criminal offenses that would likely end in a successful prosecution*: "Attorney General
       Finally Releases Rio Nuevo Report," *Arizona Daily Independent*, October 17, 2013.

155   *"tax-increment financing district"*: A major irony of Rio Nuevo is that a similar
       mechanism had been used a half century ago to build the ugly refrigerator box of
       the Tucson Convention Center at the expense of hundreds of 1880s adobe town-
       homes—exactly the kind of atrocity for which Rio Nuevo was offered up as an
       atonement.

156   *Rio Nuevo was beginning to look like a turnaround story*: Gabriela Rico, "Audit: 20
       Years Later, Rio Nuevo District Turnaround 'Truly Exceptional,'" *Arizona Daily
       Star*, December 22, 2019.

157   *and told her he was in love with her*: Julia Shumway, "Lobbyist: Ugenti-Rita Sexually
       Harassed Her before Shooter Expulsion," *Arizona Capitol Times*, February 4, 2020.

158   *an episode in which Ugenti-Rita reportedly lay on top of a bar . . .*: Dustin Gardiner
       and Yvonne Wingett Sanchez, "Arizona House Expels Rep. Don Shooter, Citing
       'Dishonorable' Pattern of Workplace Harassment," *Arizona Republic*, February 1,
       2018; Andrew Oxford, "Maricopa County Won't Pursue Charges over Explicit Pho-
       tos of Arizona Lawmaker Sent to Lobbyist," *Arizona Republic*, August 25, 2020.

161   *The FBI called the ensuing investigation Operation High Grid*: Katie Campbell,
       "Judge's Decision in Bribery Trial Opens Door on Larger Probe," *Arizona Capitol
       Times*, June 22, 2018.

163   *people whose moral sensibilities may become all too flexible in the heat of the job*: Old-
       timers liked to tell the story of a minority leader who was a vice president at Phoenix
       Children's Hospital but whose phone number wasn't in the hospital directory. An
       intern was sent down to the hospital to go find him in his office—only to find he
       didn't actually have an office there.

164   *"Serving ice cream isn't exactly like serving in state government . . ."*: Yvonne Wingett
       Sanchez and Brahm Resnik, "New Details Emerge in Ducey's Cold Stone Record,"
       Arizona Republic, August 10, 2014; Howard Koplowitz, "Who Is Doug Ducey?"
       International Business Times, August 27, 2014.

———

171   *"Wherever you go in the state of Arizona . . . of that lifetime more interesting"*: Esther
       Henderson, "U.S. 60," *Arizona Highways*, May 1956.

———

El Rey

173   *"This is not her country . . ."*: Laura Gómez, "'An Ugly Tactic': Lawsuit Questions
       Citizenship of Future Latina Lawmaker," *AZ Mirror*, November 9, 2018.

174   *stolen the office through ballot box stuffing*: "Riot Reported in Mexican Border Town,"
       Associated Press, September 16, 1985.

174 *widely suspected to be in league with drug cartels*: Morgan, *The Reaper's Line*, 173; Tim Steller, "Mayor Vicente Terán: In Agua Prieta, He's Go-To Man," *Arizona Daily Star*, June 24, 2012.

175 *and built a smelter to process copper*: Schwantes, *Vision and Enterprise*, 253. The year after a new blast furnace was installed on August 18, 1927, Edward H. Robie, associate editor of the *Engineering and Mining Journal*, came for a look at Douglas and noted "its group of smelter stacks, belching into the atmosphere all the sulphur contained in the Bisbee ores, make a distinguishing landmark."

175 *they should instead pay Phelps Dodge for the courtesy of the gunk*: Schwantes, 254. See also Wirth, *Smelter Smoke in North America*, 122–24.

175 *towering like a sundial over the working-class bungalows below*: Wirth, 137.

175 *you get could get your tickets dismissed*: Borane was a protégé of a baby-faced police chief named Percy Bowden who drove vice into the shadows but at the price of an autocratic hand. Favors and skimming became routine. "They learned the law could be traded with," said a federal official. See Morgan, *The Reaper's Line*. I had a personal experience with this. When I was a college sophomore, I got pulled over by a cop on Highway 80, not far from the smelter, while on my way to ask for a summer job at the *Douglas Dispatch*. As he handed me a ticket, the cop told me I could get it dismissed without my insurance company finding out if I appeared before a judge. And sure enough, without understanding then what was happening, I was allowed to plead to a noncriminal "wasting a finite resource" offense, and it all went away for fifty bucks in cash.

175 *charged with racketeering and money laundering*: Sam Dillon, "Small-Town Arizona Judge Amasses Fortune, and Indictment," *New York Times*, January 30, 2000. Most of the charges were dismissed amid suspicions of FBI entrapment, and Borane instead pleaded guilty to ticket-fixing.

176 *New black SUVs prowled the streets*: Louis Sahagun, "Border Town Tires of Its Corrupt Aura," *Los Angeles Times*, December 28, 1996.

176 *Judge Borane had sold this strategic parcel of land to his friend Camarena at a profit of 500 percent*: Paul Brinkley-Rogers and Keoki Skinner, "Land Deal Staining JP's Life," *Arizona Republic*, June 24, 1990.

176 *"It was as dark and dank . . ."*: Morgan, *The Reaper's Line*, 139.

176 *serious proposals to turn the tunnel into a tourist attraction*: Paul Brinkley-Rogers and Keoki Skinner, "Tunnel Vision: Douglas Eager to Dig Up Profits," *Arizona Republic*, June 10, 1990.

176 *the abandoned smelter, where lead and arsenic made some of them sick*: "The Toxic Release Inventory and Its Impact on Federal Minerals and Energy," House Resource Committee, U.S. Government Printing Office, 2003.

177 *restrictive covenants stopped them from buying homes anywhere else*: One official described it in dire terms with a splash of implied racism: "Steinbeck-esque Joad

families living in dilapidated housing, row after row of open backyard toilets, which smelled to high heaven and dust blanketed, littered streets and even dirtier alleys, and children played in a squalor that a hog raiser wouldn't tolerate in his pens." See Needham, *Power Lines*, 84.

177   *forcing Spanish-speaking voters to read words from a white card to prove their literacy*: Rehnquist had moved to Arizona after Stanford Law School for reasons aligned with the New Old West ethos exemplified by the Goldwater reformers. Arizona represented "the lost frontier in America," he told the city council, "the right to manage your own affairs as free as possible from the interference of government."

178   *"I know I didn't do the right thing in my life . . . who don't believe in politics"*: Rachel Leingang, "From Ages 18 to 65, These Arizona Voters Celebrate Their First Time Casting Ballots," *Arizona Republic*, October 29, 2020.

179   *the glories of Joe Arpaio*: This and the next three paragraphs are adapted from my op-ed "The Good, the Bad and the Ugly about Sheriff Joe Arpaio," *Arizona Daily Star*, August 30, 2017.

179   *Joe never forgot the lesson. Publicity means love*: Tom Zoellner, "Arpaio's Big Decision," *Arizona Republic*, March 3, 2002. He told the same story to Sterling and Joffe-Block, as recounted in *Driving While Brown*, 8.

179   *"I go back to the cowboy days . . . but that's the concept"*: Zoellner, "Arpaio's Big Decision."

179   *"Jerry, I never had any friends . . . in the sheriff's office"*: Sterling and Joffe-Block, *Driving While Brown*, 291.

180   *"I have no friends . . . You're my friends"*: Michael Kruse, "The Loneliest President," *Politico*, September 17, 2017.

180   *bringing anxiety that pricked the subconscious*: There was touch of vengeance in Pearce's mania to stop what he called "an invasion." In 1977 a teenager in the Mexican-Yaqui town of Guadalupe had grabbed his revolver from his holster when he was on patrol and shot off his right ring finger. Twenty-seven years later, an undocumented Mexican immigrant shot and wounded his son, also a sheriff's deputy.

180   *showy cruelty with little other benefit*: As Geraldo Cadava has observed, this dismal new direction for the Arizona Republican Party was linked with the older brand of conservatism espoused by Barry Goldwater in one important way: both relied on anti-federal rhetoric. See Geraldo L. Cadava, "Barry and Beyond: Conservatism in Arizona before, during, and after Its Most Famous Representative," *Journal of Arizona History* 61, nos. 3 and 4 (Autumn/Winter 2020): 582. For a comprehensive history of punitive state measures, see also Magaña and Silva, *Empowered!*

180   *entire vanloads of migrants on conspiracy charges*: Sterling and Joffe-Block, *Driving While Brown*, 58.

181   *He had run a frivolous "threat assessment unit" . . .*: Tom Zoellner, "Threats on Arpaio Costly," *Arizona Republic*, January 4, 2002.

181 *"Citizens here sincerely hope . . .": "*Arpaio Setting Aside Space at Tent City to Enforce SB1070," *Phoenix Business Journal*, July 21, 2010.

183 *Jerry Lewis, who viewed the mass deportations as a crime against families*: Parraz, *Dignity by Fire*, 114, 130.

183 *"We will be back, they should count on it"*: Laura Gómez and Jerod MacDonald-Evoy, "Activists Said a Proposal Was Racist. The GOP Chairman Had State Troopers Remove Them," *AZ Mirror*, February 13, 2020.

185 *"This is proof that our community can move mountains"*: Sterling and Joffe-Block, *Driving While Brown*, 249.

185 *he would win election to the Phoenix City Council*: Dianna M. Nanez, "Hecho in USA: Latinos in Politics," *USA Today*, January 7, 2020.

185 *"We seem to be traveling the same highway . . ."*: Sterling and Joffe-Block, *Driving While Brown*, 258.

186 *"I've got two new titles now," he complained . . .* : Sterling and Joffe-Block, 278.

———

189 *Picket Post served as the staging base . . .* : Redniss, *Oak Flat*, 152.

189 *showing it around to justify the expensive military presence*: Hutton, *The Apache Wars*, 123. See Chebahtah and Minor, *Chevato*, 18, for a description of Western Apache raiding philosophy.

190 *and in legends like that of Apache Leap*: Hutton, *The Apache Wars*, 10, 120.

191 *"It seemed to me . . . This country is geology by day and astronomy at night"*: Priestley, *Midnight on the Desert*, 2–3.

———

The Love Song of Interstate 10

192 *The Love Song of Interstate 10*: Revised and adapted from my article "Interstate 10: A Personal History," *Tucson Weekly*, January 10, 2019.

193 *he died consumed with survivor guilt and alcoholism ten years after the war*: "The Ballad of Ira Hayes" was written by folksinger Peter La Farge, the son of Oliver La Farge, author of the novel *Laughing Boy*.

———

199 *He had found a squeezebox of creativity at the AM radio station KCKY in Coolidge . . .* : West, *The Phoenix Sound*, 22–33.

200 *"all the colors that the desert painted . . . when I described southern Arizona to people"*: Aaron Gilbreath, "Finding the Soundtrack to My Desert Life," *Longreads*, April 2018.

200 *"Doug took in beauty everywhere . . . over acres of suburban rooftops repeating to the horizon"*: Brian Smith, "Jesus of Suburbia," *Detroit Metro Times*, December 19, 2007.

White Bones

202   *"great inland empire" in the central part of Arizona* . . . : "Great Crowds Today to Attend the Dedication of Ashurst-Hayden Dam, First Unit in San Carlos Project," *Arizona Republican*, May 10, 1922; "Diversion Dam to Be Dedicated May 10," *Casa Grande Dispatch*, April 14, 1922. How Gila River water was taken away from prosperous Pima Indian farmers, and the dam's imperfect role in restoring some version of equity, is told in David H. DeJong, *Diverting the Gila: The Pima Indians and the Florence-Casa Grande Project, 1916–1928* (Tucson: University of Arizona Press, 2021).

202   *"one of the most erratic and torrential streams in America"*: "Ashurst-Hayden Dam Dedicated," *Arizona Republican*, May 11, 1922.

203   *The population of Casa Grande quadrupled*: Melissa Keane, "Cotton and Figs: The Great Depression in the Casa Grande Valley," *Journal of Arizona History* 32, no. 3 (Autumn 1991): 267–90.

204   *But the money didn't lie*: Abrahm Lustgarten and Naveena Sadasivam, "Holy Crop: How Federal Dollars Are Financing the Water Crisis in the West," *ProPublica*, May 27, 2015.

205   *"The still waters were of a deep emerald hue . . . matched by its white reflection"*: Leopold, *Sand County Almanac*, 132.

205   *city of Yuma that today supplies 90 percent of the nation's leafy vegetables*: A labor force of approximately five thousand Latino pickers, many of whom are on H2-A visas, are bused out to the fields for long and exhausting days during the harvest, when two million pounds of lettuce are processed and shipped each day.

205   *"I am told . . . Some say we had to"*: Leopold, *Sand County Almanac*, 141.

206   *Hayden clawed his way to the chairmanship of the Senate Appropriations Committee* . . . : "Memorial Addresses and Other Tributes in the Congress of the United States on the Life and Contributions of Carl T. Hayden," Ninety-Second Congress, Second Session (Washington, D.C.: Government Printing Office, 1972), 102. See also Sheridan, *Arizona*, 341.

206   *used birthright language: "our water"*: Needham, *Power Lines*, 190, 201.

206   *"Colorado River water will someday flow . . . 'the people who are gone'"*: Quoted in Sevigny, *Mythical River*, 42.

207   *rough equivalent of streaming twenty-two thousand gallons per second over a skyscraper twice as high as the Chase Tower in downtown Phoenix*: With thanks to Reisner, *Cadillac Desert*, 282, for inspiring this comparison.

207   *into the aquifer where it could be pumped out as groundwater*: Tony Davis, "Arizona's Plan to Withdraw Years Worth of 'Banked' CAP Water Lagging," *Arizona Daily Star*, August 18, 2018.

207 *Melted snowpack represents almost three-quarters of Arizona's water consumption*: Erica R. Siirila-Woodburn, Alan M. Rhoades, Benjamin J. Hatchett, Laurie S. Huning, Julia Szinai, Christina Tague, Peter S. Nico, Daniel R. Feldman, Andrew D. Jones, William D. Collins, and Laurna Katz, "A Low-to-No Snow Future and Its Impacts on Water Resources in the Western United States," *Nature* 2 (November 2021): 800–819.

208 *"In front of us stood a grove . . . thirty feet off the ground"*: Elizabeth Kolbert, "The Lost Canyon under Lake Powell," *New Yorker*, August 9, 2021.

208 *But such prophecies are hyperbolic . . .* : Bowden, *Killing the Hidden Waters*, 130.

208 *Bringing arid lands into life is an urge . . .* : Isaiah 35:2; Kardashian, *Milk Money*, 23.

208 *"Any people who, for the first time, managed to divert a river . . ."*: Reisner, *Cadillac Desert*, 476.

209 *a rich grandfather*: McGivney, *Resurrection*, 123.

210 *"where I can get acquainted with myself . . ."*: Samuel L. Myers, "Dick Wick Hall: Humorist with a serious purpose," *Journal of Arizona History* 11, no. 4 (Winter 1970): 257. The Yuman and Mohave peoples ventured occasionally into the waterless portions of the eastern Mohave Desert, but they mainly clung to the river. The Oatman family of Illinois was traveling that path on the way to California in 1851 when they were set upon by a group of Western Yavapais who slaughtered most of them and took fourteen-year-old Olive Oatman as a captive. She was traded as chattel to the Mohaves, who treated her as an equal and gave her a blue-patterned face tattoo, a subject of national fascination when she was released back into Anglo society in her late teens. Louis L'Amour made repeated allusions to "sandy, rock-strewn wastelands" and "sun-blasted desert" in his 1957 novel *Last Stand at Papago Wells*.

210 *"so white, so bare, so endless, and so still"*: Summerhayes, *Vanished Arizona*, 132.

210 *playing on themes of grievances*: Dick Wick Hall himself had complained about the "Yumaresque" ring of politicians in his satiric *Salome Sun* newspaper in the 1920s, calling the city so inhospitable that it lost the territorial prison to Florence because prisoners refused to stay there. "Sand-swept and cursed of fate," Charles Phelps complained in an 1882 poem named for the town. "Burning, but how passionless. Barren, bald and pitiless!" Quoted in McNamee, *Named in Stone and Sky*, 19.

211 *"They were no doubt doing it for their own economic benefit . . ."*: The town of Salome has a history of scheming. In 1939 the Sheffler brothers came out from Southern California, where they had made money selling slot machines for offshore gambling, and opened Sheffler's Motel, where gambling and prostitution were part of the business plan. They tried to induce Arizona to legalize casinos, as Nevada had done, but had no luck. The motel is still in business on U.S. 60, across from Don's Cactus Bar.

211 *so he could sentence a defendant to prison for second-degree murder*: Alan Ariav, "Growing Pains: La Paz County Carving Identity," *Arizona Republic*, April 1, 1984.

211   *"You are sitting astride some of the most important and dynamic future-oriented real estate and beachfront in the Southwest"*: Joan M. Travis and John Gutekunst, "The Birth of Arizona's 15th County, Celebrating 30 Years," *Parker Pioneer*, January 2, 2013.

212   *where the big agricultural interests in Yuma no longer had a voice*: The water speculators arrived at a time when the area was falling into a depression. High commodity prices and brimming groundwater reserves had made local operators rich in the 1970s, enough for several of them to buy light aircraft to do their own crop-dusting, which could double as an easy way to fly an hour up to Las Vegas for boozy weekends. When prices dipped, some fell into trouble and bankruptcy. One of them, despondent, took his plane up and flew it into the east-facing slopes of the Harcuvar Mountains.

212   *dust storms kicked up where cotton used to grow*: Paul Bergelin, "Moderating Power: Municipal Interbasin Groundwater Transfers in Arizona," M.A. thesis, Arizona State University, 2013, 76.

213   *some of them large enough to swallow a car*: Fradkin, *A River No More*, 260.

213   *Moon complained of "widows and orphans" being trotted out to sway public opinion*: Bergelin, "Moderating Power," 138.

213   *Some residents have barely enough pressure to take a shower*: Rob O'Dell and Ian James, "In Western Arizona, Corporate Farms Turn Water into Profits, Leaving Small Towns in the Dust," *Arizona Republic*, December 15, 2019.

214   *New York hedge funds have made investments in Arizona land . . .* : Rob O'Dell and Ian James, "These 7 Industrial Farm Operations Are Draining Arizona's Aquifers, and No One Knows Exactly How Much They're Taking," *Arizona Republic*, December 5, 2021. See also "In Southeastern Arizona, Farms Drill a Half-Mile Deep While Families Pay the Price," *Arizona Republic*, February 18, 2020.

214   *"It was the farmers who pledged their land as collateral . . ."*: Phillip Bashaw, "Industrial Farms Invest in Arizona. They Don't Pirate Its Water and Resources," *Arizona Republic*, December 30, 2019.

215   *The gifts of the ice age won't last*: Sevigny, *Mythical River*, xviii.

217   *Weeds grew on murdered furrows*: Webb, *A Pima Remembers*, 122–25.

217   *"I can laugh about it now . . ."*: Roger Naylor, "Great Papago Escape: 25 German POWs Dug Their Way Out of Phoenix Prison Camp," *Arizona Republic*, December 17, 2015.

218   *"Some mapmakers acknowledge this truth . . ."*: McNamee, *Gila*, 19.

———

223   *"Behold now the happy results . . ."*: Miller, *The Arizona Story*, 39. See also Jacoby, *Shadows at Dawn*.

Windy Point

224 *Windy Point*: This essay is revised and adapted from my article "The Catalina Highway: Boosterism, Convict Labor, and the Road to Tucson's Backyard Mountain," *Journal of Arizona History* 60, no. 2 (Summer 2019): 131–57.

225 *Such was the randomness of a western place-name . . .* : Frank S. Crosswhite, "'J.G. Lemmon and Wife': Plant Explorers in California, Arizona and Nevada," *Desert Plants*, August 1979. See also Emerson Oliver Stratton Papers 1846–1918, Arizona Historical Society, MS 0770, folder 1, p. 68.

225 *"But of all the peaks . . . remote yet very near"*: Wright, *The Mine with the Iron Door*, 1.

225 *"Tucson Doomed to Be 8 Month Town unless Mountain Road Built"*: Quoted in Lawrence Cheek, "Tucson's Long and Winding Road," *Tucson Citizen*, August 2, 1990. See also "Added Cost to Taxpayers but 11 Cents per $100," *Tucson Citizen*, October 21, 1928. See "Moonshine Added Glow to Mountain Holiday," *Arizona Daily Star*, February 14, 1962; and Sonnichsen, *Tucson*, 171, for a view of early Anglo settlement.

226 *"He is inscrutable, imperturbable . . ."*: Edward G. Lowry, "Mr. Hitchcock Blows Out the Gas," *New Republic*, September 22, 1920.

226 *"He dresses immaculately . . ."*: George Max, "Ringmaster Hitchcock and His Plans for the 1936 Republican Circus," *Real America*, June 1935.

226 *Hitchcock's entry for June 8, 1930, is typical . . .* : Papers of Frank H. Hitchcock, Manuscript Division, Library of Congress, Washington, D.C., shelf 365, box 1.

226 *Coverage of airplane crashes was also discouraged . . .* : "F.H. Hitchcock Dies," *New York Times*, August 6, 1935.

226 *"I am keeping you out of the breadline . . ."*: Max, "Ringmaster Hitchcock."

227 *"Instructions have been already issued . . ."*: Hitchcock to Moeur, Western Union telegram, February 27, 1933, Papers of Frank H. Hitchcock, box 1.

227 *an urgency to get his Tucson highway project approved*: G. L. McLane, "Final Construction Report: Arizona Forest Highway Project 33, Catalina Highway, Coronado National Forest, Pima County, Arizona," U.S. Department of Commerce, Bureau of Public Roads, Division 7, 1951.

227 *thanks to the potent combination of local boosterism, federal intervention, and wartime manpower shortages*: Ingram, *Dixie Highway*, 130.

227 *When three others tried it, guards turned dogs on them*: McLane, "Final Construction Report."

228 *painted the legend "Methuselah" on its side*: McLane, 85.

228 *flags at the state capitol to be flown at half-staff*: "'Presidential Maker' Victim of Pneumonia," *Phoenix Gazette*, August 5, 1935. See also "F.H. Hitchcock Dies," *New York Times*, August 6, 1935.

228 *"When Frank Hitchcock originated the idea, . . .":* "Naming the Catalina Highway," *Arizona Daily Star*, March 31, 1936.

228 *"Dynamite—and lots of it—is building up the new Catalina highway . . .":* J. Robert Burns, *Arizona Daily Star*, August 17, 1941.

229 *"You know, I feel really sorry for you people . . .":* "Tucsonians" Oral History Project 1947–2002, Special Collections, University of Arizona Library, MS 390, Box 1.

230 *"It is a spectacle . . .":* "Desert Highway Makes Progress," *Arizona Daily Star*, undated from 1937.

230 *"a lot more turns in it than there needed to be . . . but they wanted to show off Tucson":* Barnes made this observation to me in a conversation, but she is also the author of *The Road to Mount Lemmon: A Father, a Family and the Making of Summerhaven* (University of Arizona Press, 2009).

231 *"looks out over the great valley of the Santa Cruz as lasting as time itself":* "A Fitting Memorial," *Tucson Daily Citizen*, October 13, 1948.

231 *"A city of mud boxes . . . in the glare of a southern sun":* Browne, *Adventures in the Apache Country*, 131.

232 *"It's beautiful up there . . .":* "Tucsonians" Oral History Project, box 2, folder 2.

———

234 *and invested its pillared forms with spiritual resonance:* Canadian Geographic, January/February 1998, 62.

235 *"like a palm stretched out for a fortuneteller to read . . .":* Kingsolver, *The Bean Trees*, 54.

236 *the least known of the ranges that form the walls of the Tucson valley:* These paragraphs on the Rincons are revised and adapted from my essay "Crossing the Rincons," *Zocalo Magazine*, January 2020.

237 *"Even people who have lived next door . . . unromantic as an electric oven":* Bowers, *The Mountains Next Door*, 4.

———

Gabrielle, Then and Now

241 *She twice faced an opponent who said awful things about her . . . :* Hussein Ibish, "When They Fantasize about Killing You, Believe Them," *The Atlantic*, August 21, 2021.

———

246 *one day grace a green reflective street sign in an instant neighborhood:* Roberts, *The Pueblo Revolt*, 100. An alternative explanation is that Murphey's work crews, who had grown up on Mexican farms, suggested he name a street after San Isidro Labrador, the patron saint of farmers and laborers.

———

The Red Embrace

249   *"I saw gold mining . . . but did not seem to mind it at all"*: Hislop, *An Englishman's Arizona*, 33.

250   *wagons bearing copper ore*: William Ascarza, "Mine Tales: Helvetia-Rosemont Area Is Important in Arizona's Copper Mining History," *Arizona Daily Star*, July 13, 2020.

250   *a target for wood thieves and vandals*: The Lewisohns collected fine art and underwrote the Metropolitan Opera and Columbia University with wealth derived from copper claims in the West.

250   *But there was no free method to peel back the ground for a look*: A. B. Bowman, "History, Growth and Development of a Small Mining Company," *Society for Mining, Metallurgy and Exploration* 15, no. 6 (1963): 42–49.

251   *copper at just under 1 percent purity*: Kalt, *Awake the Copper Ghosts!*

252   *washing the streets of garbage and manure*: Schwantes, *Vision and Enterprise*, 112.

253   *the most powerful man in town*: Byrkit, *Forging the Copper Collar*, 187.

253   *Copper outposts circled the capital of Phoenix in bright electron paths*: Sheridan, *Arizona*, 166.

253   *mysteriously valued for taxes at just $2 million*: Sheridan, 180.

254   *"behind-the-scenes manipulator . . . with a splendid handlebar mustache"*: Berman, *George Hunt*, 41.

254   *"you cannot compromise with a rattlesnake"*: Sheridan, *Arizona*, 191.

255   *"the frontier was a company town"*: Sheridan, 193.

257   *Pima County was soon talking to Triangle about a deal*: Tim Vanderpool, "Rosemont Rising," *Tucson Weekly*, March 8, 2007. See also Tim Vanderpool, "Nature versus Greed," *Tucson Weekly*, November 23, 2006.

258   *given less flattering names by the would-be developers*: Curt Prendergast, "Tucson Lawsuit Seeks to Protect Jaguars from Rosemont Mine," *Arizona Daily Star*, September 25, 2017.

259   *"It is almost impossible for me to imagine . . ."*: Carter, *Boom, Bust, Boom*, 246.

260   *the postmark would show what he knew when he knew it*: John R. Wilke, "Arizona Congressman Is Indicted," *Wall Street Journal*, February 23, 2008. See also "Copper Exec Says Ex-congressman Issued Land-Swap Threat," *USA Today*, May 16, 2013.

260   *"extracted, removed and marketed at a profit"*: 409 F. Supp. 3d 738 (D. Ariz. 2019), July 31, 2019.

The Green Valley Grin

268   *Seniors are expected to make up about a quarter of all Arizonans by the middle of the century*: Joel Anderson, "It's the Ultimate Retirement Showdown: Arizona vs. Florida," *Yahoo News*, September 3, 2020.

269   *"The nights were heartbreaking . . ."*: Sonnichsen, *Tucson*, 150.

269 *"a primitive, under-developed desert and hot as hell"*: Tucker, *Sun City*, 373.

270 *"But death is not as frightening to me out here . . ."*: Tucker, 56. Also quoted in Flannery Burke, "From Senior Citizen to Sun Citian," *Journal of Arizona History* 26, nos. 3 and 4 (Autumn 2020).

270 *especially those funding nearby school districts*: Calvin Trillin, "Wake Up and Live," *New Yorker*, April 4, 1964; also quoted in Burke, "From Senior Citizen to Sun Citian."

271 *mortgage that came with the cherished American idea of a reboot*: Clizbe, *This Is Green Valley*, 16–21; Dan Shearer, "The Guy Who Put GV on the Map," *Green Valley News*, October 22, 2017.

271 *the golden years sometimes bring hazy afternoons*: N. Moussa Malaak, Sean L. Simpson, Rhiannon E. Mayhugh, Michelle E. Grata, Jonathan H. Burdette, Linda J. Porrino, and Paul J. Laurienti, "Long-Term Moderate Alcohol Consumption Does Not Exacerbate Age-Related Cognitive Decline in Healthy, Community-Dwelling Older Adults," *Frontiers in Aging Neuroscience*, January 5, 2015.

272 *police charged both with disorderly conduct*: "Police: Game of Fetch Leads to Charges as Men Hit Each Other with Canes," *Sahuarita Sun*, April 8, 2019.

280 *a place of rest as a widower in a country club villa in his tenth decade*: Freisen, *Reflections at Eventide*.

———

283 *And somewhere along the way I stopped again . . .* : Zepeda, *When It Rains*, 3–4.

———

Lechuguilla

290 *The creator god I'itoi lives in a cave near its base*: Nabhan, *The Desert Smells Like Rain*, 14.

291 *a traditional last stop to light a votive candle and pray for a safe crossing*: Will Grant, "Altar: The Town Where Migrants Shop for a Perilous Journey," BBC News, April 8, 2014.

291 *Water companies in Altar . . .* : De León, *The Land of Open Graves*, 191.

294 *a combination of "harboring" and "conspiracy" that could net him twenty years*: Ryan Devereaux, "Humanitarian Volunteer Scott Warren Reflects on the Borderlands and Two Years of Government Persecution," *The Intercept*, November 23, 2019.

294 *they pay extravagant amounts of taxes*: Judith Gans, "Immigrants in Arizona: Fiscal and Economic Impacts," Udall Center for Studies in Public Policy, University of Arizona, 2008.

294 *border towns are statistically among the safest in Arizona*: Dennis Welch, "Border Towns as Safe as Anywhere in Arizona," *AZ Family*, January 18, 2017.

294 *smuggled through well-guarded official ports of entry*: "Illicit Drug Smuggling between Ports of Entry and Border Barriers," Congressional Research Service, February 7, 2020.

294　*Border patrol agents are arrested at twice the rate of their errant counterparts in city police departments*: Garrett M. Graff, "The Green Monster: How the Border Patrol Became America's Most Out-of-Control Law Enforcement Agency," *Politico*, November/December 2014.

295　*Now it's everywhere*: David Folkenflik, "Tensions Rise at Fox News over Coverage and Rhetoric Surrounding Migrant Caravan," National Public Radio, October 30, 2018.

295　*"This is an invasion . . ."*: Glenn Beck, "This Is Not a Caravan. It's an INVASION," glennbeck.com, October 23, 2018.

295　*"America cannot allow this invasion"*: "Trump Ad Recycles Anti-immigration Video," Associated Press, November 2, 2018.

295　*"I'm protesting the invasion . . ."*: Michael Martinez, Holly Yan, and Catherine E. Shoichet, "Growing Protests over Where to Shelter Immigrant Children Hits Arizona," CNN, July 16, 2014.

295　*"I have noticed a change in people . . ."*: "Pittsburgh Suspect Echoed Talking Point That Dominated Fox News Airwaves," WTVA.com, October 30, 2018.

295　*"This attack is a response to the Hispanic invasion of Texas"*: Peter Baker and Michael D. Shear, "El Paso Shooting Suspect's Manifesto Echoes Trump's Language," *New York Times*, August 4, 2019.

295　*"a volatile mix of wannabe vigilante soldier-boys and Southern tobacco-stain-chinned rednecks"*: Morgan, *The Reaper's Line*, 503.

295　*they commit violent crimes at a far higher rate than the migrants they delight in hounding*: Media-friendly kindergarten teacher Chris Simcox ran a group called the Minutemen Project out of Tombstone before he went to prison on child molestation charges. One of his deputies, Shawna Forde, was convicted of double murder after she and three accomplices broke into the home of Raul Flores while "looking for illegal drugs" and ended up killing Flores and his daughter, then burglarizing the house. Another of his associates, J.T. Ready, was a neo-Nazi who shot and killed his girlfriend and three other occupants at her house before turning the gun on himself. Tim Foley set himself up in the ranching town of Arivaca as the leader of the Arizona Border Recon militia—one of its members went to prison after federal agents arrested him for running a "gun factory" out of his home. Megan Cassidy, "Ex-Minuteman Chris Simcox Sentenced to 19.5 Years in Child Sex-Abuse Case," *Arizona Republic*, July 11, 2016.

295　*seven Arizona facilities run by the private company Southwest Key*: Kristin Myers, "Migrant 'Children in Cages' Costs American Taxpayers more than $4.5 Million Daily," by Yahoo News, July 5, 2019.

296　*most of which are strategically located*: Dana Nickel, "Who Profits from Migrant Detention in the US?" *Globe Post*, August 22, 2019.

296　*"The men and women held behind the perimeter fences . . ."*: Barry, *Border Wars*, 45.

298   *they aim to rob the migrants or the dope mules*: Broyles and McManus, *A Visitor's Guide.*

298   *he went to fetch more water, and then never came back*: Urrea, *The Devil's Highway.*

298   *"Have you ever seen a mummy . . .":* "14 Die in Border Crossing," Associated Press, May 14, 2001.

298   *they were trying to "get a grip" on the influx of migrants*: Broyles, *Desert Duty*, 16.

299   *scooped up pieces of older metal barriers and sold them*: Nathan O'Neal, "Border Barriers Sold as Scrap Metal," KOB4, October 2, 2020.

300   *An official from the International Boundary Commission counted sixty-five graves . . .*: Broyles and McManus, *A Visitor's Guide.*

301   *there were no other human beings in the universe*: Smith, *Gold on the Desert*, 40.

301   *few plants capable of growing in the valley create a thin illusion of green*: Broyles and McManus, *A Visitor's Guide.*

301   *small cavities called tafone that look like a thousand empty eye sockets*: Broyles et al., *Last Water*, 15.

302   *a cauldron loaded with fermenting carbon material*: Broyles et al., 23.

302   *They died next to it . . .* : International Boundary Commission, *Report*, 25.

302   *a coyote howled and the sound echoed in the natural amphitheater*: Near this mesa in 1906, geologist W. J. McGee shared some sheep jerky with a hardy miner named Pablo Valencia, who left the next morning with full canteens. Eight days later, McGee heard a horrific sound outside his tent walls and found Valencia nearly dead outside. "His lips had disappeared as if amputated, leaving low edges of blackened tissue," wrote McGee in a scientific article published the next year. "His teeth and gums projected like those of a skinned animal, but the flesh was black and dry as a hank of jerky; his nose was withered and shrunken to half its length." W. J. McGee, "Desert Thirst as Disease," *Interstate Medical Journal* 13 (1906).

303   *lest they trigger a long-dormant fuse and get their hands blown off*: On the west side of the Tinajas Altas, the Marine Corps built a fake city out of shipping containers for pilots to practice their warfare maneuvers over populated areas like Damascus or Baghdad. Officially known as an Urban Target Complex, the perpetually doomed city is known as Yodaville for a legendary pilot's call sign. Unwitting pedestrians from Mexico, twenty miles south, risk getting strafed by bullets, blinded by lasers, or atomized by air-to-ground shells.

304   *"You could simply go to sleep under that ironwood tree . . .":* Smith, *Gold on the Desert*, 247.

———

Notes on Sources

315   *Leslie Marmon Silko has observed . . .* : Silko, "Language and Literature from a Pueblo Indian Perspective."

317 *"fat on flowery phrases, woefully thin on factual presentation"*: Ruffner, *All Hell Needs Is Water*, 59.

318 *"idealism and good business rarely go hand in hand"*: Lyon, *Those Old Yellow Dog Days*, 84.

318 *Its name was shortened to the more ecumenical* Republic *in 1929*: Zarbin, *All the Time a Newspaper*.

318 *more than seven hundred titles, most out of print—to a lasting digital format*: Robrt L. Pela, "Paper Chase: Librarian Sativa Peterson Keeps the Past in the Basement," *Phoenix New Times*, August 19, 2019.

BIBLIOGRAPHY

Albright, Horace, and Marian Albright Schenck. *Creating the National Park Service: The Missing Years*. Norman: University of Oklahoma Press, 1999.

Anzaldúa, Gloria. *Borderlands: The New Mestiza = La Frontera*. San Francisco: Spinsters/ Aunt Lute, 1987.

Arellano, Gustavo. *Taco USA: How Mexican Food Conquered America*. New York: Scribner, 2012.

Ashworth, Donna. *Biography of a Small Mountain*. Flagstaff: Small Mountain Press, 1991.

Barry, Tom. *Border Wars*. Boston: Boston Review Books, 2011.

Berger, Bruce. *A Desert Harvest: New and Selected Essays*. New York: Farrar, Straus and Giroux, 2019.

Black, John A. *Arizona: The Land of Sunshine and Silver, Health and Prosperity, the Place for Ideal Homes*. Tucson: Republican Book and Job Print, 1890.

Bowers, Janice Emily. *The Mountains Next Door*. Tucson: University of Arizona Press, 1991.

Browne, J. Ross. *Adventures in the Apache Country: A Tour through Arizona and Sonora, 1864*. New York: Harper and Brothers, 1869.

Broyles, Bill, and Mark Haynes. *Desert Duty: On the Line with the U.S. Border Patrol*. Austin: University of Texas Press, 2010.

Broyles, Bill, and Roger McManus. *A Visitor's Guide to El Camino del Diablo*. Tucson: Friends of the Sonoran Desert, 2016.

Broyles, Bill, Gayle Harrison Hartman, Thomas E. Sheridan, Gary Paul Nabhan, and Mary Charlotte Thurtle. *Last Water on the Devil's Highway*. Tucson: University of Arizona Press, 2012.

Burns, Mike. *The Only One Living to Tell: The Autobiography of a Yavapai Indian*. Edited by Gregory McNamee. Tucson: University of Arizona Press, 2012.

Burroughs, John. *Time and Change*. New York: Houghton Mifflin, 1912.

Byrkit, James W. *Forging the Copper Collar: Arizona's Labor-Management War of 1901–1921*. Tucson: University of Arizona Press, 1982.

Carter, Bill. *Boom, Bust, Boom: A Story about Copper, the Metal That Runs the World*. New York: Scribner, 2012.

Chebahtah, William, and Nancy Minor. *Chevato: The Story of the Apache Warrior Who Captured Herma*. Lincoln: University of Nebraska Press, 2009.

Childs, Craig. *The Secret Knowledge of Water: Discovering the Essence of the American Desert*. New York: Back Bay, 2001.

Clarke, James W. *Last Rampage: The Escape of Gary Tison* Tucson: University of Arizona Press, 1988.

Clizbe, George A. *This is Green Valley*. Tucson: Shandling Lithographing, 1971.

Cobb, Irwin J. *Roughing It De Luxe*. New York: George H. Doran, 1914.

Cremony, John C. *Life among the Apaches*. San Francisco: A. Roman, 1868.

De León, Jason. *The Land of Open Graves: Living and Dying on the Migrant Trail*. Berkeley: University of California Press, 2015.

Dillard, Annie. *Teaching a Stone to Talk: Expeditions and Encounters*. New York: Harper Perennial, 2013.

Duany, Andres, Elizabeth Plater-Zybek, and Jeff Speck. *Suburban Nation: The Rise of Sprawl and the Decline of the American Dream*. New York: North Point, 2000.

Dutton, Clarence. *Tertiary History of the Grand Cañon District*. Washington, D.C.: Government Printing Office, 1882.

Engel-Pearson, Kim. *Writing Arizona: 1912–2012*. Norman: University of Oklahoma Press, 2017.

Forrest, Earle R. *Arizona's Dark and Bloody Ground*. Caldwell, Idaho: Caxton, 1936.

Fradkin, Philip L. *A River No More: The Colorado River and the West*. Berkeley: University of California Press, 1968.

Frazier, Ian. *On the Rez*. New York: Picador, 2001.

Freisen, Eugene. *Reflections at Eventide: A Grandfather Shares His Story with His Grandchildren*. Tucson: Wheatmark, 2018.

Gammage, Grady, Jr. *Phoenix in Perspective: Reflections on Developing the Desert*. Phoenix: Herberger Center for Design, 1999.

Gantenbein, Douglas. *A Season of Fire: Four Months on the Firing Line of America's Forests*. New York: Tarcher, 2003.

George, Diane Hume. *Koyaanisqatsi: Poems*. Sunderland, Mass.: Heatherstone Press, 2011.

Ghiglieri, Michael, and Thomas M. Myers. *Over the Edge: Death in Grand Canyon*. Puma Press, 2001.

Gilbert, Matthew Sakiestewa. *Hopi Runners: Crossing the Terrain between Indian and American*. Lawrence: University Press of Kansas, 2018.

Gillette, Frank V. *Pleasant Valley*. Phoenix: F. V. Gillette, 1984.

Glotfelty, Cheryll, and Harold Fromm, eds. *The Ecocriticism Reader: Landmarks in Literary Ecology*. Athens: University of Georgia Press, 1996.

Goff, John S. *Charles Poston*. Cave Creek: Black Mountain Press, 1995.

Goldberg, Robert Alan. *Barry Goldwater*. New Haven: Yale University Press, 1995.

Higgins, Charles. *The Grand Canyon of Arizona: Being a Book of Words from Many Pens*. Topeka: Passenger Department of the Atchison, Topeka and Santa Fe Railroad, 1909.

Hutton, Paul Andrew. *The Apache Wars: The Hunt for Geronimo, the Apache Kid, and the Captive Boy Who Started the Longest War in American History.* New York: Broadway, 2016.

Ingram, Tammy. *Dixie Highway: Road Building and the Making of the Modern South, 1900–1930.* Chapel Hill: University of North Carolina Press, 2014.

International Boundary Commission. *Report of the Boundary Commission upon the Survey and Remarking of the Boundary between the United States and Mexico West of the Rio Grande, 1892–1896.* Washington, D.C.: U.S. Government Printing Office, 1898.

Iverson, Peter. *Barry Goldwater, Native Arizonan.* Norman: University of Oklahoma Press, 1997.

Jacoby, Karl. *Shadows at Dawn: An Apache Massacre and the Violence of History.* New York: Penguin, 2009.

Kalt, William D. *Awake the Copper Ghosts! The History of Banner Mining Company and the Treasure of Twin Buttes.* Tucson: Banner Copper, 1968.

Kardashian, Kirk. *Milk Money: Cash, Cows, and the Death of the American Dairy Farm.* Hanover: University Press of New England, 2012.

Kelley, Klara, and Harris Francis. *A Diné History of Navajoland.* Tucson: University of Arizona Press, 2019.

Kinsey, Joni. *The Majesty of the Grand Canyon: 150 Years in Art.* Petaluma: Pomegranate, 2004.

Kluckhohn, Clyde, and Dorothea Leighton. *The Navaho.* Cambridge: Harvard University Press, 1974.

Lamberton, Ken. *Chasing Arizona: One Man's Yearlong Obsession with the Grand Canyon State.* Tucson: University of Arizona Press, 2015.

Lazar, Zachary. *Evening's Empire: The Story of My Father's Murder.* New York: Little, Brown, 2009.

Lopez, Barry. *Crossing Open Ground.* New York: Vintage, 1989.

Lopez, Barry, ed. *Home Ground: Language for an American Landscape.* San Antonio: Trinity University Press, 2006.

Luckingham, Bradford. *Phoenix: The History of a Southwestern Metropolis.* Tucson: University of Arizona Press, 1989.

Lummis, Charles Fletcher. *Mesa, Cañon and Pueblo.* New York: Century, 1925.

Lyon, William H. *Those Old Yellow Dog Days: Frontier Journalism in Arizona, 1859–1912.* Tucson: Arizona Historical Society, 1994.

Magaña, Lisa, and César S. Silva. *Empowered! Latinos Transforming Arizona Politics.* Tucson: University of Arizona Press, 2021.

Magrane, Eric, and Christopher Cokinos, eds. *The Sonoran Desert: A Literary Field Guide.* Tucson: University of Arizona Press, 2016.

Marder, Michael. *The Philosopher's Plant: An Intellectual Herbarium.* New York: Columbia University Press, 2014.

McGivney, Annette. *Resurrection: Glen Canyon and a New Vision for the American West*. Seattle: Braided River, 2009.

McNamee, Gregory. *Gila: The Life and Death of an American River*. Albuquerque: University of New Mexico Press, 1998.

McNamee, Gregory. *Named in Stone and Sky: An Arizona Anthology*. Tucson: University of Arizona Press, 1993.

McNamee, Gregory. *Tortillas, Tiswin, and T-Bones: A Food History of the Southwest*. Albuquerque: University of New Mexico Press, 2017.

Miller, Joseph, ed. *The Arizona Story*. New York: Hastings House, 1952.

Miller, Tom, ed. *Arizona: The Land and the People*. Tucson: University of Arizona Press, 1986.

Moore, Richard D. *Too Tough to Tame*. Bloomington, Ind.: Author House, 2009.

Morgan, Lee, II. *The Reaper's Line: Life and Death on the Mexican Border*. Tucson: Rio Nuevo, 2006.

Murphy, Thomas D., *Three Wonderlands of the American West*. Boston: L. C. Page, 1913.

Nabakov, Peter. *Indian Running: Native American History and Tradition*. Santa Fe: Ancient City Press, 1981.

Nabakov, Peter. *Where the Lightning Strikes: The Lives of American Indian Sacred Places*. New York: Penguin, 2007.

Nabhan, Gary Paul. *The Desert Smells Like Rain: A Naturalist in O'odham Country*. Tucson: University of Arizona Press, 1982.

Needham, Andrew. *Power Lines: Phoenix and the Making of the Modern Southwest*. Princeton: Princeton University Press, 2014.

Nelson, Matthew. *Your Complete Guide to the Arizona National Scenic Trail*. Birmingham, Ala.: Wilderness Press, 2014.

Neumann, Mark. *On the Rim: Looking for the Grand Canyon*. Minneapolis: University of Minnesota Press, 2001.

Newberry, J. S., and J. N. Macomb. *Report of the Exploring Expedition from Santa Fe, New Mexico, to the Junction of the Grand and Green Rivers othe Great Colorado of the West, in 1859 under the Command of Capt. J. N. Macomb*. Washington, D.C.: U.S. Army Corps of Engineers, 1876.

Niethammer, Carolyn. *A Desert Feast: Celebrating Tucson's Culinary Heritage*. Tucson: University of Arizona Press, 2020.

Otero, Lydia. *La Calle: Spatial Conflicts and Urban Renewal in a Southwest City*. Tucson: University of Arizona Press, 2010.

Owen, David. *Where the Water Goes: Life and Death along the Colorado River*. New York: Riverhead, 2017.

Palmer, Carol. *The City of Surprise: History in Progress*. Phoenix: Heritage, 2010.

Parraz, Randy. *Dignity by Fire: Dismantling Arizona's Anti-Immigrant Machine*. Phoenix: Randy Parraz, 2021.

Peabody, Henry Greenwood. *Glimpses of the Grand Canyon of Arizona*. Kansas City: Fred Harvey, 1902.

Perlstein, Rick. *Before the Storm: Barry Goldwater and the Unmaking of the American Consensus*. New York: Nation, 2001.

Poirier, Mark Jude. *Naked Pueblo: Stories*. New York: Hyperion, 2009.

Powell, John Wesley. *Exploration of the Colorado River of the West and Its Tributaries*. Washington, D.C.: U.S. Government Printing Office, 1875.

Powell, Lawrence Clark. *Southwest: Three Definitions*. Benson: Singing Wind Bookshop, 1990.

Preistley, J. B. *Midnight on the Desert*. New York: Harper and Brothers, 1977.

Pyne, Stephen. *How the Canyon Became Grand: A Short History*. New York: Viking, 1998.

Redniss, Laura. *Oak Flat: A Fight for Sacred Land in the American West*. New York: Penguin Random House, 2021.

Reisner, Marc. *Cadillac Desert: The American West and Its Disappearing Water*. New York: Viking, 1986.

Roberts, David. *The Pueblo Revolt: The Secret Rebellion That Drove the Spanish out of the Southwest*. New York: Simon and Schuster, 2004.

Ross, Andrew. *Bird on Fire: Lessons from the World's Least Sustainable City*. Oxford: Oxford University Press, 2011.

Ruffner, Budge. *All Hell Needs Is Water*. Tucson: University of Arizona Press, 1972.

Salmon, Enrique. *Eating the Landscape: American Indian Stories of Food, Identity, and Resilience*. Tucson: University of Arizona Press, 2012.

Santos, Fernanda. *The Fire Line: The Story of the Granite Mountain Hotshots and One of the Deadliest Days in American Firefighting*. New York: Flatiron Books, 2016.

Sauder, Robert. *The Yuma Reclamation Project: Irrigation, Indian Allotment, and Settlement along the Lower Colorado River*. Reno: University of Nevada Press, 2009.

Schullery, Paul. *Grand Canyon: Early Impressions*. Portland, Ore.: Westwinds, 1989.

Schwantes, Carlos A. *Vision and Enterprise: Exploring the History of Phelps Dodge Corporation*. Tucson: University of Arizona Press, 2000.

Schwarz, Maureen Trudelle. *Molded in the Image of Changing Woman: Navajo Views on the Human Body and Personhood*. Tucson: University of Arizona Press, 1997.

Sevigny, Melissa L. *Mythical River: Chasing the Mirage of New Water in the American Southwest*. Iowa City: University of Iowa Press, 2016.

Shelton, Richard. *Going Back to Bisbee*. Tucson: University of Arizona Press, 1992.

Sheridan, Thomas E. *Arizona: A History*. Tucson: University of Arizona Press, 2012.

Shermer, Elizabeth Tandy. *Sunbelt Capitalism: Phoenix and the Transformation of American Politics*. Philadelphia: University of Pennsylvania Press, 2013.

Sides, Hampton. *Blood and Thunder: An Epic of the American West*. New York: Doubleday, 2006.

Silko, Leslie Marmon. "Language and Literature from a Pueblo Indian Perspective." In *English Literature: Opening up the Canon*, edited by Leslie A. Fielder and Houston A. Baker, 54–72. Baltimore: Johns Hopkins University Press, 1981.

Silko, Leslie Marmon. *Yellow Woman and a Beauty of the Spirit*. New York: Simon and Schuster, 1996.

Simenon, Georges. *Maigret at the Coroner's*. New York: Harcourt Brace Jovanovich, 1952.

Simpson, W. H. *El Tovar: A New Hotel at Grand Canyon of Arizona*. Topeka: Passenger Department of the Atchison, Topeka and Santa Fe Railroad, 1909.

Smith, Brian Jabas. *Tucson Salvage: Tales and Recollections from La Frontera*. London: Eyewear Publishing, 2018.

Smith, Olga Wright. *Gold on the Desert*. 1956.

Sonnichsen, C. L. *Tucson: The Life and Times of an American City*. Norman: University of Oklahoma Press, 1987.

Sterling, Terry Greene, and Jude Joffe-Block. *Driving While Brown: Sheriff Joe Arpaio Versus The Latino Resistance*. Berkeley: University of California Press, 2021.

Talayesva, Don. *Sun Chief: The Autobiography of a Hopi Indian*. New Haven: Yale University Press, 1942.

Talton, Jon. *A Brief History of Phoenix*. Charleston: History Press, 2015.

Thybony, Scott. *Burntwater*. Tucson: University of Arizona Press, 1997.

Tobin, Mitch. *Endangered: Biodiversity on the Brink*. Golden: Fulcrum, 2010.

Torres, Alva B., and Lydia Otero, eds. *Notitas: Select Columns from the* Tucson Citizen. Tucson: Planet Earth Press, 2021.

Trimble, Marshall. *A Roadside History of Arizona*. Missoula: Mountain Press, 2004.

Tucker, Jack M. *Sun City: 60-Plus and Hanging Tough*. Phoenix: Quail Run, 1985.

Underhill, Ruth. *The Navajos*. Norman: University of Oklahoma Press, 1956.

Urrea, Luis Alberto. *The Devil's Highway: A True Story*. New York: Little, Brown, 2008.

Van Dyke, Henry. *The Grand Canyon and Other Poems*. New York: Scribner, 1914.

Webb, George. *A Pima Remembers*. Tucson: University of Arizona Press, 1959.

West, Jim. *The Phoenix Sound: A History of Twang and Rockabilly Music in Arizona*. Charleston: History Press, 2015.

Willink, Roseann S., and Paul G. Zolbrod. *Weaving a World: Textiles and the Navajo Way of Seeing*. Santa Fe: Museum of New Mexico Press, 1996.

Wirth, John D. *Smelter Smoke in North America: The Politics of Transborder Pollution*. Lawrence: University of Kansas Press, 2000.

Wright, Harold Bell. *The Mine with the Iron Door*. New York: D. Appleton, 1923.

Wykoff, William. *Riding Shotgun with Norman Wallace: Rephotographing the Arizona Landscape*. Albuquerque: University of New Mexico Press, 2020.

Yetman, David. *Natural Landmarks of Arizona*. Tucson: University of Arizona Press, 2021.

Yetman, David, Alberto Búrquez, Kevin Hultine, and Michael Sanderson. *The Saguaro Cactus: A Natural History*. Tucson: University of Arizona Press, 2020.

Zarbin, Earl. *All the Time a Newspaper: The First 100 Years of the Arizona Republic.* Phoenix: Arizona Republic, 1990.

Zarbin, Earl. *Roosevelt Dam: A History to 1911.* Phoenix: Salt River Project, 1984.

Zepeda, Ofelia. *When It Rains: Tohono O'odham and Pima Poetry.* Tucson: University of Arizona Press, 2019.

Zoellner, Tom. *A Safeway in Arizona: What the Gabrielle Giffords Shooting Tells Us about the Grand Canyon State and Life in America.* New York: Viking, 2012.

INDEX

ABOUT THE AUTHOR

Tom Zoellner, a fifth-generation Arizonan, is the author of eight nonfiction books, including *The Heartless Stone, Uranium, A Safeway in Arizona, The National Road*, and *Island on Fire*, which won the 2020 National Book Critics Circle Award and was a finalist for the Bancroft Prize.